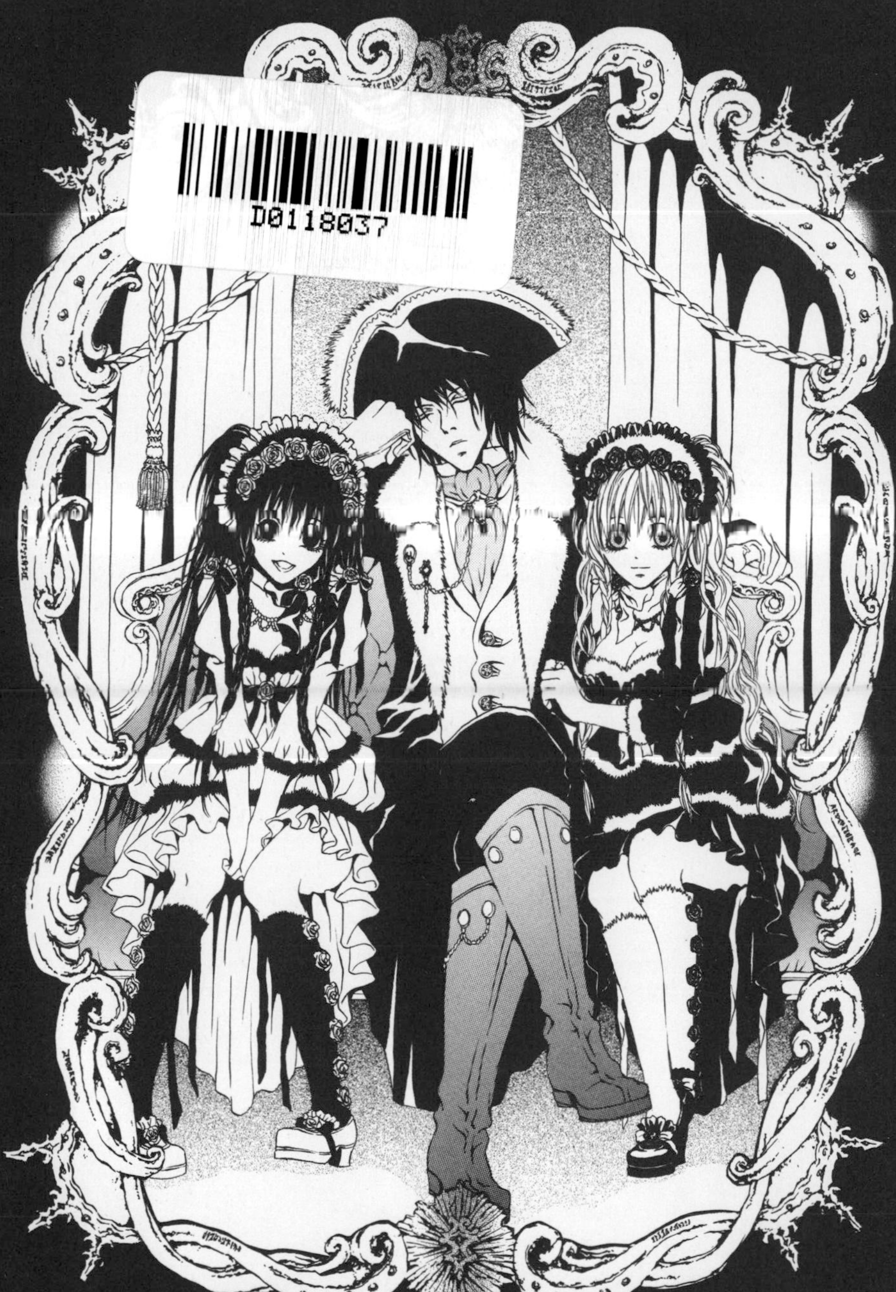

Doors of Chaos Volume 1
Created by Ryoko Mitsuki

Translation - Adrienne Beck
English Adaptation - Shannon Foreman
Retouch and Lettering - Star Print Brokers
Production Artist - Katherine Schilling
Graphic Designer - James Lee

Editor - Katherine Schilling
Digital Imaging Manager - Chris Buford
Pre-Production Supervisor - Erika Terriquez
Production Manager - Elisabeth Brizzi
Managing Editor - Vy Nguyen
Creative Director - Anne Marie Horne
Editor-in-Chief - Rob Tokar
Publisher - Mike Kiley
President and C.O.O. - John Parker
C.E.O. and Chief Creative Officer - Stuart Levy

A **TOKYOPOP** Manga

TOKYOPOP Inc.
5900 Wilshire Blvd. Suite 2000
Los Angeles, CA 90036

E-mail: info@TOKYOPOP.com
Come visit us online at www.TOKYOPOP.com

ISBN: 978-1-4278-0734-2

First TOKYOPOP printing: February 2008
10 9 8 7 6 5 4 3 2 1
Printed in the USA

Doors of Chaos

Volume One
By Ryoko Mitsuki

HAMBURG // LONDON // LOS ANGELES // TOKYO

~Table of Contents~

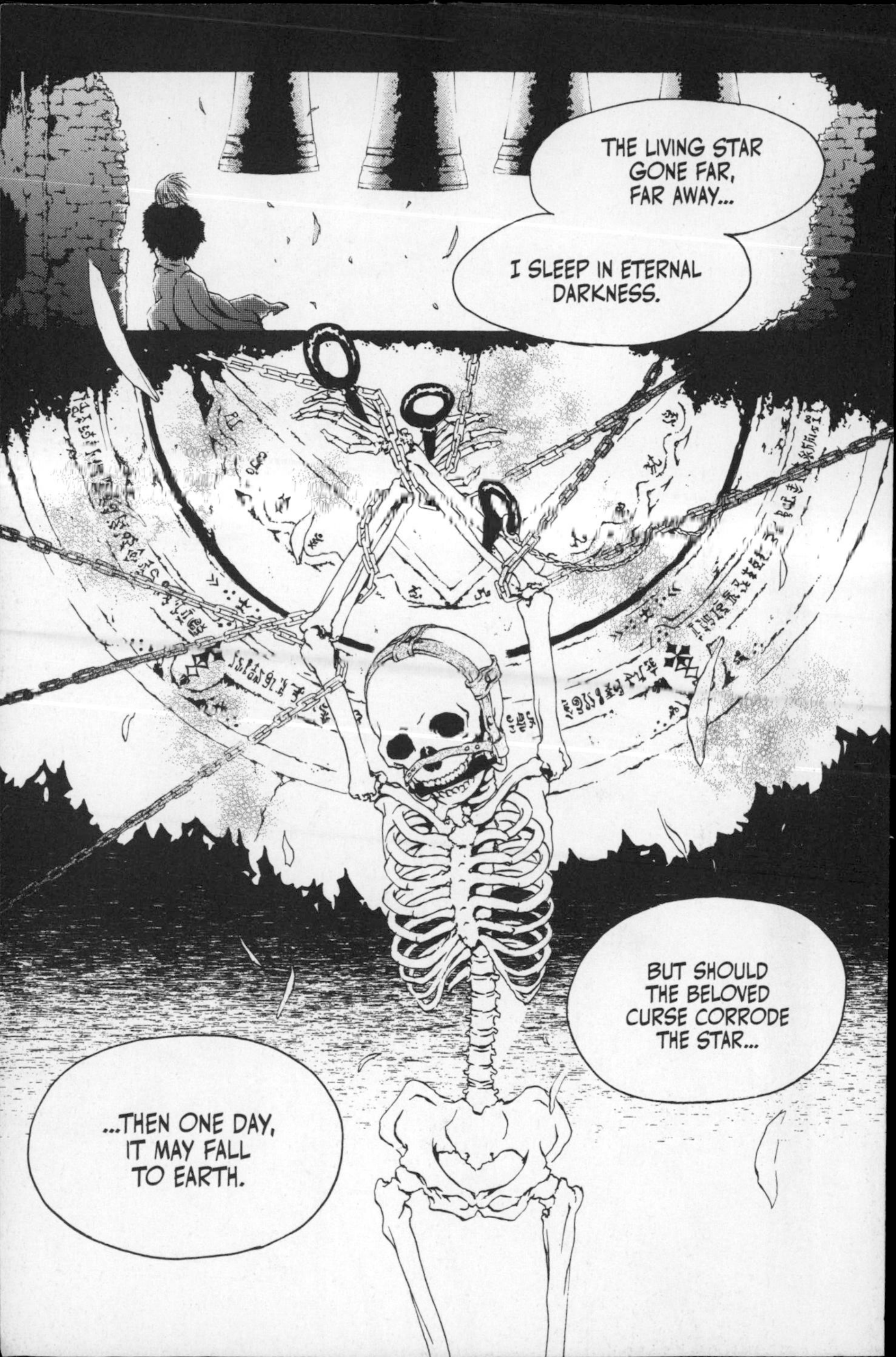
THE LIVING STAR GONE FAR, FAR AWAY...
I SLEEP IN ETERNAL DARKNESS.
BUT SHOULD THE BELOVED CURSE CORRODE THE STAR...
...THEN ONE DAY, IT MAY FALL TO EARTH.

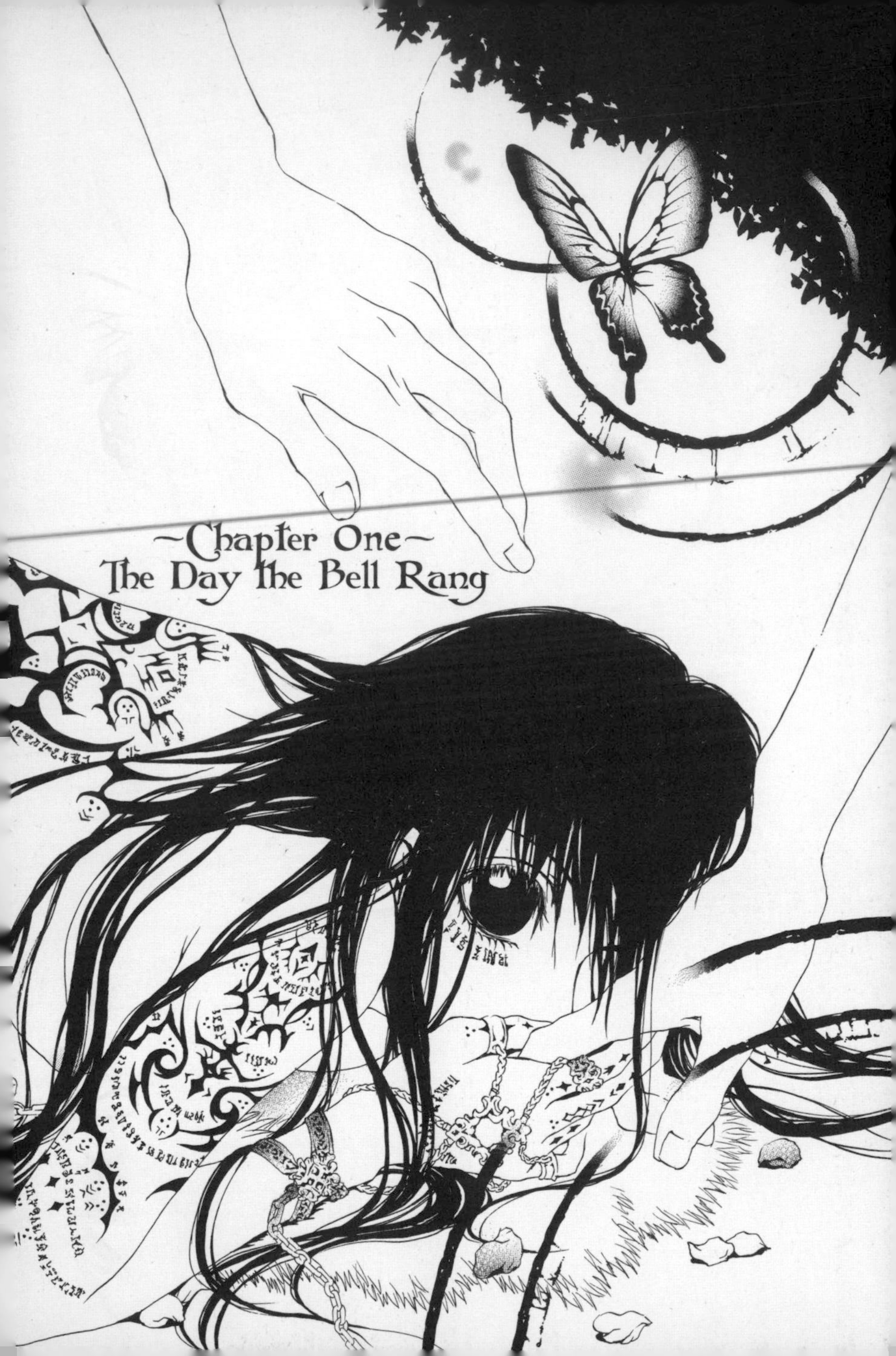
~Chapter One~
The Day The Bell Rang

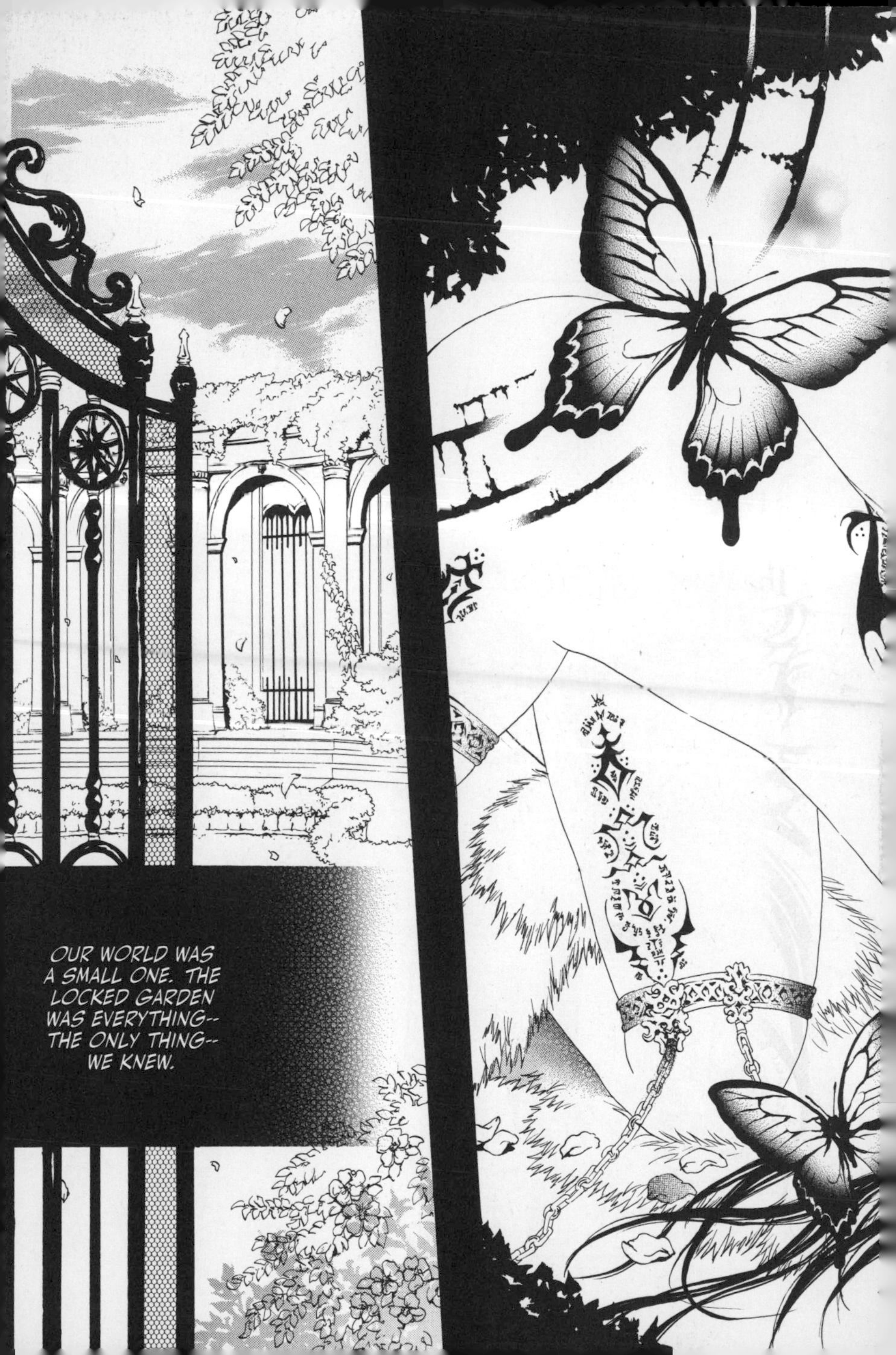
OUR WORLD WAS A SMALL ONE. THE LOCKED GARDEN WAS EVERYTHING-- THE ONLY THING-- WE KNEW.

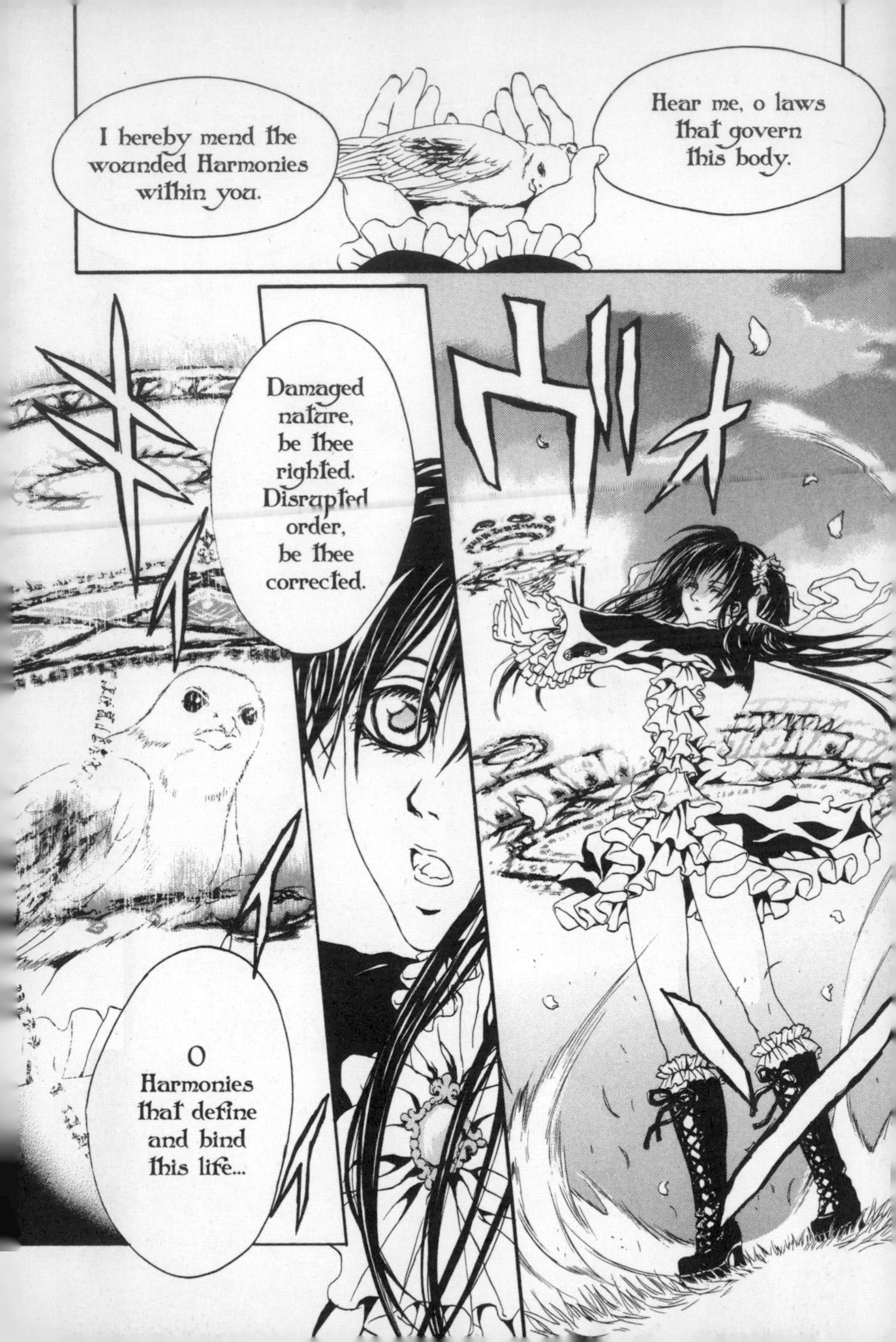
Hear me, o laws that govern this body.
I hereby mend the wounded Harmonies within you.
Damaged nature, be thee righted. Disrupted order, be thee corrected.
O Harmonies that define and bind this life...

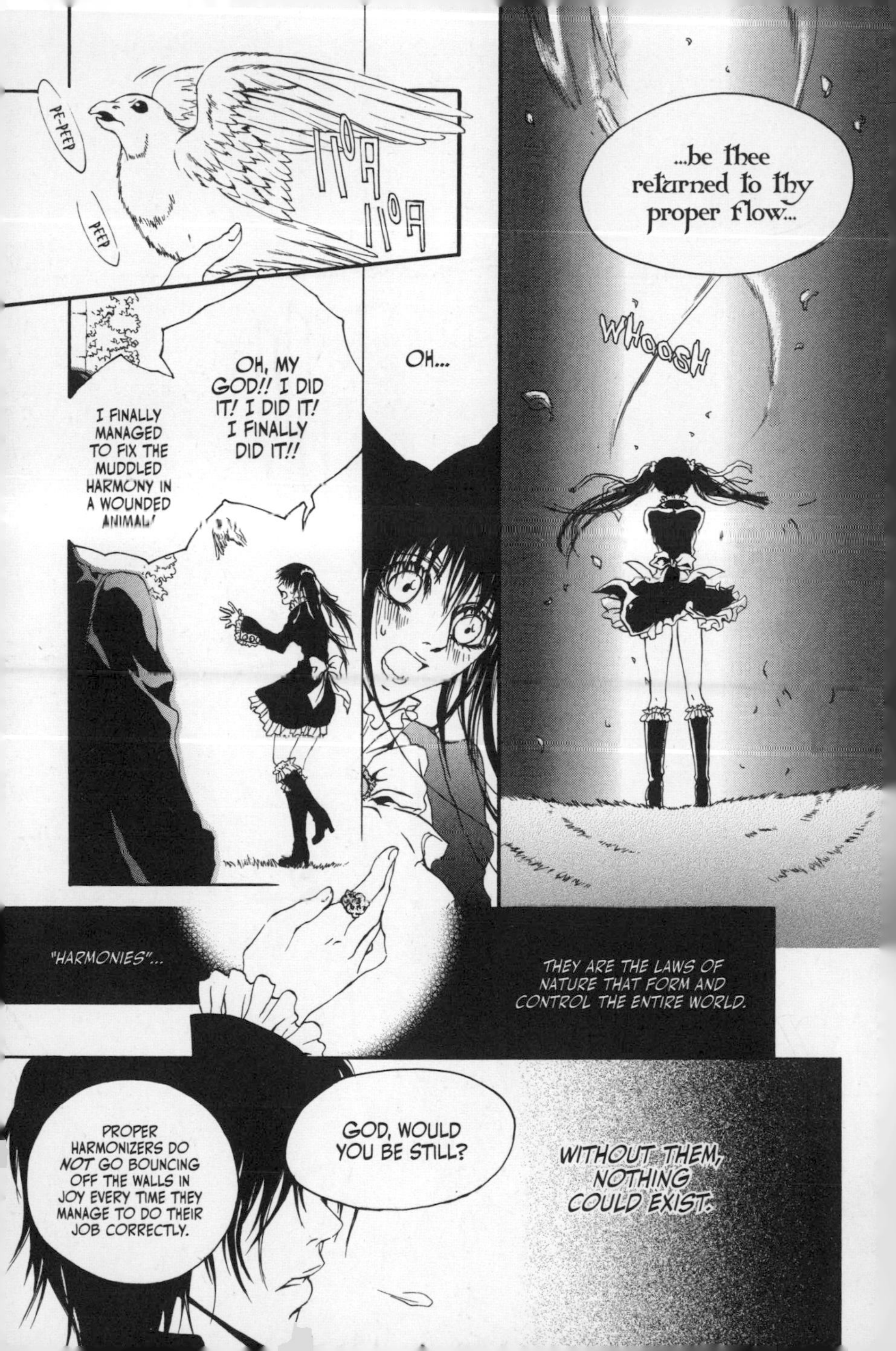
...be thee returned to thy proper flow...
WHOOSH
PE-PEEP
PEEP
FOA!!
FOA!!
OH...
OH, MY GOD!! I DID IT! I DID IT! I FINALLY DID IT!!
I FINALLY MANAGED TO FIX THE MUDDLED HARMONY IN A WOUNDED ANIMAL!
"HARMONIES"...
THEY ARE THE LAWS OF NATURE THAT FORM AND CONTROL THE ENTIRE WORLD.
WITHOUT THEM, NOTHING COULD EXIST.
GOD, WOULD YOU BE STILL?
PROPER HARMONIZERS DO *NOT* GO BOUNCING OFF THE WALLS IN JOY EVERY TIME THEY MANAGE TO DO THEIR JOB CORRECTLY.

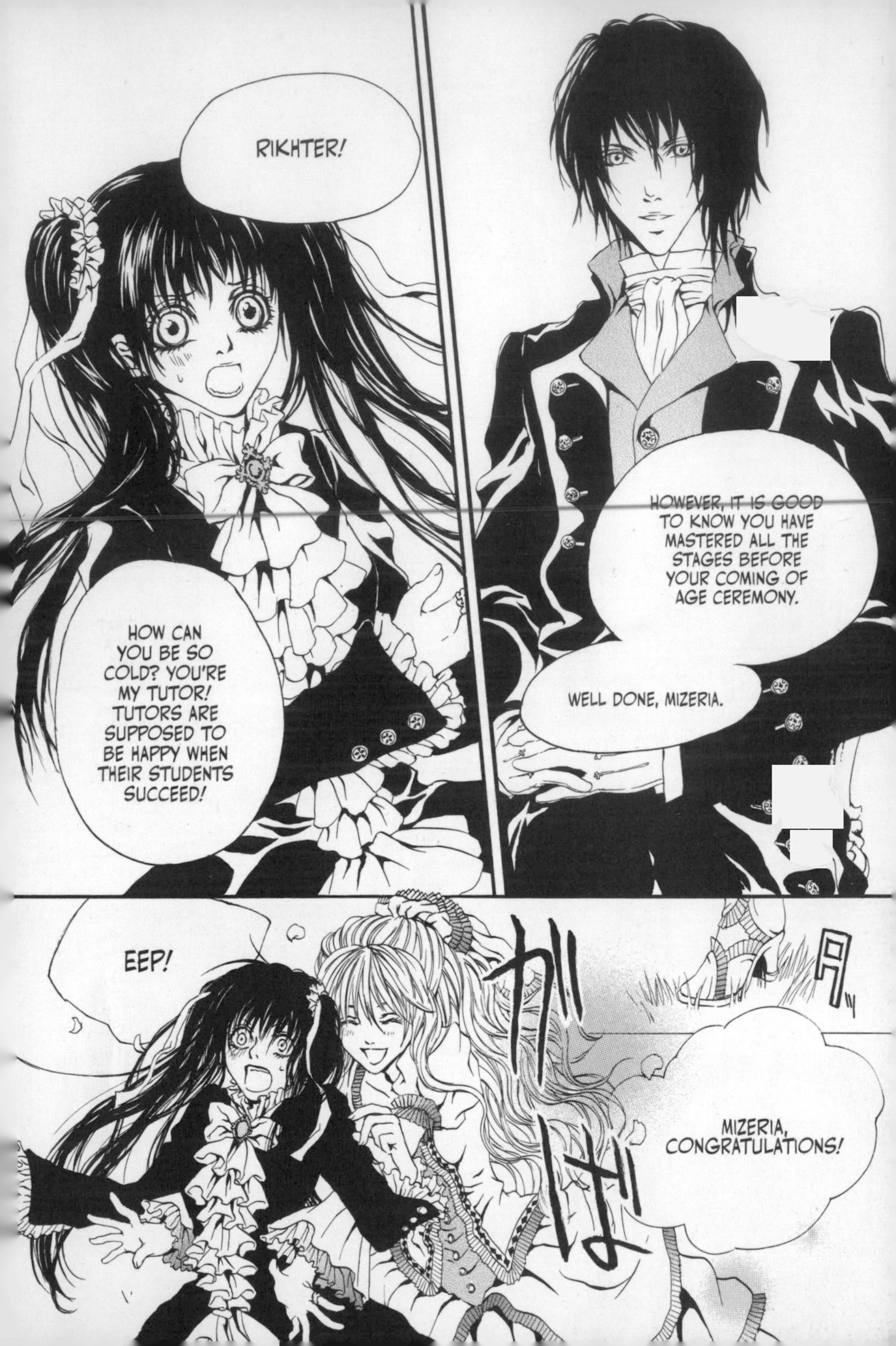
HOWEVER, IT IS GOOD TO KNOW YOU HAVE MASTERED ALL THE STAGES BEFORE YOUR COMING OF AGE CEREMONY.
WELL DONE, MIZERIA.
RIKHTER!
HOW CAN YOU BE SO COLD? YOU'RE MY TUTOR! TUTORS ARE SUPPOSED TO BE HAPPY WHEN THEIR STUDENTS SUCCEED!
MIZERIA, CONGRATULATIONS!
EEP!

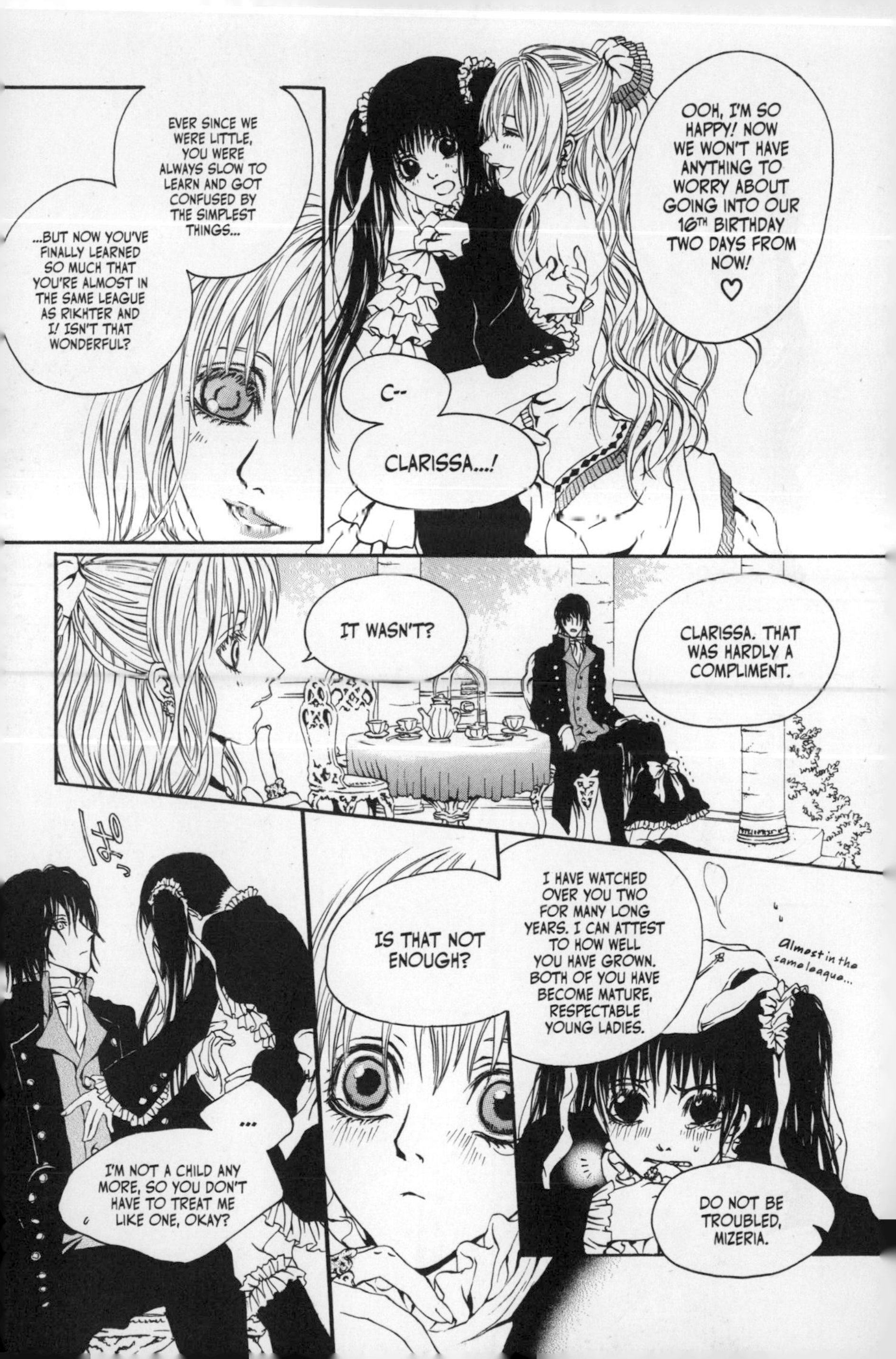
OOH, I'M SO HAPPY! NOW WE WON'T HAVE ANYTHING TO WORRY ABOUT GOING INTO OUR 16TH BIRTHDAY TWO DAYS FROM NOW! ♡
C-- CLARISSA...!
EVER SINCE WE WERE LITTLE, YOU WERE ALWAYS SLOW TO LEARN AND GOT CONFUSED BY THE SIMPLEST THINGS...
...BUT NOW YOU'VE FINALLY LEARNED SO MUCH THAT YOU'RE ALMOST IN THE SAME LEAGUE AS RIKHTER AND I! ISN'T THAT WONDERFUL?
CLARISSA. THAT WAS HARDLY A COMPLIMENT.
IT WASN'T?
Almost in the same league...
DO NOT BE TROUBLED, MIZERIA.
I HAVE WATCHED OVER YOU TWO FOR MANY LONG YEARS. I CAN ATTEST TO HOW WELL YOU HAVE GROWN. BOTH OF YOU HAVE BECOME MATURE, RESPECTABLE YOUNG LADIES.
IS THAT NOT ENOUGH?
...
I'M NOT A CHILD ANY MORE, SO YOU DON'T HAVE TO TREAT ME LIKE ONE, OKAY?

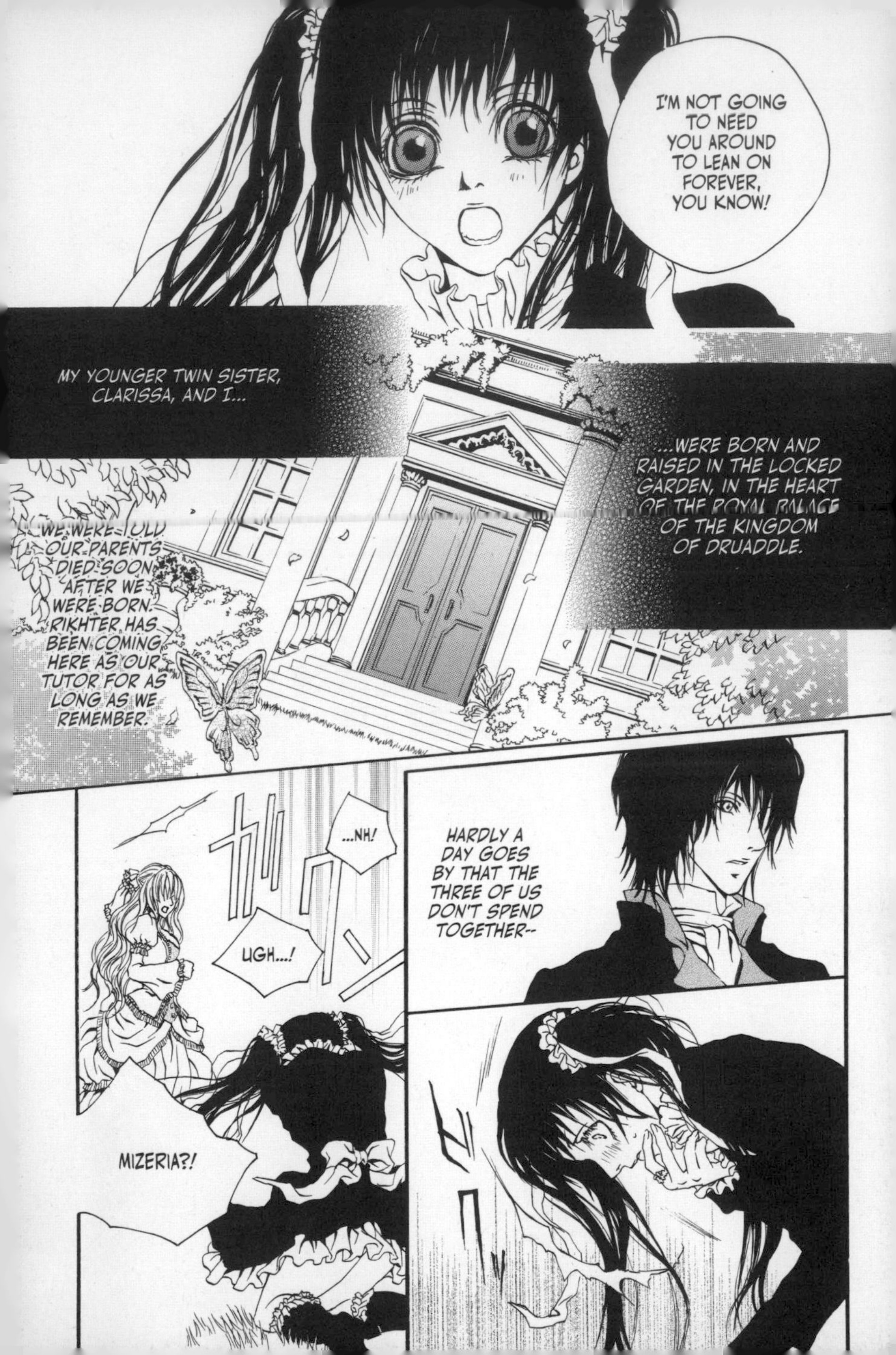
I'M NOT GOING TO NEED YOU AROUND TO LEAN ON FOREVER, YOU KNOW!
MY YOUNGER TWIN SISTER, CLARISSA, AND I...
...WERE BORN AND RAISED IN THE LOCKED GARDEN, IN THE HEART OF THE ROYAL PALACE OF THE KINGDOM OF DRUADDLE.
WE WERE TOLD OUR PARENTS DIED SOON AFTER WE WERE BORN. RIKHTER HAS BEEN COMING HERE AS OUR TUTOR FOR AS LONG AS WE REMEMBER.
HARDLY A DAY GOES BY THAT THE THREE OF US DON'T SPEND TOGETHER--
...NH!
UGH...!
MIZERIA?!

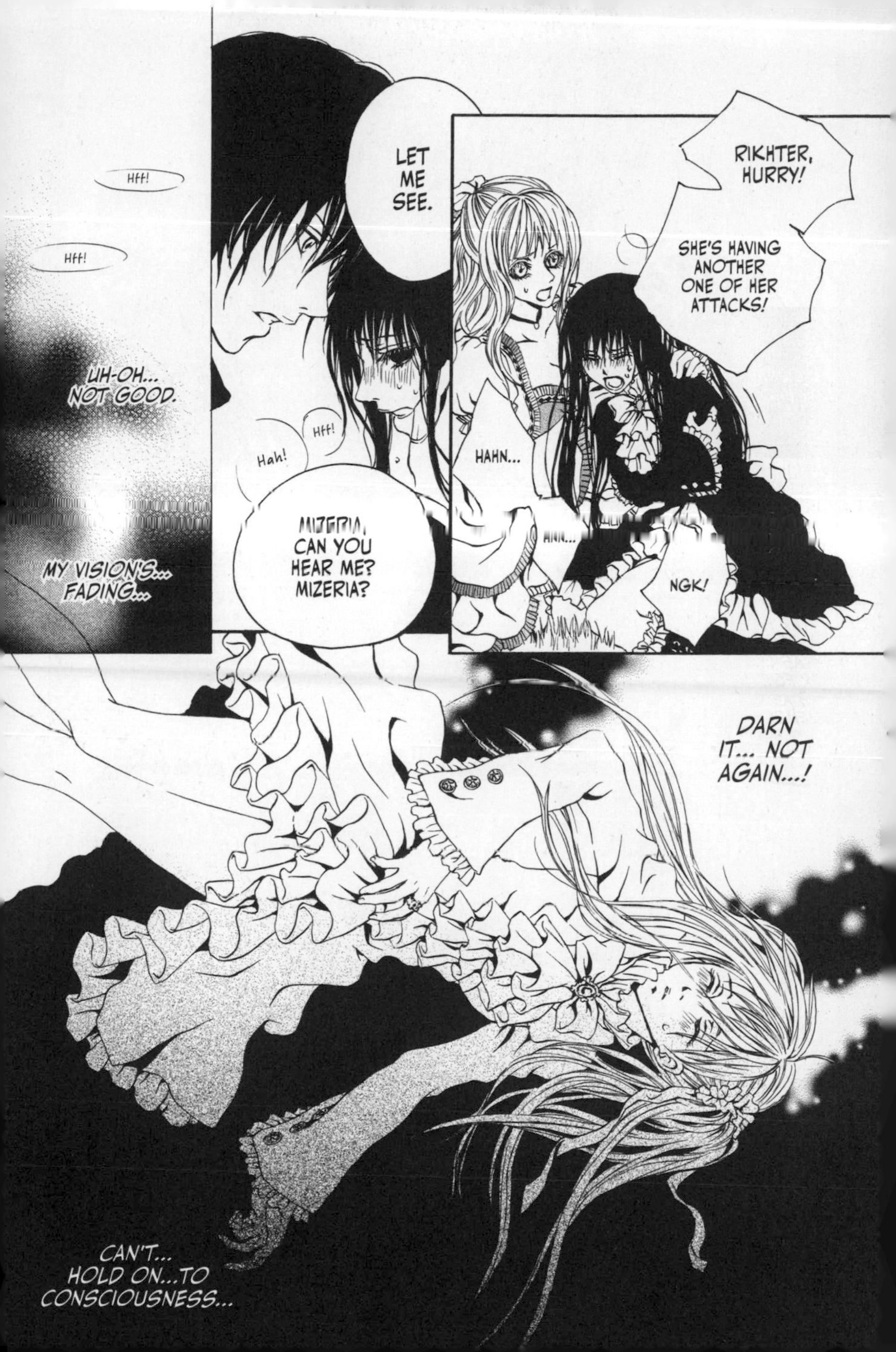
RIKHTER, HURRY!
SHE'S HAVING ANOTHER ONE OF HER ATTACKS!
HAHN...
NGK!
LET ME SEE.
Hff!
Hah!
MIZERIA, CAN YOU HEAR ME? MIZERIA?
Hff!
Hff!
UH-OH... NOT GOOD.
MY VISION'S... FADING...
DARN IT... NOT AGAIN...!
CAN'T... HOLD ON...TO CONSCIOUSNESS...

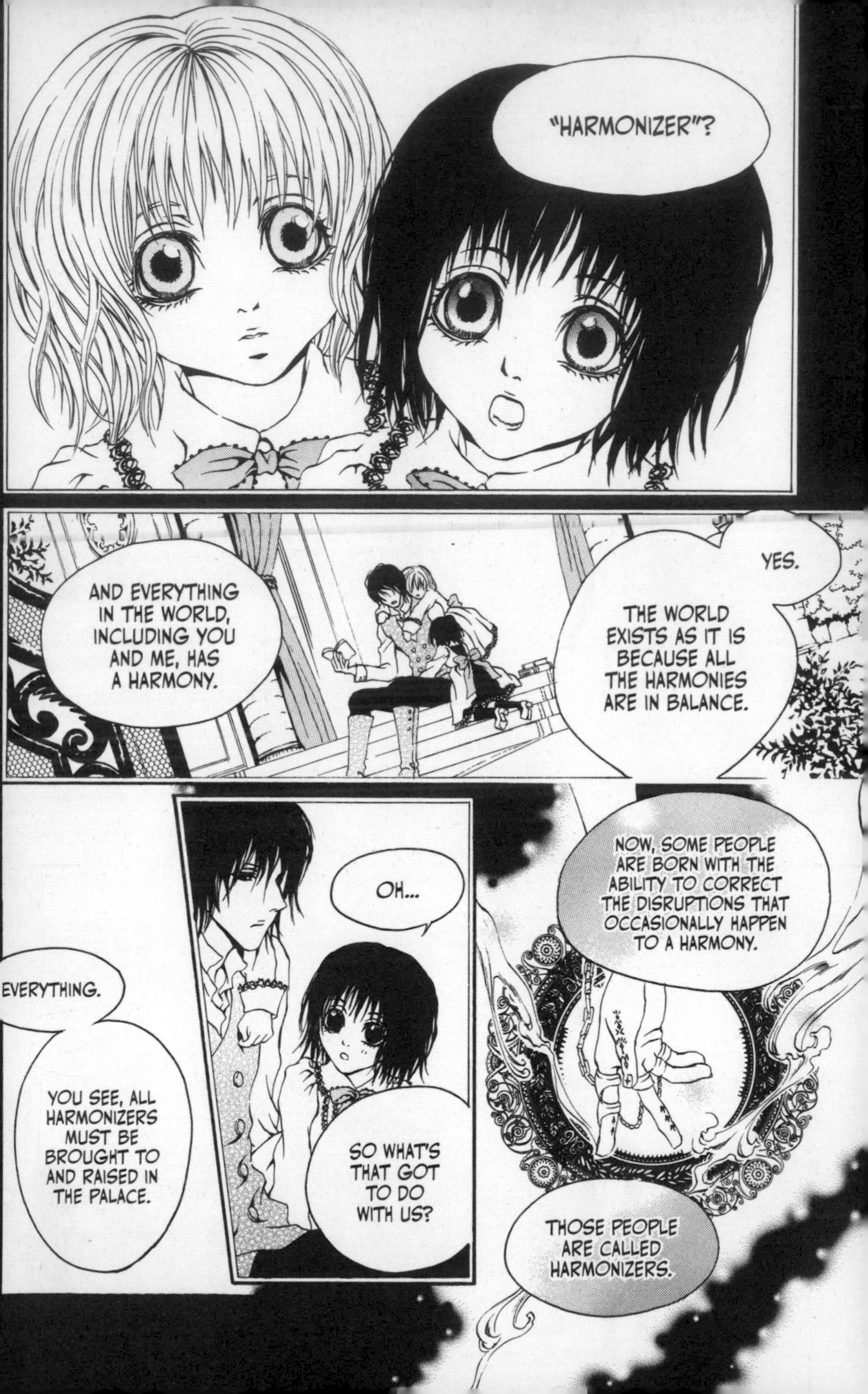
"HARMONIZER"?
YES.
THE WORLD EXISTS AS IT IS BECAUSE ALL THE HARMONIES ARE IN BALANCE.
AND EVERYTHING IN THE WORLD, INCLUDING YOU AND ME, HAS A HARMONY.
NOW, SOME PEOPLE ARE BORN WITH THE ABILITY TO CORRECT THE DISRUPTIONS THAT OCCASIONALLY HAPPEN TO A HARMONY.
THOSE PEOPLE ARE CALLED HARMONIZERS.
OH...
SO WHAT'S THAT GOT TO DO WITH US?
EVERYTHING.
YOU SEE, ALL HARMONIZERS MUST BE BROUGHT TO AND RAISED IN THE PALACE.

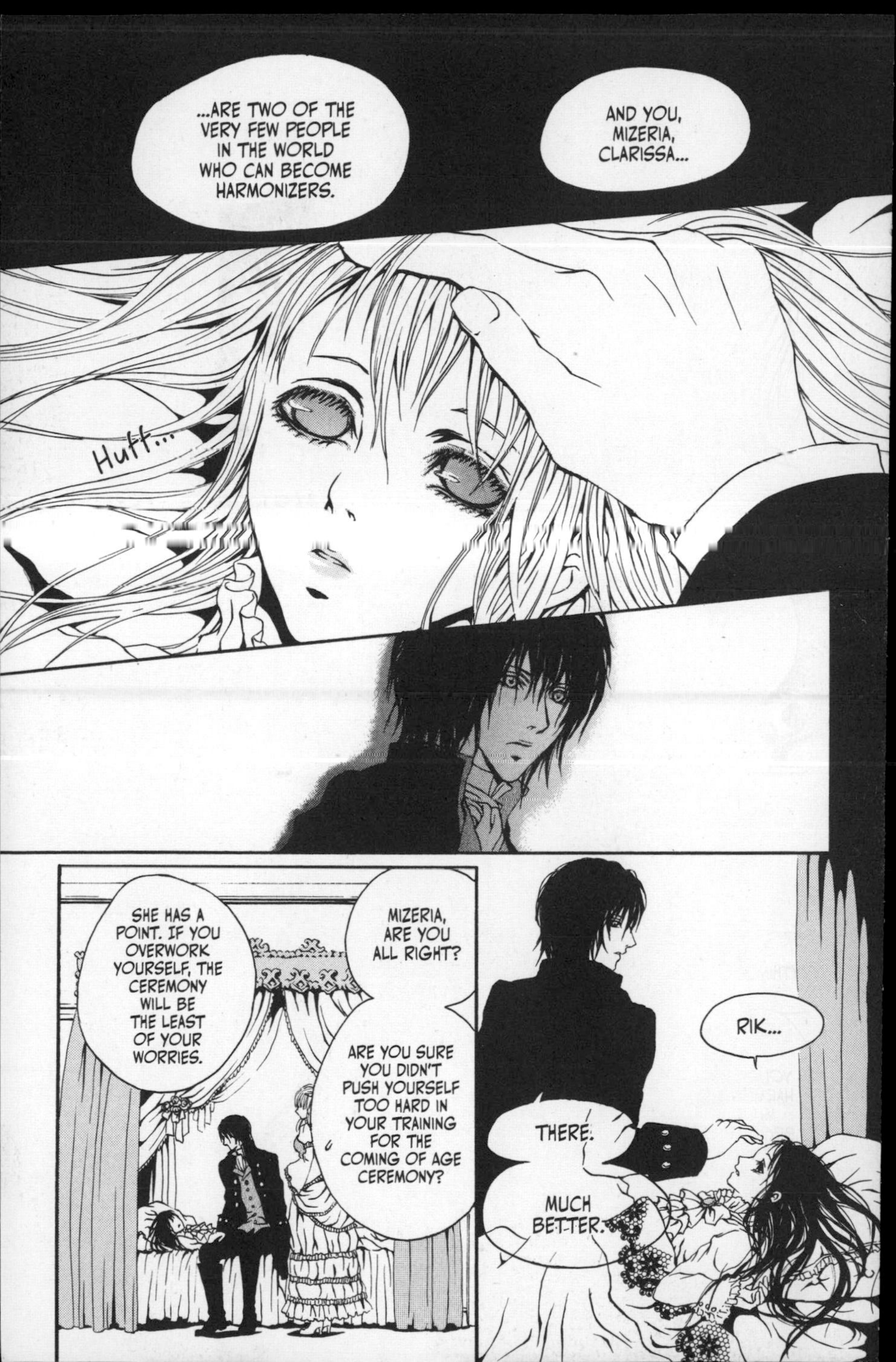
AND YOU, MIZERIA, CLARISSA...
...ARE TWO OF THE VERY FEW PEOPLE IN THE WORLD WHO CAN BECOME HARMONIZERS.
Huff...
RIK...
THERE.
MUCH BETTER.
MIZERIA, ARE YOU ALL RIGHT?
ARE YOU SURE YOU DIDN'T PUSH YOURSELF TOO HARD IN YOUR TRAINING FOR THE COMING OF AGE CEREMONY?
SHE HAS A POINT. IF YOU OVERWORK YOURSELF, THE CEREMONY WILL BE THE LEAST OF YOUR WORRIES.

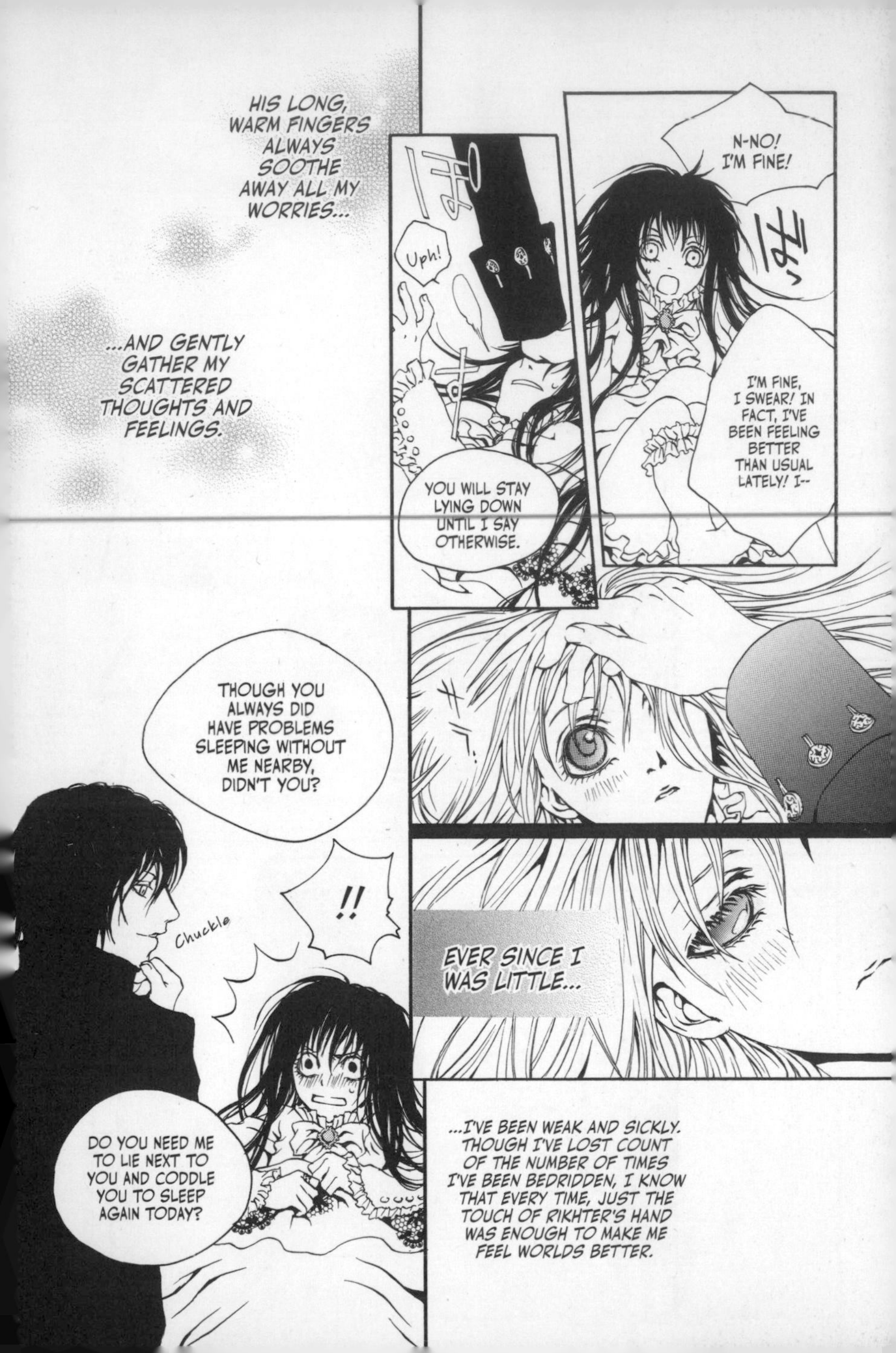
N-NO! I'M FINE!
I'M FINE, I SWEAR! IN FACT, I'VE BEEN FEELING BETTER THAN USUAL LATELY! I--
Uph!
YOU WILL STAY LYING DOWN UNTIL I SAY OTHERWISE.
HIS LONG, WARM FINGERS ALWAYS SOOTHE AWAY ALL MY WORRIES...
...AND GENTLY GATHER MY SCATTERED THOUGHTS AND FEELINGS.
EVER SINCE I WAS LITTLE...
...I'VE BEEN WEAK AND SICKLY. THOUGH I'VE LOST COUNT OF THE NUMBER OF TIMES I'VE BEEN BEDRIDDEN, I KNOW THAT EVERY TIME, JUST THE TOUCH OF RIKHTER'S HAND WAS ENOUGH TO MAKE ME FEEL WORLDS BETTER.
THOUGH YOU ALWAYS DID HAVE PROBLEMS SLEEPING WITHOUT ME NEARBY, DIDN'T YOU?
!!
Chuckle
DO YOU NEED ME TO LIE NEXT TO YOU AND CODDLE YOU TO SLEEP AGAIN TODAY?

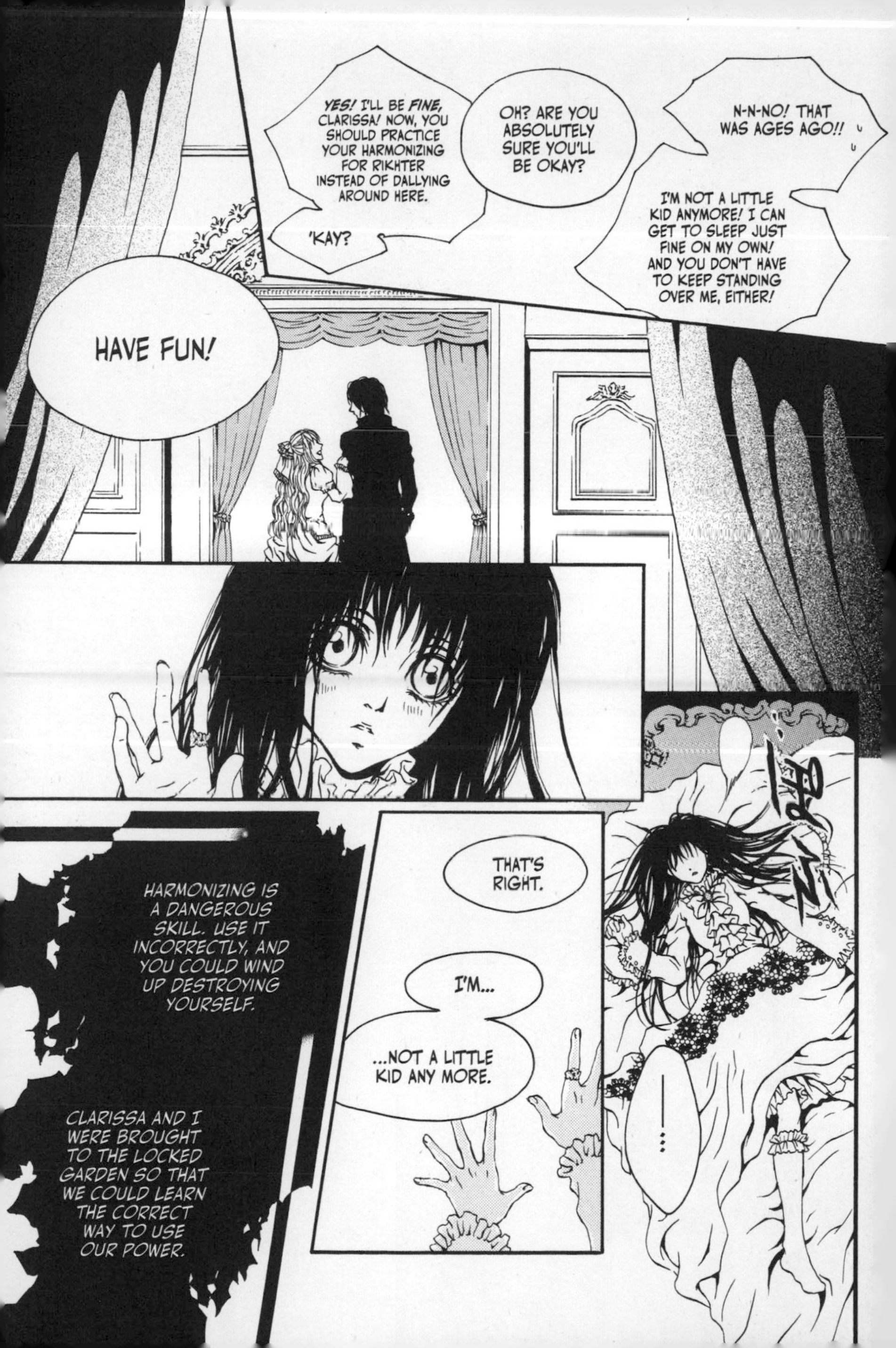
N-N-NO! THAT WAS AGES AGO!!
I'M NOT A LITTLE KID ANYMORE! I CAN GET TO SLEEP JUST FINE ON MY OWN! AND YOU DON'T HAVE TO KEEP STANDING OVER ME, EITHER!
OH? ARE YOU ABSOLUTELY SURE YOU'LL BE OKAY?
YES! I'LL BE *FINE,* CLARISSA! NOW, YOU SHOULD PRACTICE YOUR HARMONIZING FOR RIKHTER INSTEAD OF DALLYING AROUND HERE.
'KAY?
HAVE FUN!
...
THAT'S RIGHT.
I'M...
...NOT A LITTLE KID ANY MORE.
HARMONIZING IS A DANGEROUS SKILL. USE IT INCORRECTLY, AND YOU COULD WIND UP DESTROYING YOURSELF.
CLARISSA AND I WERE BROUGHT TO THE LOCKED GARDEN SO THAT WE COULD LEARN THE CORRECT WAY TO USE OUR POWER.

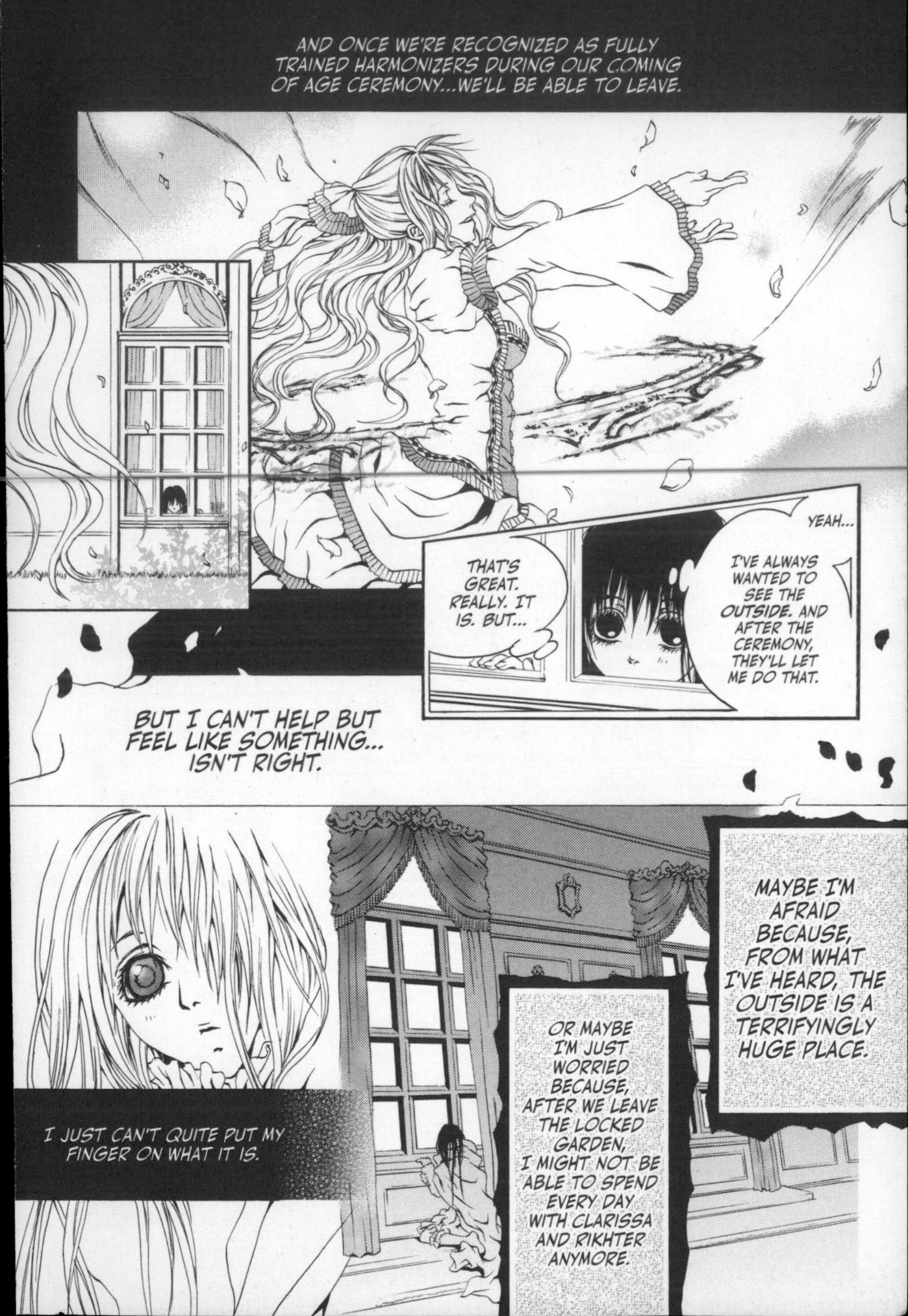
AND ONCE WE'RE RECOGNIZED AS FULLY TRAINED HARMONIZERS DURING OUR COMING OF AGE CEREMONY...WE'LL BE ABLE TO LEAVE.
YEAH...
I'VE ALWAYS WANTED TO SEE THE OUTSIDE. AND AFTER THE CEREMONY, THEY'LL LET ME DO THAT.
THAT'S GREAT. REALLY. IT IS. BUT...
BUT I CAN'T HELP BUT FEEL LIKE SOMETHING... ISN'T RIGHT.
MAYBE I'M AFRAID BECAUSE, FROM WHAT I'VE HEARD, THE OUTSIDE IS A TERRIFYINGLY HUGE PLACE.
OR MAYBE I'M JUST WORRIED BECAUSE, AFTER WE LEAVE THE LOCKED GARDEN, I MIGHT NOT BE ABLE TO SPEND EVERY DAY WITH CLARISSA AND RIKHTER ANYMORE.
I JUST CAN'T QUITE PUT MY FINGER ON WHAT IT IS.

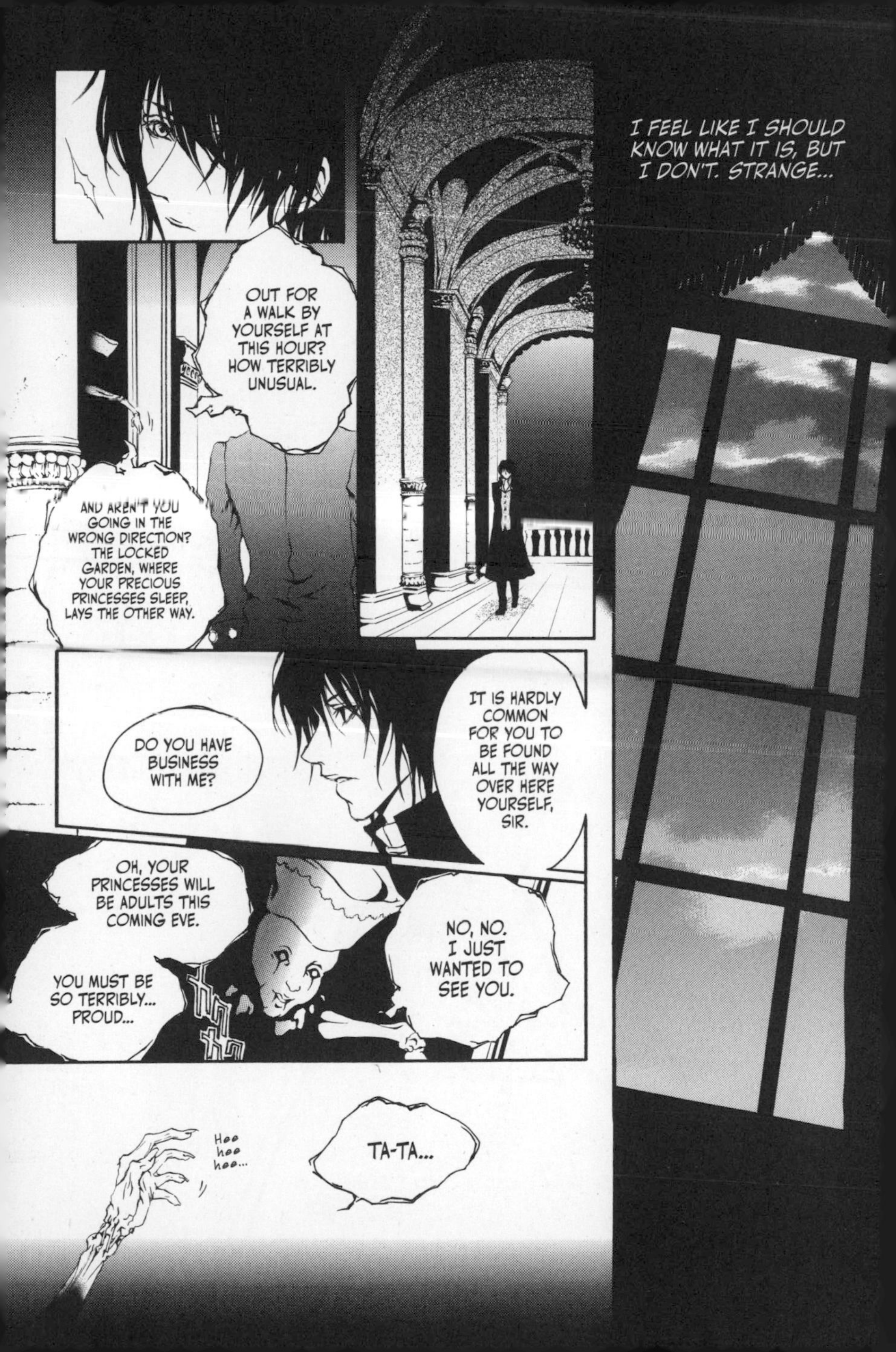
I FEEL LIKE I SHOULD KNOW WHAT IT IS, BUT I DON'T. STRANGE...
OUT FOR A WALK BY YOURSELF AT THIS HOUR? HOW TERRIBLY UNUSUAL.
AND AREN'T YOU GOING IN THE WRONG DIRECTION? THE LOCKED GARDEN, WHERE YOUR PRECIOUS PRINCESSES SLEEP, LAYS THE OTHER WAY.
IT IS HARDLY COMMON FOR YOU TO BE FOUND ALL THE WAY OVER HERE YOURSELF, SIR.
DO YOU HAVE BUSINESS WITH ME?
NO, NO. I JUST WANTED TO SEE YOU.
OH, YOUR PRINCESSES WILL BE ADULTS THIS COMING EVE.
YOU MUST BE SO TERRIBLY... PROUD...
TA-TA...
Hee hee hee...

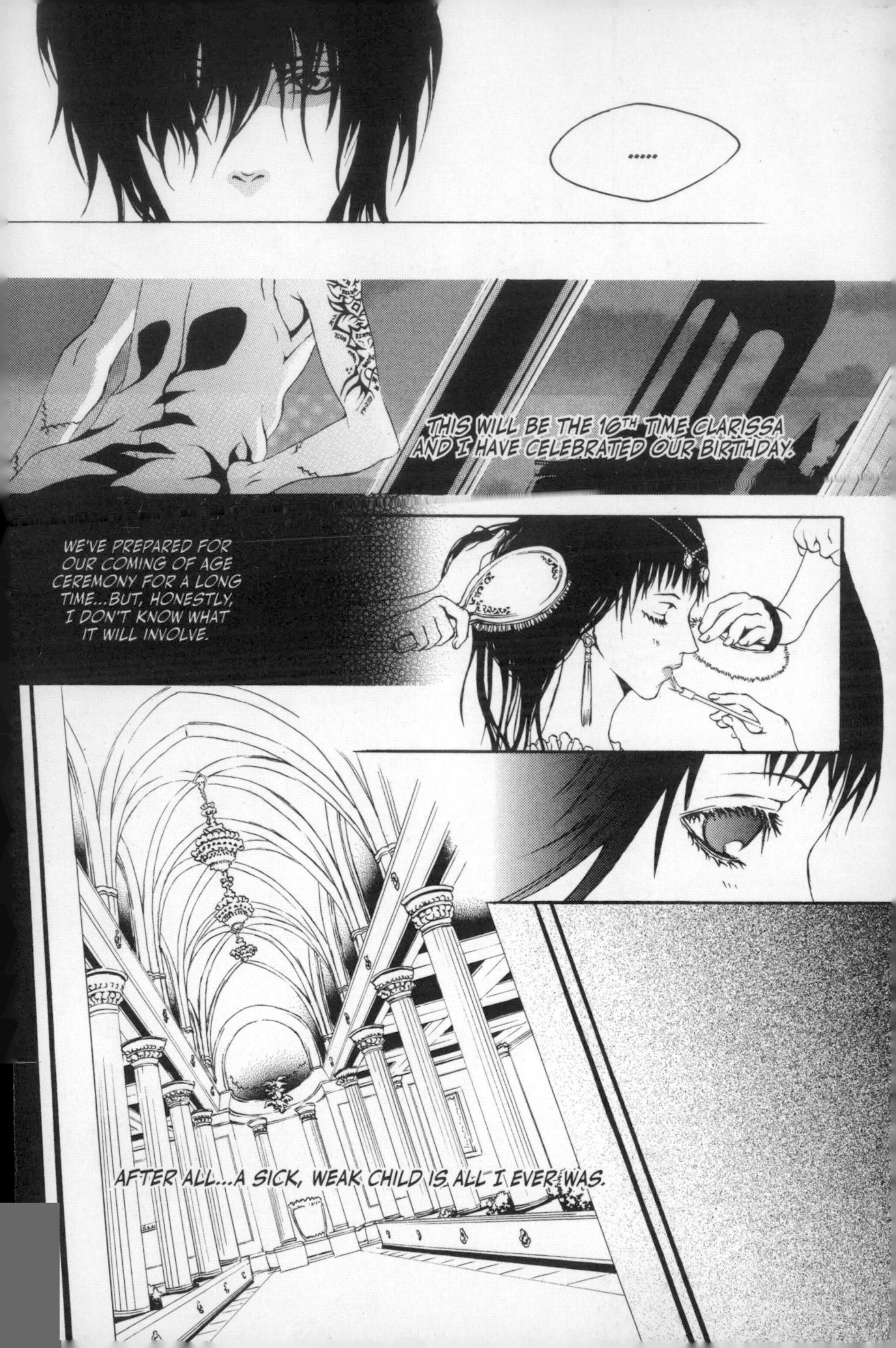

......
THIS WILL BE THE 16TH TIME CLARISSA AND I HAVE CELEBRATED OUR BIRTHDAY.
WE'VE PREPARED FOR OUR COMING OF AGE CEREMONY FOR A LONG TIME...BUT, HONESTLY, I DON'T KNOW WHAT IT WILL INVOLVE.
AFTER ALL...A SICK, WEAK CHILD IS ALL I EVER WAS.

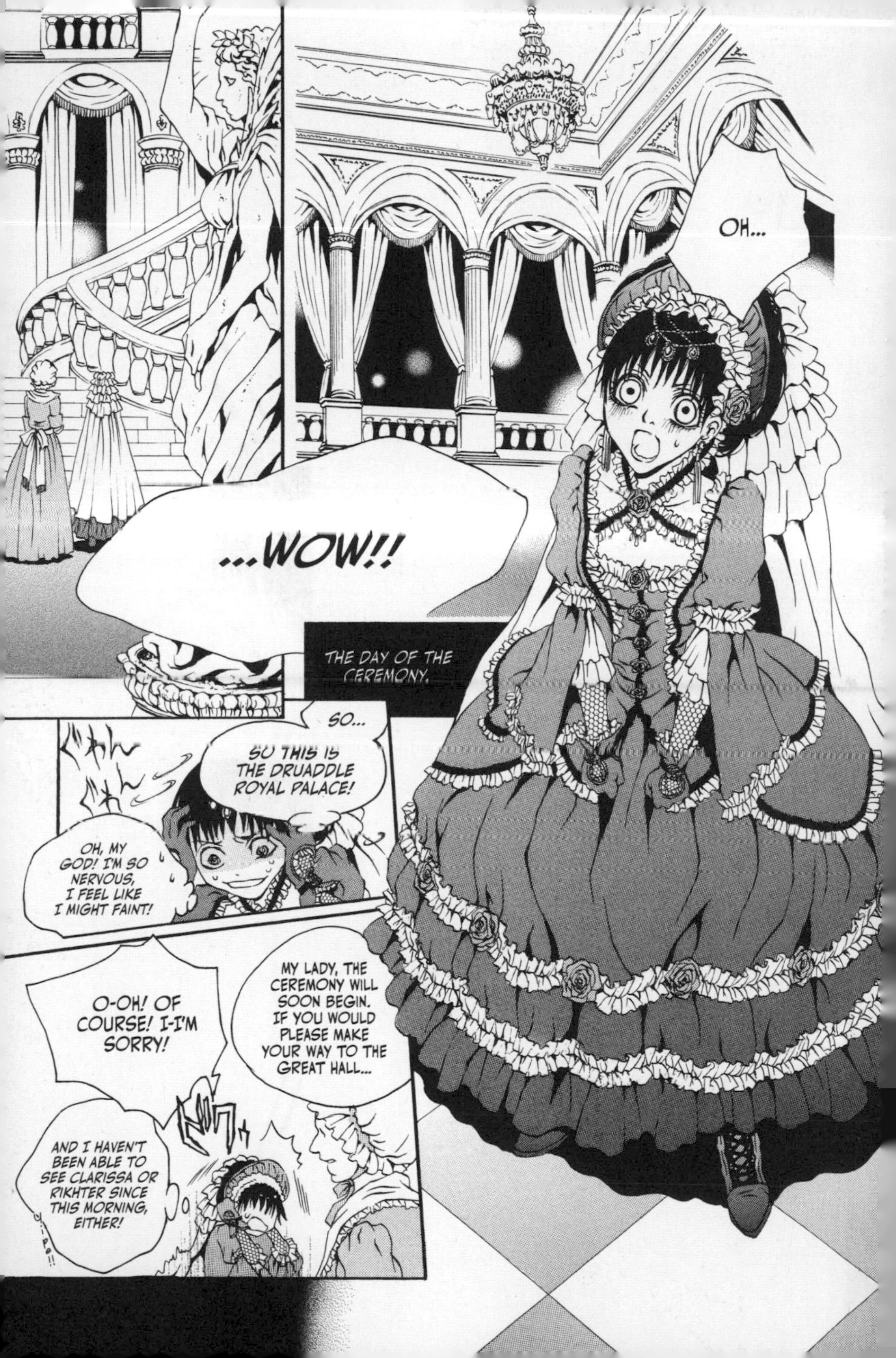
OH...
...WOW!!
THE DAY OF THE CEREMONY.
SO...
SO THIS IS THE DRUADDLE ROYAL PALACE!
OH, MY GOD! I'M SO NERVOUS, I FEEL LIKE I MIGHT FAINT!
MY LADY, THE CEREMONY WILL SOON BEGIN. IF YOU WOULD PLEASE MAKE YOUR WAY TO THE GREAT HALL...
O-OH! OF COURSE! I-I'M SORRY!
AND I HAVEN'T BEEN ABLE TO SEE CLARISSA OR RIKHTER SINCE THIS MORNING, EITHER!

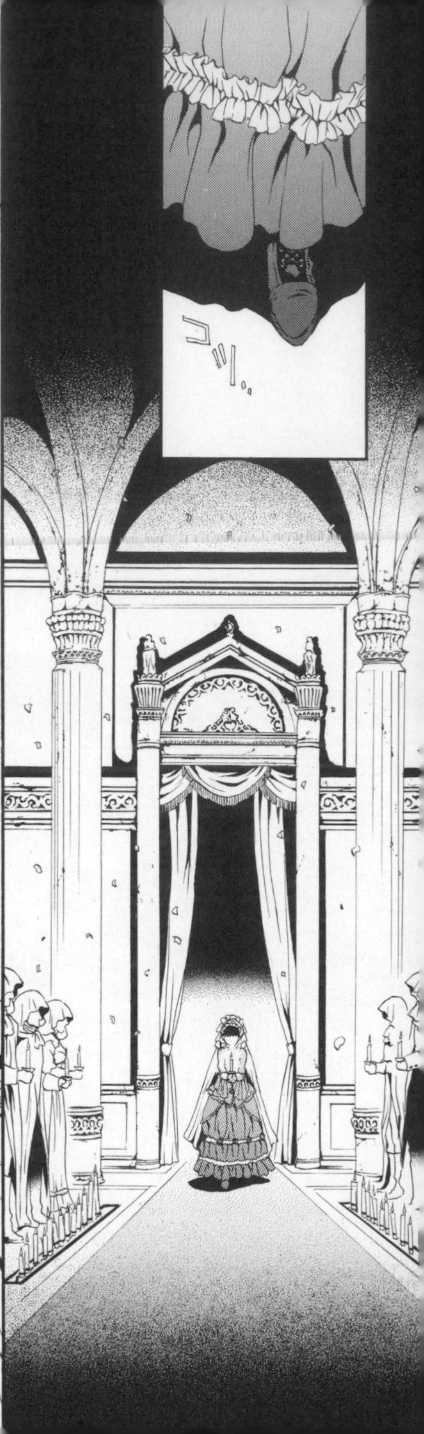
コッ…
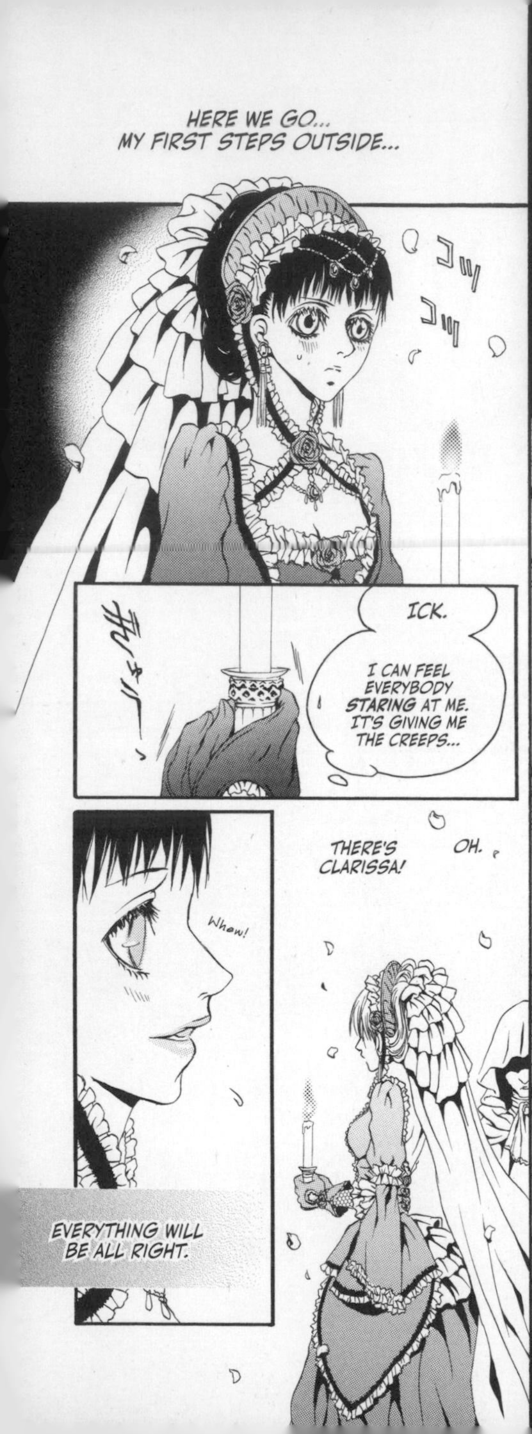
HERE WE GO... MY FIRST STEPS OUTSIDE...
コッ
コッ
ICK.
I CAN FEEL EVERYBODY STARING AT ME. IT'S GIVING ME THE CREEPS...
OH.
THERE'S CLARISSA!
Whew!
EVERYTHING WILL BE ALL RIGHT.

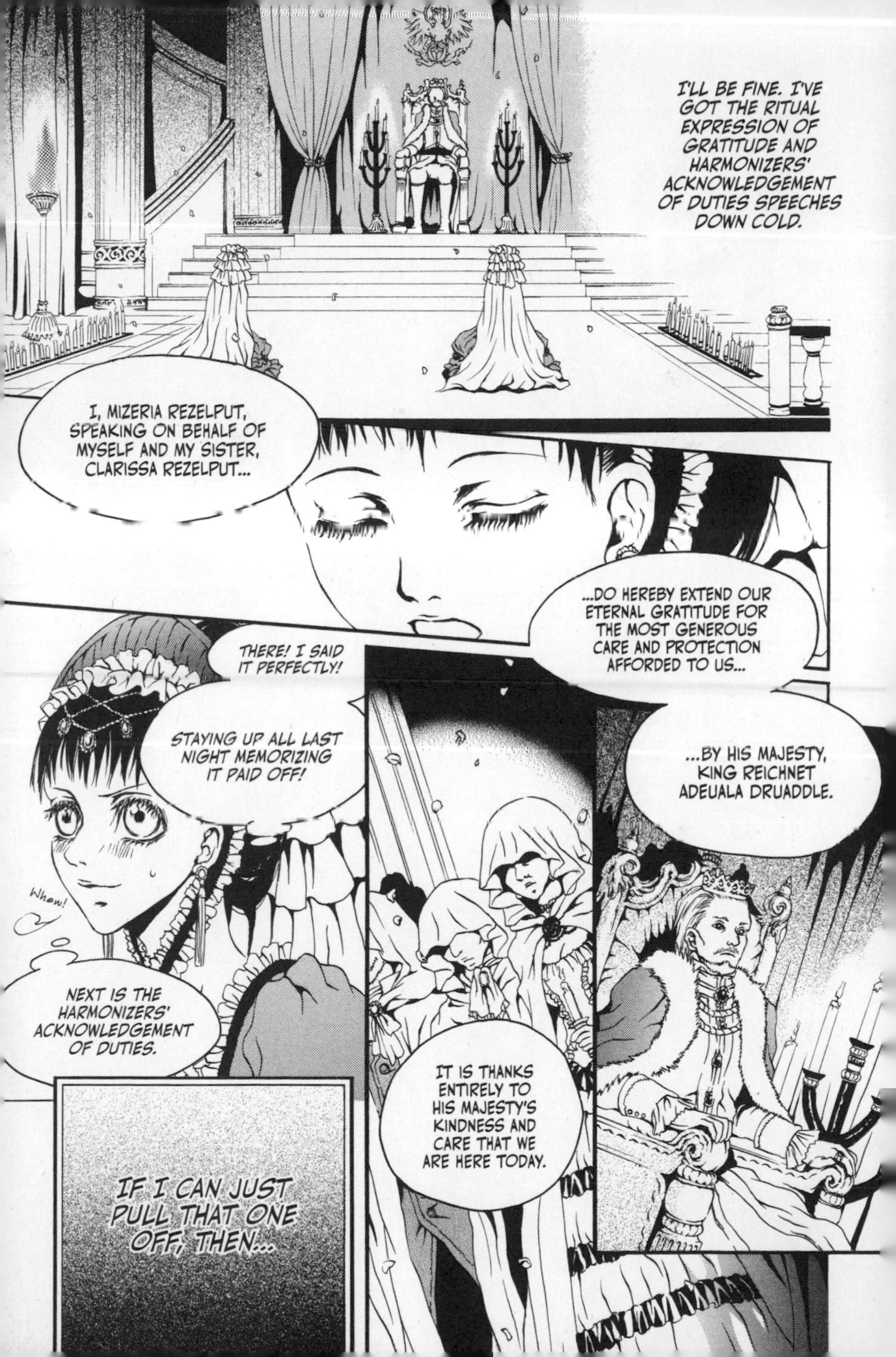
I'LL BE FINE. I'VE GOT THE RITUAL EXPRESSION OF GRATITUDE AND HARMONIZERS' ACKNOWLEDGEMENT OF DUTIES SPEECHES DOWN COLD.
I, MIZERIA REZELPUT, SPEAKING ON BEHALF OF MYSELF AND MY SISTER, CLARISSA REZELPUT...
...DO HEREBY EXTEND OUR ETERNAL GRATITUDE FOR THE MOST GENEROUS CARE AND PROTECTION AFFORDED TO US...
...BY HIS MAJESTY, KING REICHNET ADEUALA DRUADDLE.
IT IS THANKS ENTIRELY TO HIS MAJESTY'S KINDNESS AND CARE THAT WE ARE HERE TODAY.
THERE! I SAID IT PERFECTLY!
STAYING UP ALL LAST NIGHT MEMORIZING IT PAID OFF!
Whew!
NEXT IS THE HARMONIZERS' ACKNOWLEDGEMENT OF DUTIES.
IF I CAN JUST PULL THAT ONE OFF, THEN...

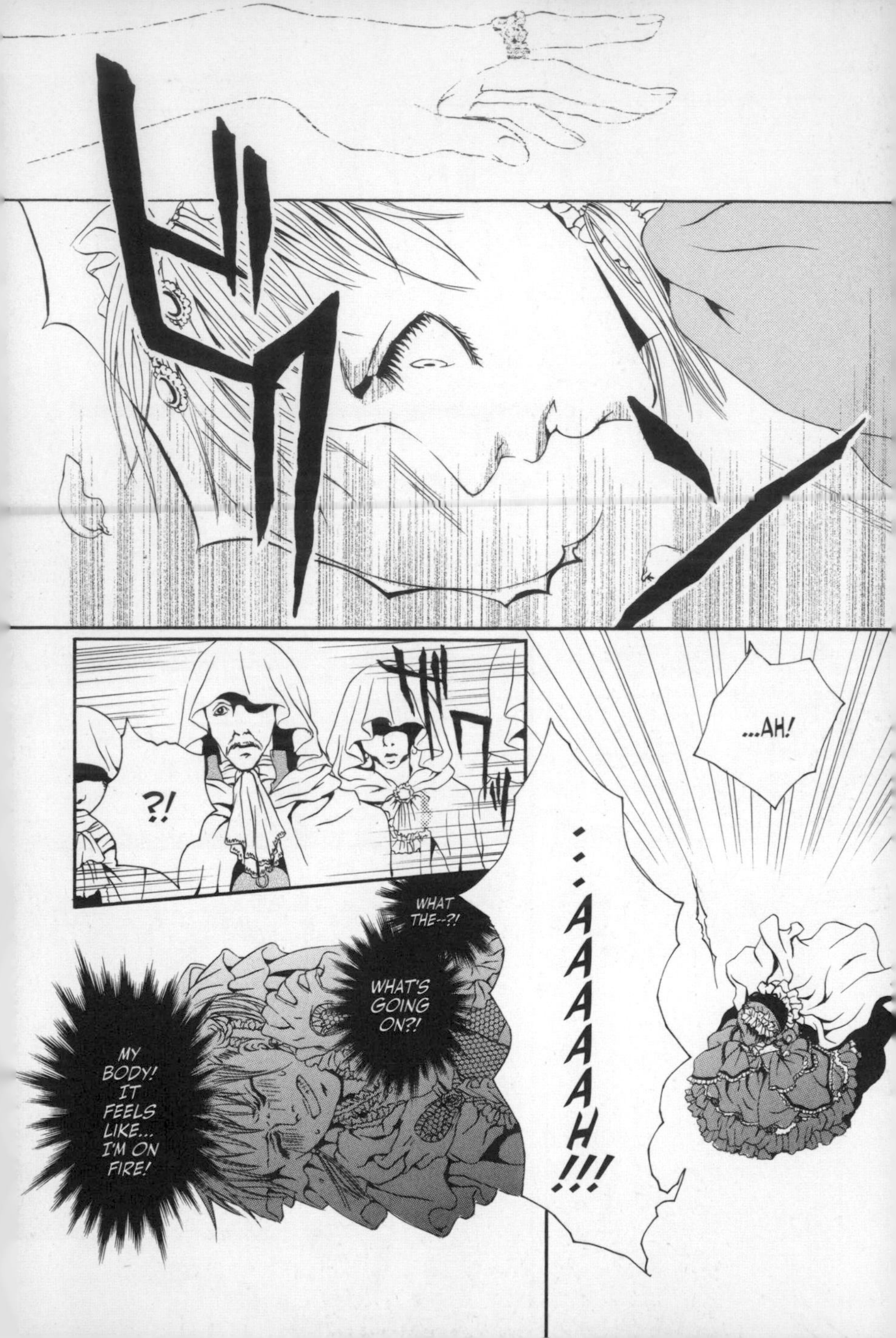
...AH!
?!
...AAAAAAH!!!
WHAT THE--?!
WHAT'S GOING ON?!
MY BODY! IT FEELS LIKE... I'M ON FIRE!

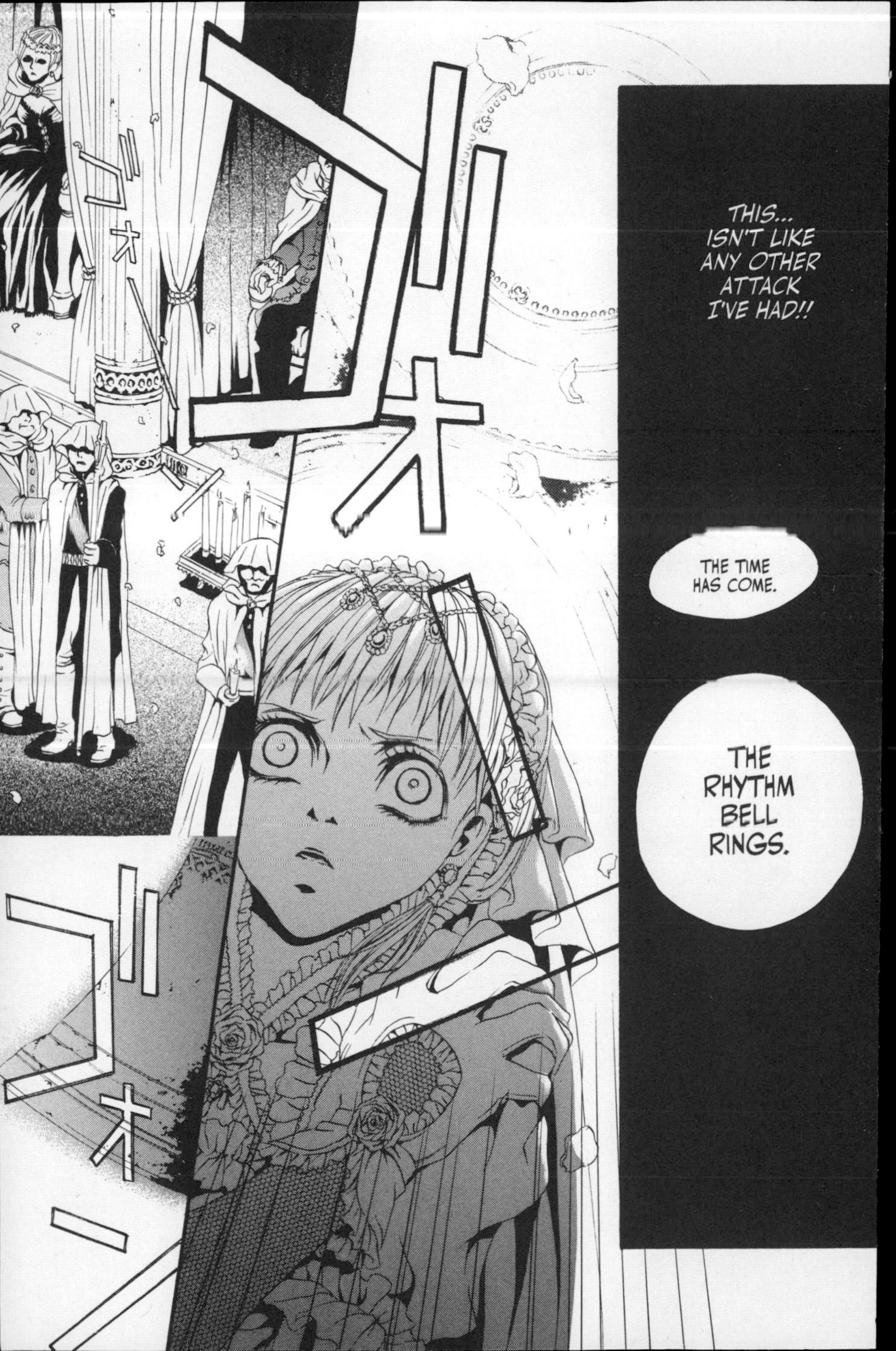
THIS... ISN'T LIKE ANY OTHER ATTACK I'VE HAD!!
THE TIME HAS COME.
THE RHYTHM BELL RINGS.
ゴォ
ゴォ
ゴォー

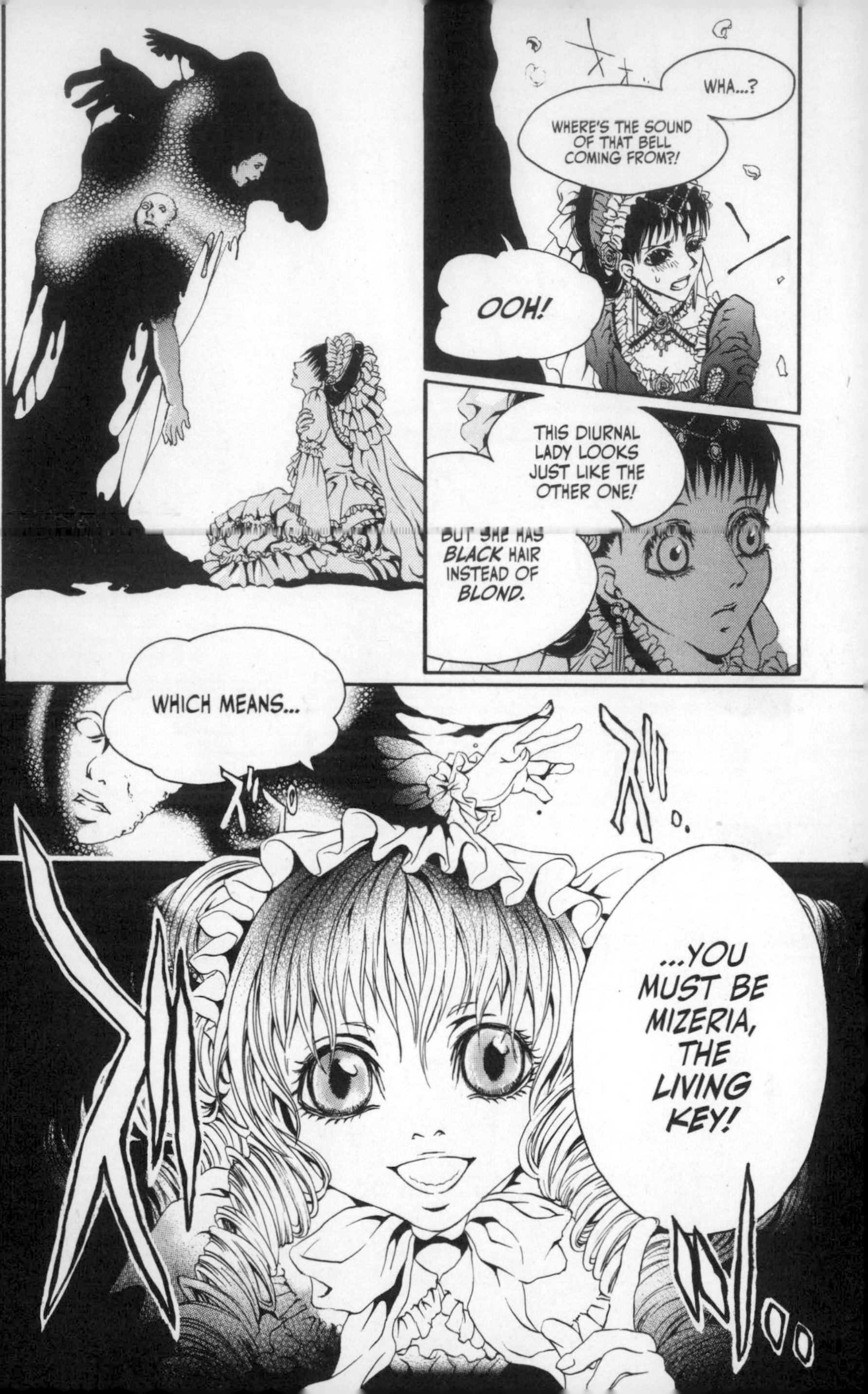
WHA...?
WHERE'S THE SOUND OF THAT BELL COMING FROM?!
OOH!
THIS DIURNAL LADY LOOKS JUST LIKE THE OTHER ONE!
BUT SHE HAS BLACK HAIR INSTEAD OF BLOND.
WHICH MEANS...
...YOU MUST BE MIZERIA, THE LIVING KEY!

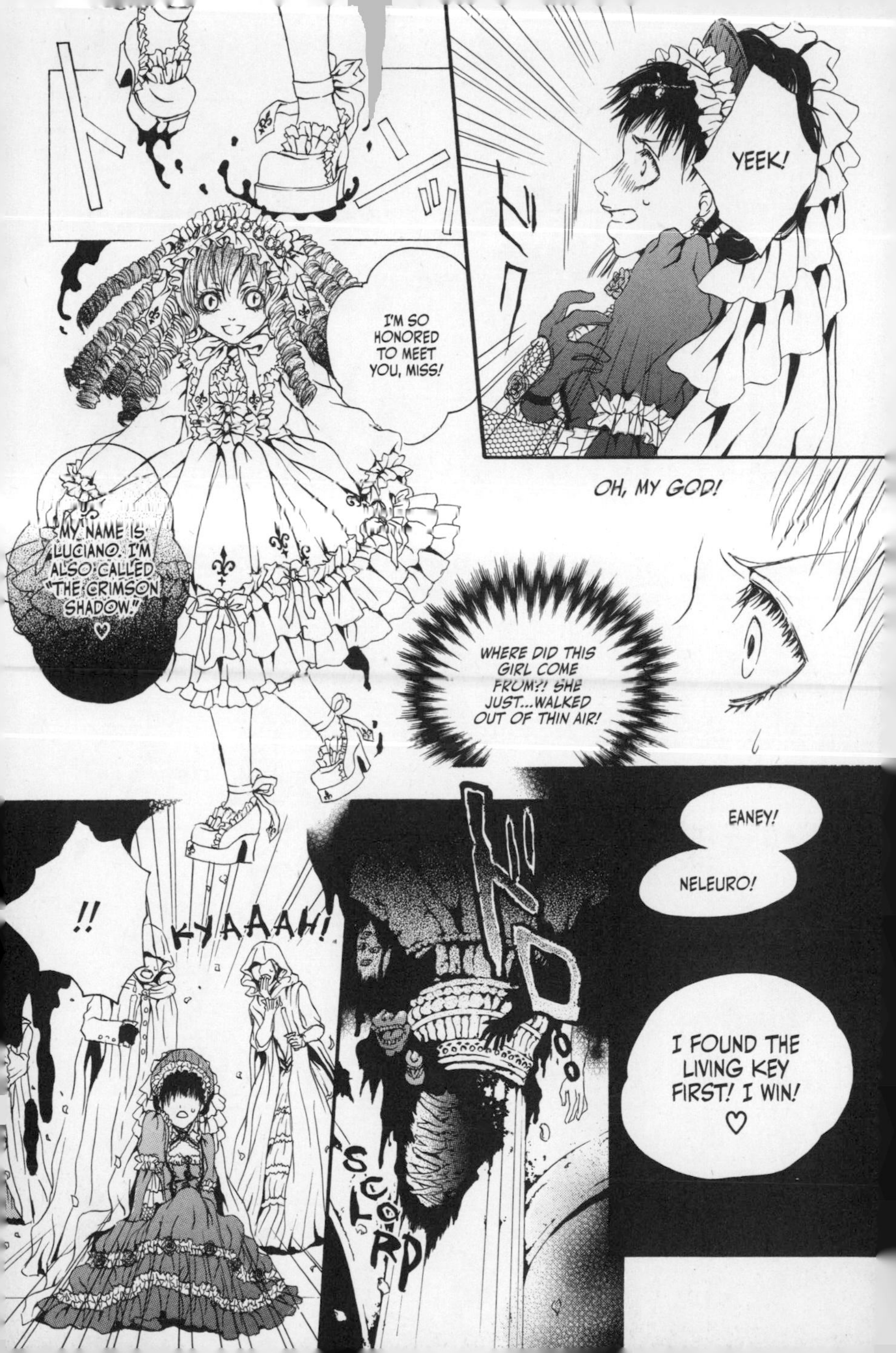
YEEK!
OH, MY GOD!
WHERE DID THIS GIRL COME FROM?! SHE JUST...WALKED OUT OF THIN AIR!
I'M SO HONORED TO MEET YOU, MISS!
MY NAME IS LUCIANO. I'M ALSO CALLED "THE CRIMSON SHADOW." ♡
EANEY!
NELEURO!
I FOUND THE LIVING KEY FIRST! I WIN! ♡
SCLORP
!!
KYAAAAH!

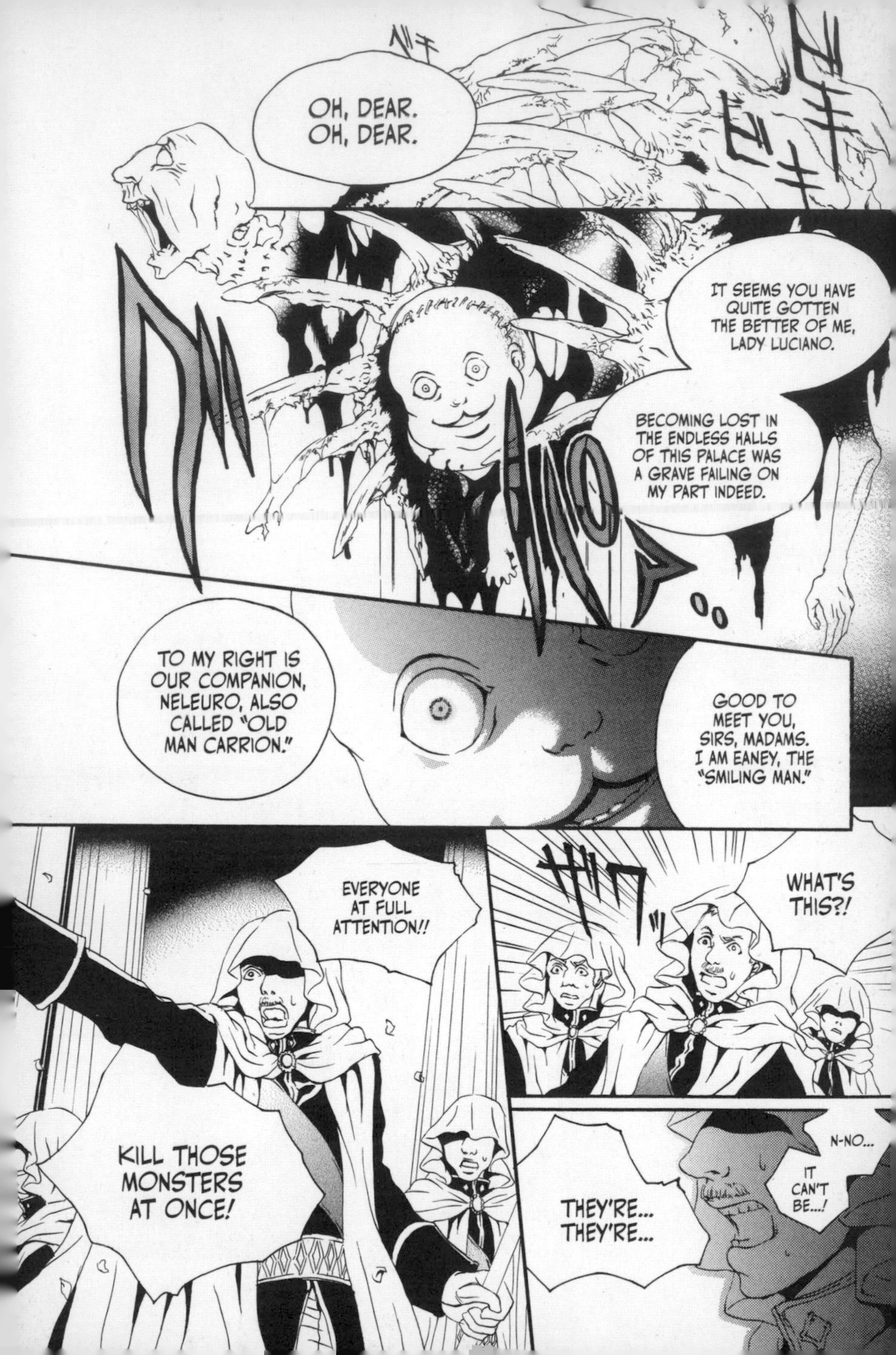
OH, DEAR.
OH, DEAR.
IT SEEMS YOU HAVE QUITE GOTTEN THE BETTER OF ME, LADY LUCIANO.
BECOMING LOST IN THE ENDLESS HALLS OF THIS PALACE WAS A GRAVE FAILING ON MY PART INDEED.
GOOD TO MEET YOU, SIRS, MADAMS. I AM EANEY, THE "SMILING MAN."
TO MY RIGHT IS OUR COMPANION, NELEURO, ALSO CALLED "OLD MAN CARRION."
WHAT'S THIS?!
N-NO...
IT CAN'T BE...!
THEY'RE... THEY'RE...
EVERYONE AT FULL ATTENTION!!
KILL THOSE MONSTERS AT ONCE!

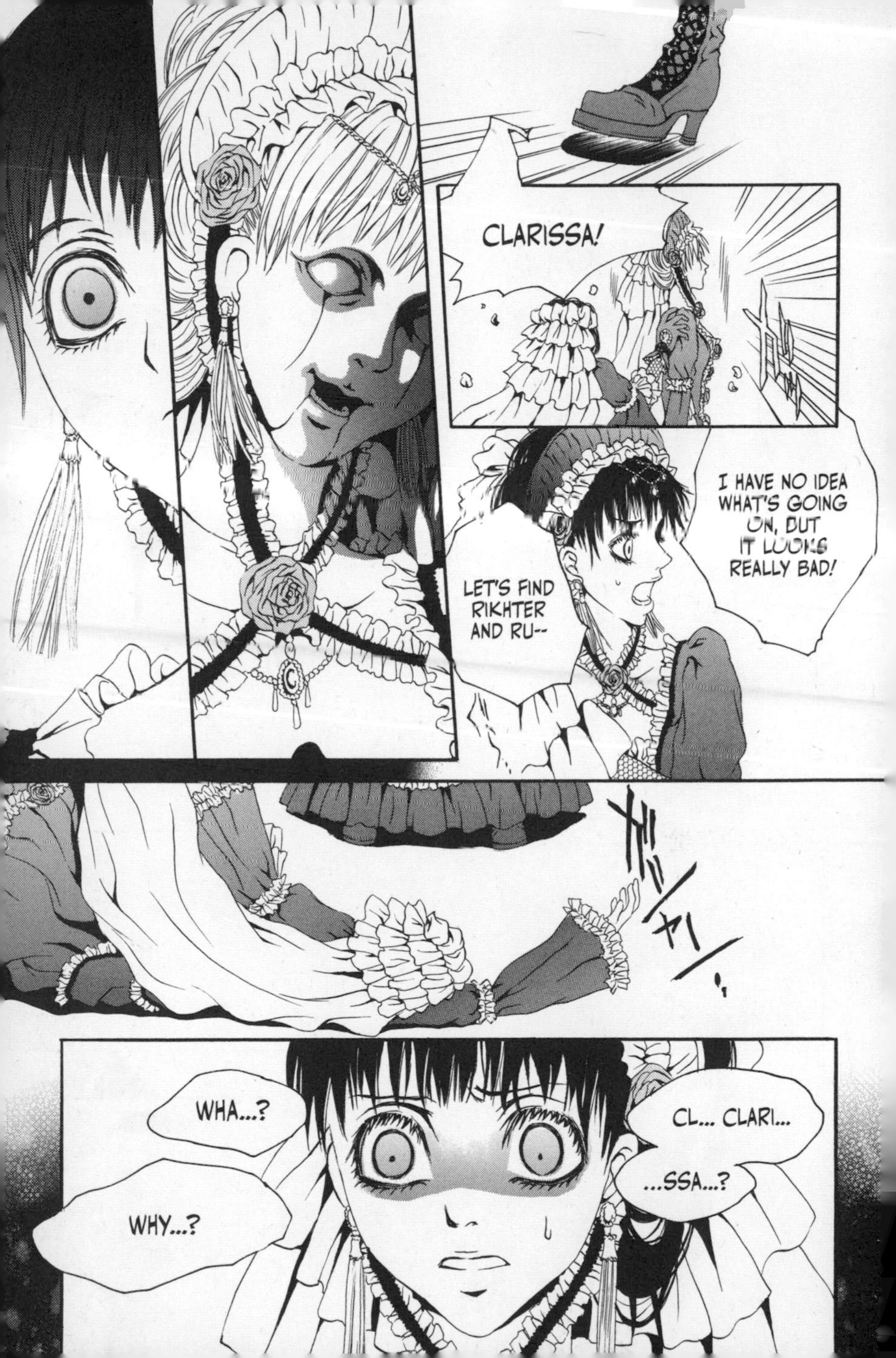
CLARISSA!
I HAVE NO IDEA WHAT'S GOING ON, BUT IT LOOKS REALLY BAD!
LET'S FIND RIKHTER AND RU--
CL... CLARI...
...SSA...?
WHA...?
WHY...?

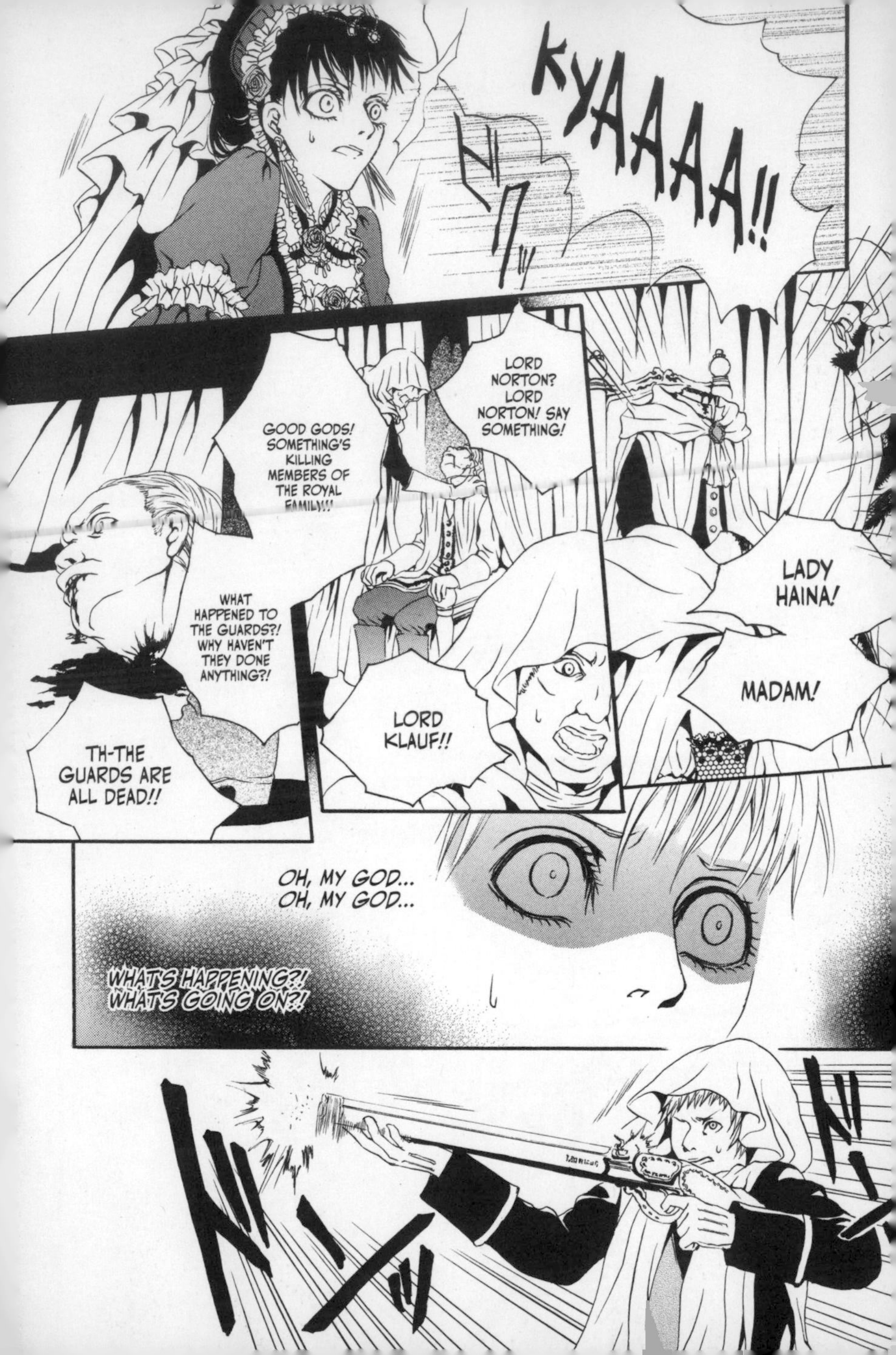
KYAAAAA!!
LADY HAINA!
MADAM!
LORD NORTON? LORD NORTON! SAY SOMETHING!
LORD KLAUF!!
GOOD GODS! SOMETHING'S KILLING MEMBERS OF THE ROYAL FAMILY!!!
WHAT HAPPENED TO THE GUARDS?! WHY HAVEN'T THEY DONE ANYTHING?!
TH-THE GUARDS ARE ALL DEAD!!
OH, MY GOD... OH, MY GOD...
WHAT'S HAPPENING?! WHAT'S GOING ON?!

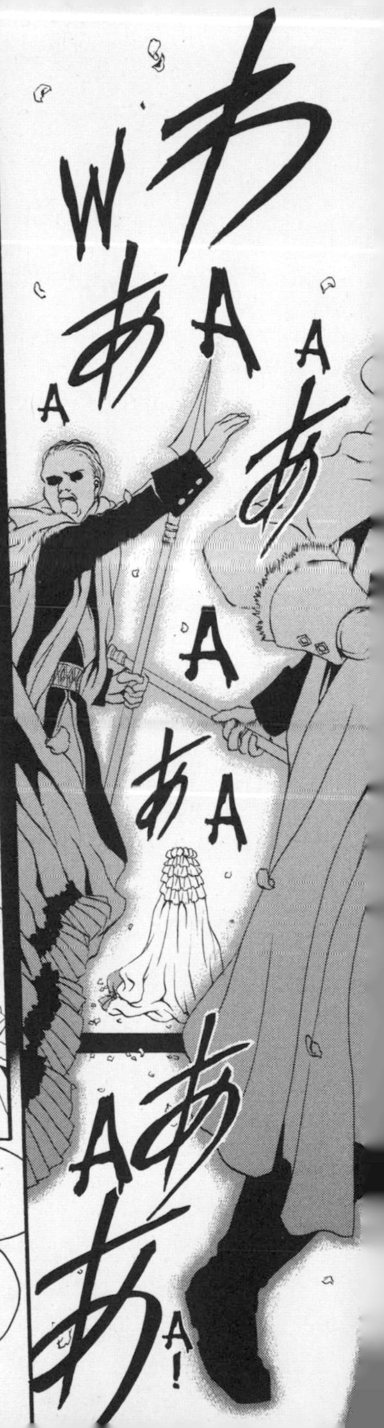
わ
W
あ
A
A
A
あ
A
あ
A
A
あ
A
あ
A!

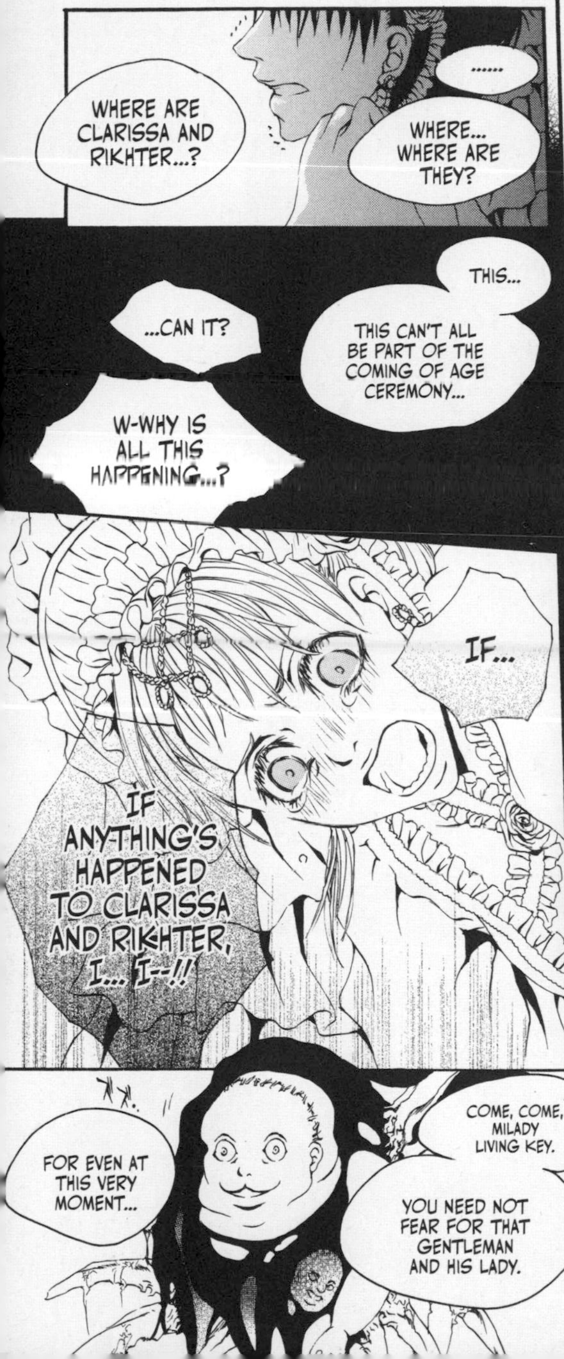
......
WHERE ARE CLARISSA AND RIKHTER...?
WHERE... WHERE ARE THEY?
THIS...
THIS CAN'T ALL BE PART OF THE COMING OF AGE CEREMONY...
...CAN IT?
W-WHY IS ALL THIS HAPPENING...?
IF...
IF ANYTHING'S HAPPENED TO CLARISSA AND RIKHTER, I... I--!!
COME, COME, MILADY LIVING KEY.
YOU NEED NOT FEAR FOR THAT GENTLEMAN AND HIS LADY.
FOR EVEN AT THIS VERY MOMENT...

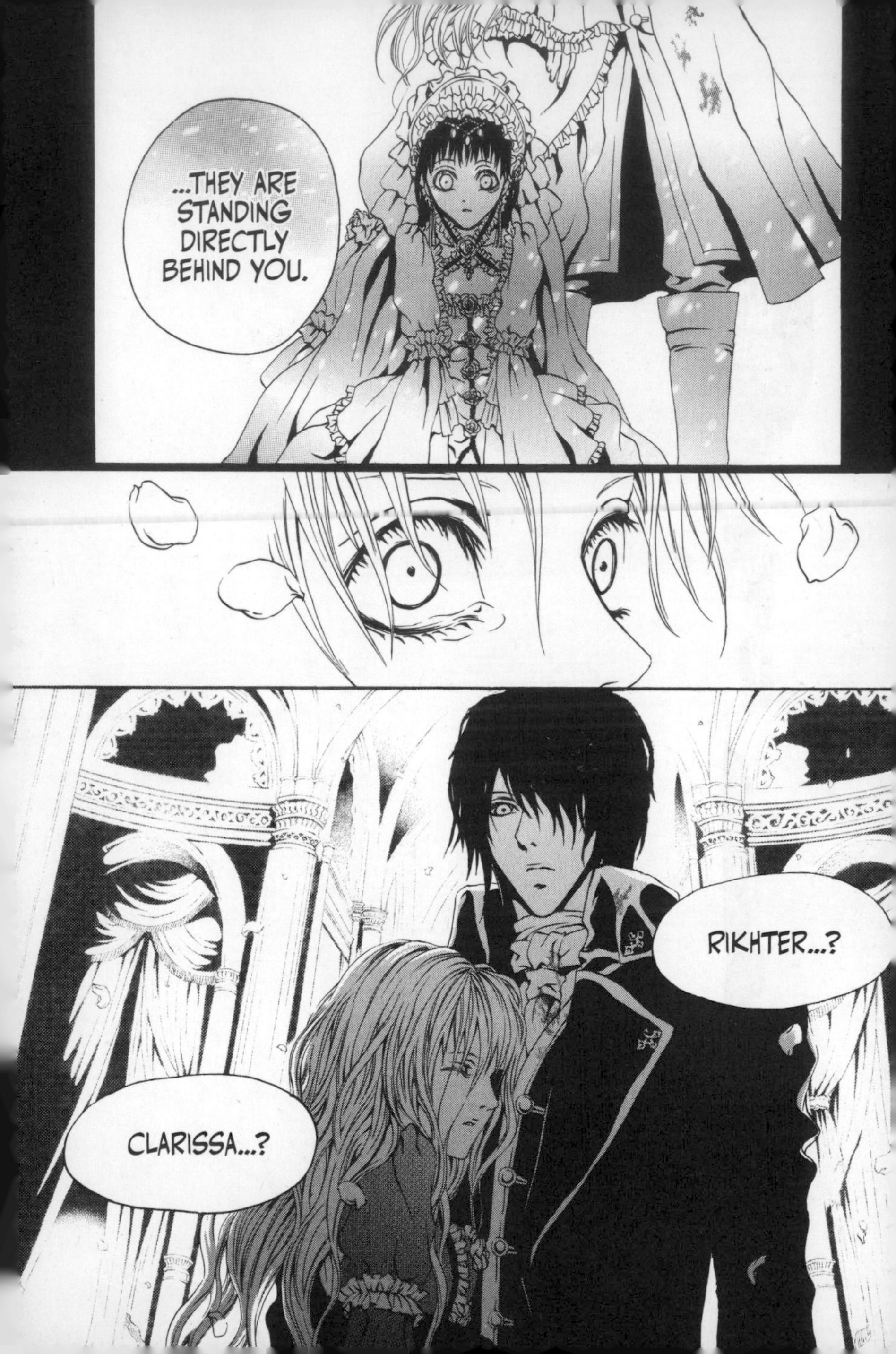
...THEY ARE STANDING DIRECTLY BEHIND YOU.
RIKHTER...?
CLARISSA...?

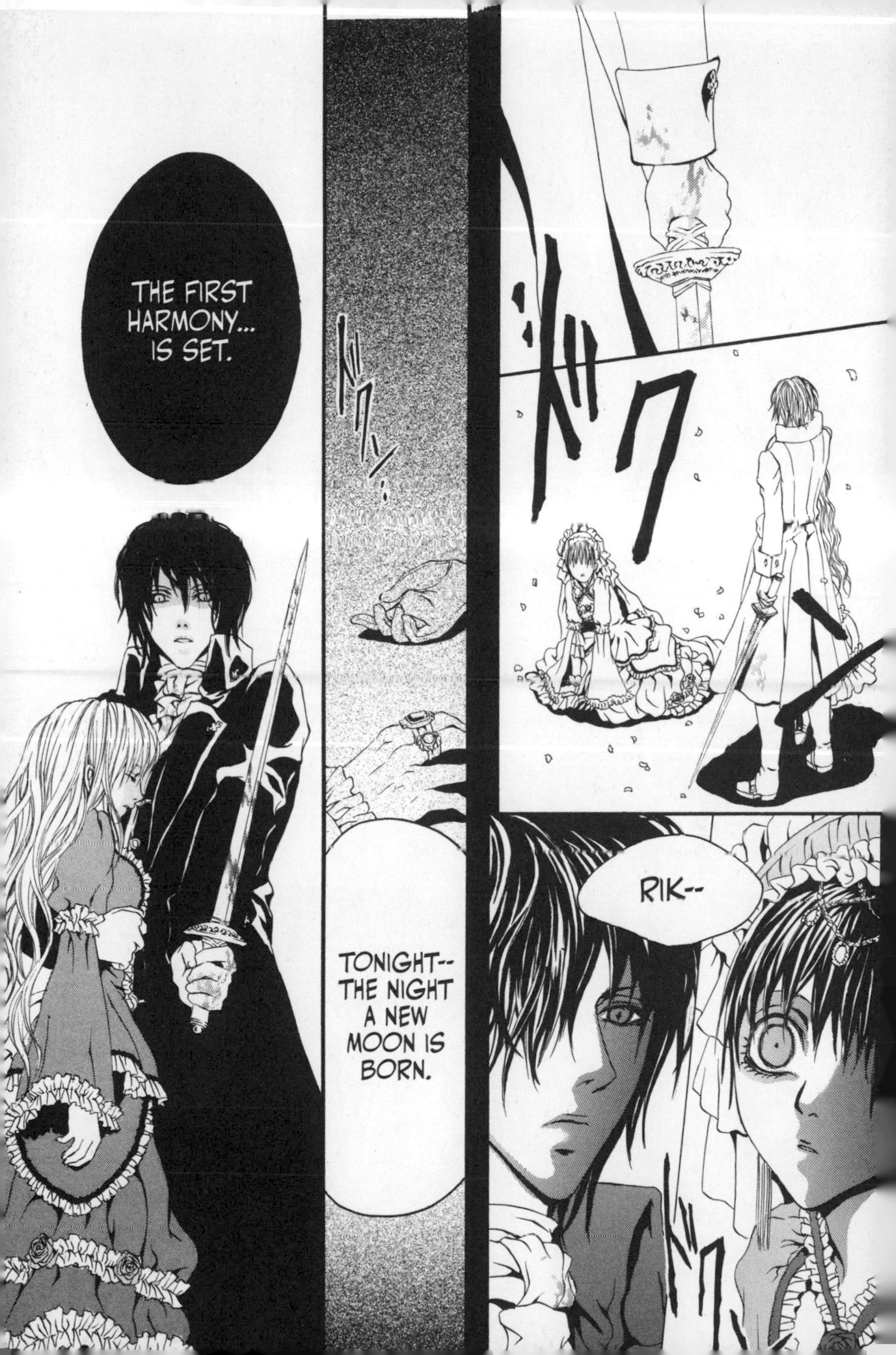
ドク
RIK--
ドク
ドクン
TONIGHT-- THE NIGHT A NEW MOON IS BORN.
THE FIRST HARMONY... IS SET.

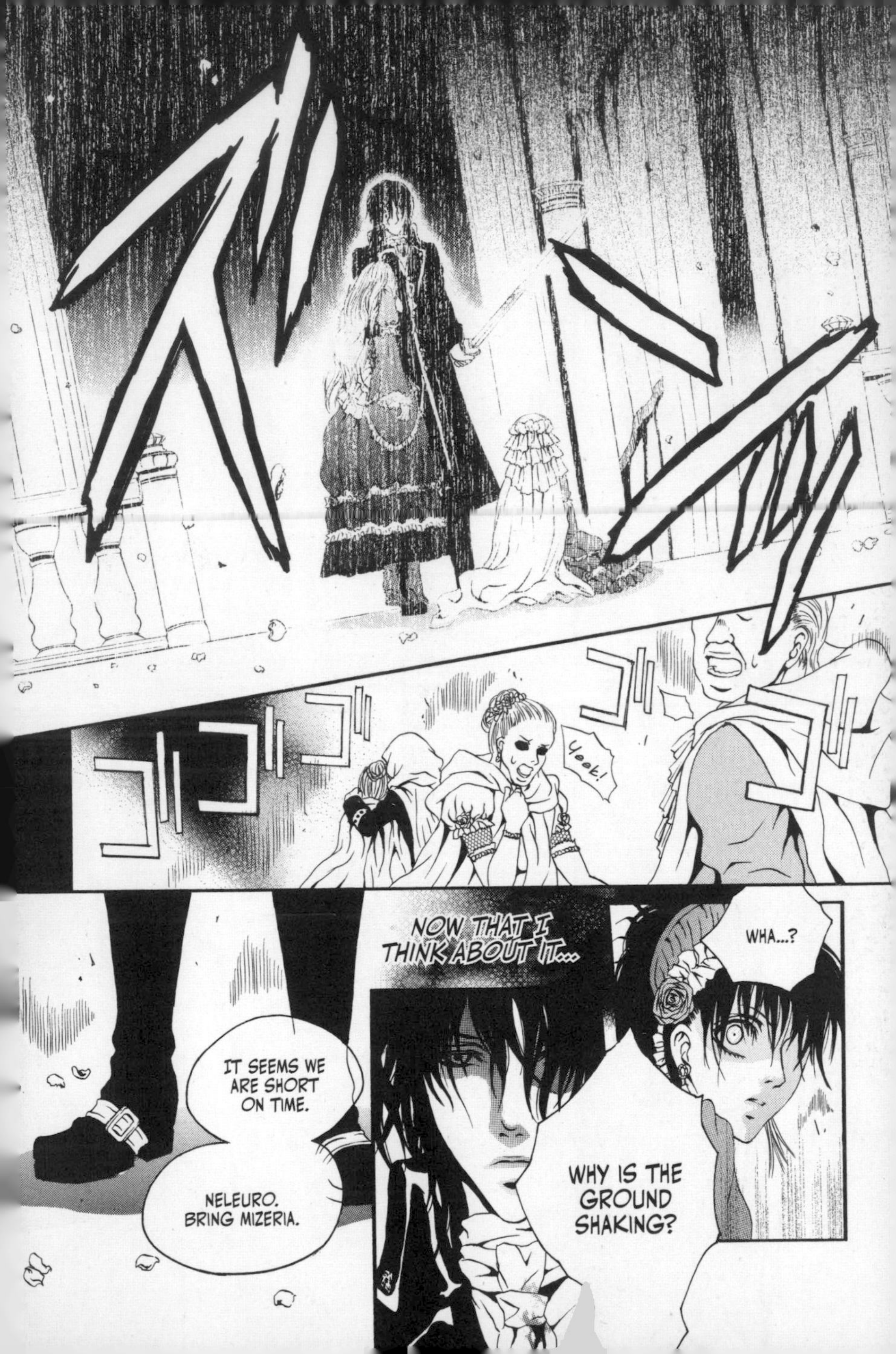
Yeek!
WHA...?
NOW THAT I THINK ABOUT IT...
WHY IS THE GROUND SHAKING?
IT SEEMS WE ARE SHORT ON TIME.
NELEURO. BRING MIZERIA.

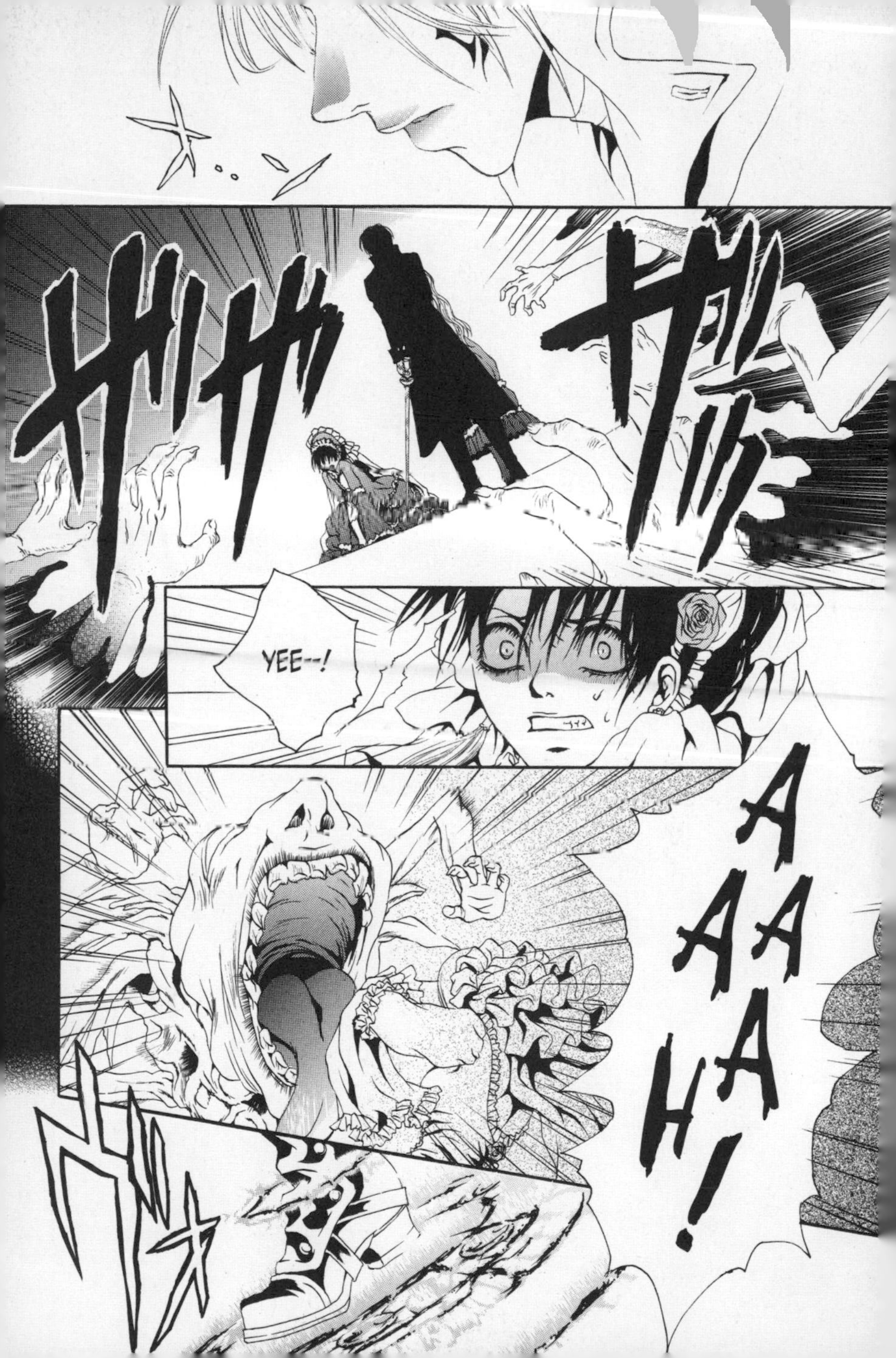
YEE--!
AAAAAH!

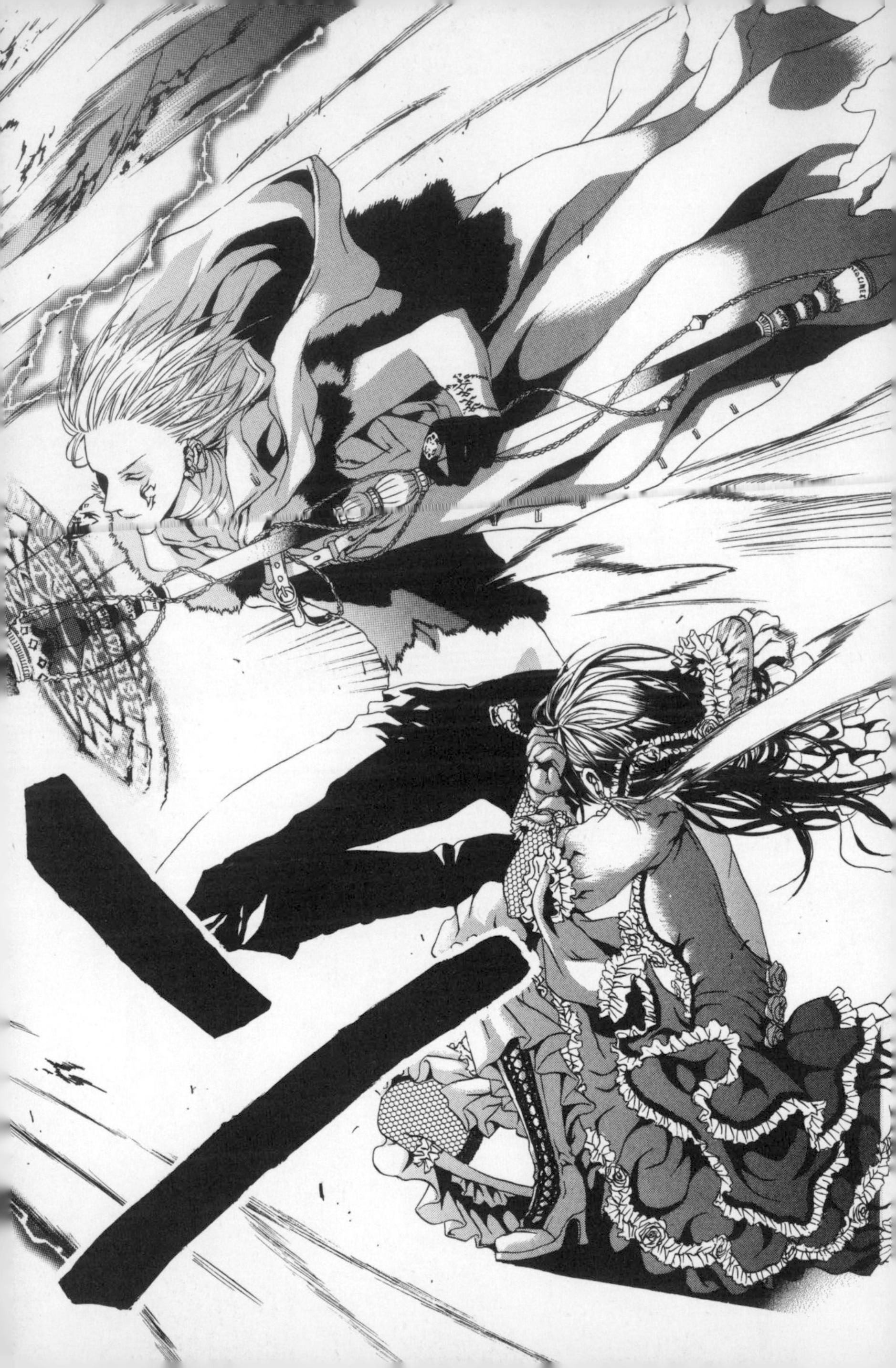

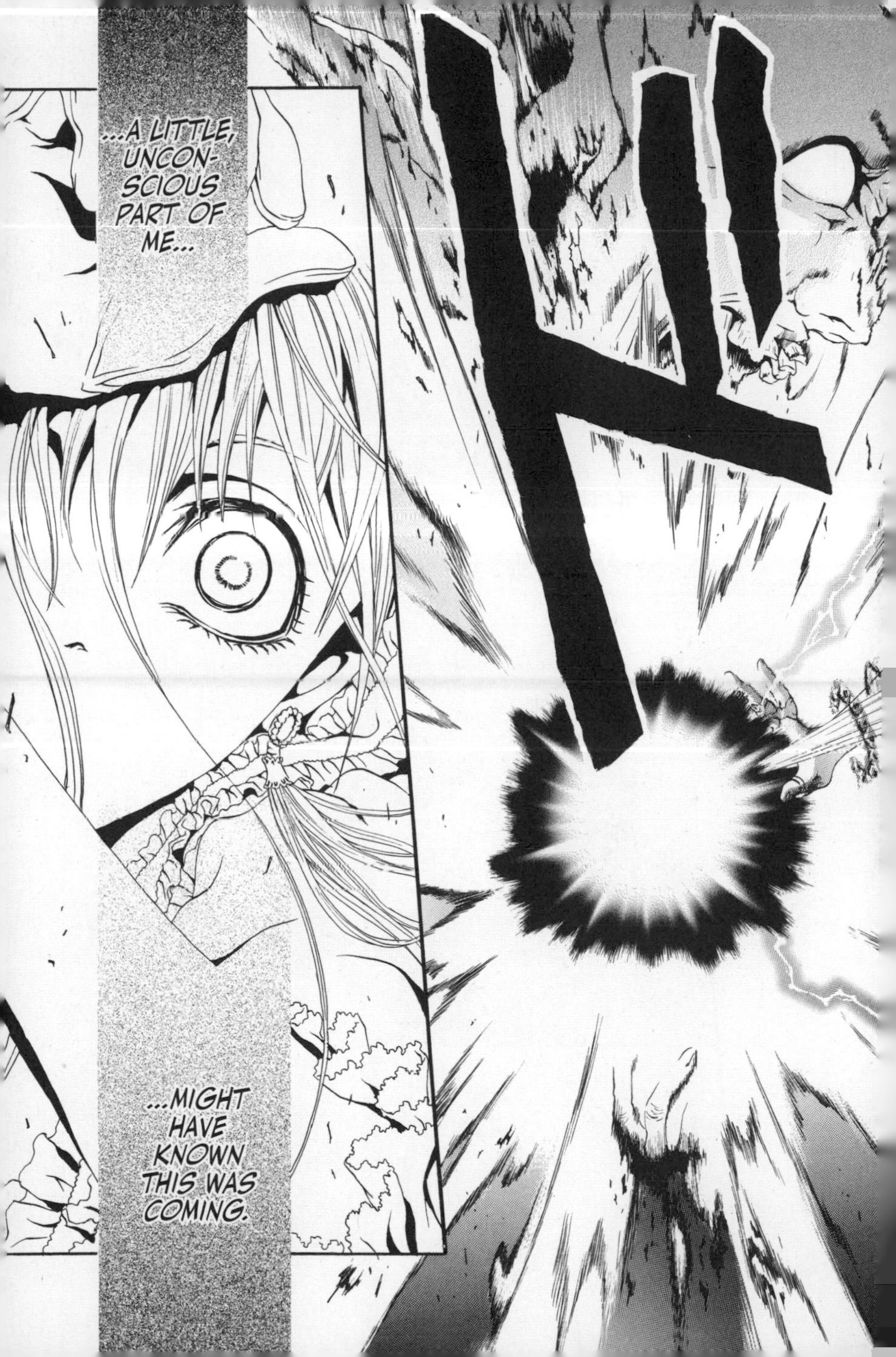
...A LITTLE, UNCON- SCIOUS PART OF ME...
...MIGHT HAVE KNOWN THIS WAS COMING.

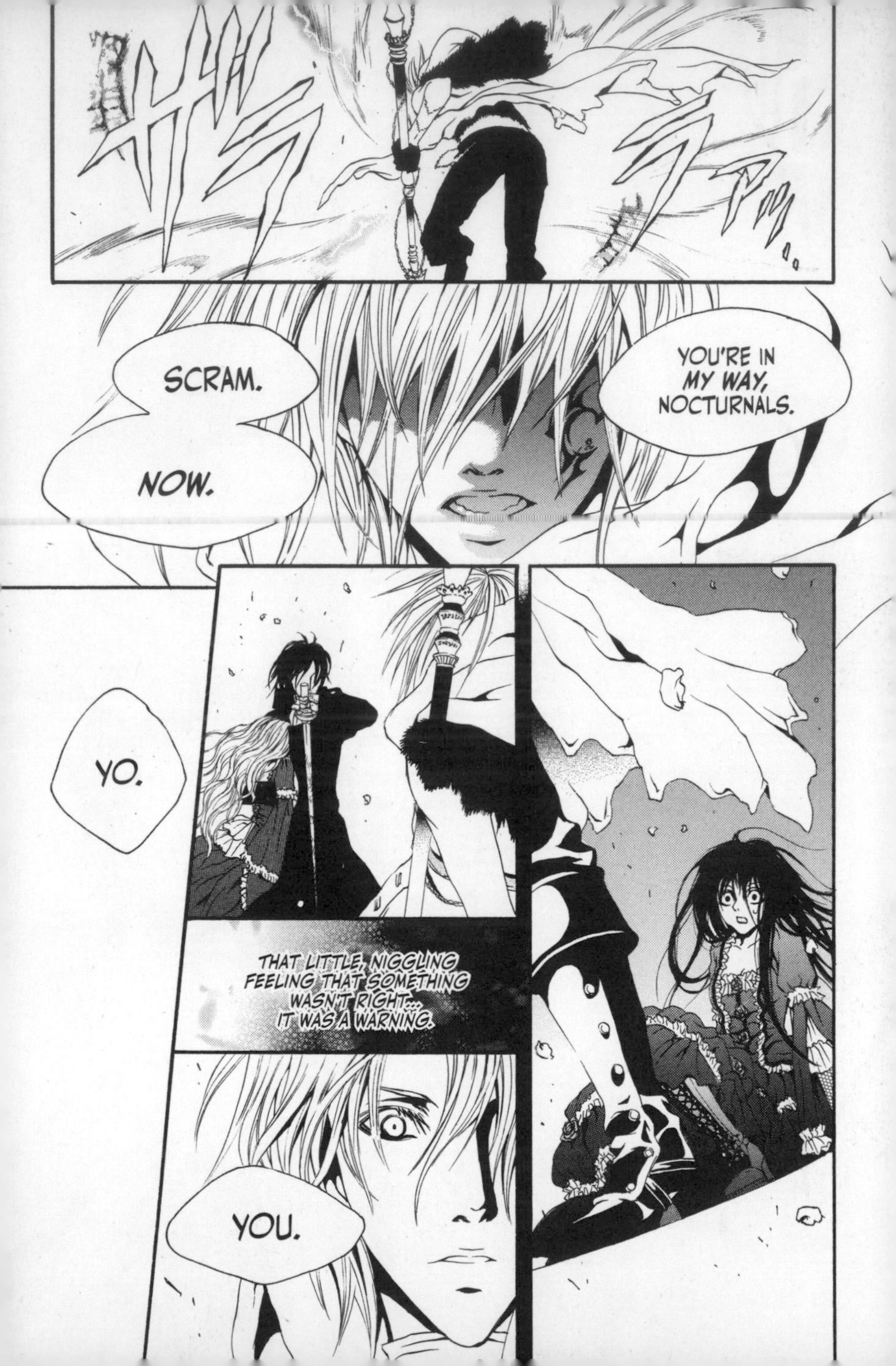
YOU'RE IN MY WAY, NOCTURNALS.
SCRAM.
NOW.
YO.
THAT LITTLE, NIGGLING FEELING THAT SOMETHING WASN'T RIGHT... IT WAS A WARNING.
YOU.

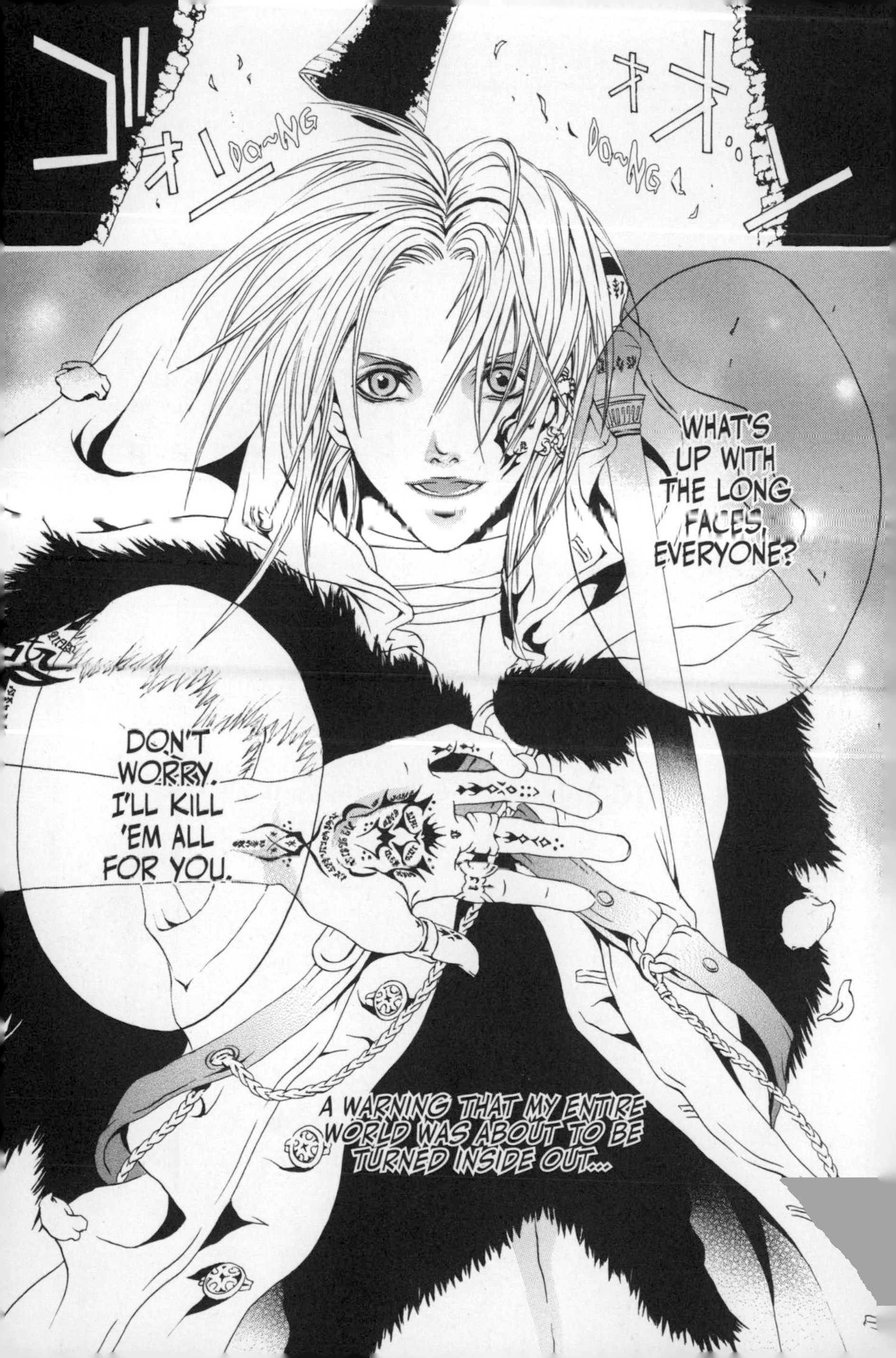
DO~NG
DO~NG
WHAT'S UP WITH THE LONG FACES, EVERYONE?
DON'T WORRY. I'LL KILL 'EM ALL FOR YOU.
A WARNING THAT MY ENTIRE WORLD WAS ABOUT TO BE TURNED INSIDE OUT...

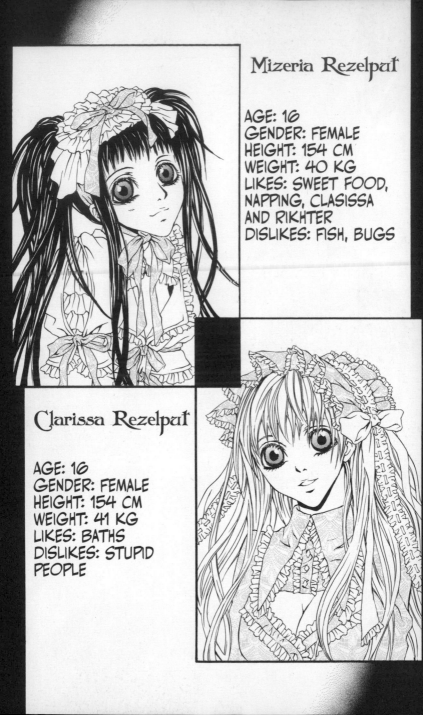

Mizeria Rezelput

AGE: 16
GENDER: FEMALE
HEIGHT: 154 CM
WEIGHT: 40 KG
LIKES: SWEET FOOD, NAPPING, CLASISSA AND RIKHTER
DISLIKES: FISH, BUGS

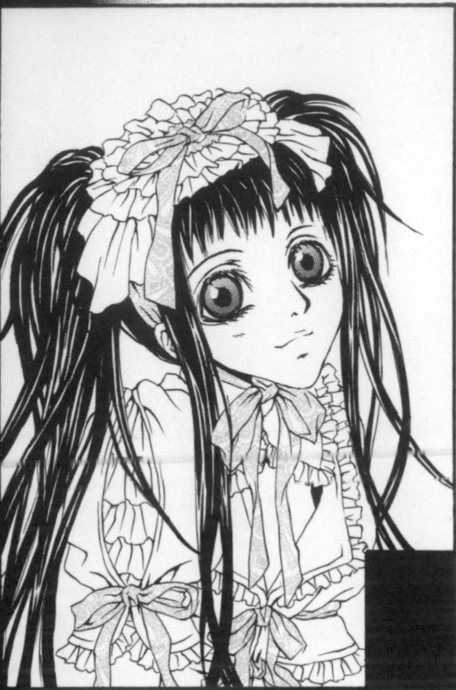

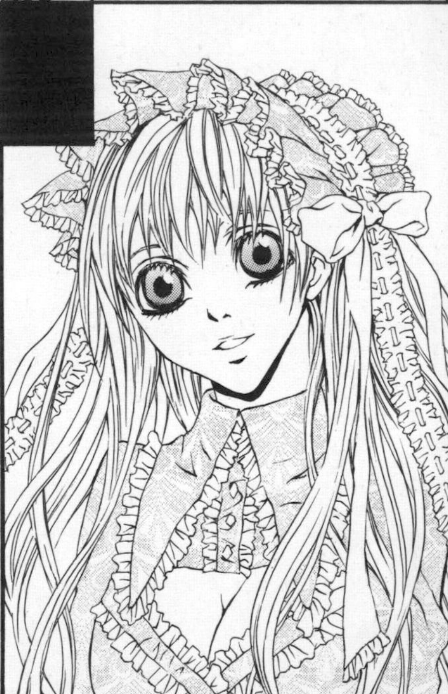

Clarissa Rezelput

AGE: 16
GENDER: FEMALE
HEIGHT: 154 CM
WEIGHT: 41 KG
LIKES: BATHS
DISLIKES: STUPID PEOPLE

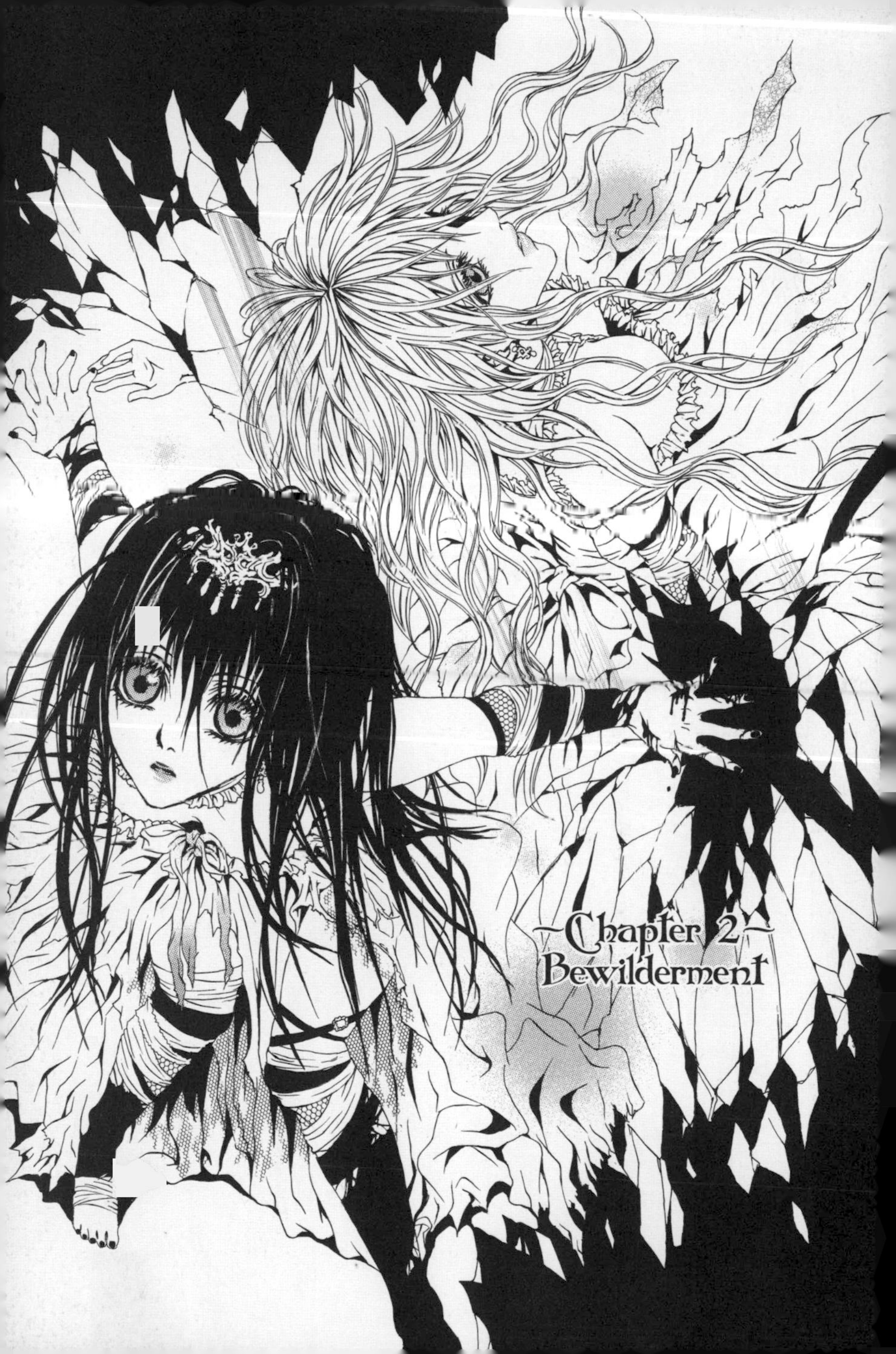
~Chapter 2~
Bewilderment

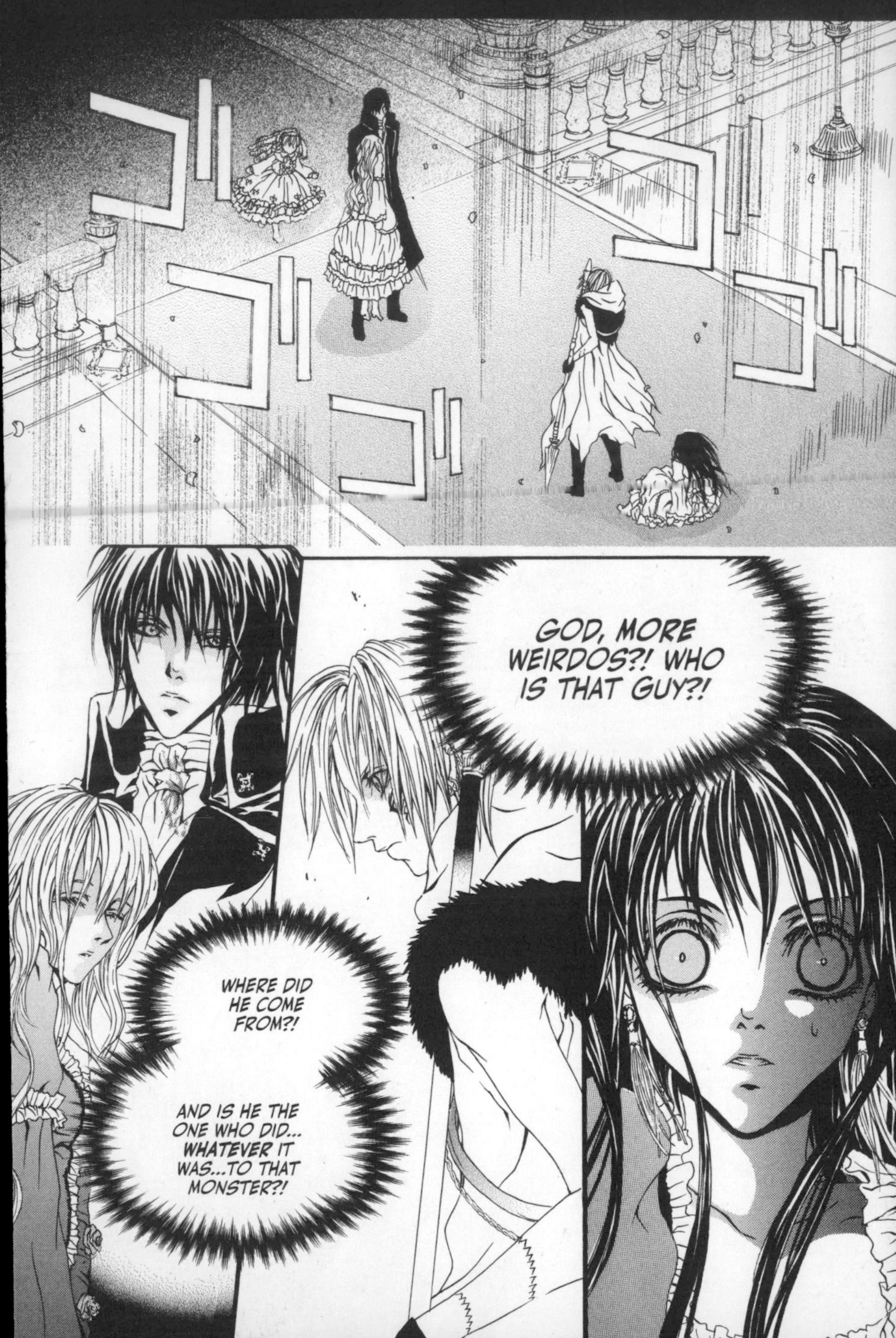
GOD, MORE WEIRDOS?! WHO IS THAT GUY?!
WHERE DID HE COME FROM?!
AND IS HE THE ONE WHO DID... WHATEVER IT WAS...TO THAT MONSTER?!

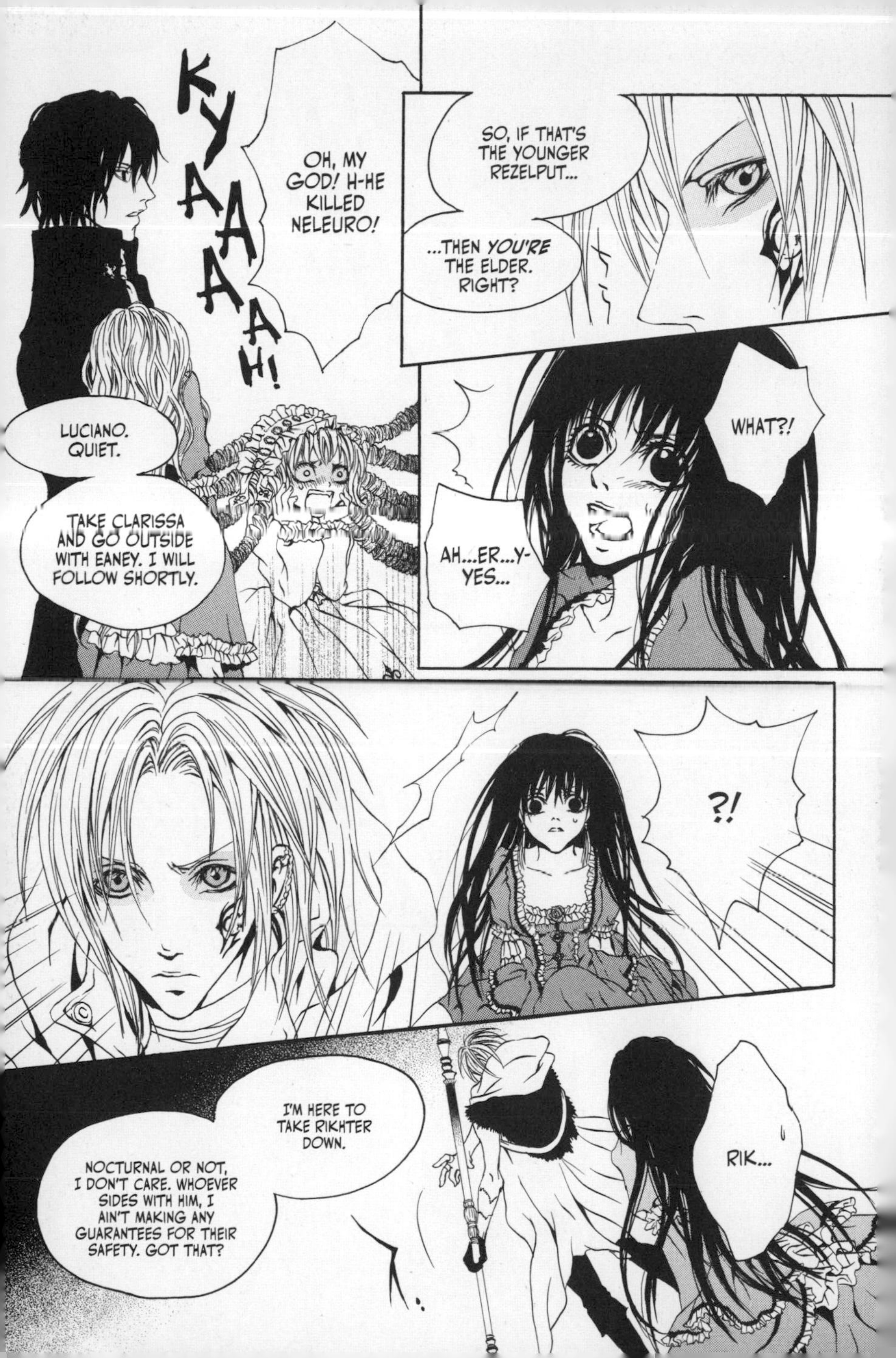

SO, IF THAT'S THE YOUNGER REZELPUT...
...THEN *YOU'RE* THE ELDER. RIGHT?
WHAT?!
AH...ER...Y-YES...
OH, MY GOD! H-HE KILLED NELEURO!
KYAAAAH!
LUCIANO. QUIET.
TAKE CLARISSA AND GO OUTSIDE WITH EANEY. I WILL FOLLOW SHORTLY.
?!
RIK...
I'M HERE TO TAKE RIKHTER DOWN.
NOCTURNAL OR NOT, I DON'T CARE. WHOEVER SIDES WITH HIM, I AIN'T MAKING ANY GUARANTEES FOR THEIR SAFETY. GOT THAT?

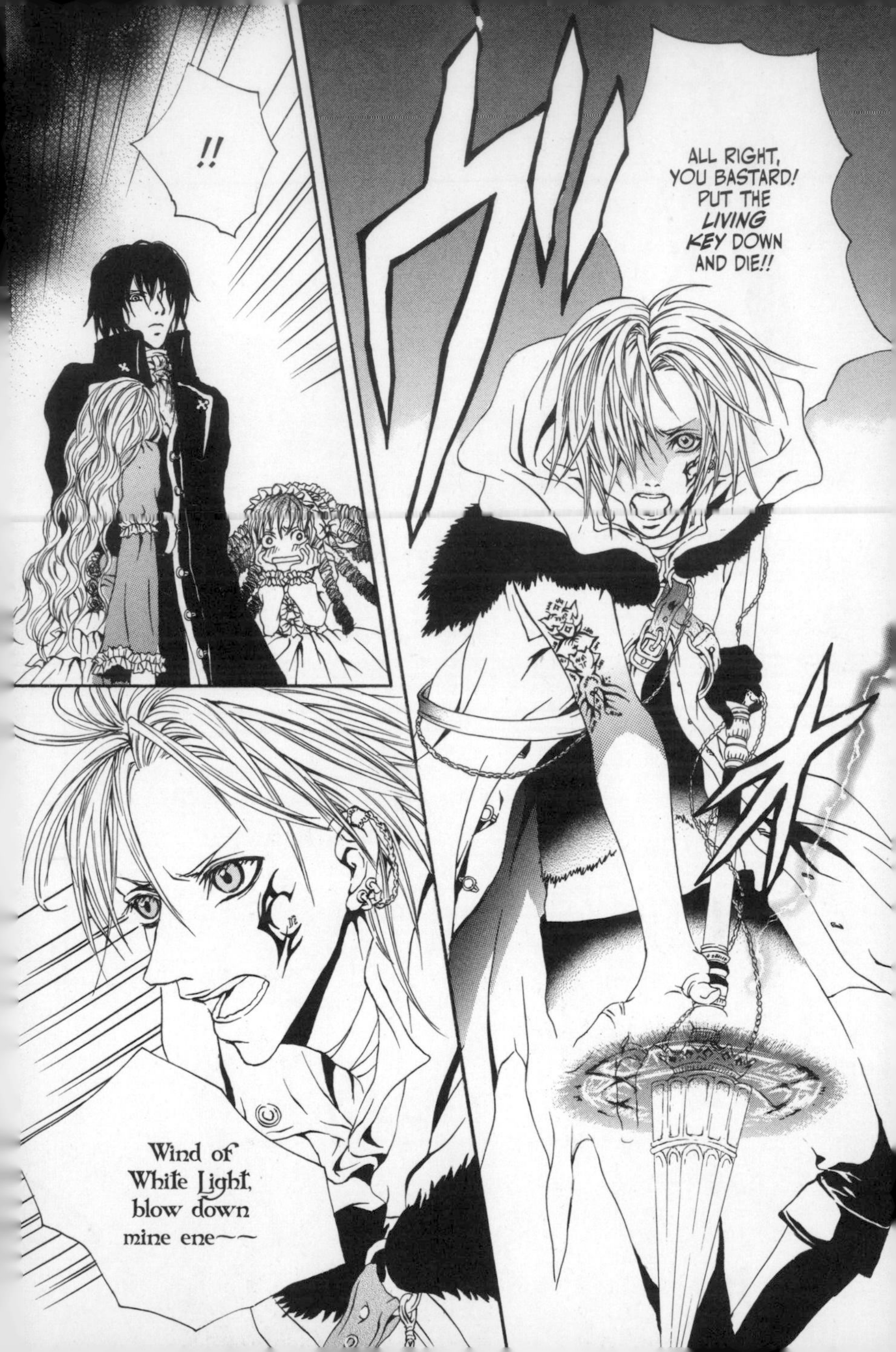
ALL RIGHT, YOU BASTARD! PUT THE *LIVING KEY* DOWN AND DIE!!
!!
Wind of White Light, blow down mine ene~~

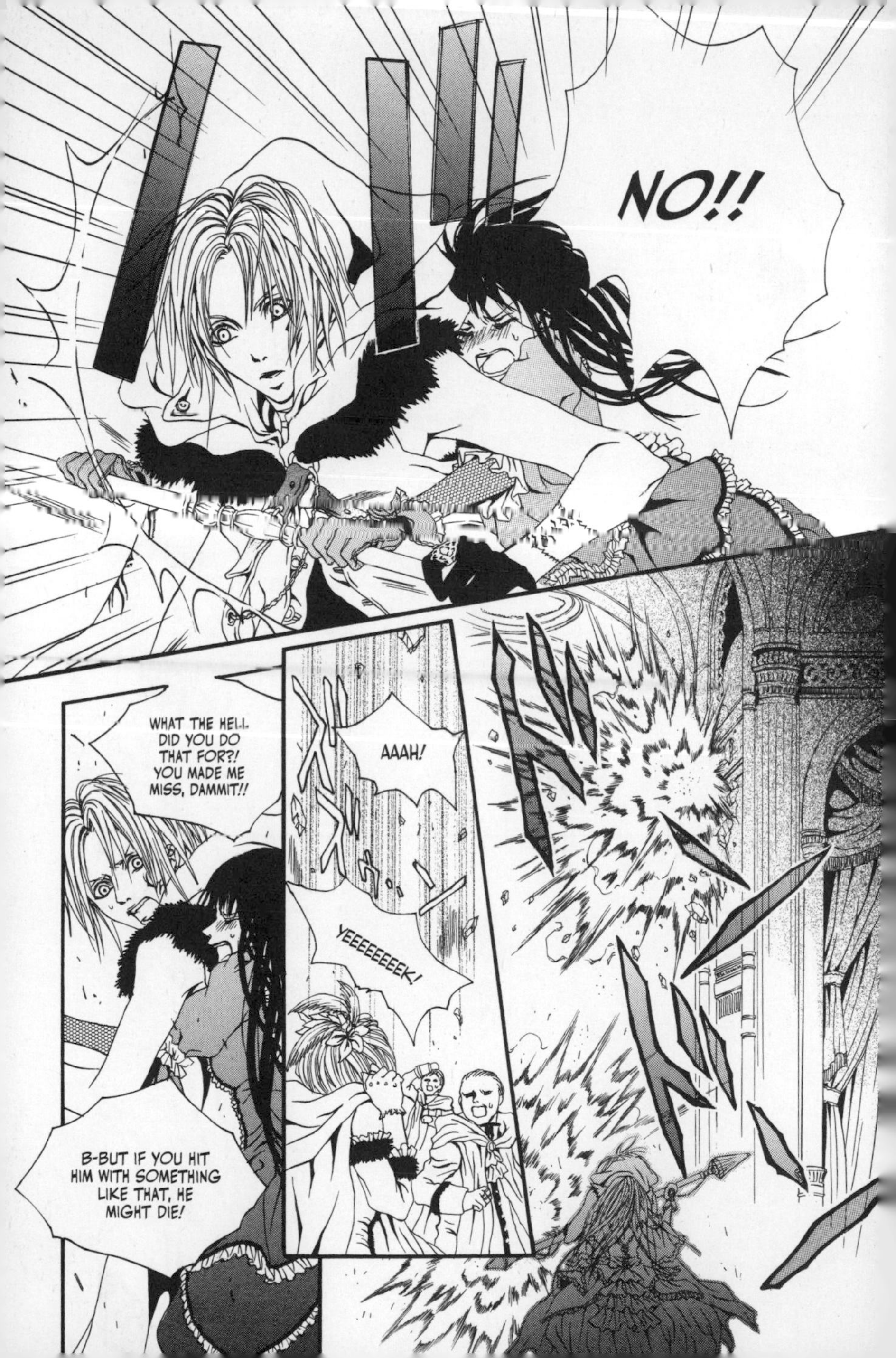
NO!!
AAAH!
YEEEEEEEEK!
WHAT THE HELL DID YOU DO THAT FOR?! YOU MADE ME MISS, DAMMIT!!
B-BUT IF YOU HIT HIM WITH SOMETHING LIKE THAT, HE MIGHT DIE!

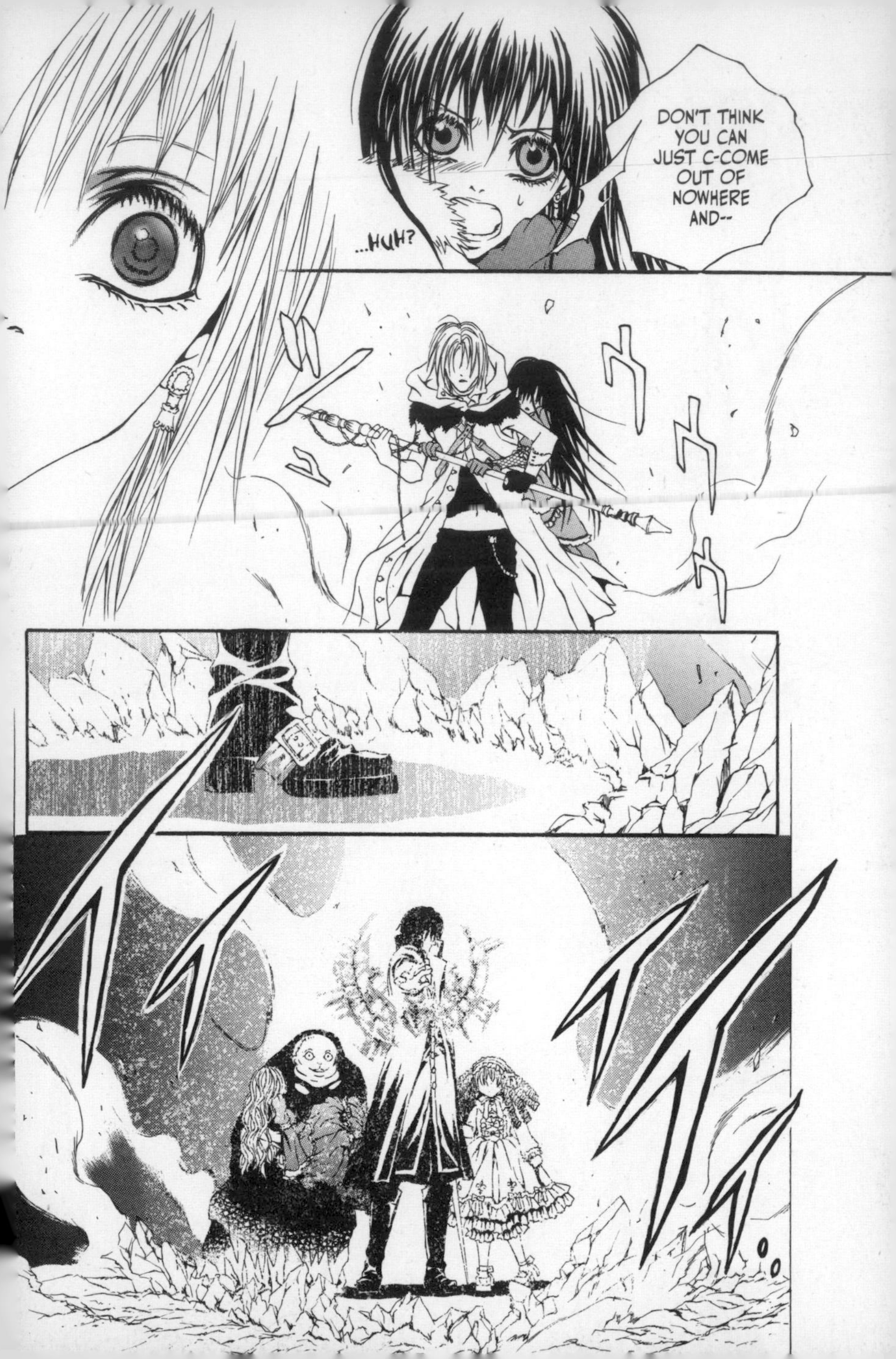
DON'T THINK YOU CAN JUST C-COME OUT OF NOWHERE AND--
...HUH?

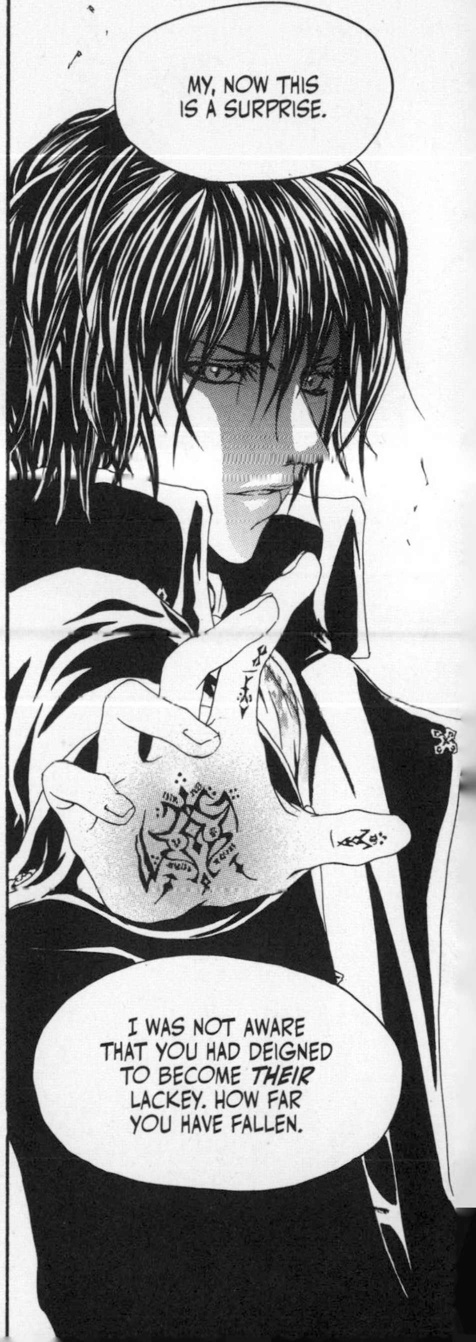
MY, NOW THIS IS A SURPRISE.
I WAS NOT AWARE THAT YOU HAD DEIGNED TO BECOME *THEIR* LACKEY. HOW FAR YOU HAVE FALLEN.
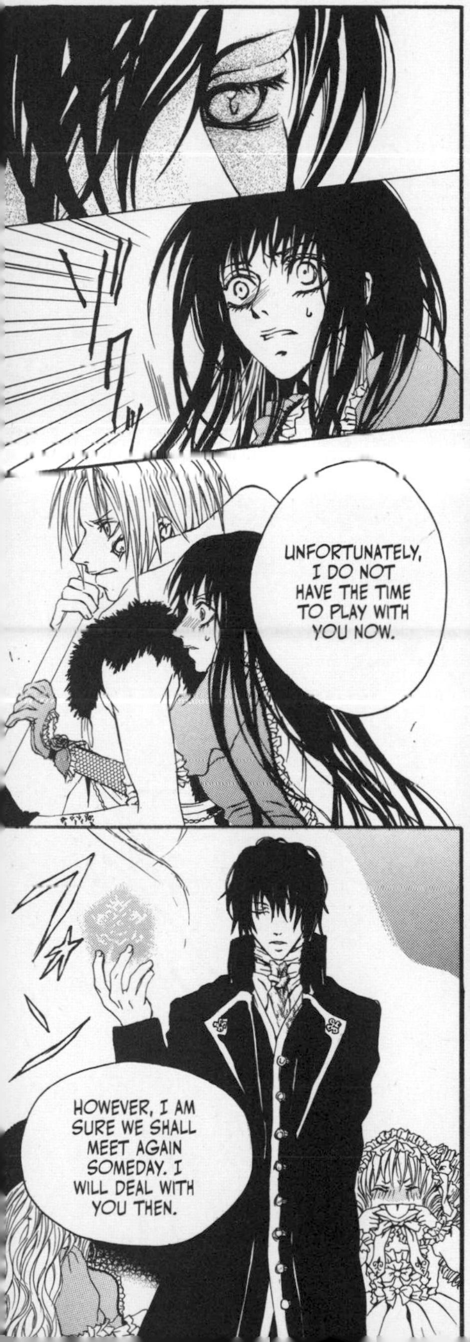
UNFORTUNATELY, I DO NOT HAVE THE TIME TO PLAY WITH YOU NOW.
HOWEVER, I AM SURE WE SHALL MEET AGAIN SOMEDAY. I WILL DEAL WITH YOU THEN.

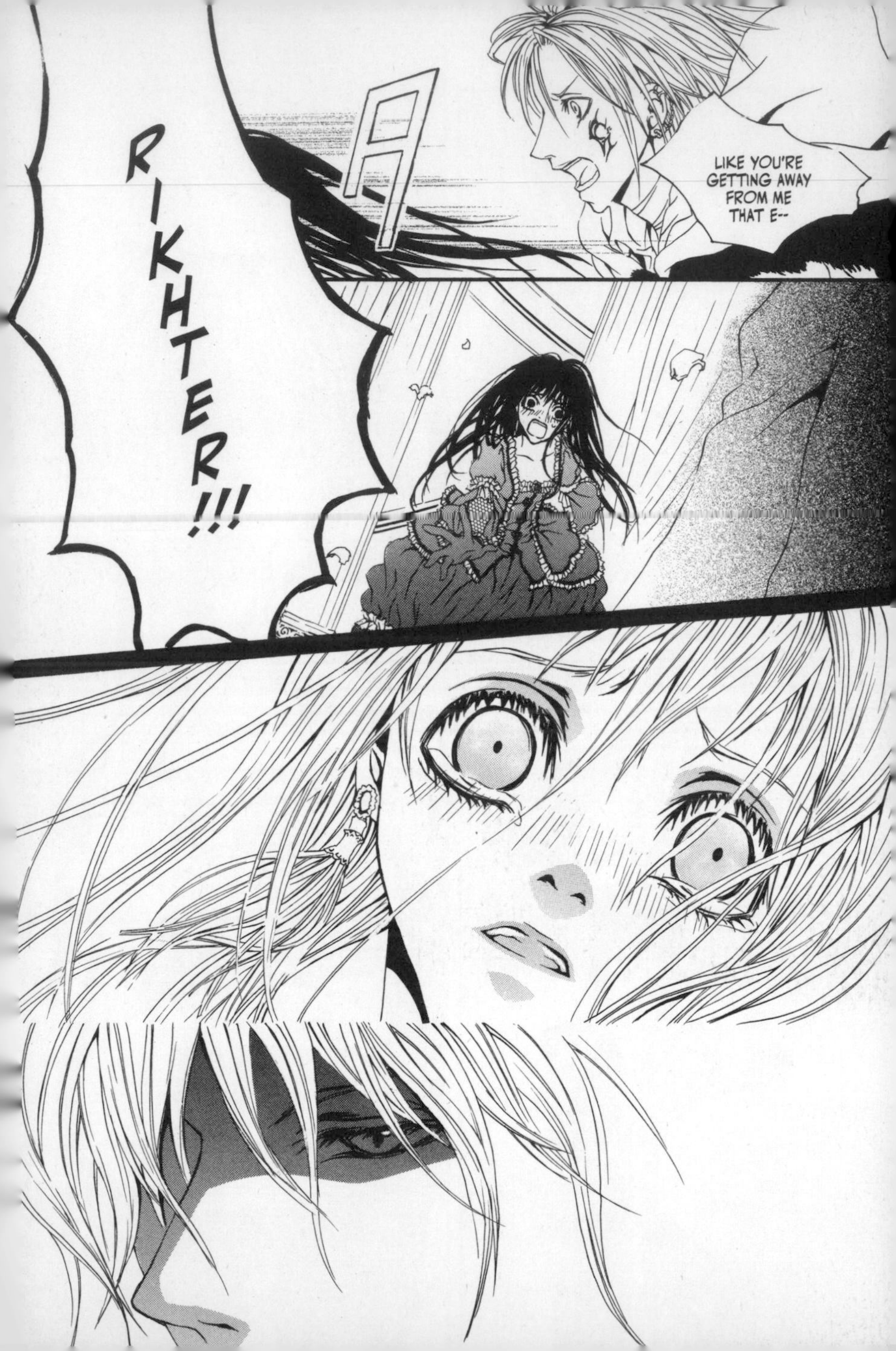
LIKE YOU'RE GETTING AWAY FROM ME THAT E--
RIKHTER!!!

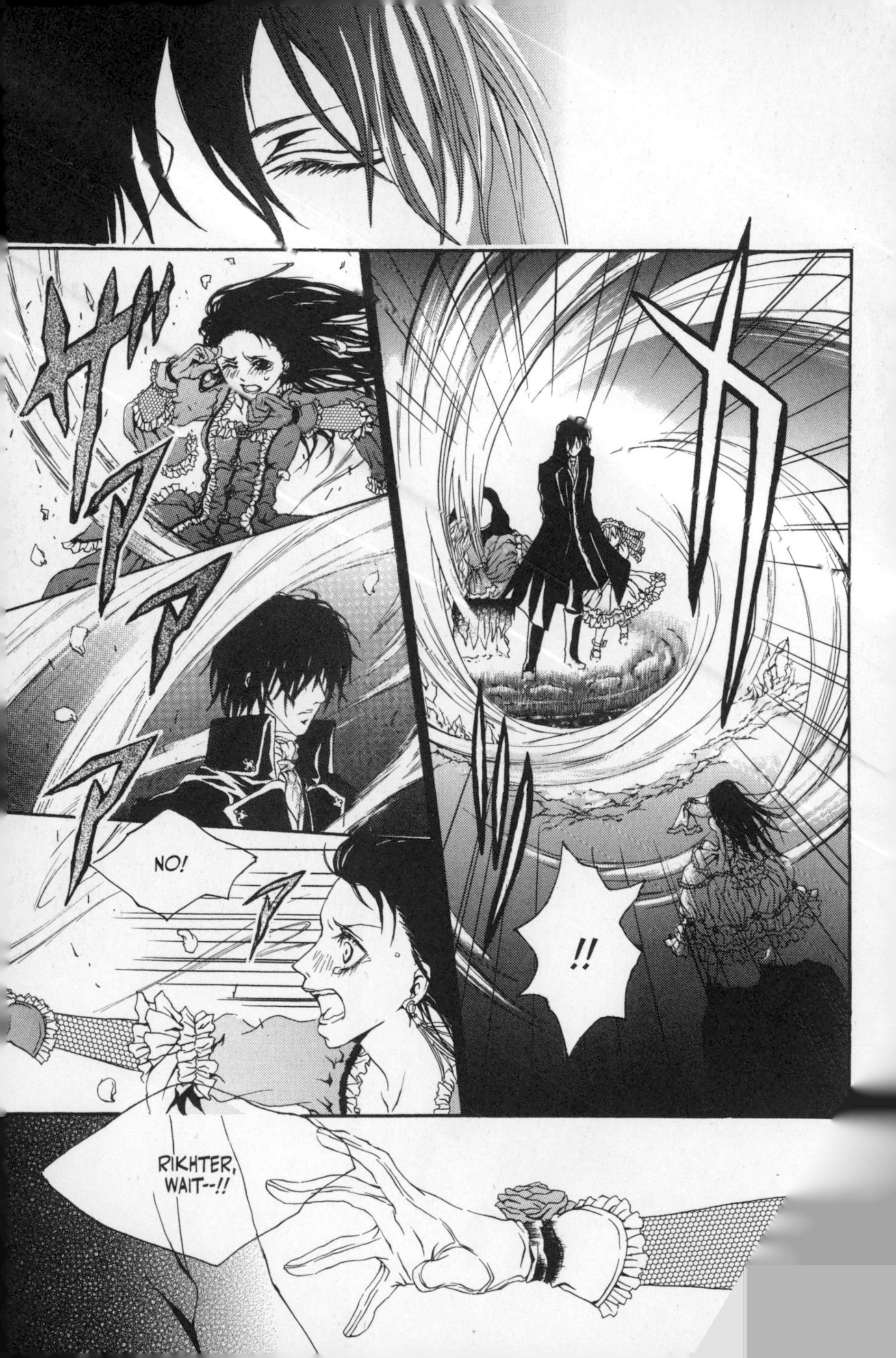
!!
NO!
RIKHTER, WAIT--!!

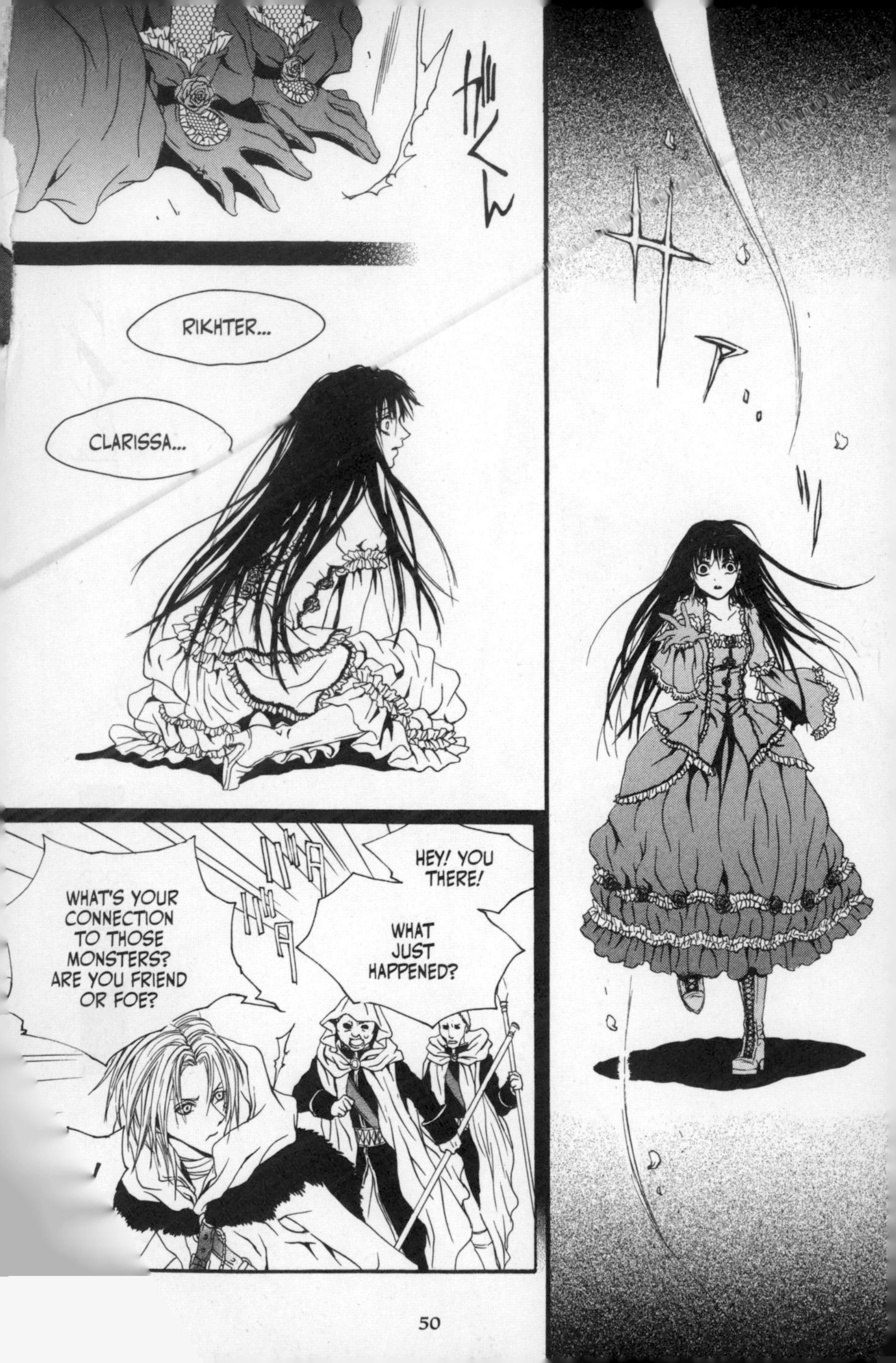
がくん
RIKHTER...
CLARISSA...
HEY! YOU THERE!
WHAT JUST HAPPENED?
WHAT'S YOUR CONNECTION TO THOSE MONSTERS? ARE YOU FRIEND OR FOE?

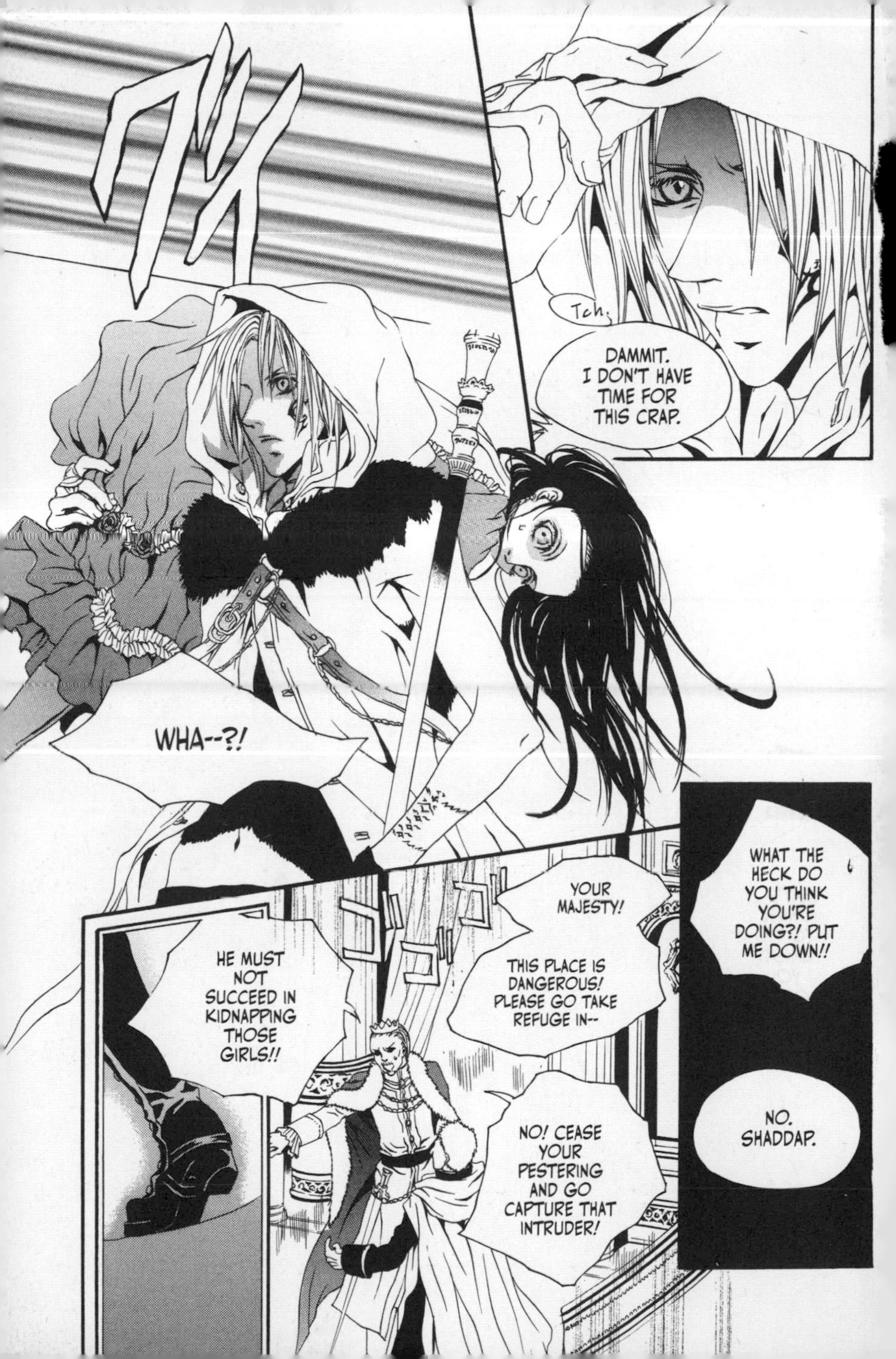
Tch.
DAMMIT. I DON'T HAVE TIME FOR THIS CRAP.
WHA--?!
WHAT THE HECK DO YOU THINK YOU'RE DOING?! PUT ME DOWN!!
NO. SHADDAP.
YOUR MAJESTY!
THIS PLACE IS DANGEROUS! PLEASE GO TAKE REFUGE IN--
HE MUST NOT SUCCEED IN KIDNAPPING THOSE GIRLS!!
NO! CEASE YOUR PESTERING AND GO CAPTURE THAT INTRUDER!

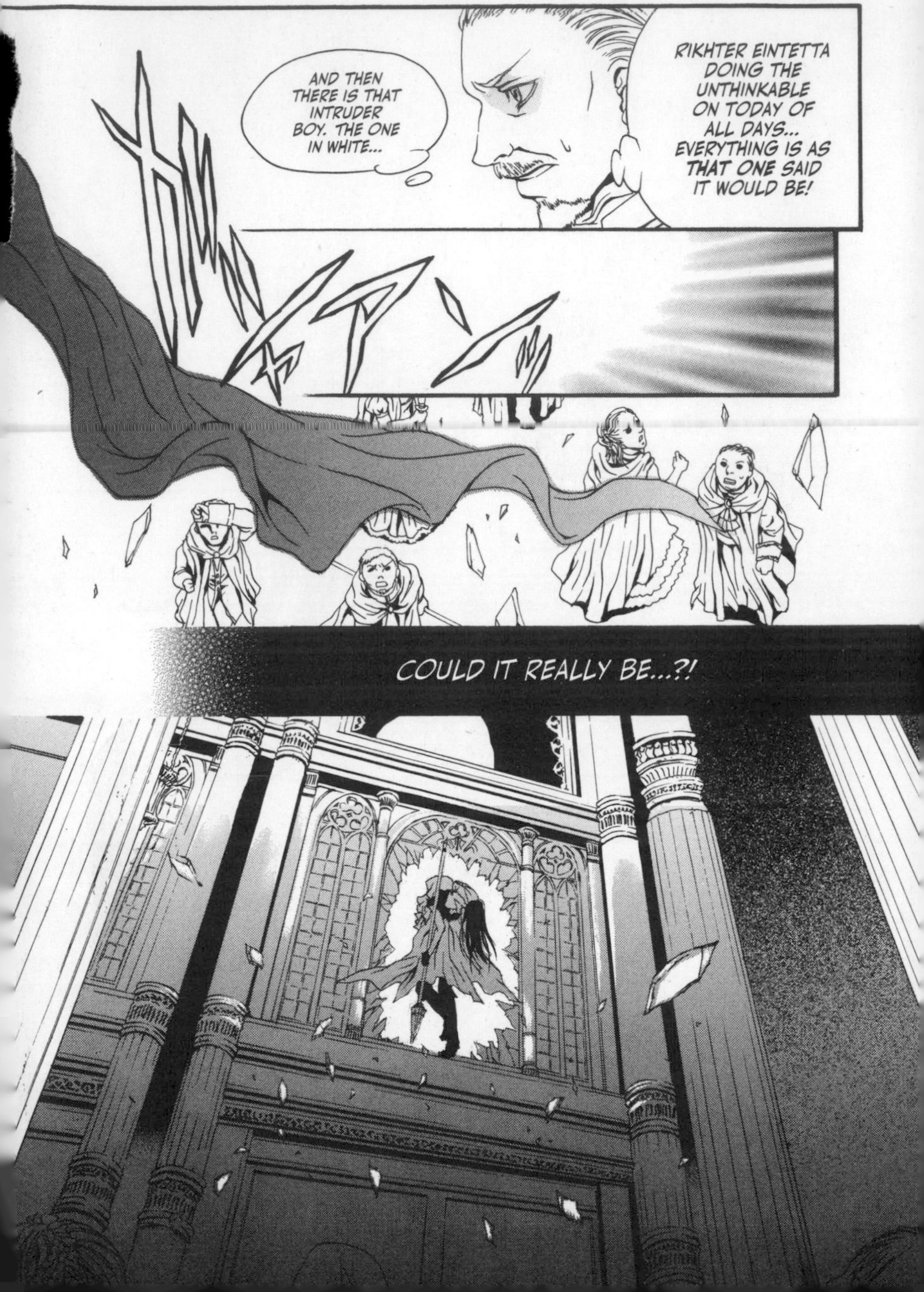
RIKHTER EINTETTA DOING THE UNTHINKABLE ON TODAY OF ALL DAYS... EVERYTHING IS AS THAT ONE SAID IT WOULD BE!
AND THEN THERE IS THAT INTRUDER BOY. THE ONE IN WHITE...
COULD IT REALLY BE...?!

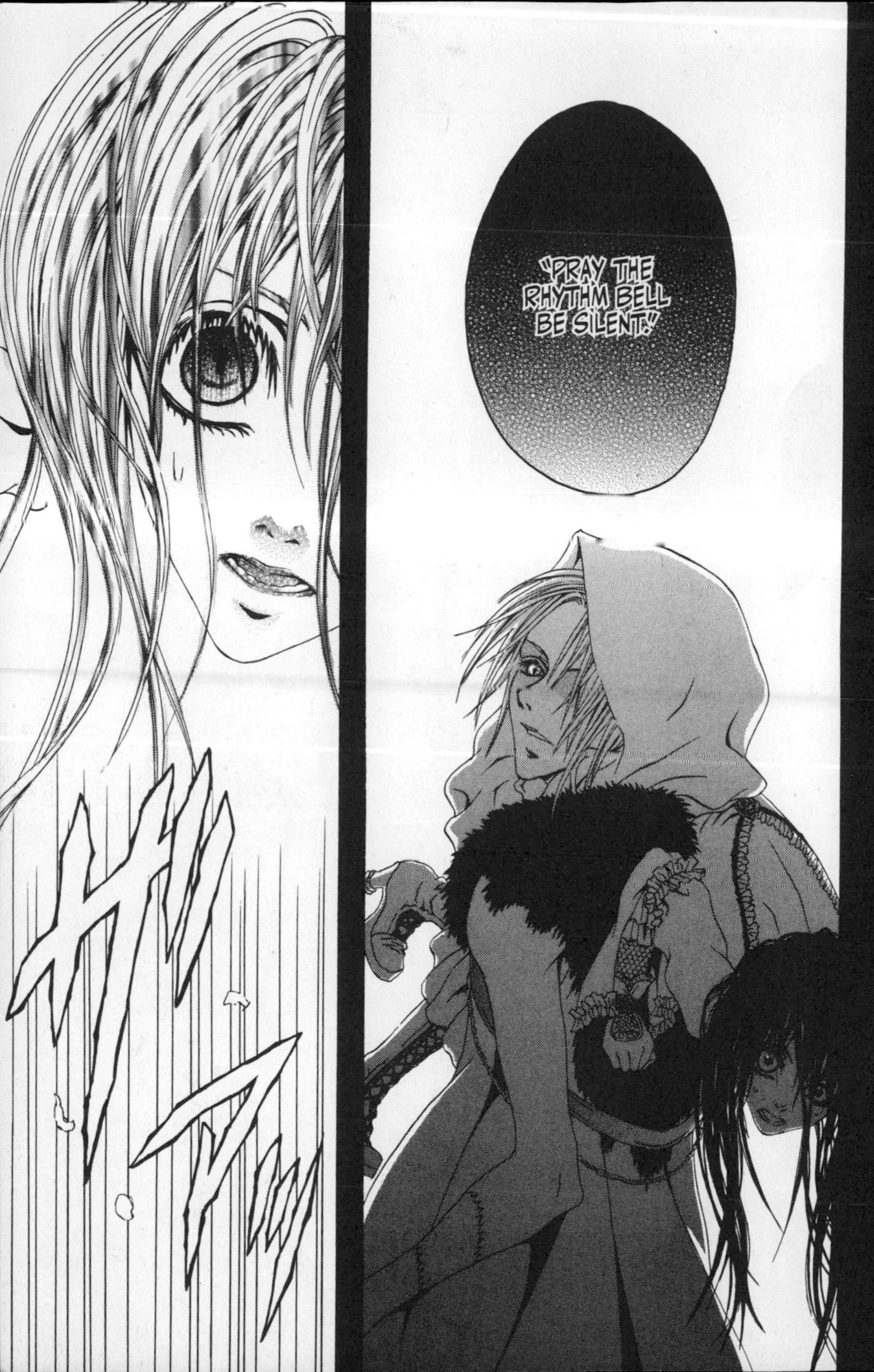
"PRAY THE RHYTHM BELL BE SILENT."

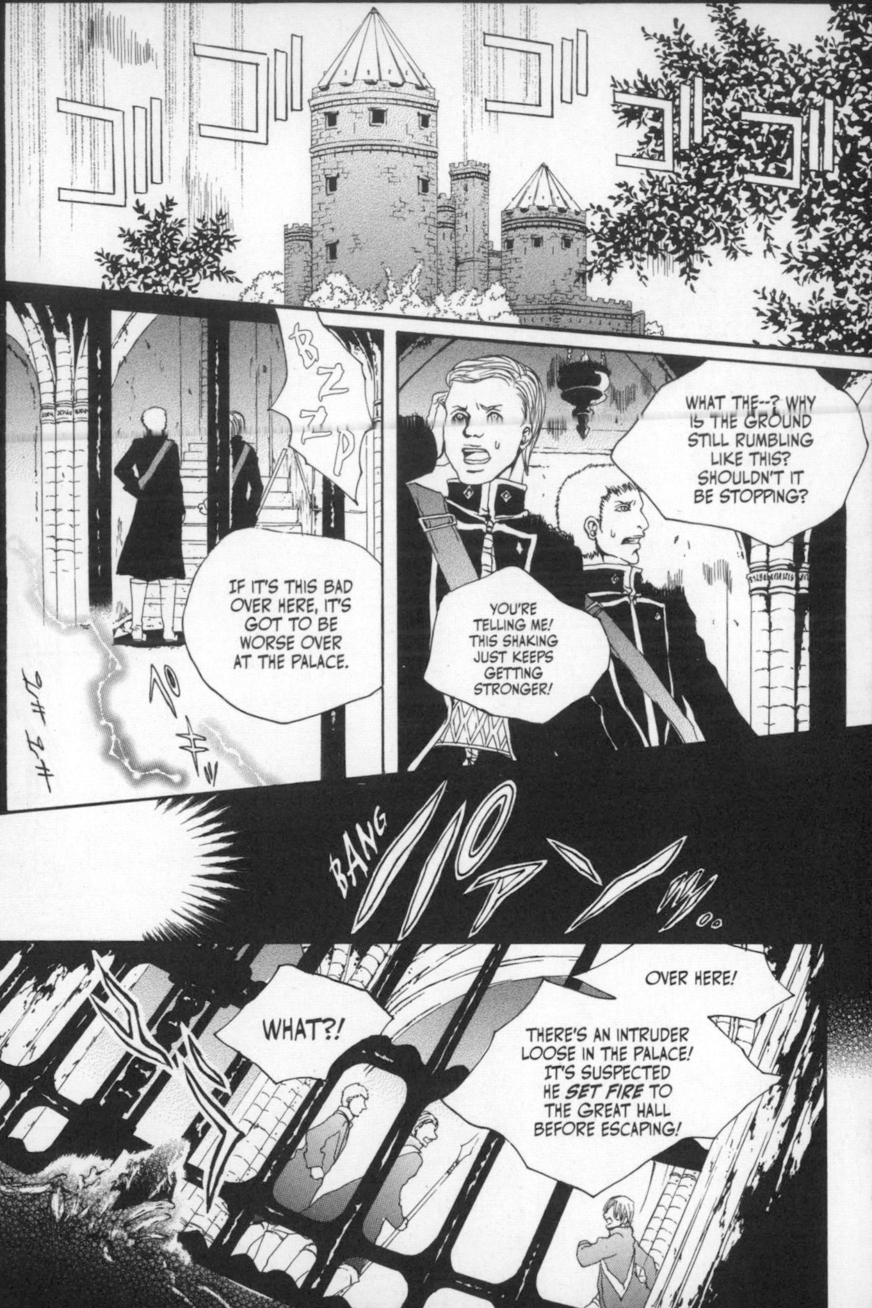
WHAT THE--? WHY IS THE GROUND STILL RUMBLING LIKE THIS? SHOULDN'T IT BE STOPPING?
YOU'RE TELLING ME! THIS SHAKING JUST KEEPS GETTING STRONGER!
BZZP
IF IT'S THIS BAD OVER HERE, IT'S GOT TO BE WORSE OVER AT THE PALACE.
BANG
OVER HERE!
THERE'S AN INTRUDER LOOSE IN THE PALACE! IT'S SUSPECTED HE SET FIRE TO THE GREAT HALL BEFORE ESCAPING!
WHAT?!

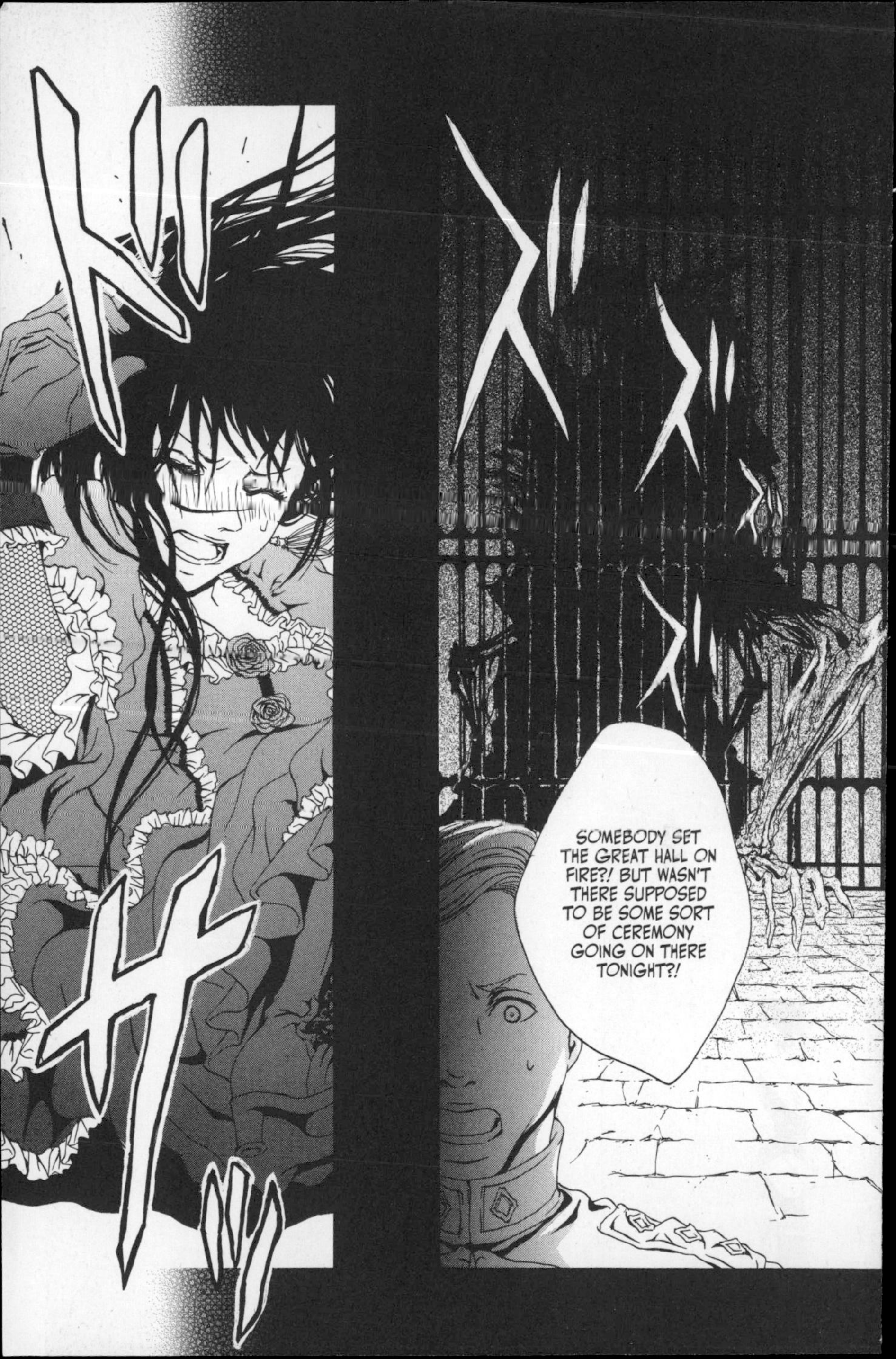
SOMEBODY SET THE GREAT HALL ON FIRE?! BUT WASN'T THERE SUPPOSED TO BE SOME SORT OF CEREMONY GOING ON THERE TONIGHT?!

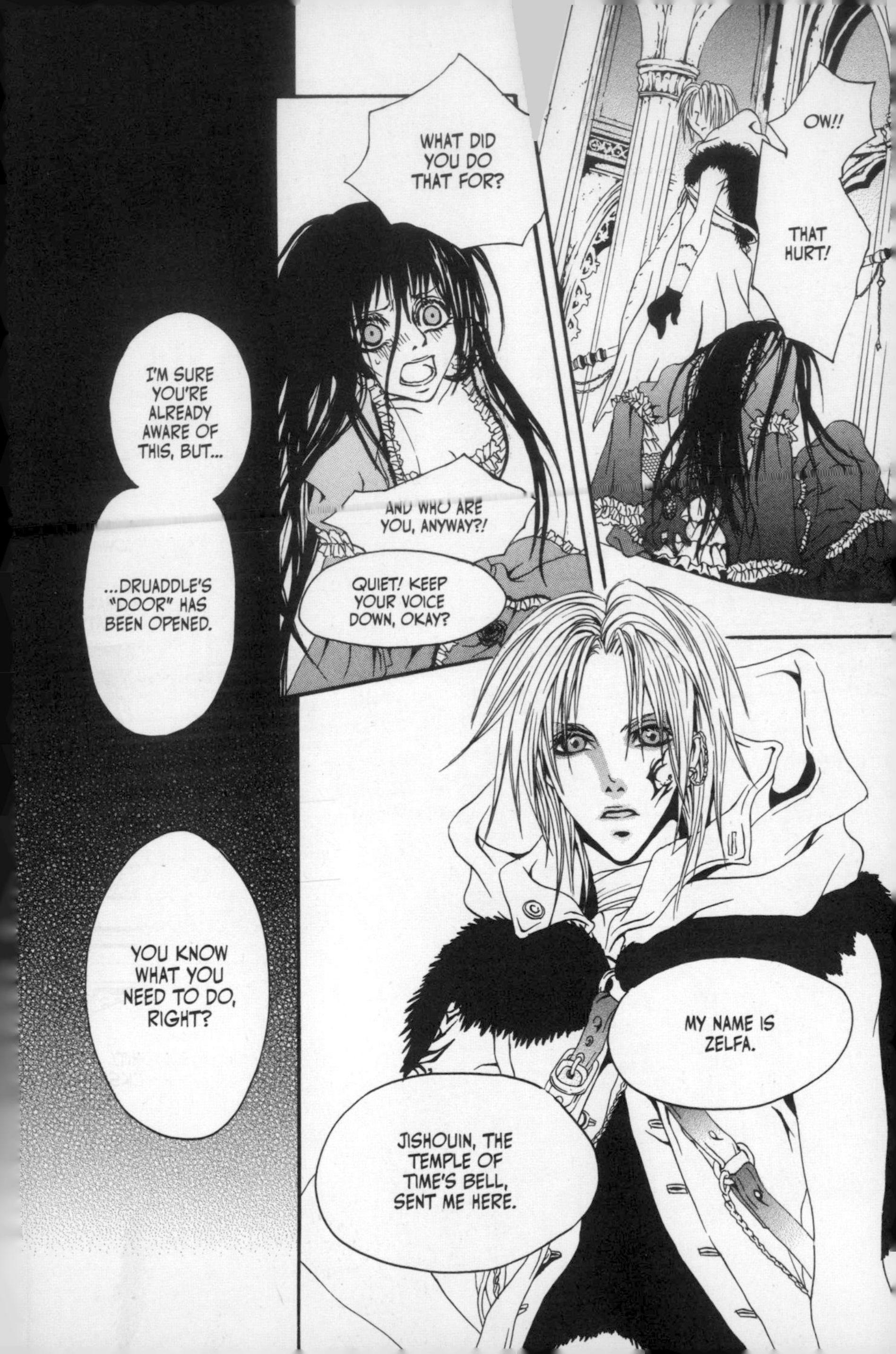
OW!!
THAT HURT!
WHAT DID YOU DO THAT FOR?
AND WHO ARE YOU, ANYWAY?!
QUIET! KEEP YOUR VOICE DOWN, OKAY?
MY NAME IS ZELFA.
JISHOUIN, THE TEMPLE OF TIME'S BELL, SENT ME HERE.
I'M SURE YOU'RE ALREADY AWARE OF THIS, BUT...
...DRUADDLE'S "DOOR" HAS BEEN OPENED.
YOU KNOW WHAT YOU NEED TO DO, RIGHT?

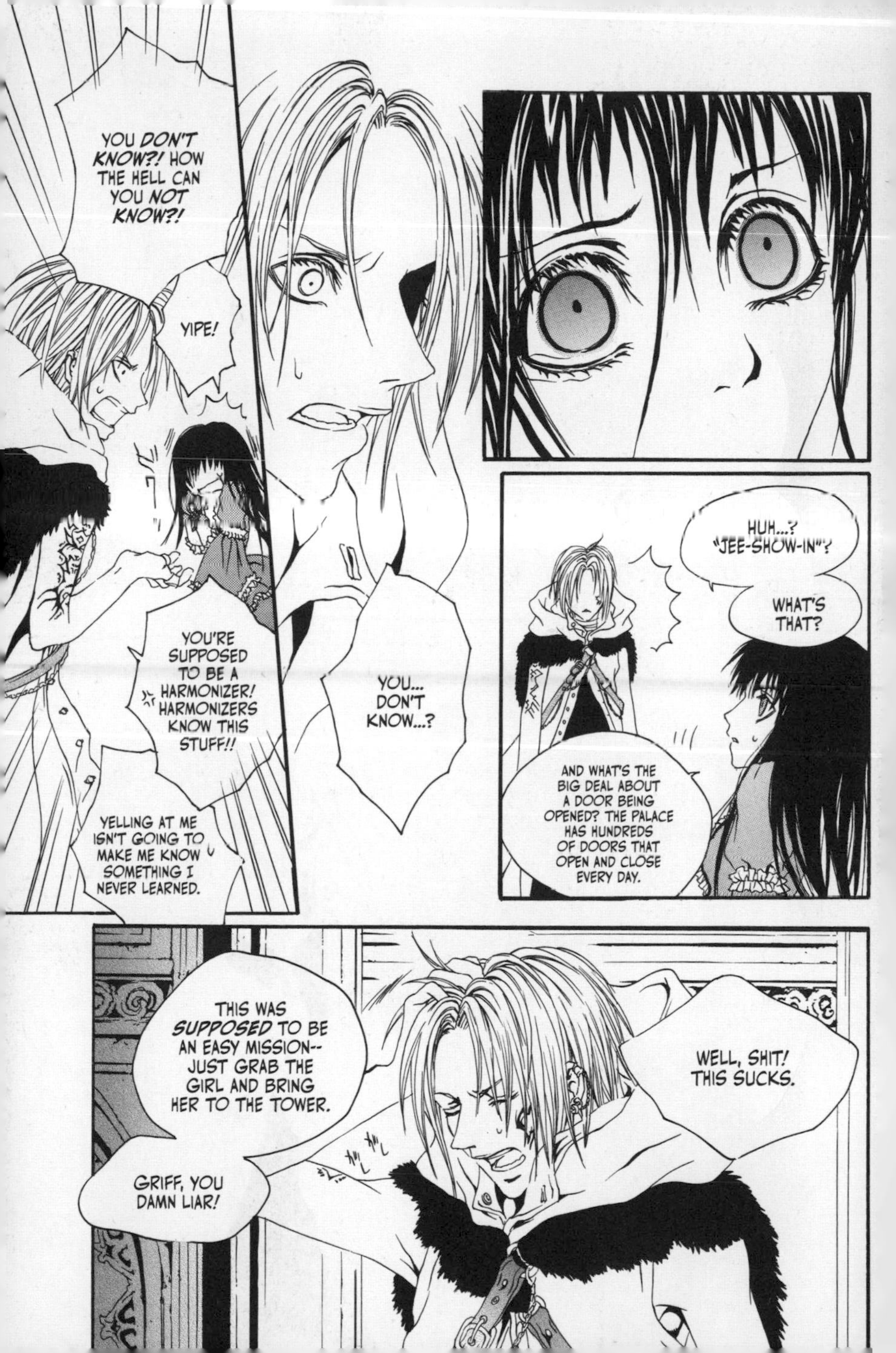
HUH...? "JEE-SHOW-IN"?
WHAT'S THAT?
AND WHAT'S THE BIG DEAL ABOUT A DOOR BEING OPENED? THE PALACE HAS HUNDREDS OF DOORS THAT OPEN AND CLOSE EVERY DAY.
YOU... DON'T KNOW...?
YOU *DON'T KNOW?!* HOW THE HELL CAN YOU *NOT KNOW?!*
YIPE!
YOU'RE SUPPOSED TO BE A HARMONIZER! HARMONIZERS KNOW THIS STUFF!!
YELLING AT ME ISN'T GOING TO MAKE ME KNOW SOMETHING I NEVER LEARNED.
WELL, SHIT! THIS SUCKS.
THIS WAS *SUPPOSED* TO BE AN EASY MISSION-- JUST GRAB THE GIRL AND BRING HER TO THE TOWER.
GRIFF, YOU DAMN LIAR!

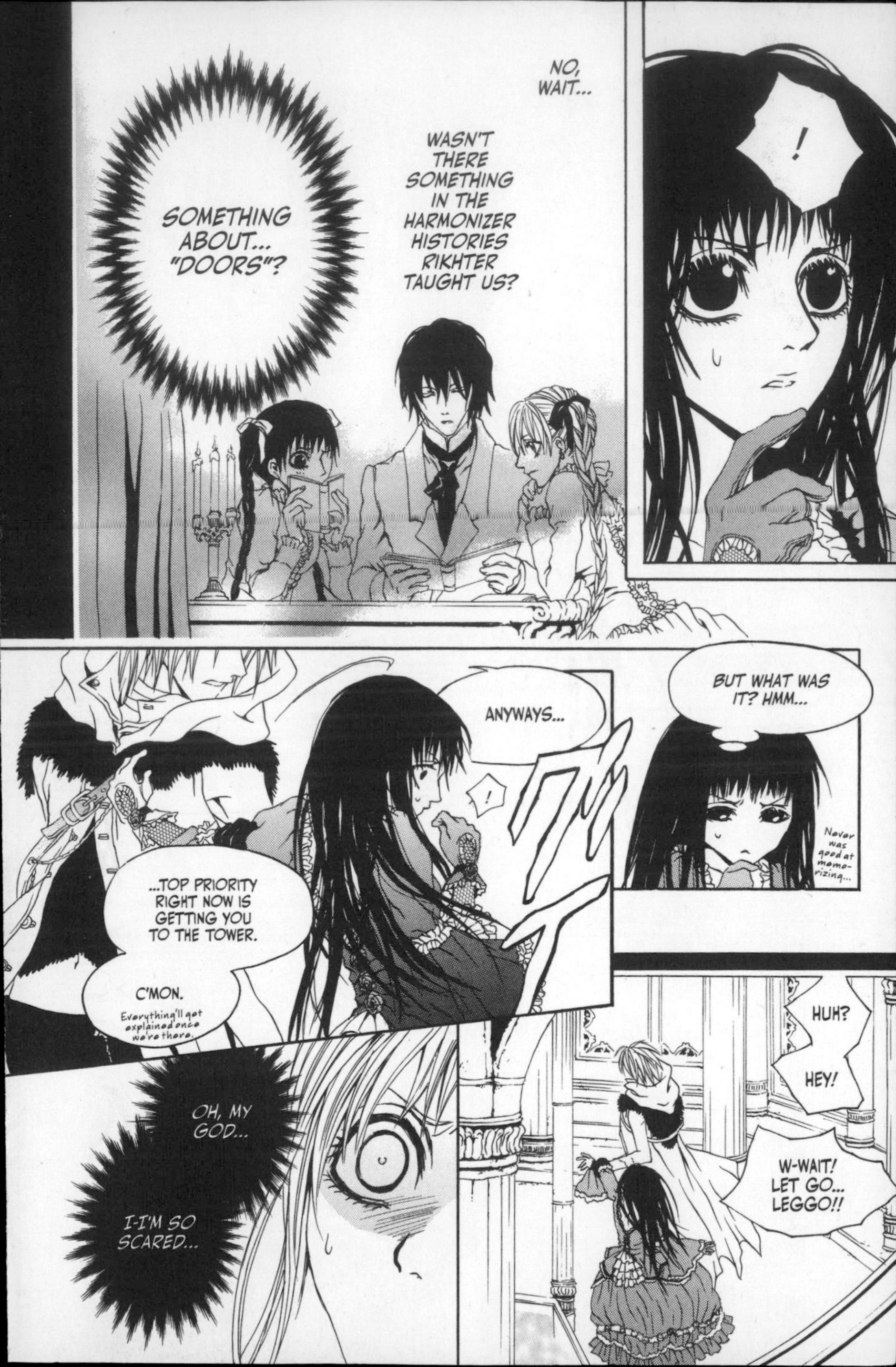
!
NO, WAIT...
WASN'T THERE SOMETHING IN THE HARMONIZER HISTORIES RIKHTER TAUGHT US?
SOMETHING ABOUT... "DOORS"?
BUT WHAT WAS IT? HMM...
Never was good at memorizing...
ANYWAYS...
!
...TOP PRIORITY RIGHT NOW IS GETTING YOU TO THE TOWER.
C'MON.
Everything'll get explained once we're there.
HUH?
HEY!
W-WAIT! LET GO... LEGGO!!
OH, MY GOD...
I-I'M SO SCARED...

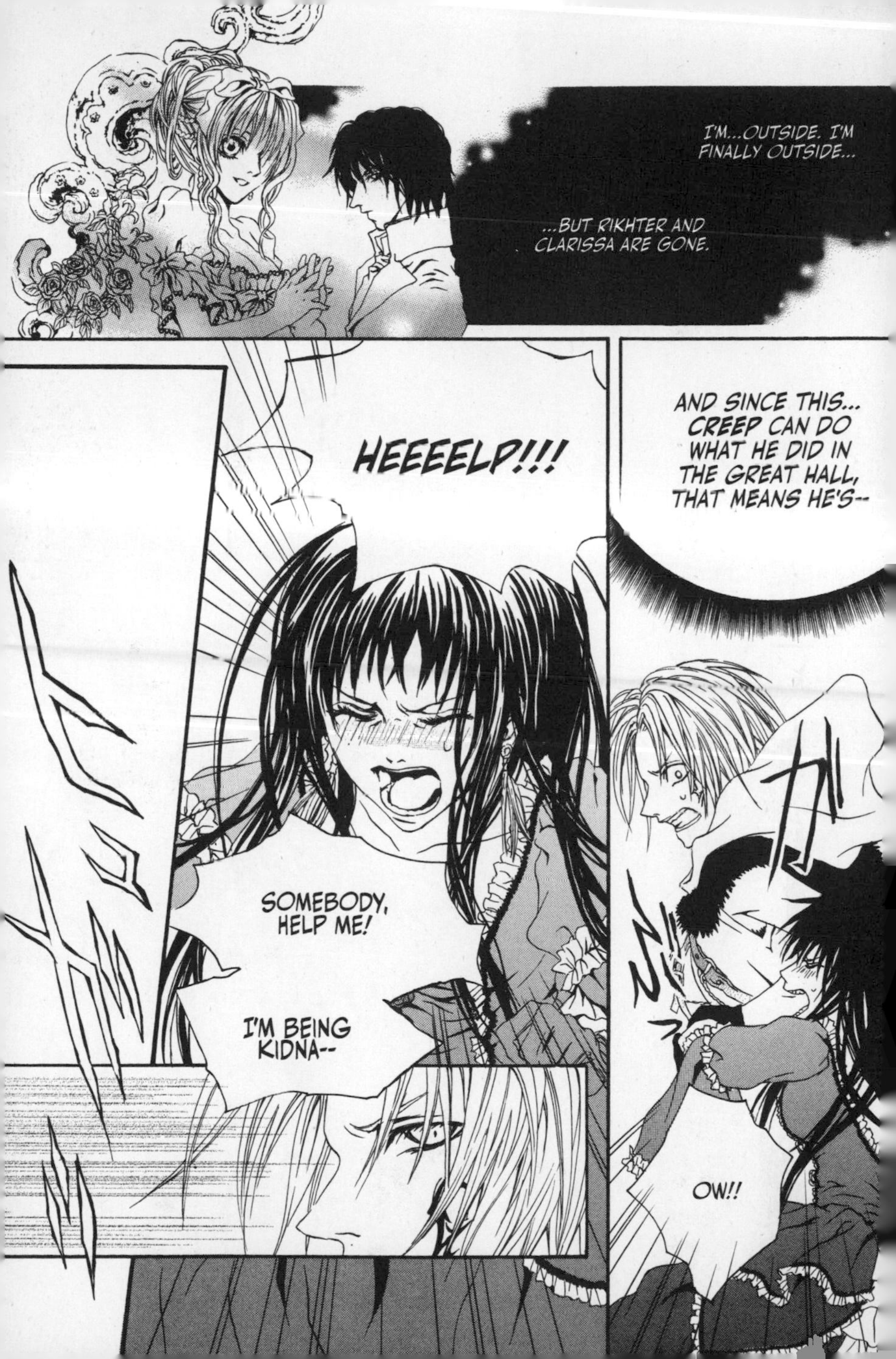
I'M...OUTSIDE. I'M FINALLY OUTSIDE...
...BUT RIKHTER AND CLARISSA ARE GONE.
AND SINCE THIS... CREEP CAN DO WHAT HE DID IN THE GREAT HALL, THAT MEANS HE'S--
OW!!
HEEEELP!!!
SOMEBODY, HELP ME!
I'M BEING KIDNA--

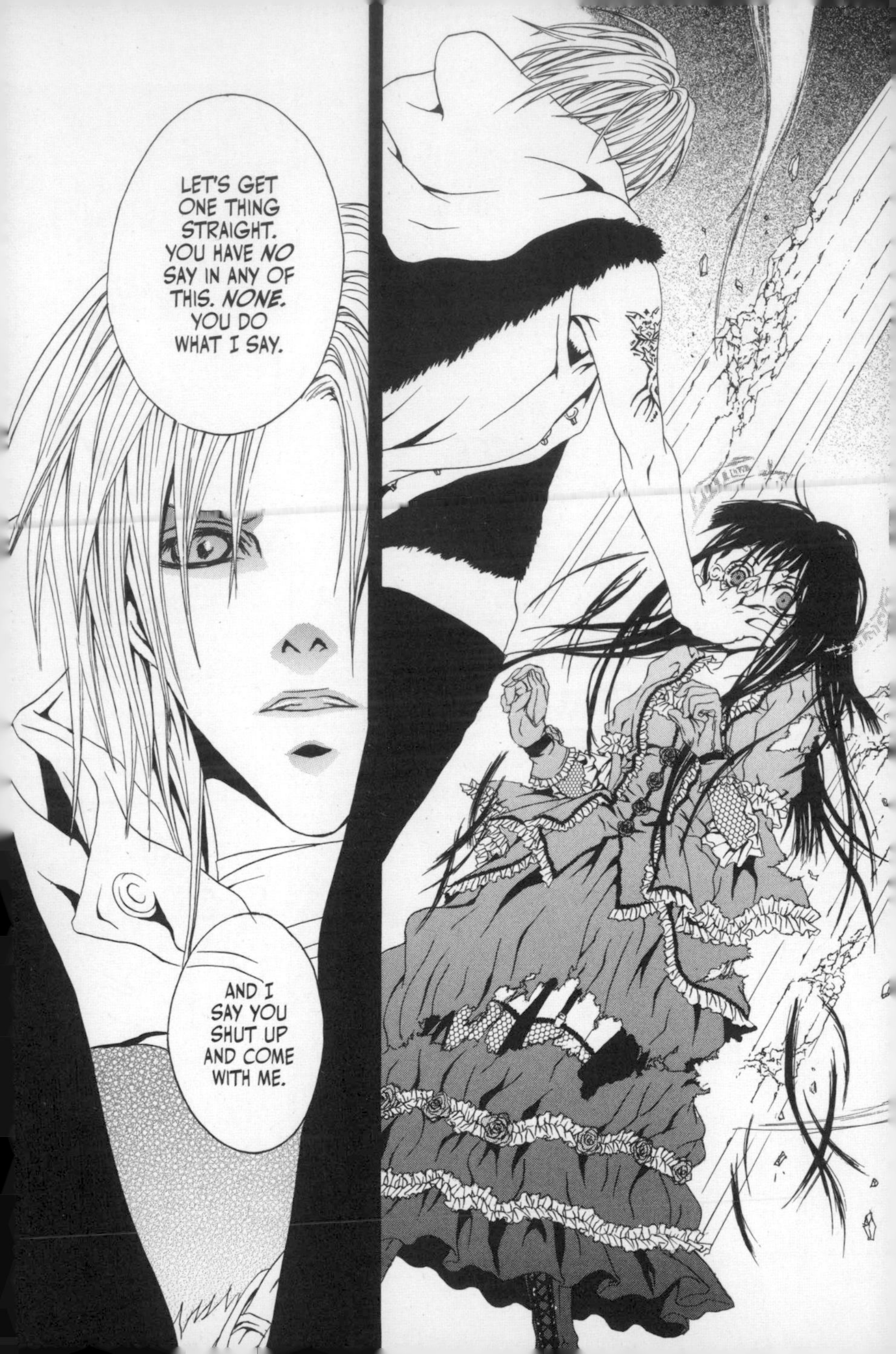
LET'S GET ONE THING STRAIGHT. YOU HAVE *NO* SAY IN ANY OF THIS. *NONE.* YOU DO WHAT I SAY.
AND I SAY YOU SHUT UP AND COME WITH ME.

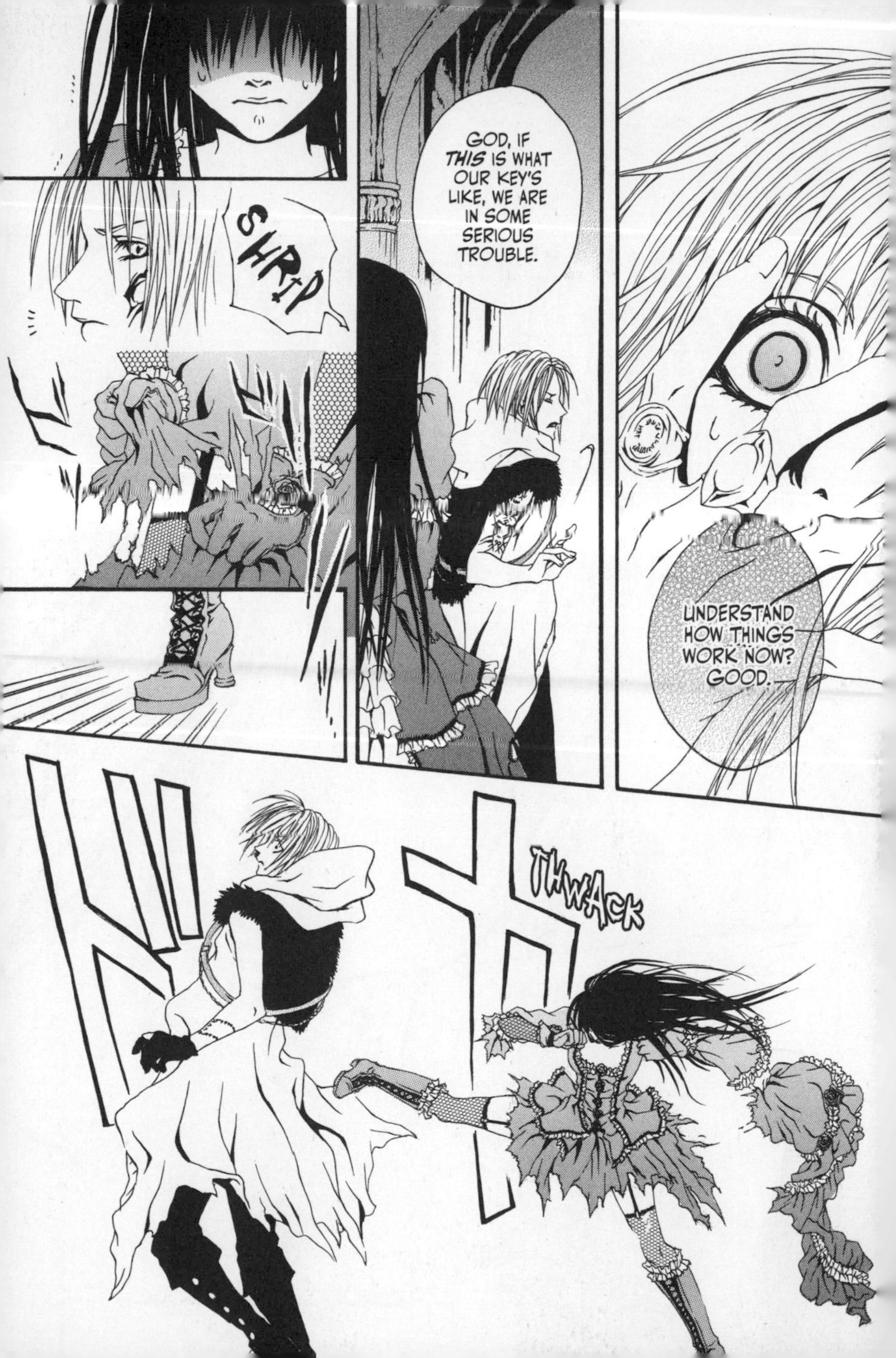
UNDERSTAND HOW THINGS WORK NOW? GOOD.
GOD, IF THIS IS WHAT OUR KEY'S LIKE, WE ARE IN SOME SERIOUS TROUBLE.
SHRIP
THWACK

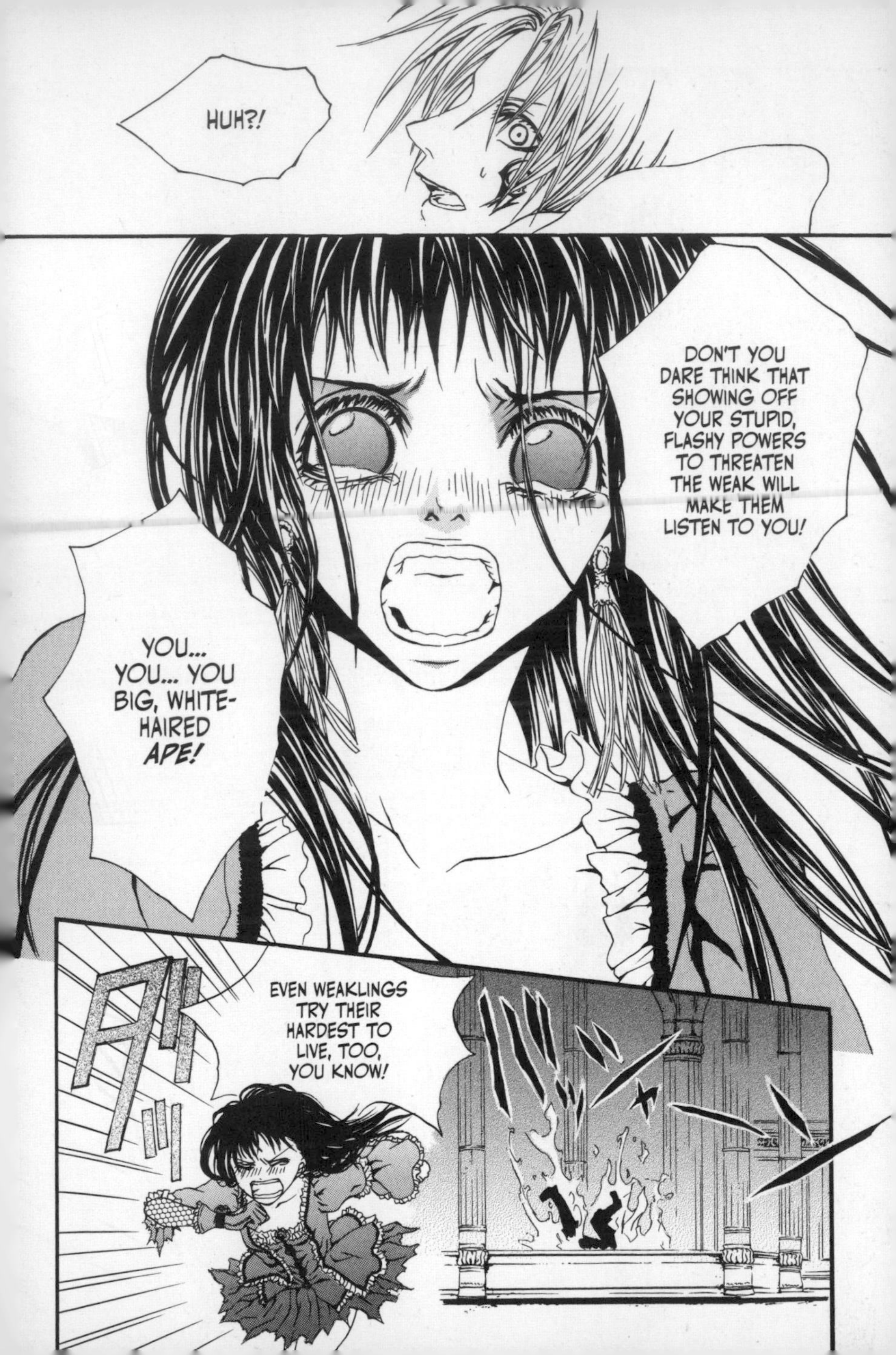
HUH?!
DON'T YOU DARE THINK THAT SHOWING OFF YOUR STUPID, FLASHY POWERS TO THREATEN THE WEAK WILL MAKE THEM LISTEN TO YOU!
YOU... YOU... YOU BIG, WHITE-HAIRED *APE!*
EVEN WEAKLINGS TRY THEIR HARDEST TO LIVE, TOO, YOU KNOW!

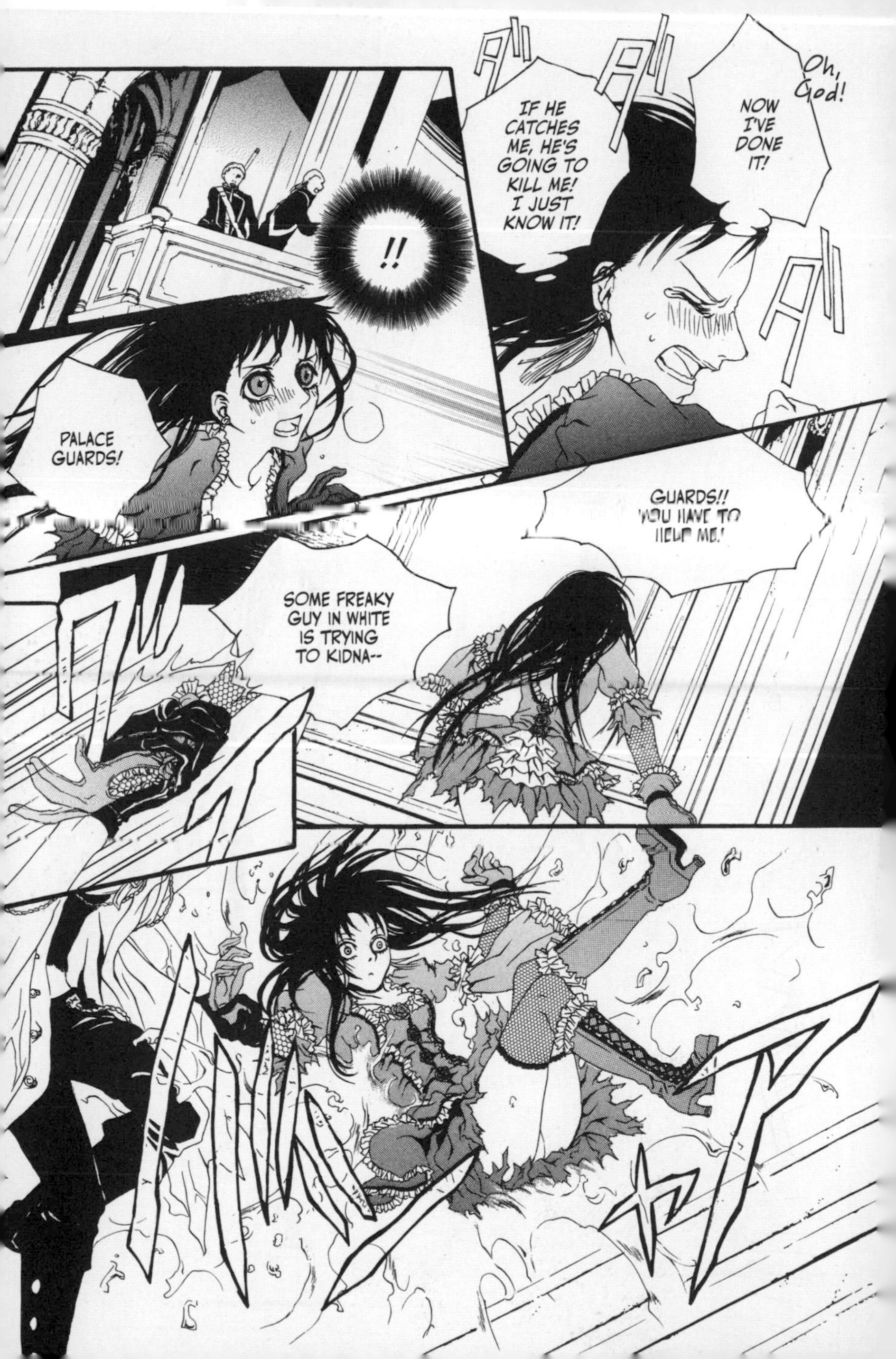
Oh, God!
NOW I'VE DONE IT!
IF HE CATCHES ME, HE'S GOING TO KILL ME! I JUST KNOW IT!
!!
PALACE GUARDS!
GUARDS!! YOU HAVE TO HELP ME!
SOME FREAKY GUY IN WHITE IS TRYING TO KIDNA--

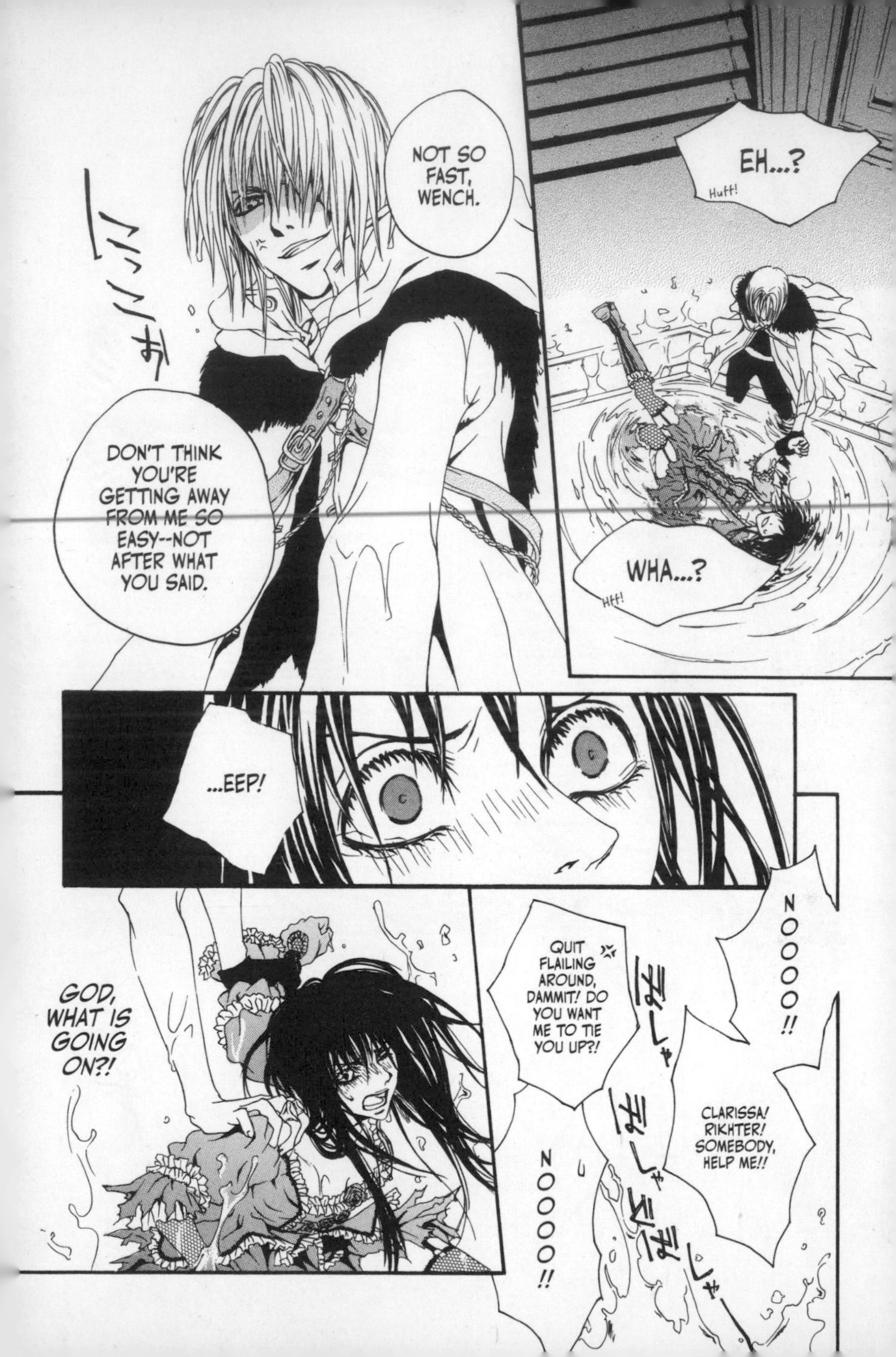
EH...?
Huff!
WHA...?
Hff!
NOT SO FAST, WENCH.
DON'T THINK YOU'RE GETTING AWAY FROM ME SO EASY--NOT AFTER WHAT YOU SAID.
...EEP!
NOOOO!!
QUIT FLAILING AROUND, DAMMIT! DO YOU WANT ME TO TIE YOU UP?!
CLARISSA! RIKHTER! SOMEBODY, HELP ME!!
NOOOO!!
GOD, WHAT IS GOING ON?!

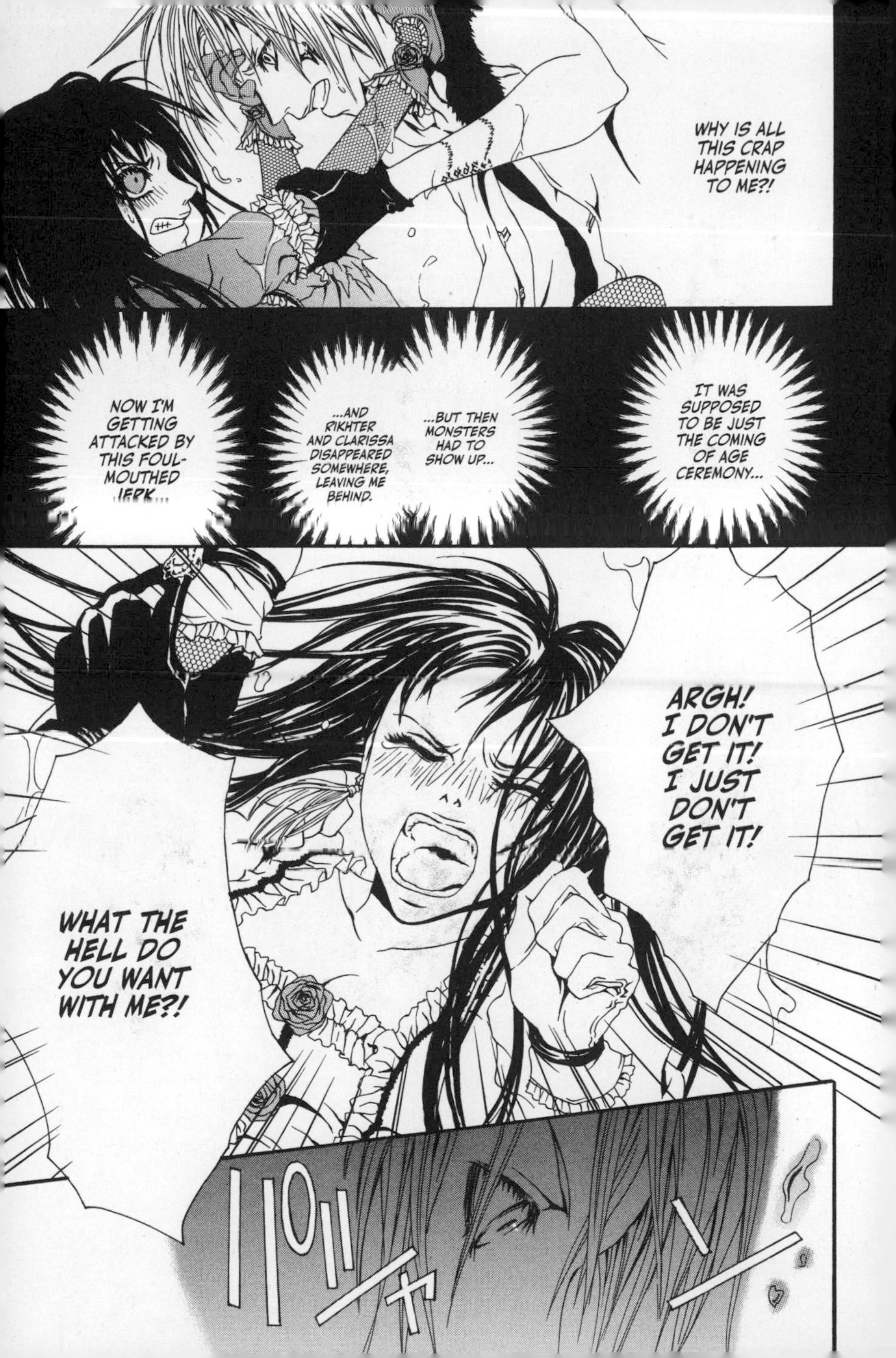
WHY IS ALL THIS CRAP HAPPENING TO ME?!
IT WAS SUPPOSED TO BE JUST THE COMING OF AGE CEREMONY...
...BUT THEN MONSTERS HAD TO SHOW UP...
...AND RIKHTER AND CLARISSA DISAPPEARED SOMEWHERE, LEAVING ME BEHIND.
NOW I'M GETTING ATTACKED BY THIS FOUL-MOUTHED JERK...
ARGH! I DON'T GET IT! I JUST DON'T GET IT!
WHAT THE HELL DO YOU WANT WITH ME?!

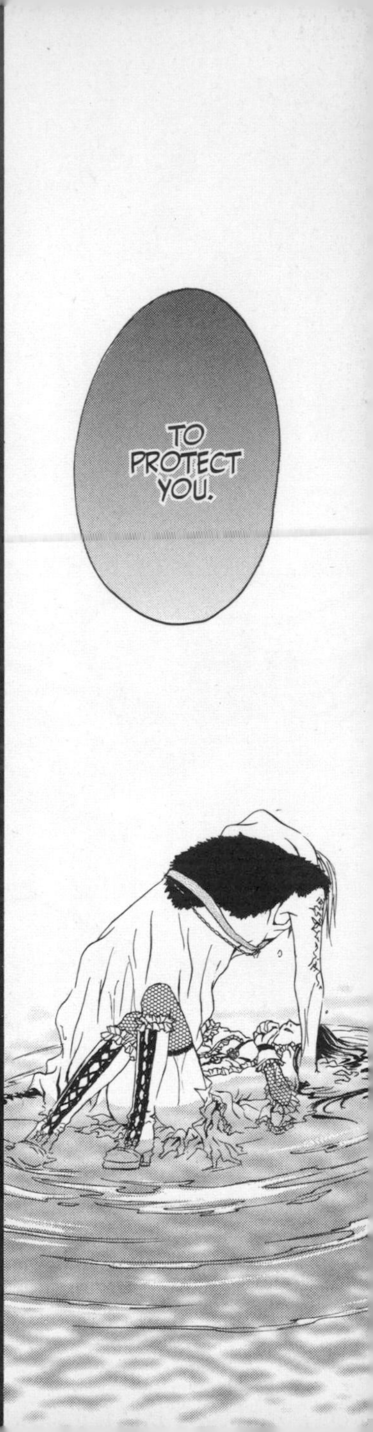
TO PROTECT YOU.
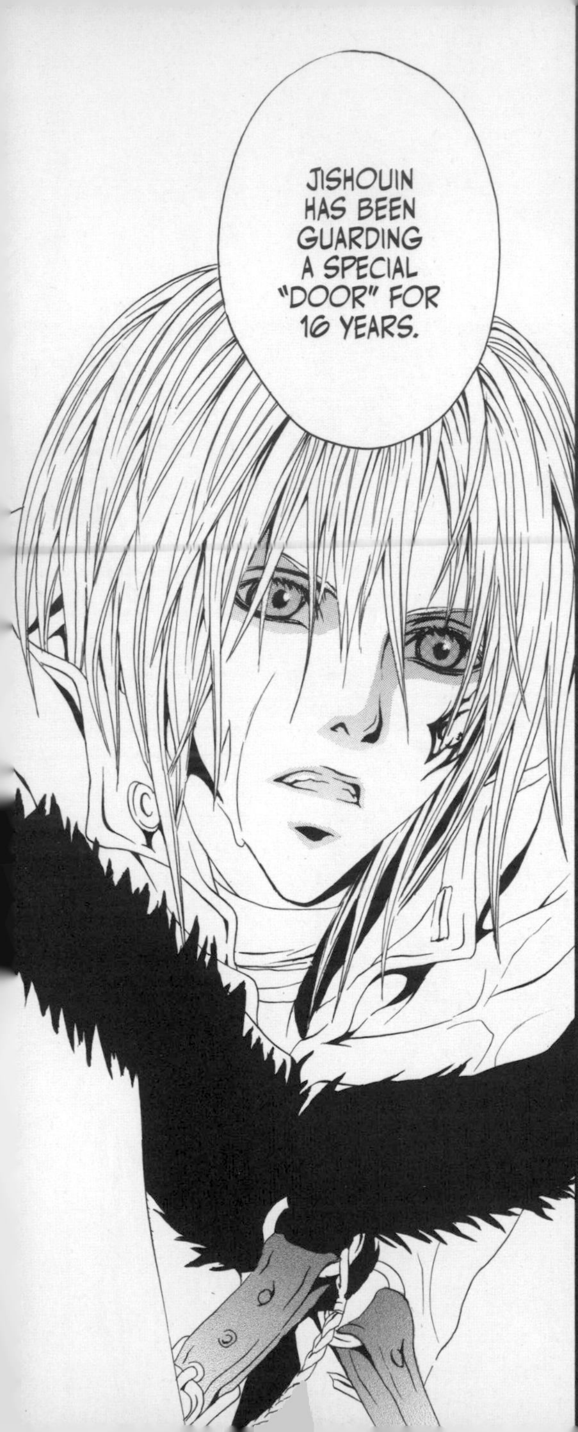
JISHOUIN HAS BEEN GUARDING A SPECIAL "DOOR" FOR 16 YEARS.

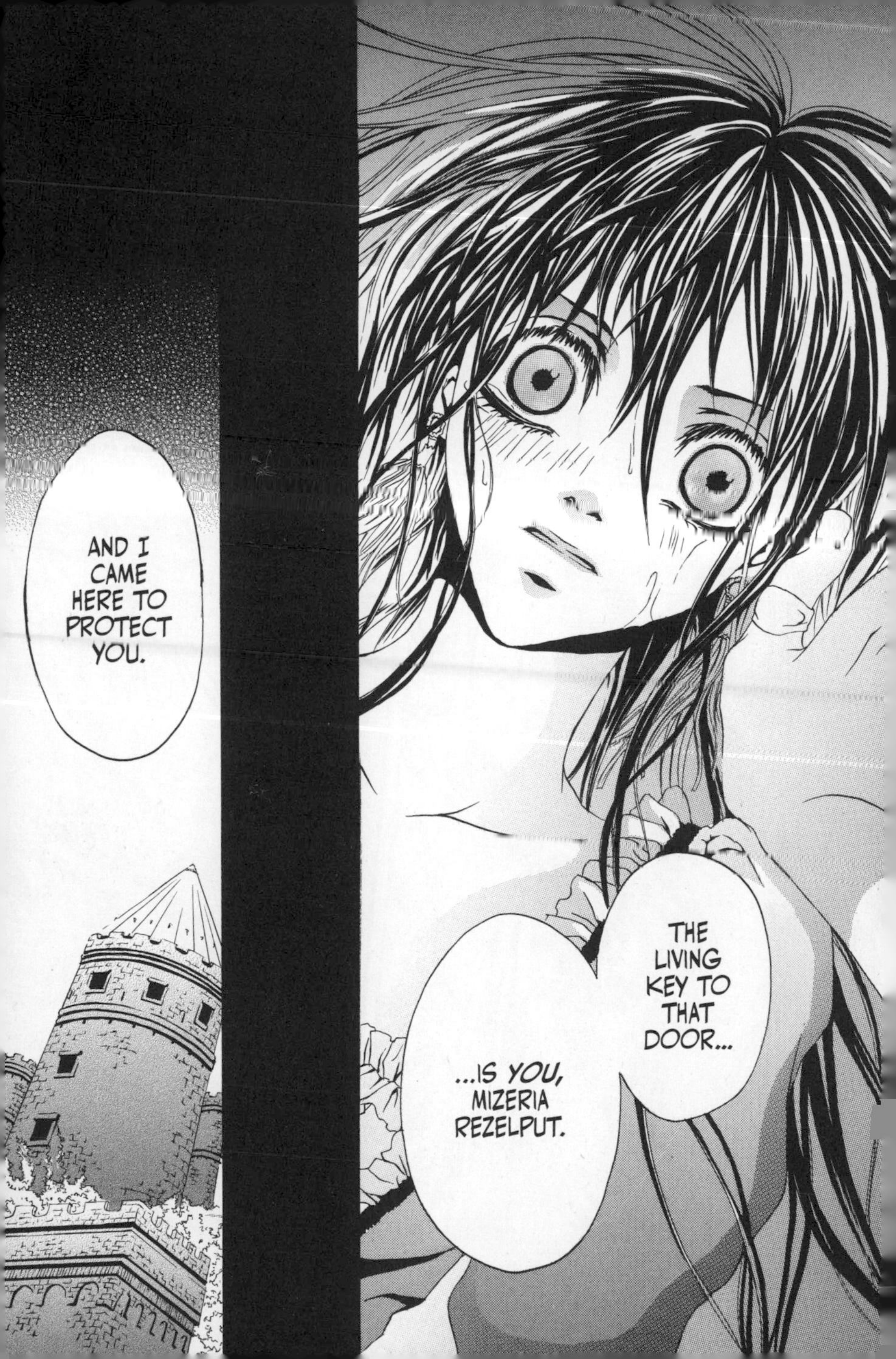
THE LIVING KEY TO THAT DOOR...
...IS *YOU*, MIZERIA REZELPUT.
AND I CAME HERE TO PROTECT YOU.

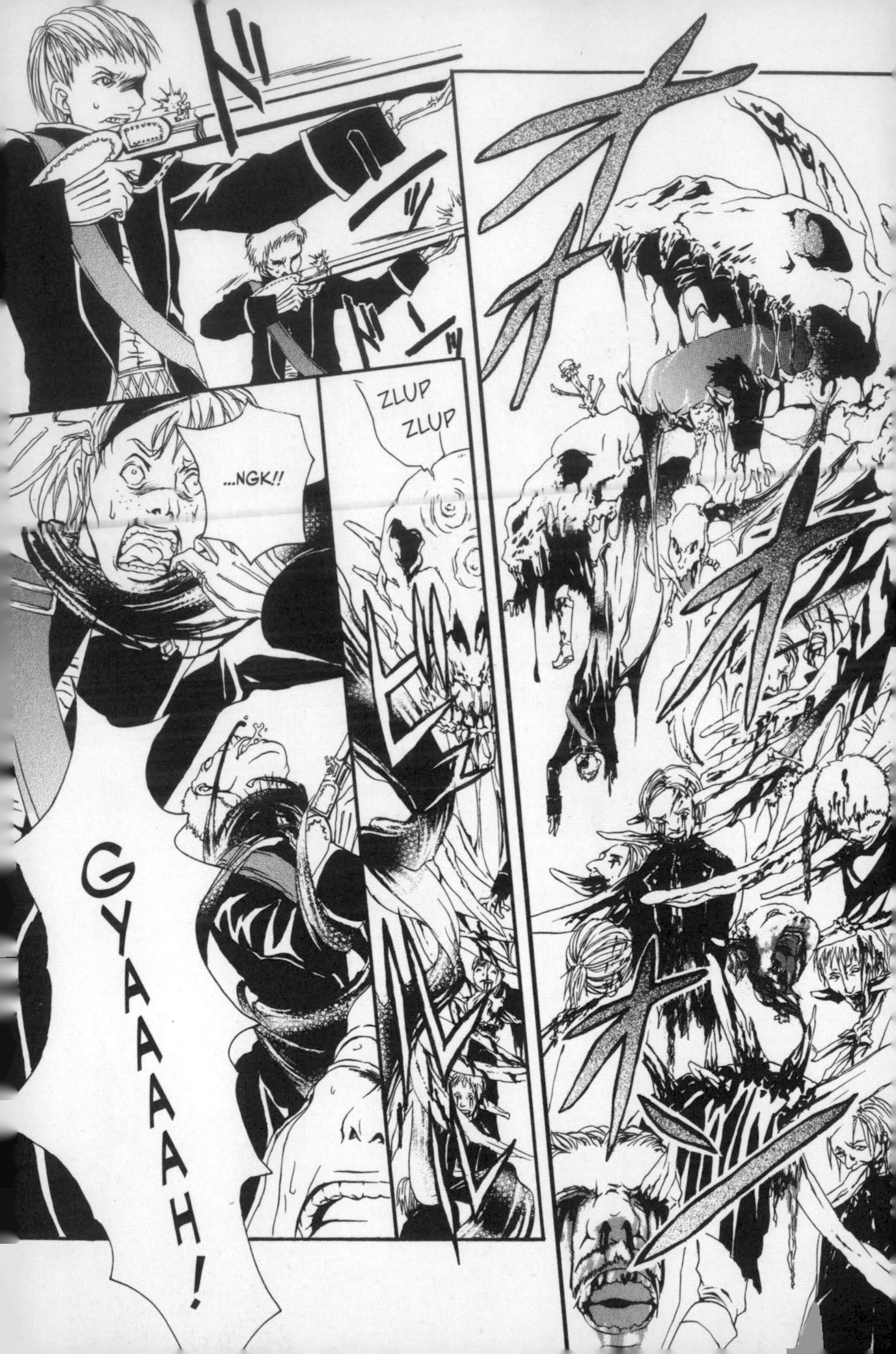
ZLUP
ZLUP
...NGK!!
GYAAAAH!

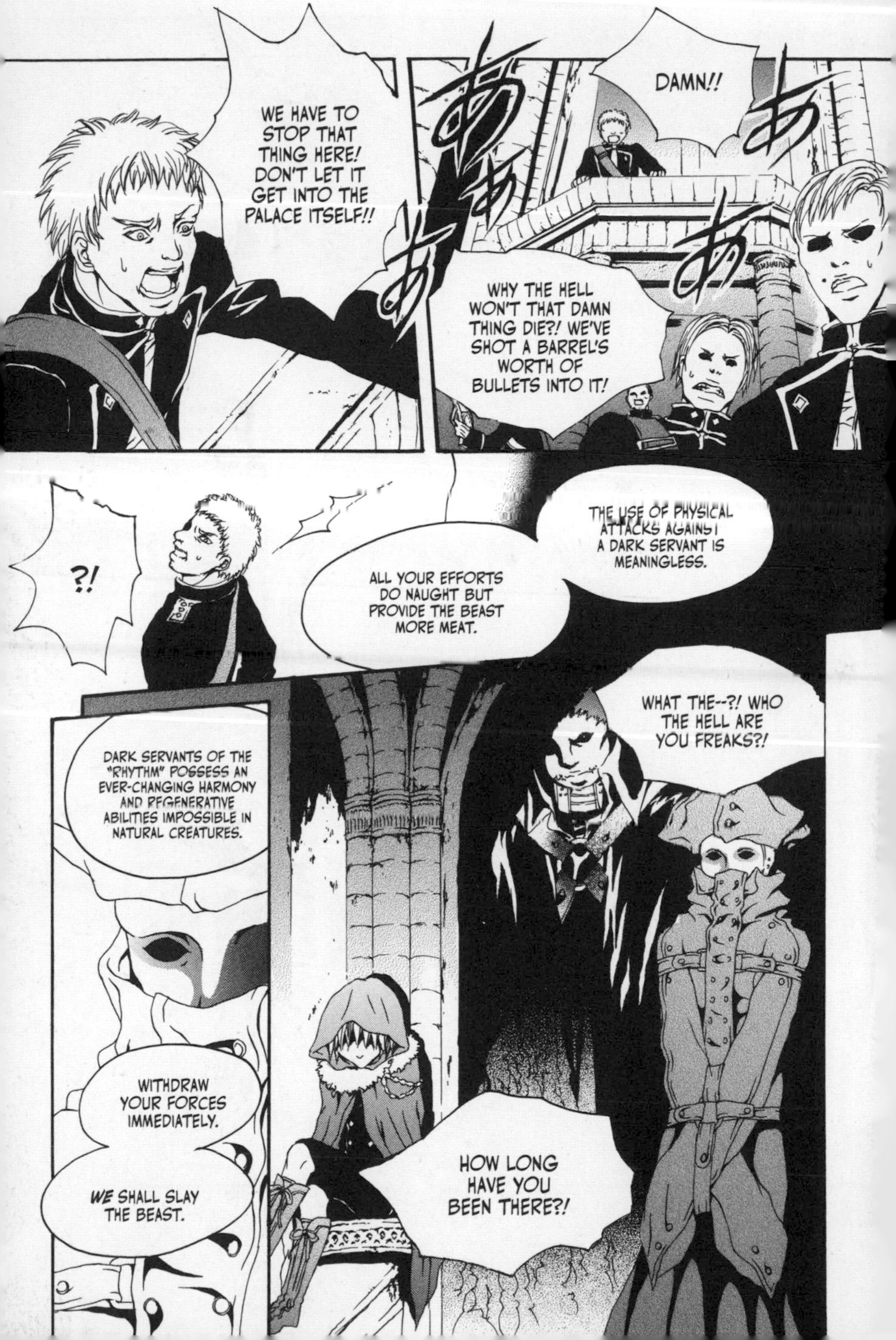

DAMN!!
ああ
あああ
WHY THE HELL WON'T THAT DAMN THING DIE?! WE'VE SHOT A BARREL'S WORTH OF BULLETS INTO IT!
WE HAVE TO STOP THAT THING HERE! DON'T LET IT GET INTO THE PALACE ITSELF!!
THE USE OF PHYSICAL ATTACKS AGAINST A DARK SERVANT IS MEANINGLESS.
ALL YOUR EFFORTS DO NAUGHT BUT PROVIDE THE BEAST MORE MEAT.
?!
WHAT THE--?! WHO THE HELL ARE YOU FREAKS?!
HOW LONG HAVE YOU BEEN THERE?!
DARK SERVANTS OF THE "RHYTHM" POSSESS AN EVER-CHANGING HARMONY AND REGENERATIVE ABILITIES IMPOSSIBLE IN NATURAL CREATURES.
WITHDRAW YOUR FORCES IMMEDIATELY.
WE SHALL SLAY THE BEAST.

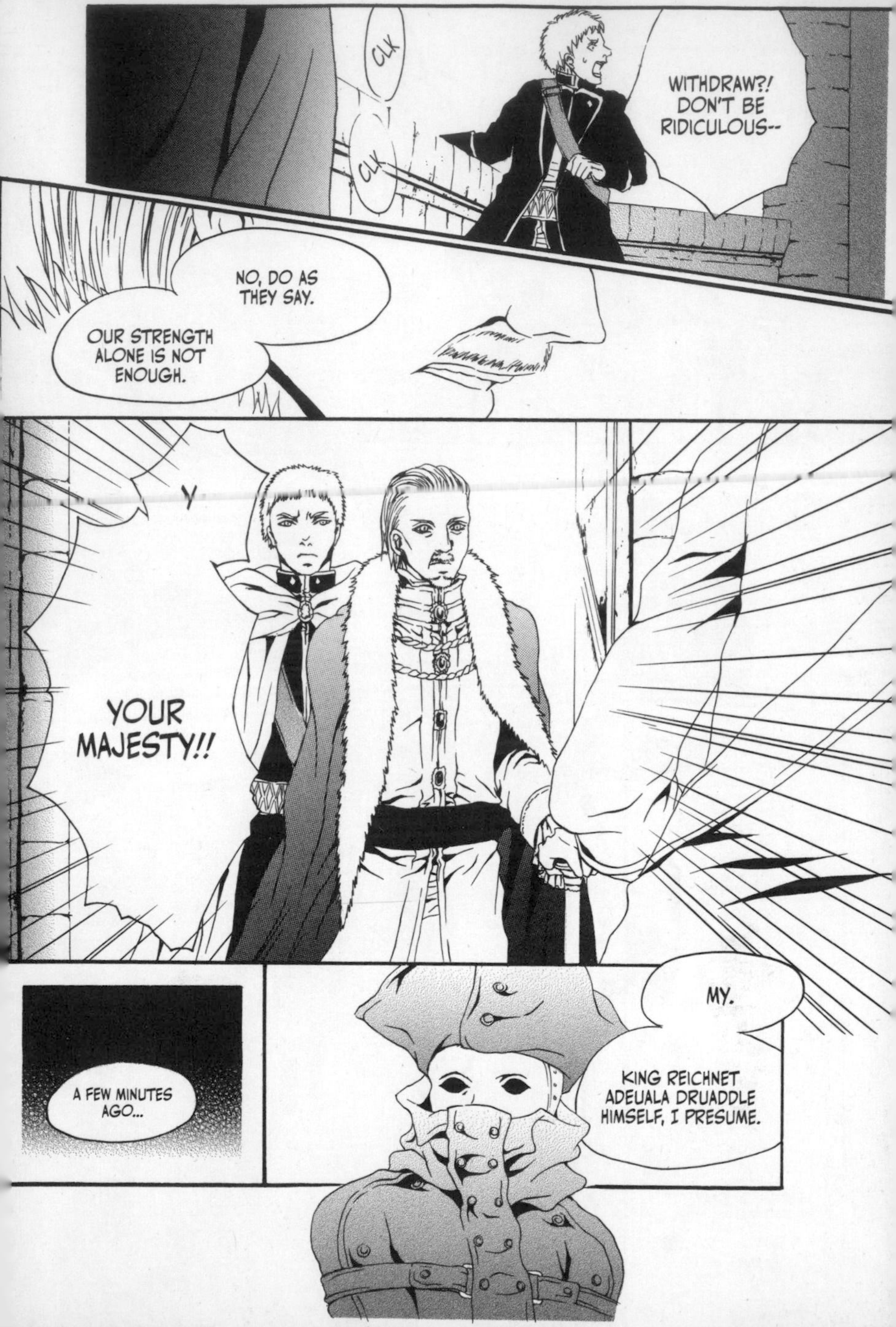
WITHDRAW?! DON'T BE RIDICULOUS--
CLK
CLK
NO, DO AS THEY SAY.
OUR STRENGTH ALONE IS NOT ENOUGH.
Y
YOUR MAJESTY!!
MY.
KING REICHNET ADEUALA DRUADDLE HIMSELF, I PRESUME.
A FEW MINUTES AGO...

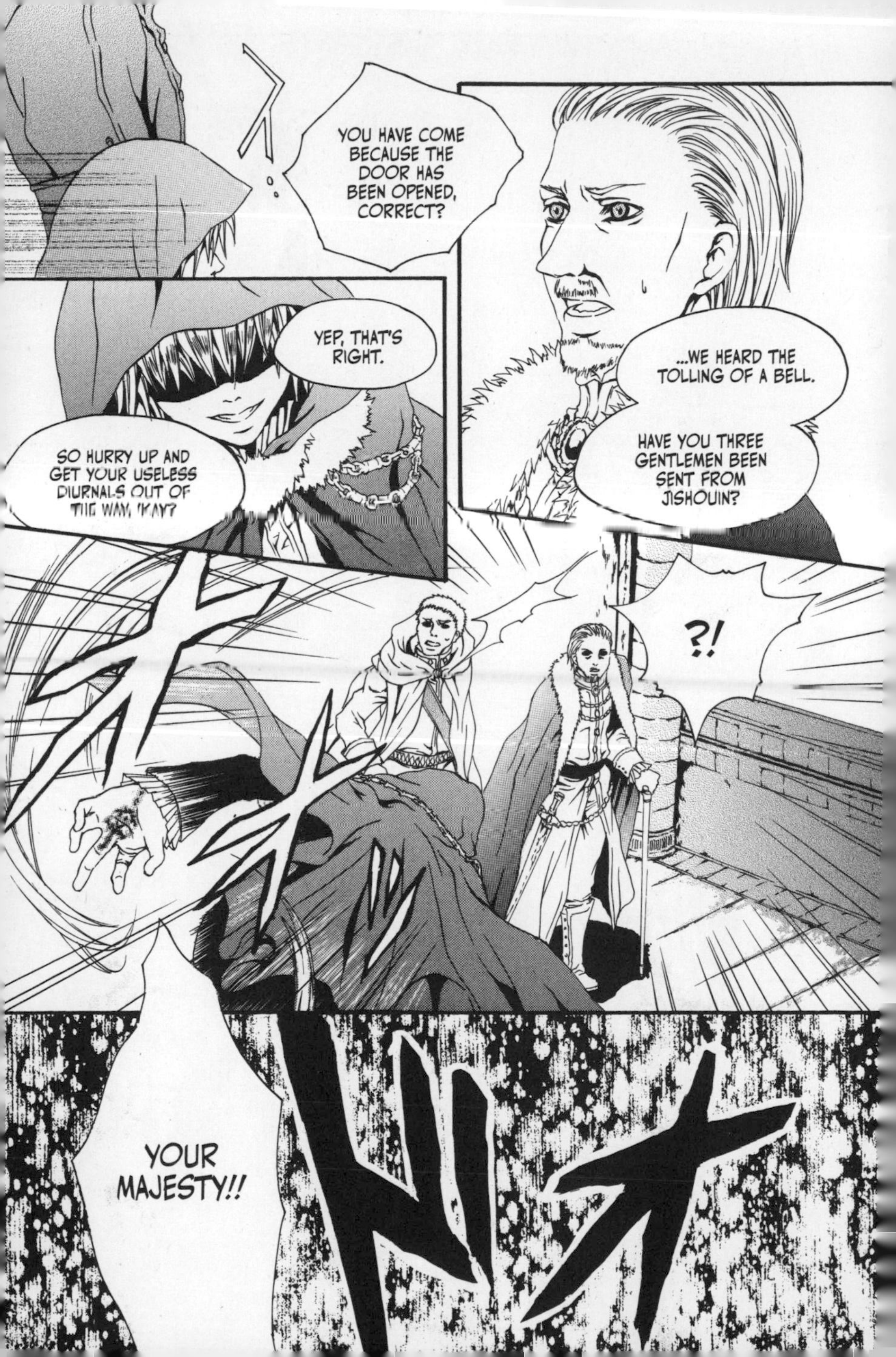
...WE HEARD THE TOLLING OF A BELL.
HAVE YOU THREE GENTLEMEN BEEN SENT FROM JISHOUIN?
YOU HAVE COME BECAUSE THE DOOR HAS BEEN OPENED, CORRECT?
YEP, THAT'S RIGHT.
SO HURRY UP AND GET YOUR USELESS DIURNALS OUT OF THE WAY, 'KAY?
?!
YOUR MAJESTY!!

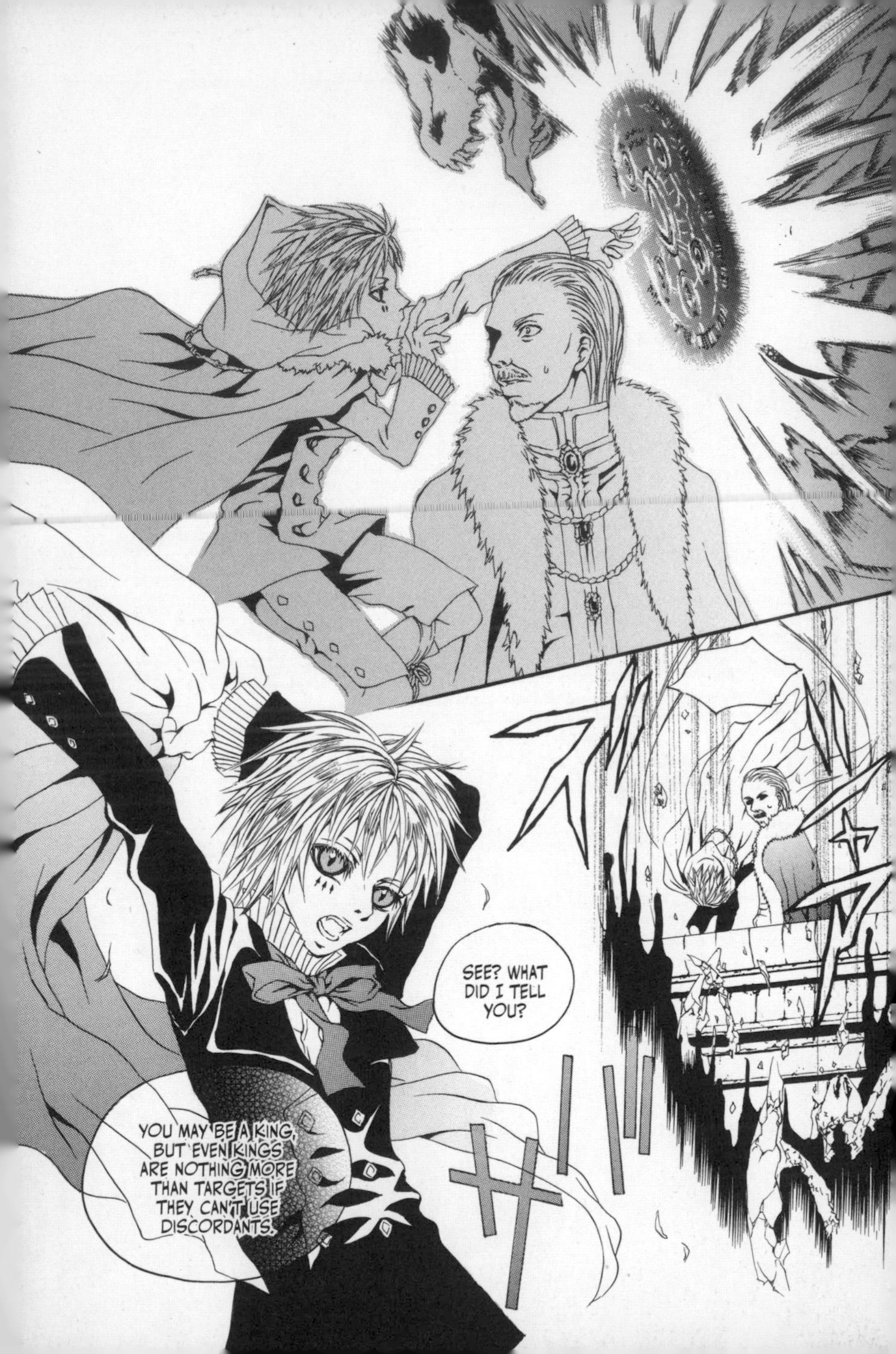
SEE? WHAT DID I TELL YOU?
YOU MAY BE A KING, BUT EVEN KINGS ARE NOTHING MORE THAN TARGETS IF THEY CAN'T USE DISCORDANTS.

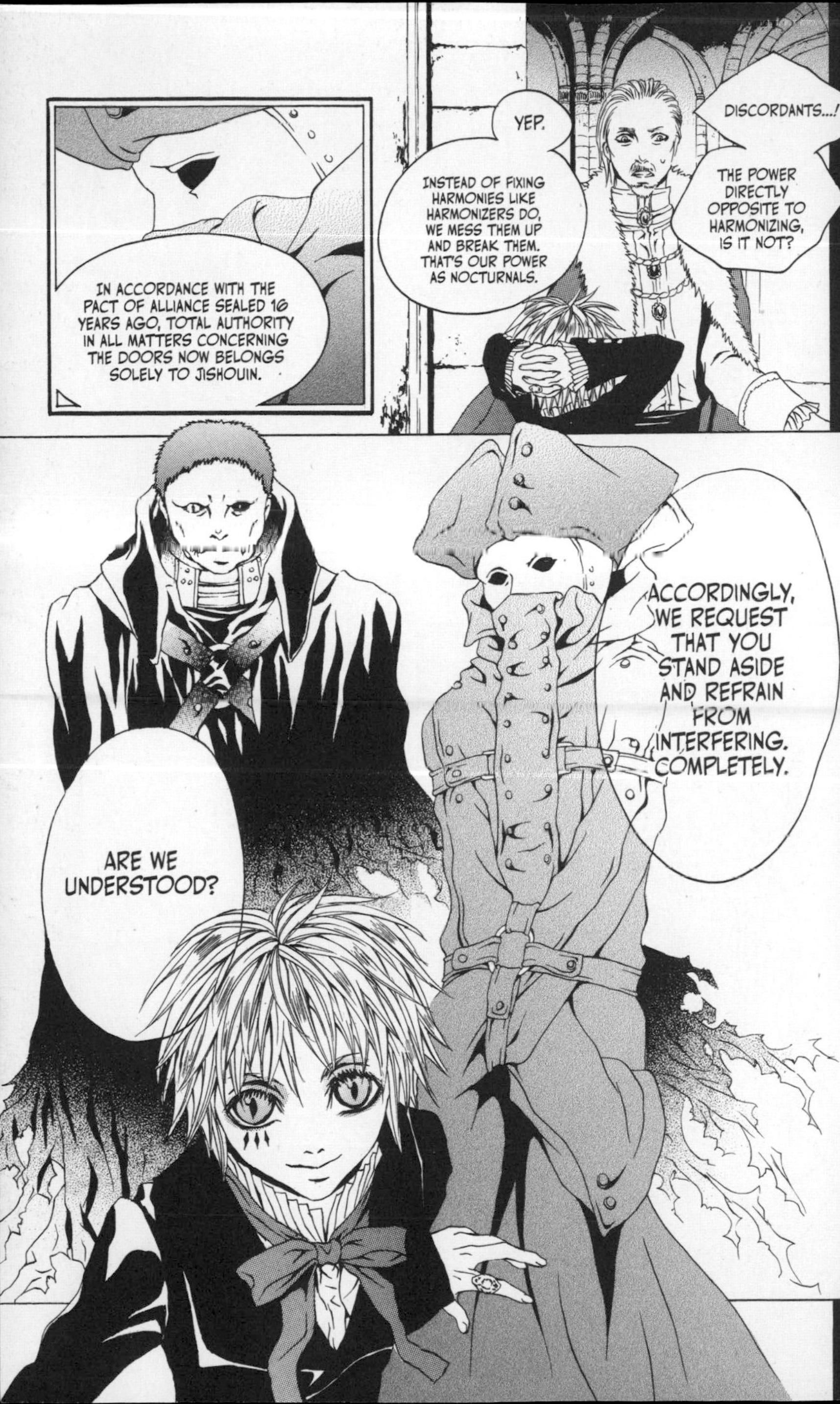
DISCORDANTS...!
THE POWER DIRECTLY OPPOSITE TO HARMONIZING, IS IT NOT?
YEP.
INSTEAD OF FIXING HARMONIES LIKE HARMONIZERS DO, WE MESS THEM UP AND BREAK THEM. THAT'S OUR POWER AS NOCTURNALS.
IN ACCORDANCE WITH THE PACT OF ALLIANCE SEALED 16 YEARS AGO, TOTAL AUTHORITY IN ALL MATTERS CONCERNING THE DOORS NOW BELONGS SOLELY TO JISHOUIN.
ACCORDINGLY, WE REQUEST THAT YOU STAND ASIDE AND REFRAIN FROM INTERFERING. COMPLETELY.
ARE WE UNDERSTOOD?

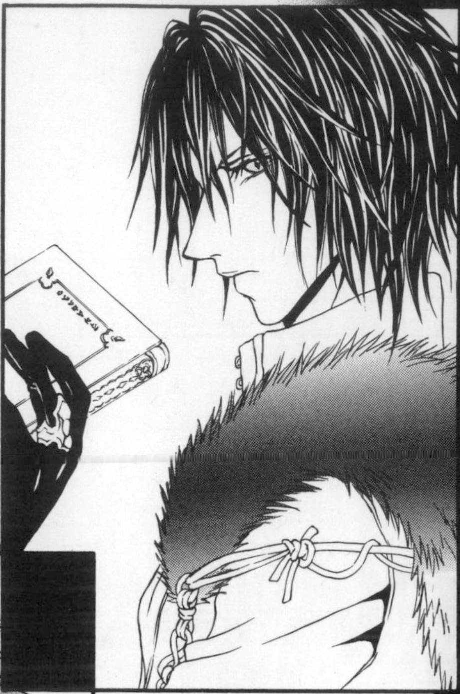

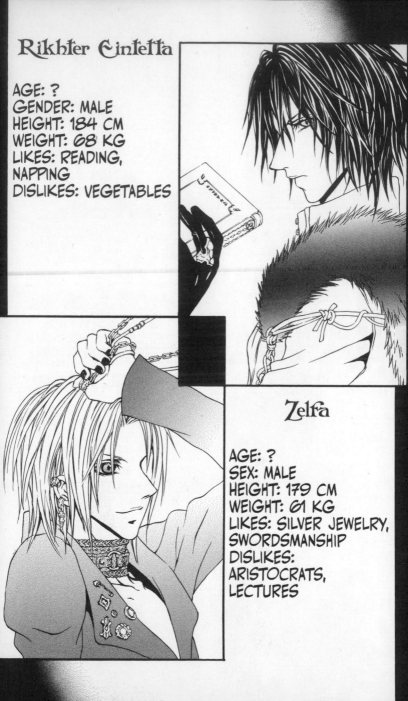

Rikhter Eintetta

AGE: ?
GENDER: MALE
HEIGHT: 184 CM
WEIGHT: 68 KG
LIKES: READING, NAPPING
DISLIKES: VEGETABLES

Zelfa

AGE: ?
SEX: MALE
HEIGHT: 179 CM
WEIGHT: 61 KG
LIKES: SILVER JEWELRY, SWORDSMANSHIP
DISLIKES: ARISTOCRATS, LECTURES

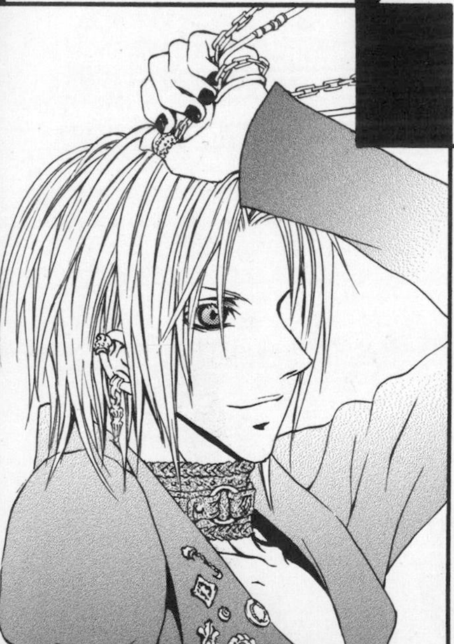

~Chapter 3~
Those Who Silence the Bells

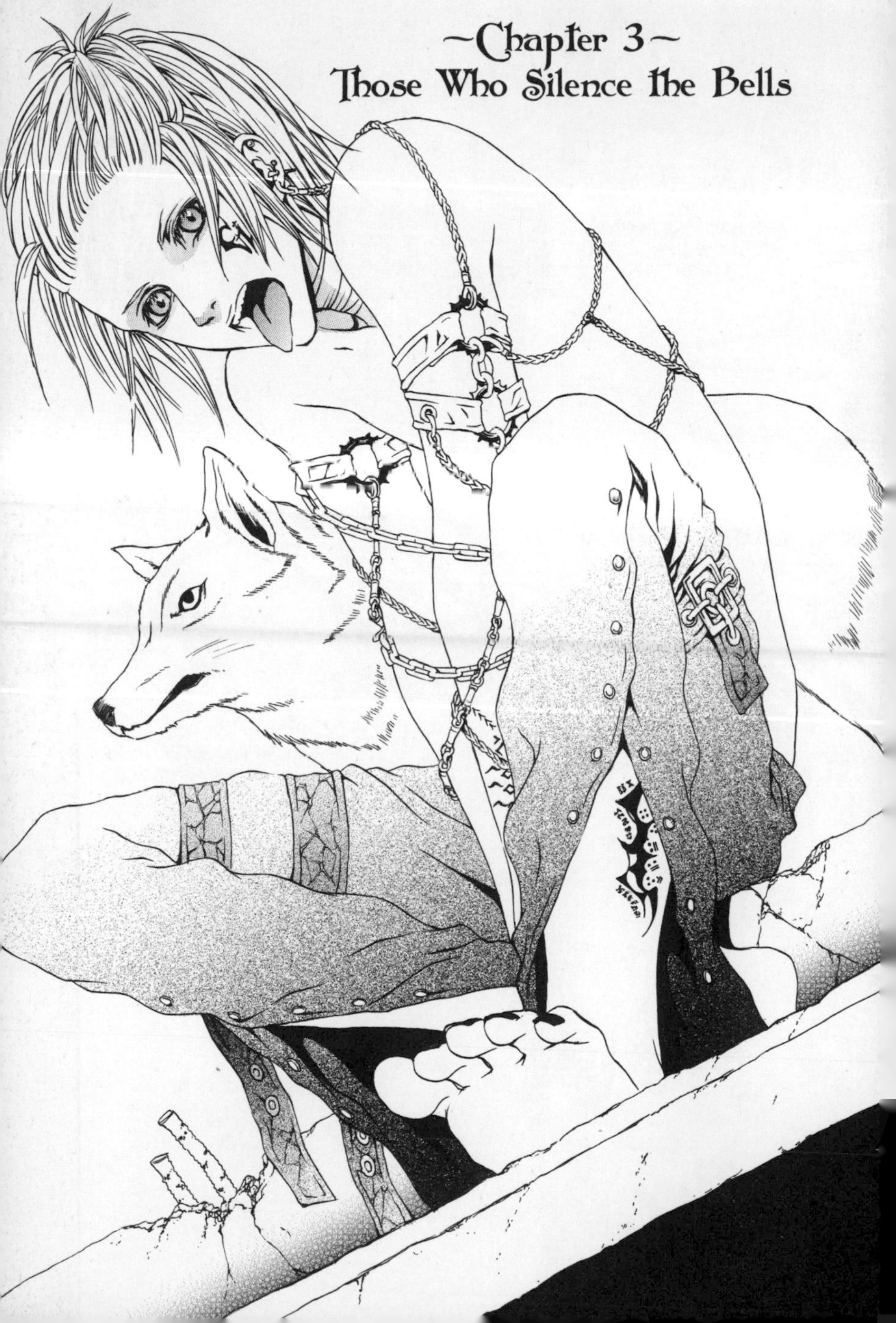

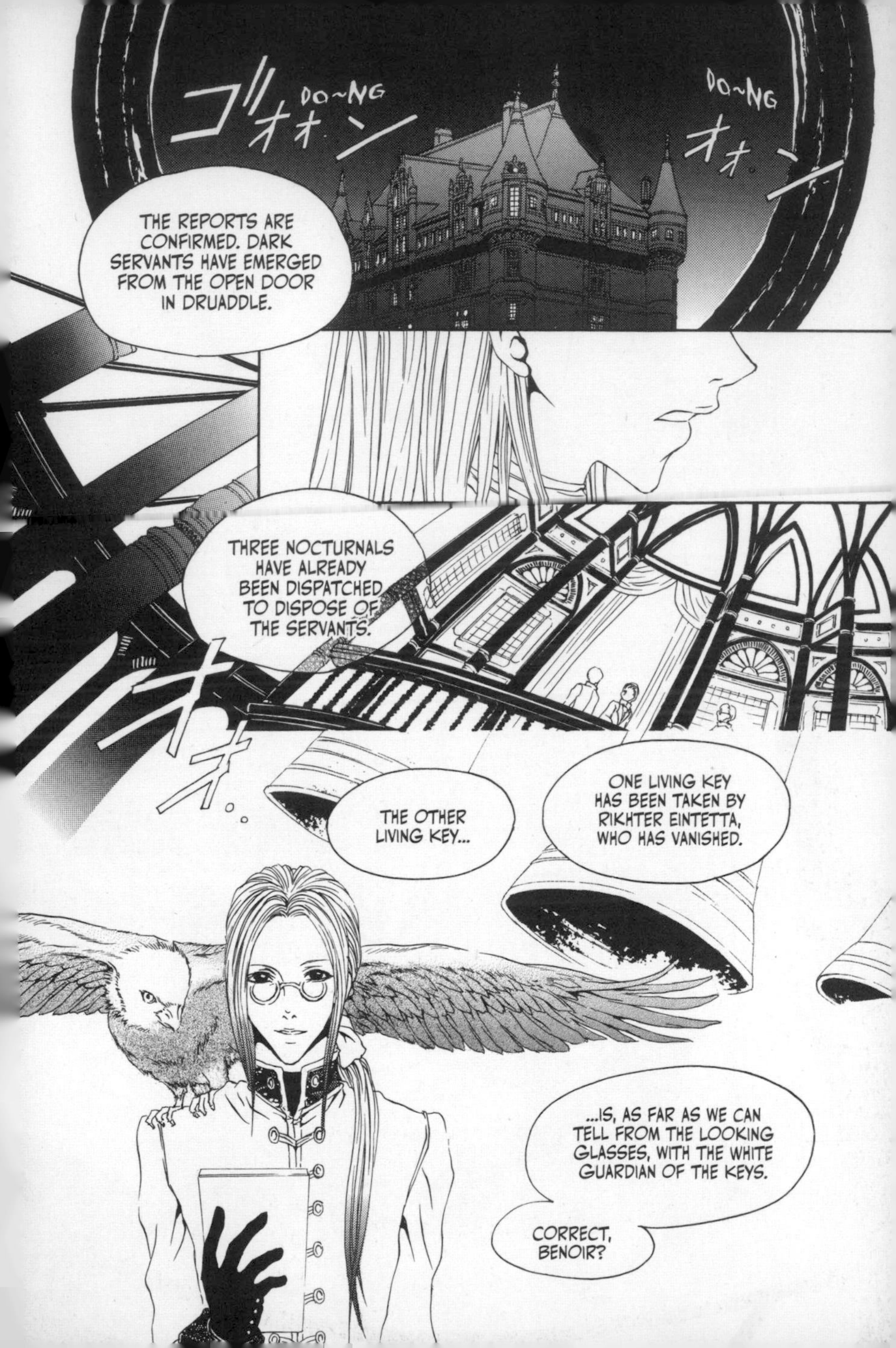
DO~NG
オオン
ゴオオン
DO~NG
THE REPORTS ARE CONFIRMED. DARK SERVANTS HAVE EMERGED FROM THE OPEN DOOR IN DRUADDLE.
THREE NOCTURNALS HAVE ALREADY BEEN DISPATCHED TO DISPOSE OF THE SERVANTS.
オオ
ONE LIVING KEY HAS BEEN TAKEN BY RIKHTER EINTETTA, WHO HAS VANISHED.
THE OTHER LIVING KEY...
...IS, AS FAR AS WE CAN TELL FROM THE LOOKING GLASSES, WITH THE WHITE GUARDIAN OF THE KEYS.
CORRECT, BENOIR?

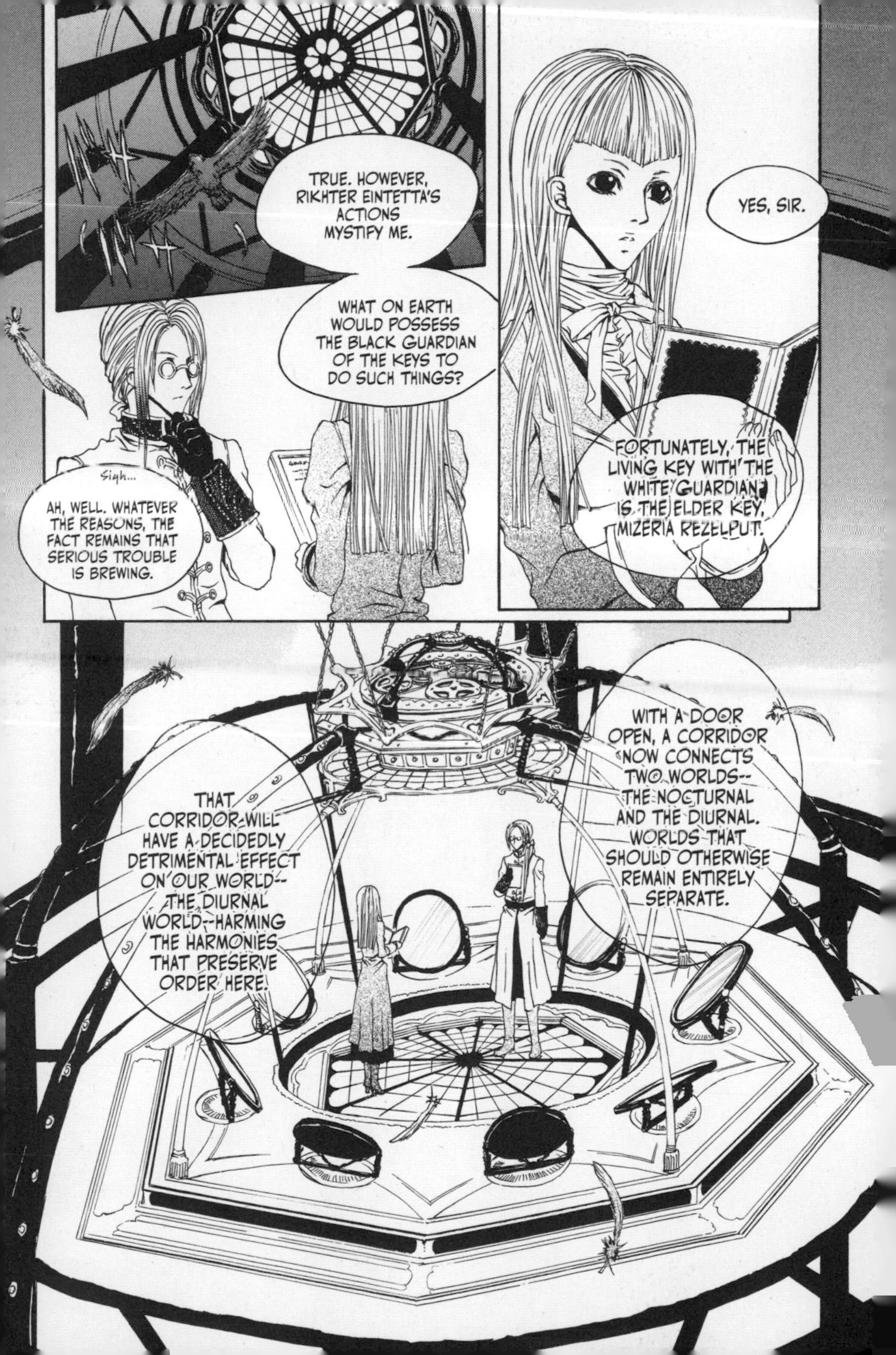
YES, SIR.
FORTUNATELY, THE LIVING KEY WITH THE WHITE GUARDIAN IS THE ELDER KEY, MIZERIA REZELPUT.
TRUE. HOWEVER, RIKHTER EINTETTA'S ACTIONS MYSTIFY ME.
WHAT ON EARTH WOULD POSSESS THE BLACK GUARDIAN OF THE KEYS TO DO SUCH THINGS?
Sigh...
AH, WELL. WHATEVER THE REASONS, THE FACT REMAINS THAT SERIOUS TROUBLE IS BREWING.
WITH A DOOR OPEN, A CORRIDOR NOW CONNECTS TWO WORLDS--THE NOCTURNAL AND THE DIURNAL. WORLDS THAT SHOULD OTHERWISE REMAIN ENTIRELY SEPARATE.
THAT CORRIDOR WILL HAVE A DECIDEDLY DETRIMENTAL EFFECT ON OUR WORLD--THE DIURNAL WORLD--HARMING THE HARMONIES THAT PRESERVE ORDER HERE.

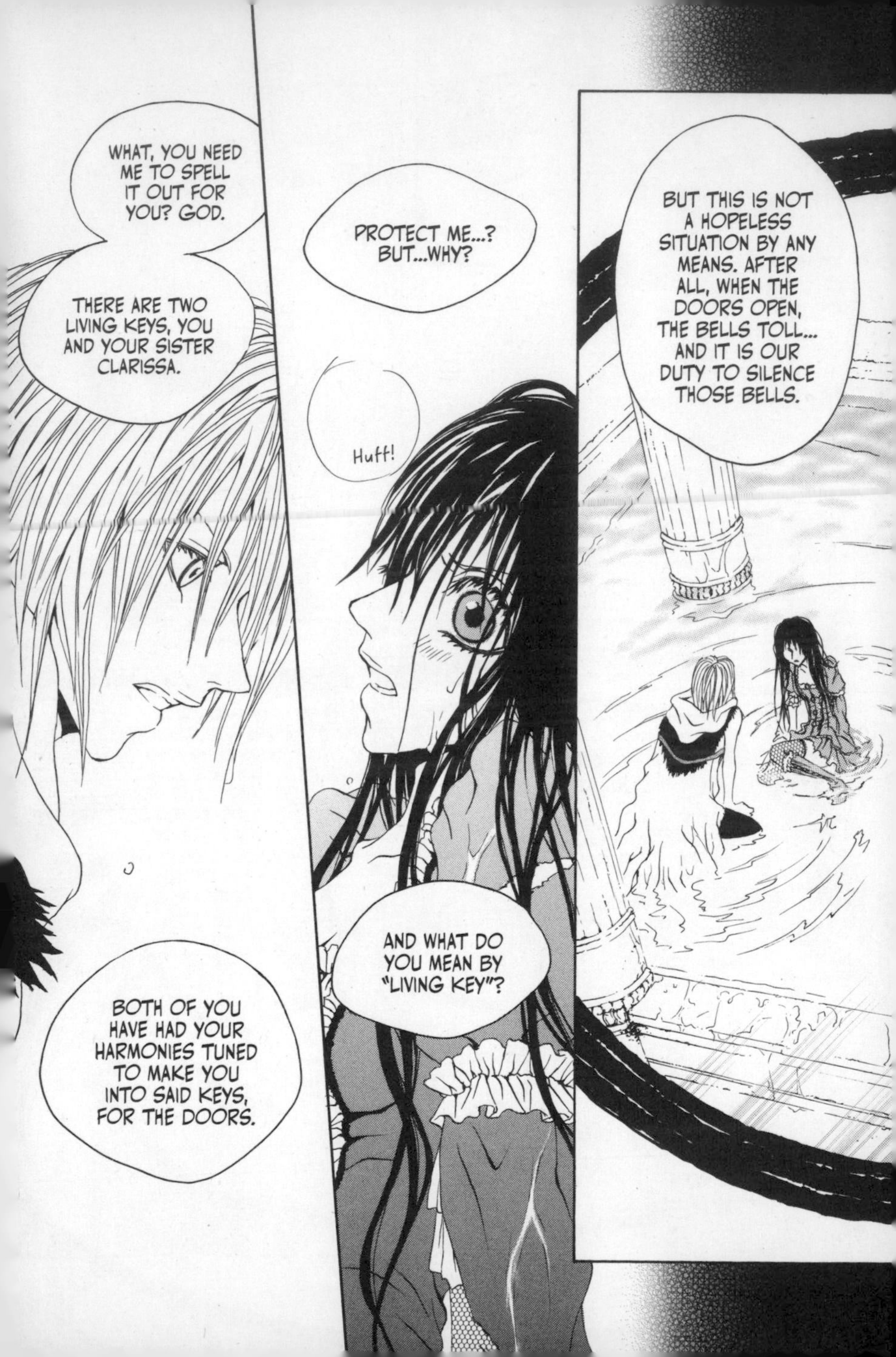
BUT THIS IS NOT A HOPELESS SITUATION BY ANY MEANS. AFTER ALL, WHEN THE DOORS OPEN, THE BELLS TOLL... AND IT IS OUR DUTY TO SILENCE THOSE BELLS.
PROTECT ME...? BUT...WHY?
Huff!
AND WHAT DO YOU MEAN BY "LIVING KEY"?
WHAT, YOU NEED ME TO SPELL IT OUT FOR YOU? GOD.
THERE ARE TWO LIVING KEYS, YOU AND YOUR SISTER CLARISSA.
BOTH OF YOU HAVE HAD YOUR HARMONIES TUNED TO MAKE YOU INTO SAID KEYS, FOR THE DOORS.

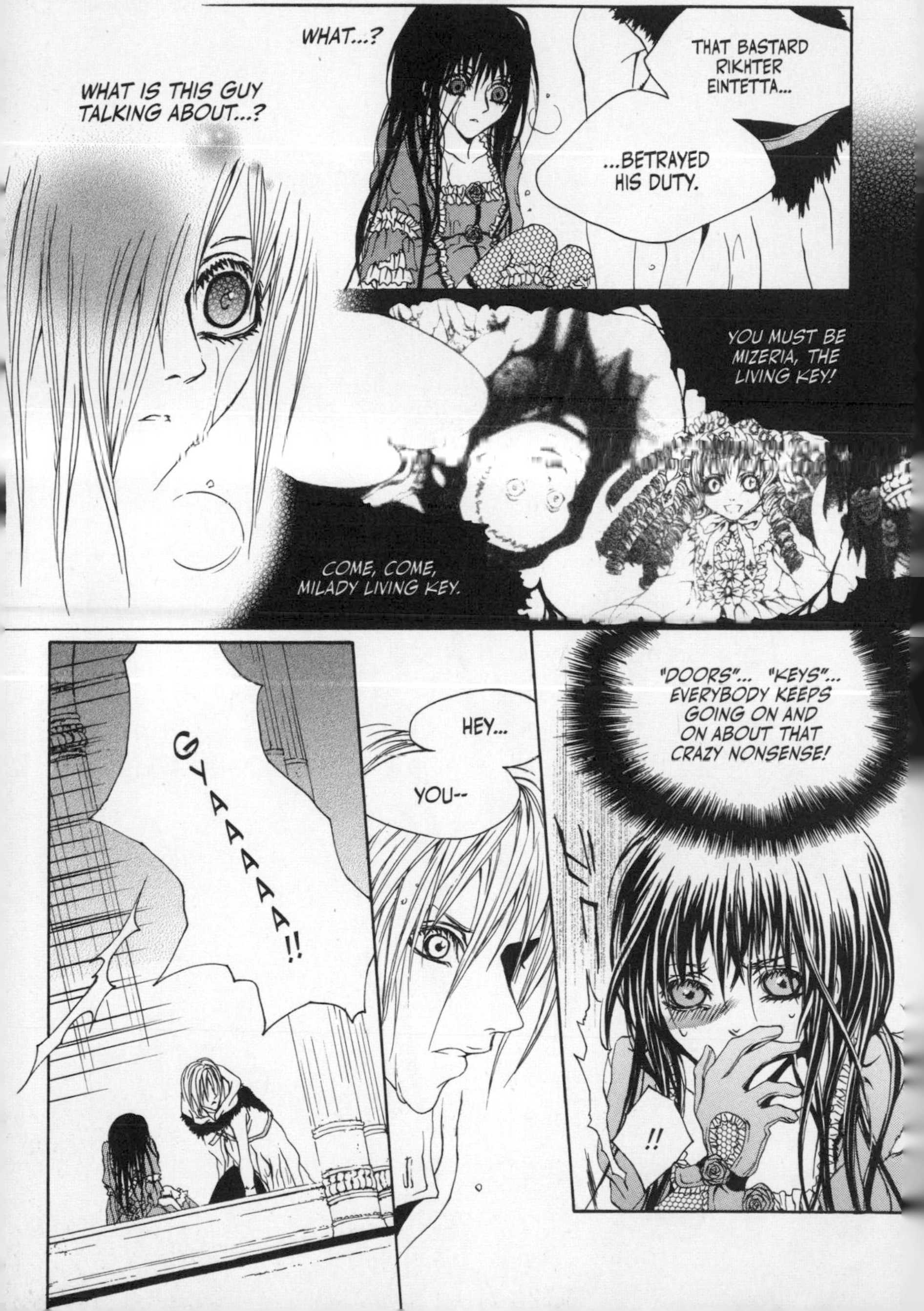
THAT BASTARD RIKHTER EINTETTA...
...BETRAYED HIS DUTY.
WHAT...?
WHAT IS THIS GUY TALKING ABOUT...?
YOU MUST BE MIZERIA, THE LIVING KEY!
COME, COME, MILADY LIVING KEY.
"DOORS"... "KEYS"... EVERYBODY KEEPS GOING ON AND ON ABOUT THAT CRAZY NONSENSE!
!!
HEY...
YOU--
GYAAAAAA!!

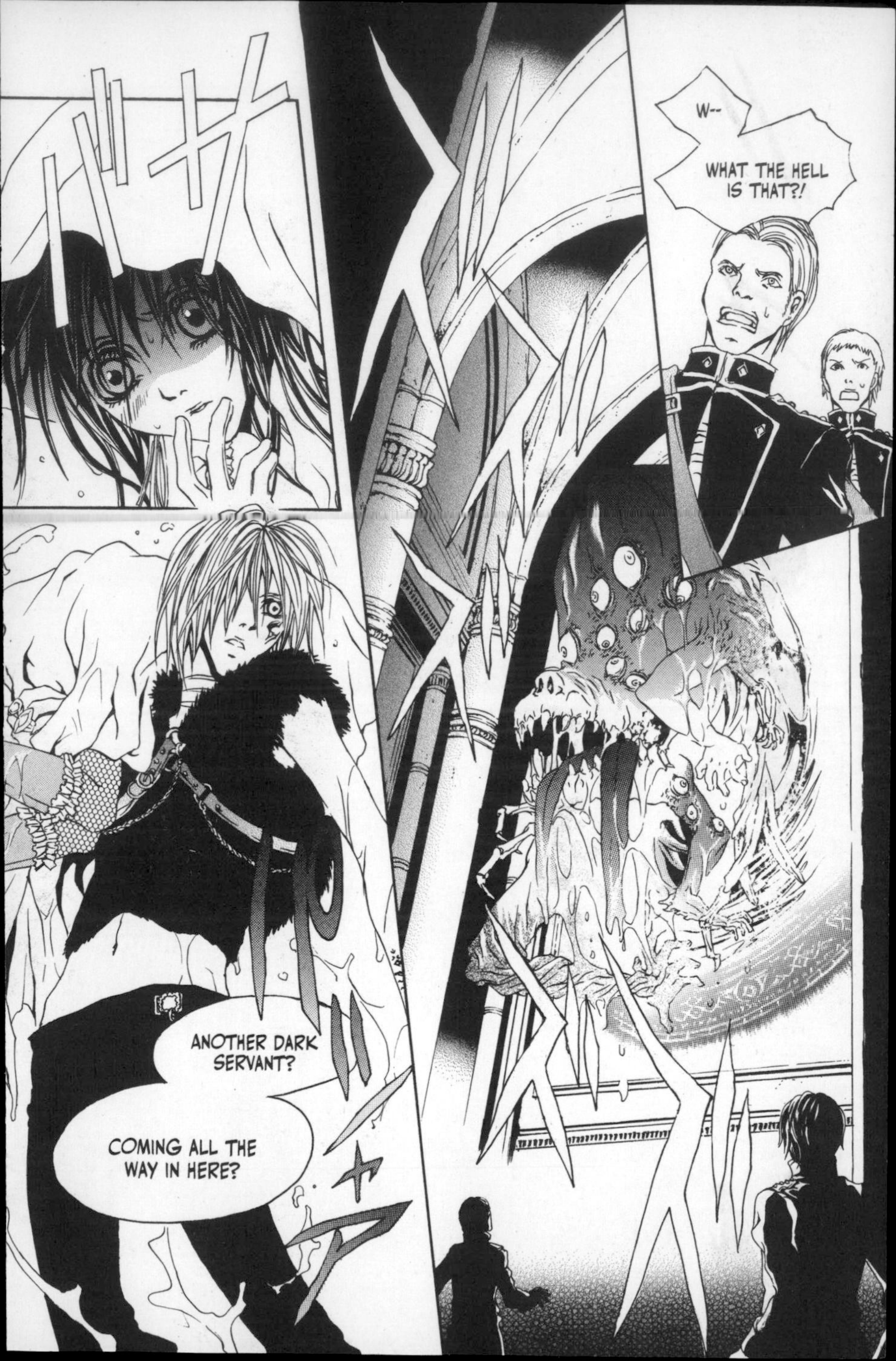
W--
WHAT THE HELL IS THAT?!
ANOTHER DARK SERVANT?
COMING ALL THE WAY IN HERE?

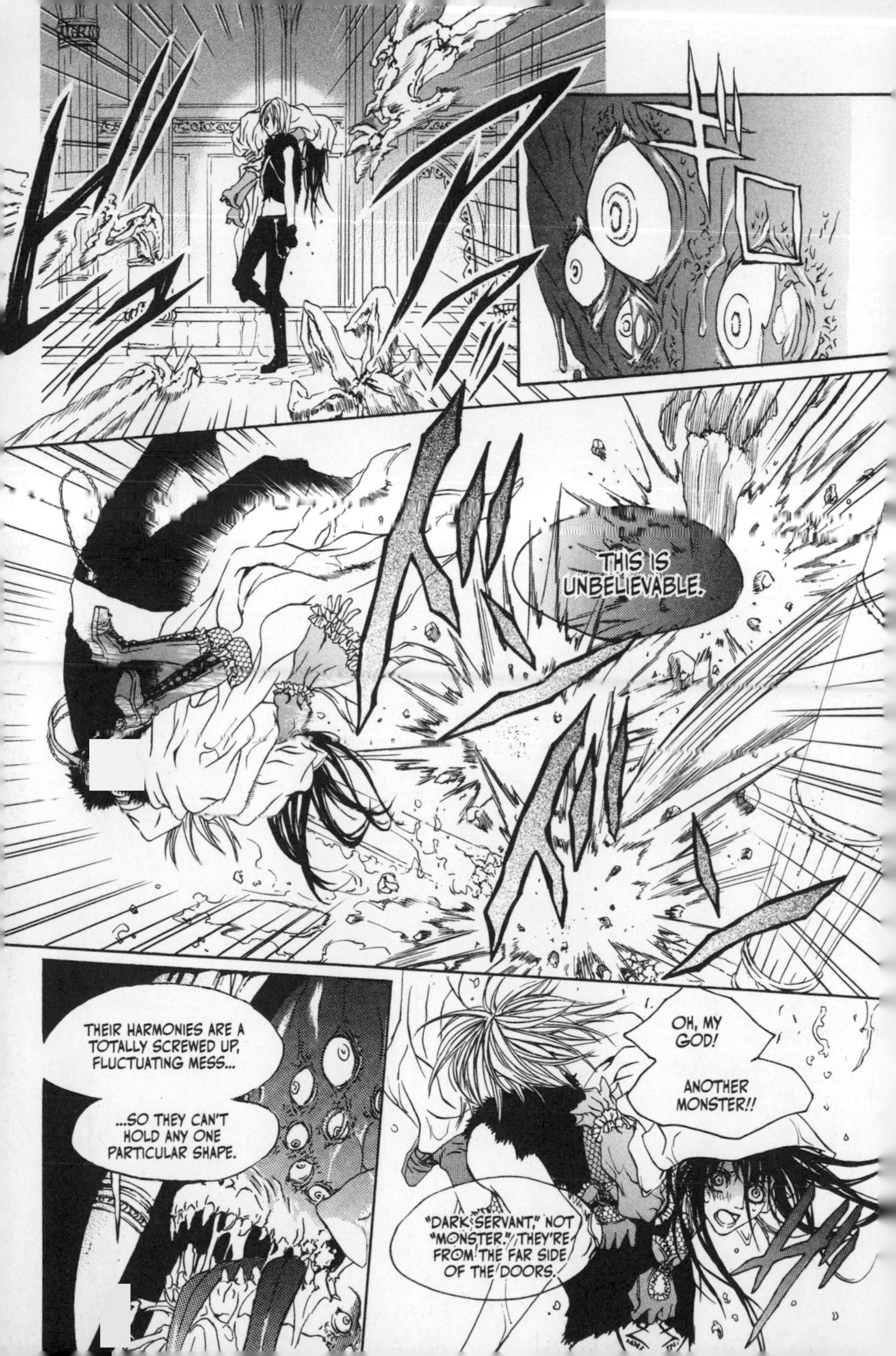
THIS IS UNBELIEVABLE.
OH, MY GOD!
ANOTHER MONSTER!!
"DARK SERVANT," NOT "MONSTER." THEY'RE FROM THE FAR SIDE OF THE DOORS.
THEIR HARMONIES ARE A TOTALLY SCREWED UP, FLUCTUATING MESS...
...SO THEY CAN'T HOLD ANY ONE PARTICULAR SHAPE.

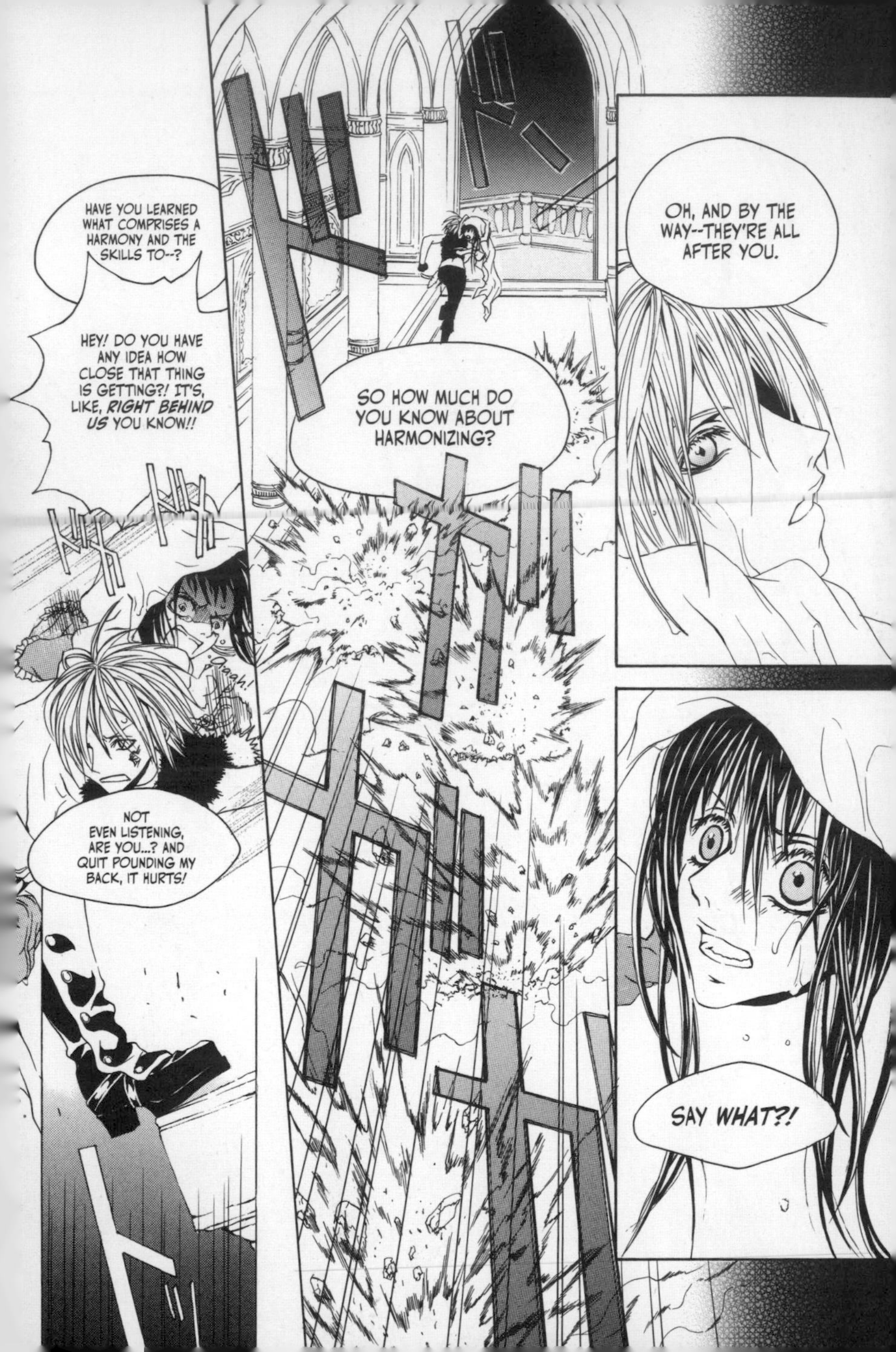
OH, AND BY THE WAY--THEY'RE ALL AFTER YOU.
SAY WHAT?!
SO HOW MUCH DO YOU KNOW ABOUT HARMONIZING?
HAVE YOU LEARNED WHAT COMPRISES A HARMONY AND THE SKILLS TO--?
HEY! DO YOU HAVE ANY IDEA HOW CLOSE THAT THING IS GETTING?! IT'S, LIKE, RIGHT BEHIND US YOU KNOW!!
Aaagh!
NOT EVEN LISTENING, ARE YOU...? AND QUIT POUNDING MY BACK, IT HURTS!

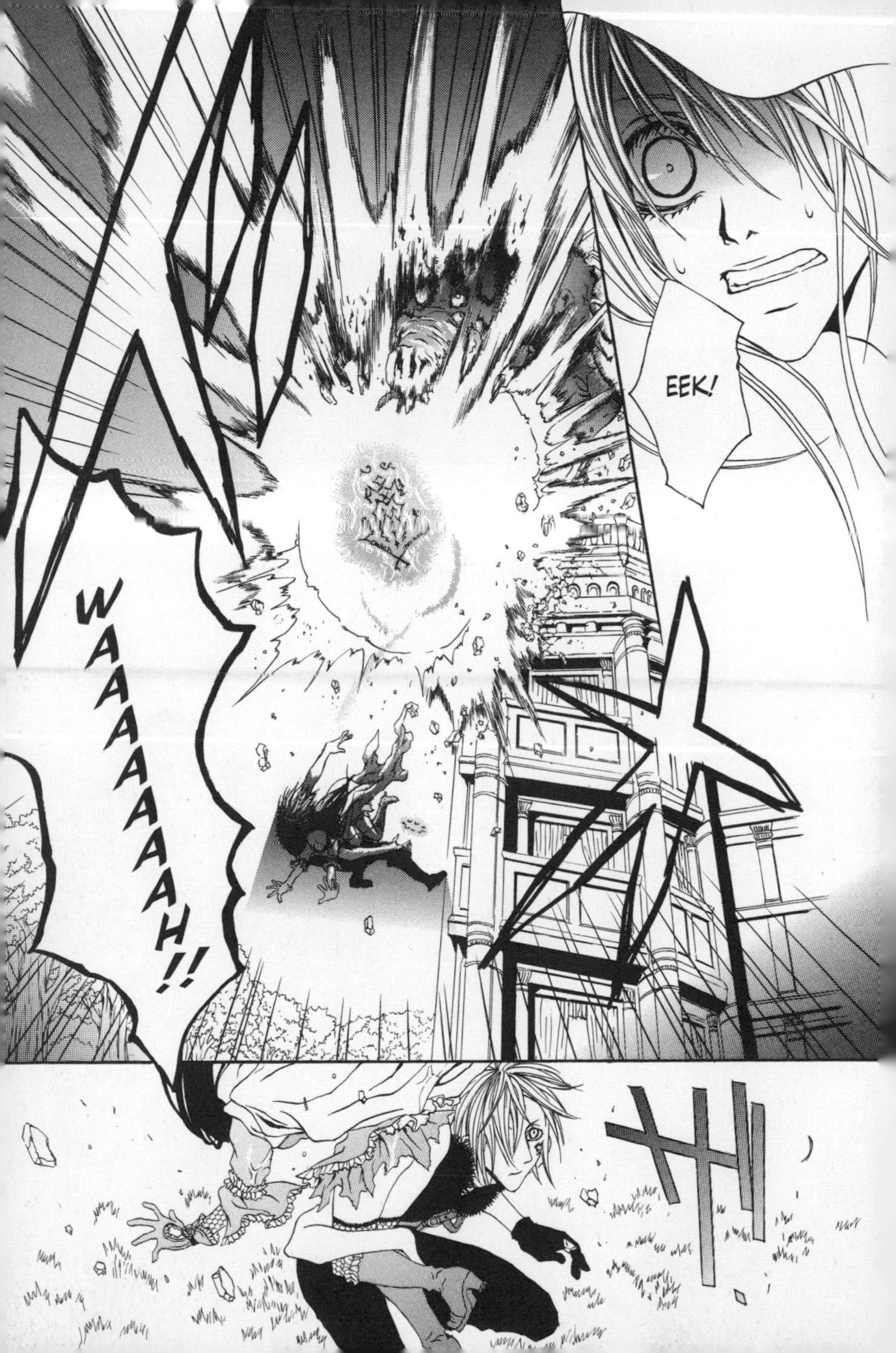
EEK!
WAAAAAAAH!!

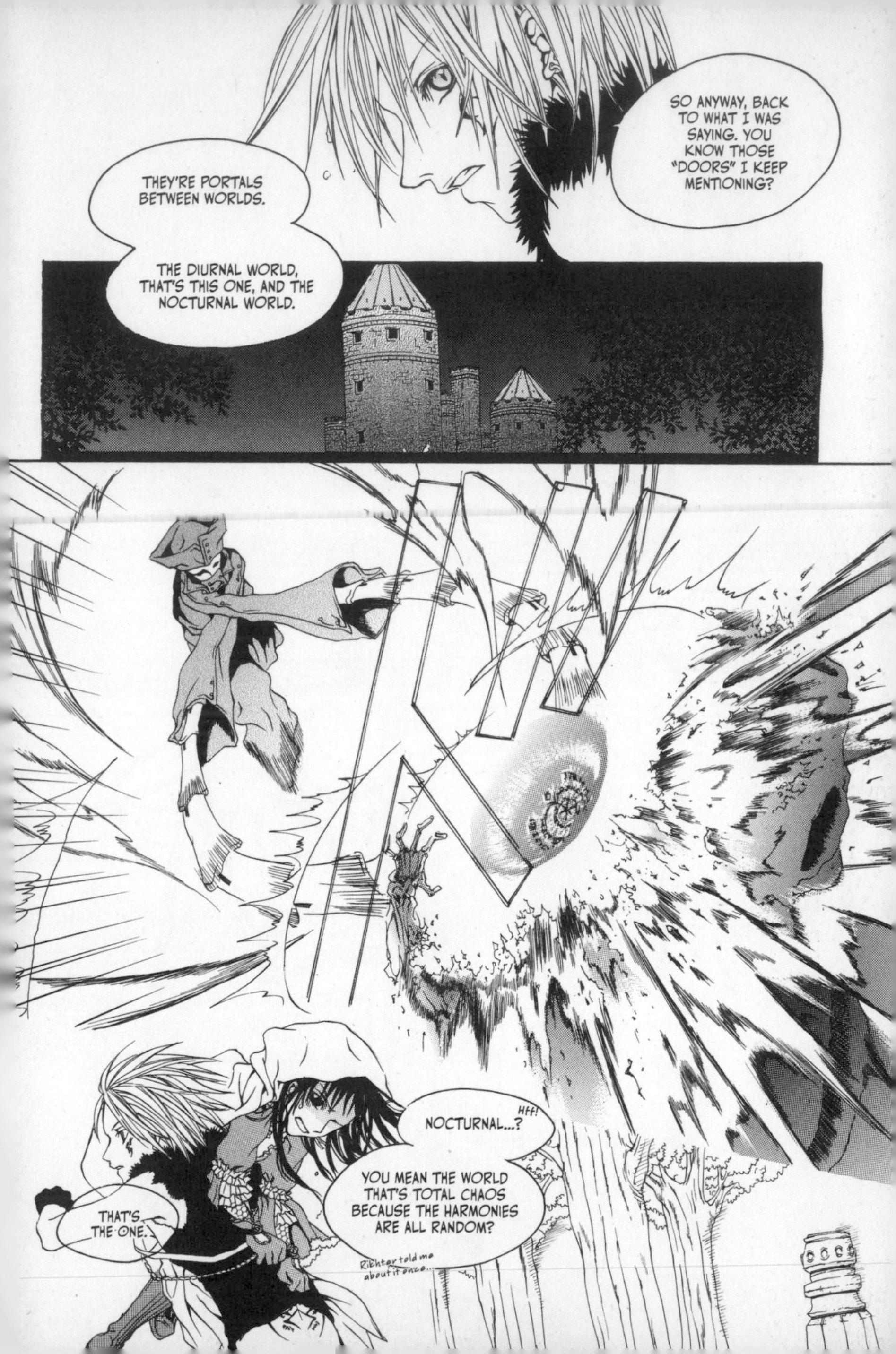
SO ANYWAY, BACK TO WHAT I WAS SAYING. YOU KNOW THOSE "DOORS" I KEEP MENTIONING?
THEY'RE PORTALS BETWEEN WORLDS.
THE DIURNAL WORLD, THAT'S THIS ONE, AND THE NOCTURNAL WORLD.
NOCTURNAL...?
Hff!
YOU MEAN THE WORLD THAT'S TOTAL CHAOS BECAUSE THE HARMONIES ARE ALL RANDOM?
Richter told me about it once...
THAT'S THE ONE.

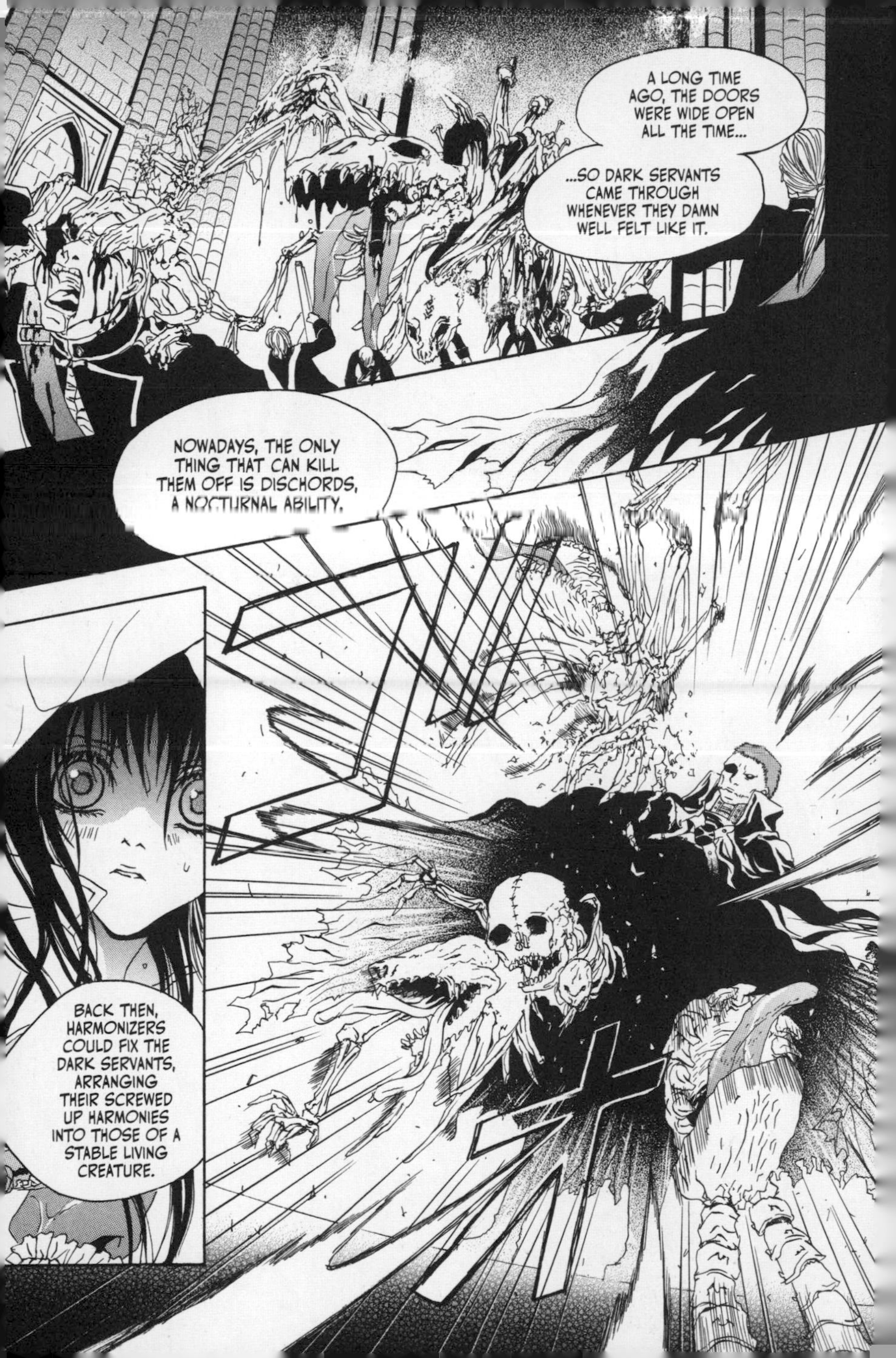
A LONG TIME AGO, THE DOORS WERE WIDE OPEN ALL THE TIME...
...SO DARK SERVANTS CAME THROUGH WHENEVER THEY DAMN WELL FELT LIKE IT.
NOWADAYS, THE ONLY THING THAT CAN KILL THEM OFF IS DISCHORDS, A NOCTURNAL ABILITY.
BACK THEN, HARMONIZERS COULD FIX THE DARK SERVANTS, ARRANGING THEIR SCREWED UP HARMONIES INTO THOSE OF A STABLE LIVING CREATURE.

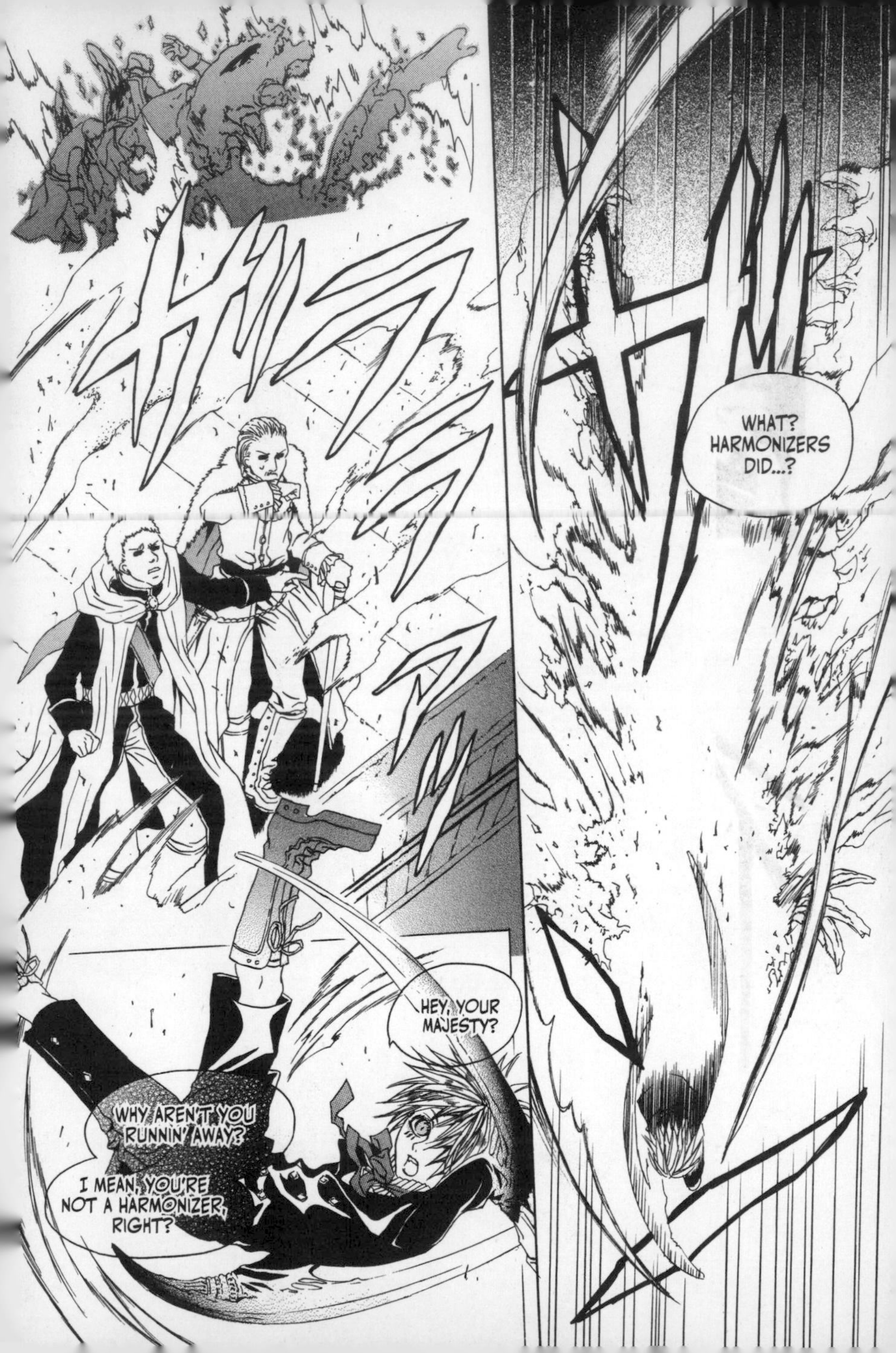
WHAT? HARMONIZERS DID...?
HEY, YOUR MAJESTY?
WHY AREN'T YOU RUNNIN' AWAY?
I MEAN, YOU'RE NOT A HARMONIZER, RIGHT?

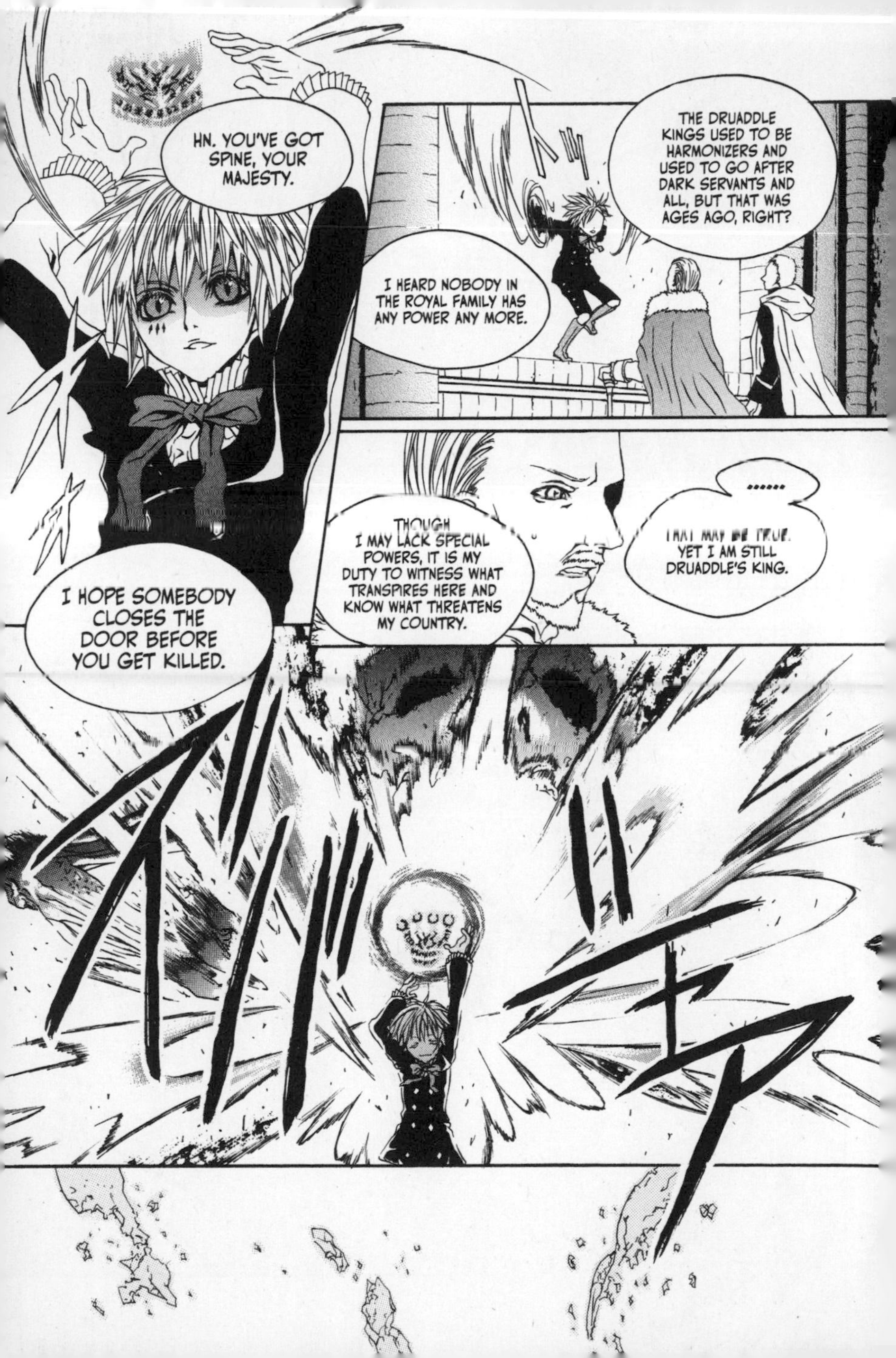
THE DRUADDLE KINGS USED TO BE HARMONIZERS AND USED TO GO AFTER DARK SERVANTS AND ALL, BUT THAT WAS AGES AGO, RIGHT?
I HEARD NOBODY IN THE ROYAL FAMILY HAS ANY POWER ANY MORE.
......
THAT MAY BE TRUE. YET I AM STILL DRUADDLE'S KING.
THOUGH I MAY LACK SPECIAL POWERS, IT IS MY DUTY TO WITNESS WHAT TRANSPIRES HERE AND KNOW WHAT THREATENS MY COUNTRY.
HN. YOU'VE GOT SPINE, YOUR MAJESTY.
I HOPE SOMEBODY CLOSES THE DOOR BEFORE YOU GET KILLED.

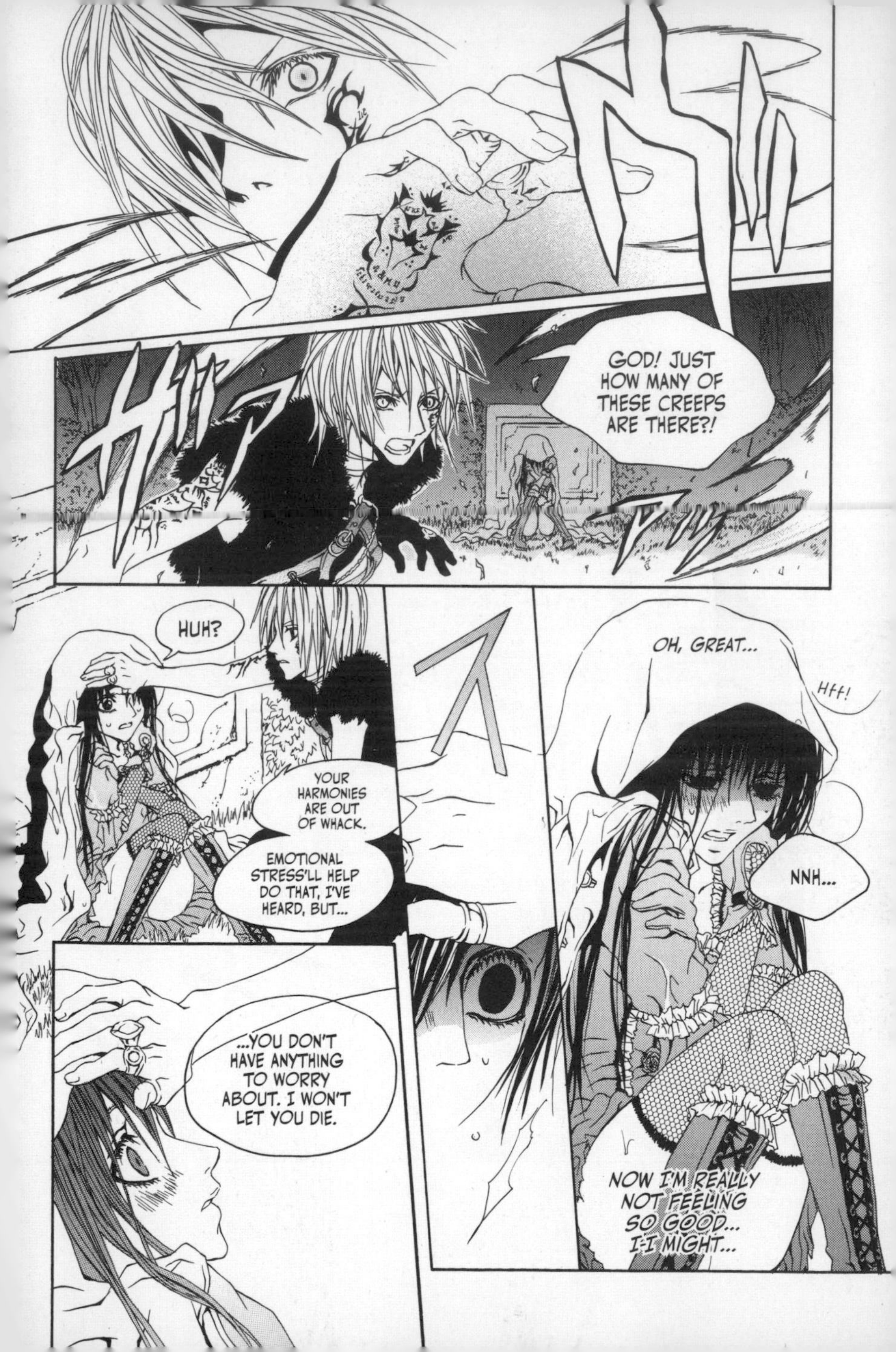
GOD! JUST HOW MANY OF THESE CREEPS ARE THERE?!
OH, GREAT...
Hff!
NNH...
NOW I'M REALLY NOT FEELING SO GOOD... I-I MIGHT...
HUH?
YOUR HARMONIES ARE OUT OF WHACK.
EMOTIONAL STRESS'LL HELP DO THAT, I'VE HEARD, BUT...
...YOU DON'T HAVE ANYTHING TO WORRY ABOUT. I WON'T LET YOU DIE.

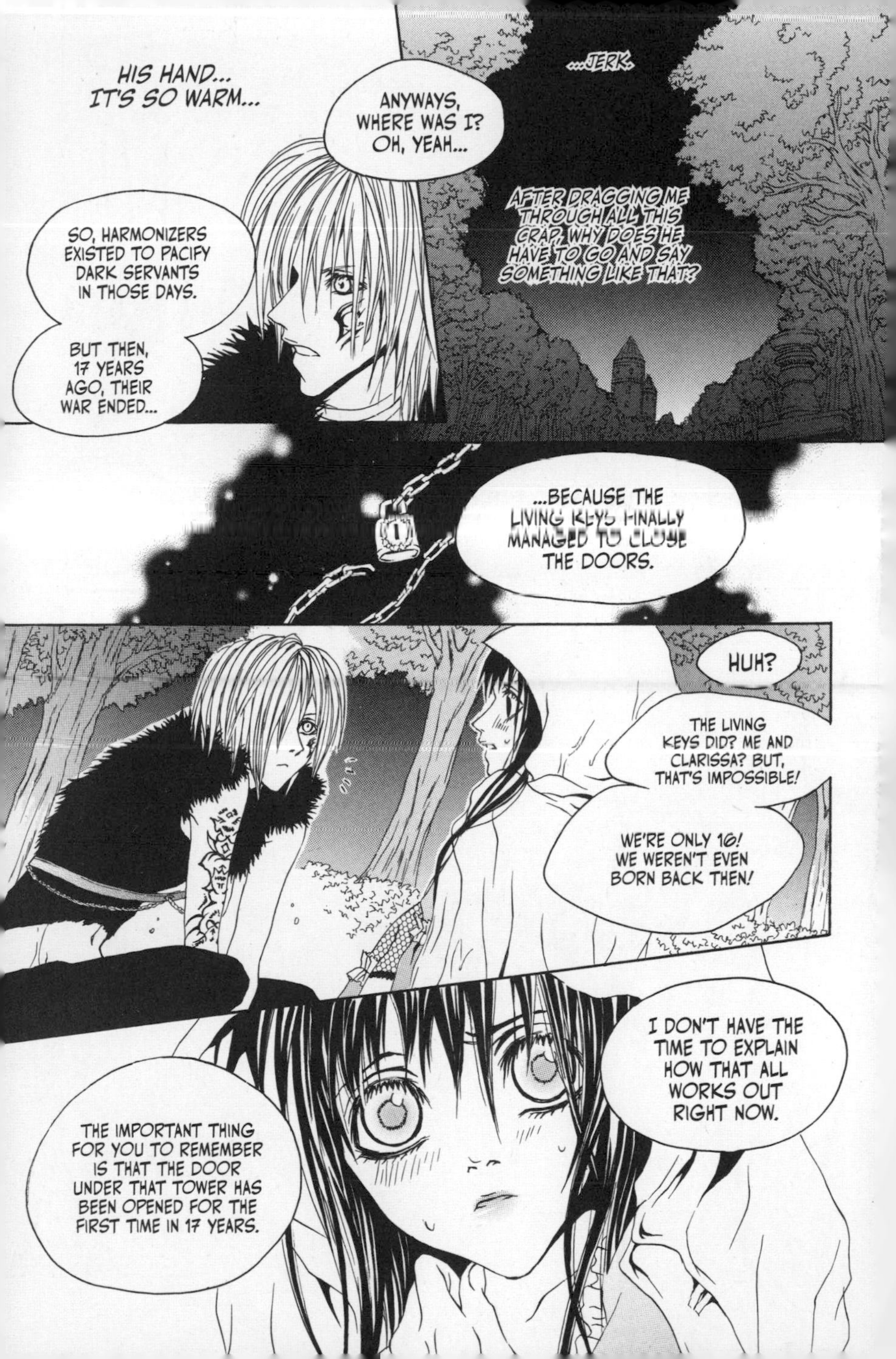

...JERK.
AFTER DRAGGING ME THROUGH ALL THIS CRAP, WHY DOES HE HAVE TO GO AND SAY SOMETHING LIKE THAT?
HIS HAND... IT'S SO WARM...
ANYWAYS, WHERE WAS I? OH, YEAH...
SO, HARMONIZERS EXISTED TO PACIFY DARK SERVANTS IN THOSE DAYS.
BUT THEN, 17 YEARS AGO, THEIR WAR ENDED...
...BECAUSE THE LIVING KEYS FINALLY MANAGED TO CLOSE THE DOORS.
HUH?
THE LIVING KEYS DID? ME AND CLARISSA? BUT, THAT'S IMPOSSIBLE!
WE'RE ONLY 16! WE WEREN'T EVEN BORN BACK THEN!
I DON'T HAVE THE TIME TO EXPLAIN HOW THAT ALL WORKS OUT RIGHT NOW.
THE IMPORTANT THING FOR YOU TO REMEMBER IS THAT THE DOOR UNDER THAT TOWER HAS BEEN OPENED FOR THE FIRST TIME IN 17 YEARS.

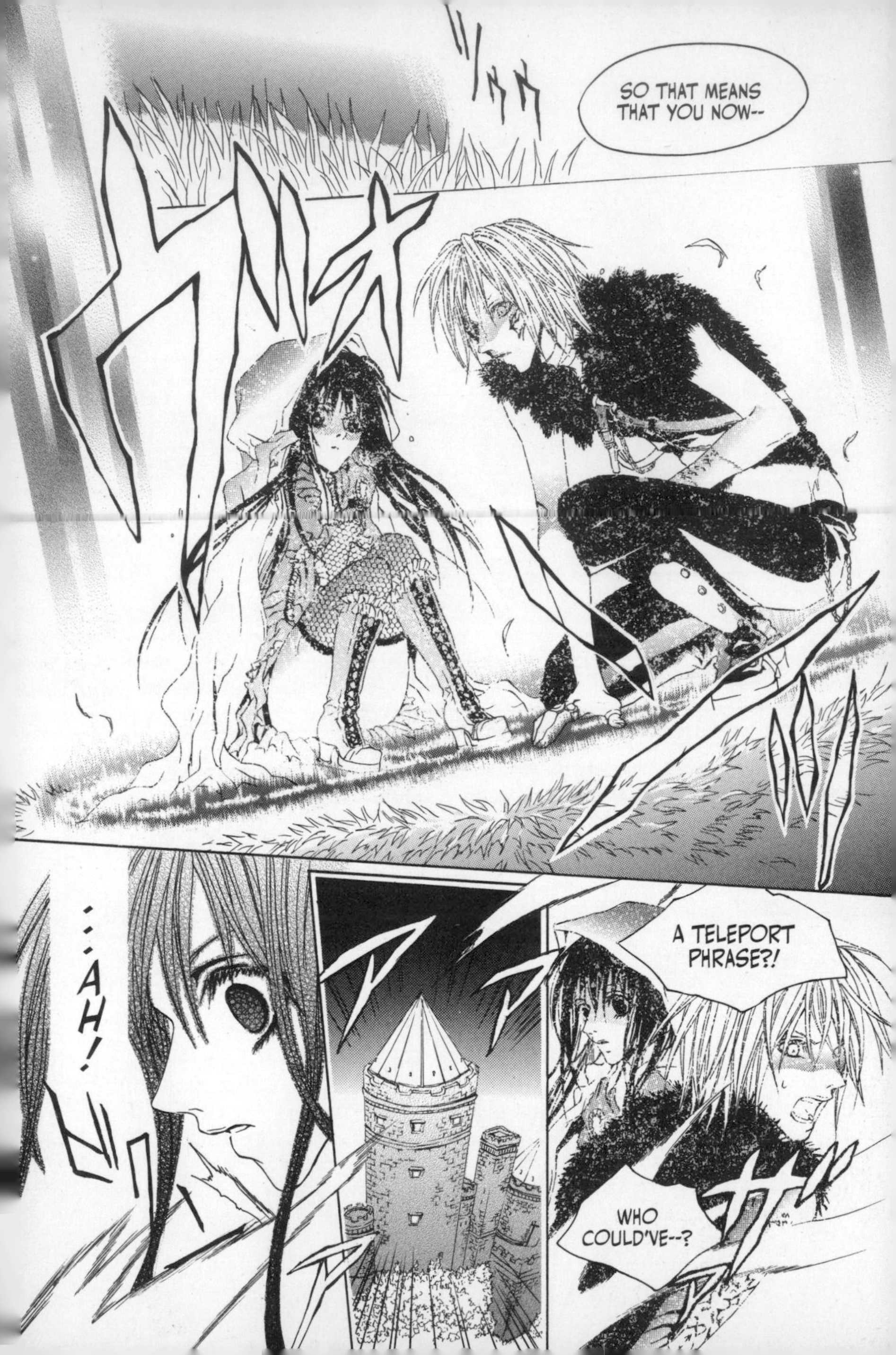
SO THAT MEANS THAT YOU NOW--
A TELEPORT PHRASE?!
WHO COULD'VE--?
...AH!

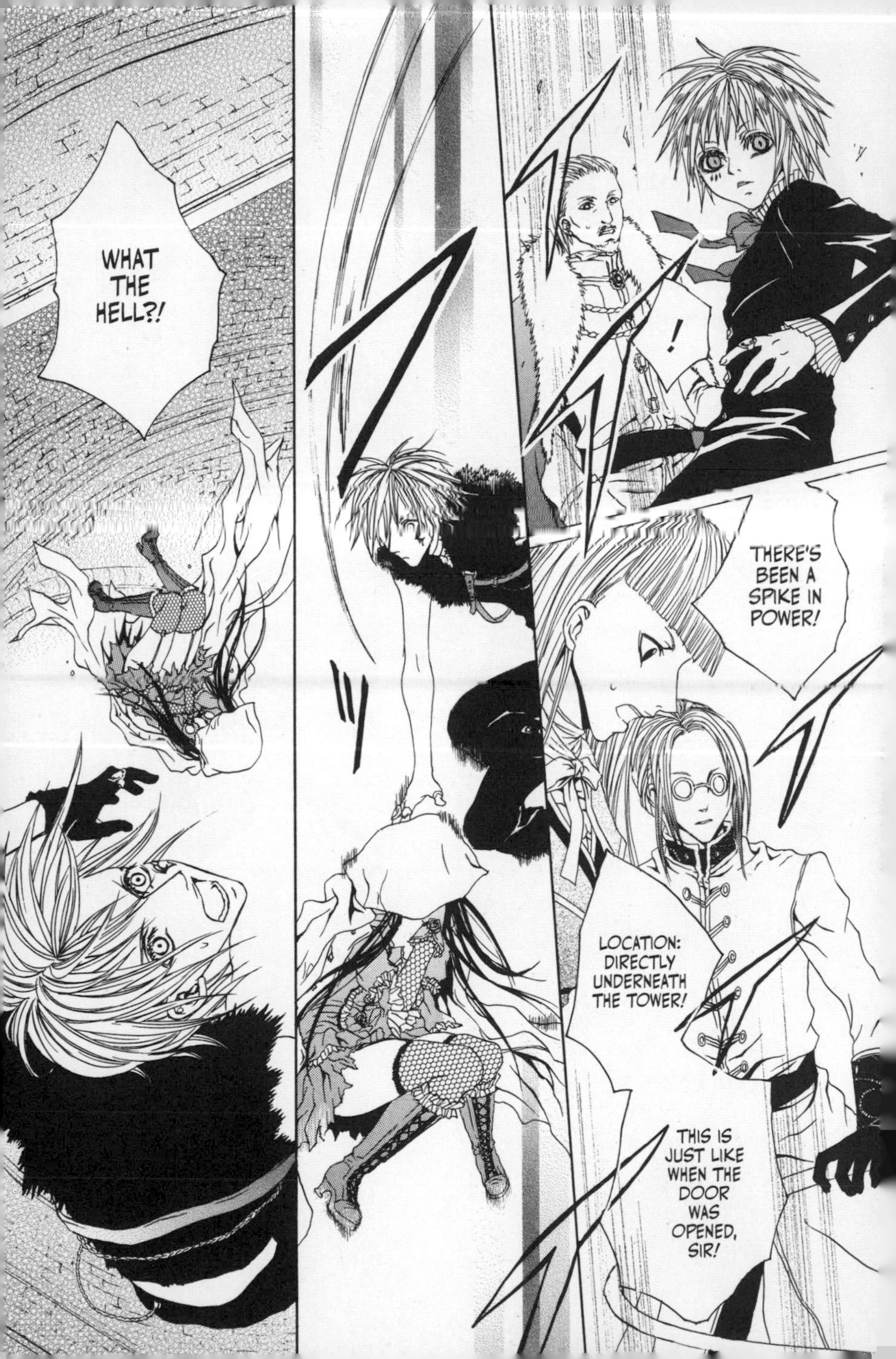
!
THERE'S BEEN A SPIKE IN POWER!
LOCATION: DIRECTLY UNDERNEATH THE TOWER!
THIS IS JUST LIKE WHEN THE DOOR WAS OPENED, SIR!
WHAT THE HELL?!

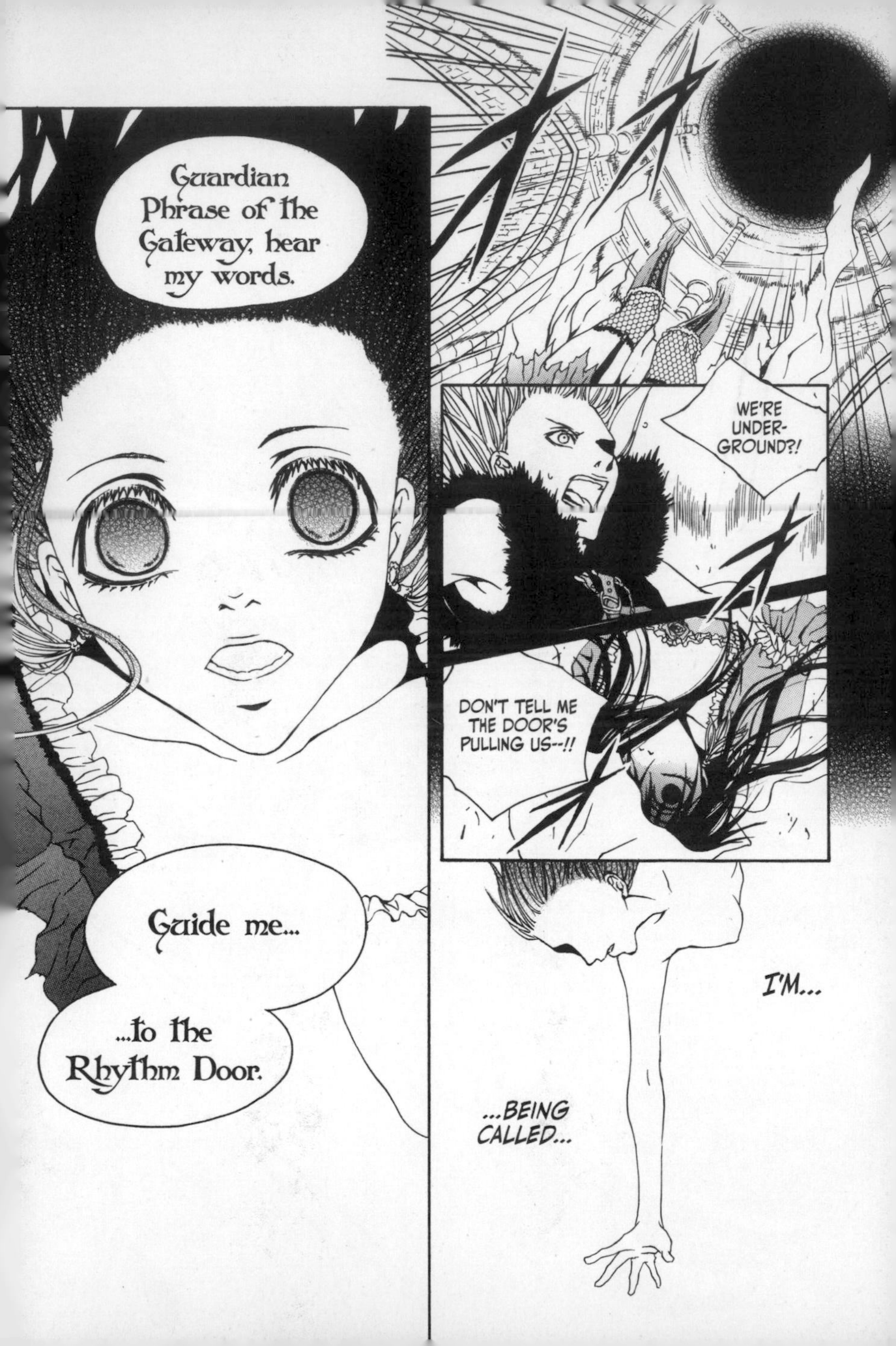
WE'RE UNDER-GROUND?!
DON'T TELL ME THE DOOR'S PULLING US--!!
I'M...
...BEING CALLED...
Guardian Phrase of the Gateway, hear my words.
Guide me...
...to the Rhythm Door.

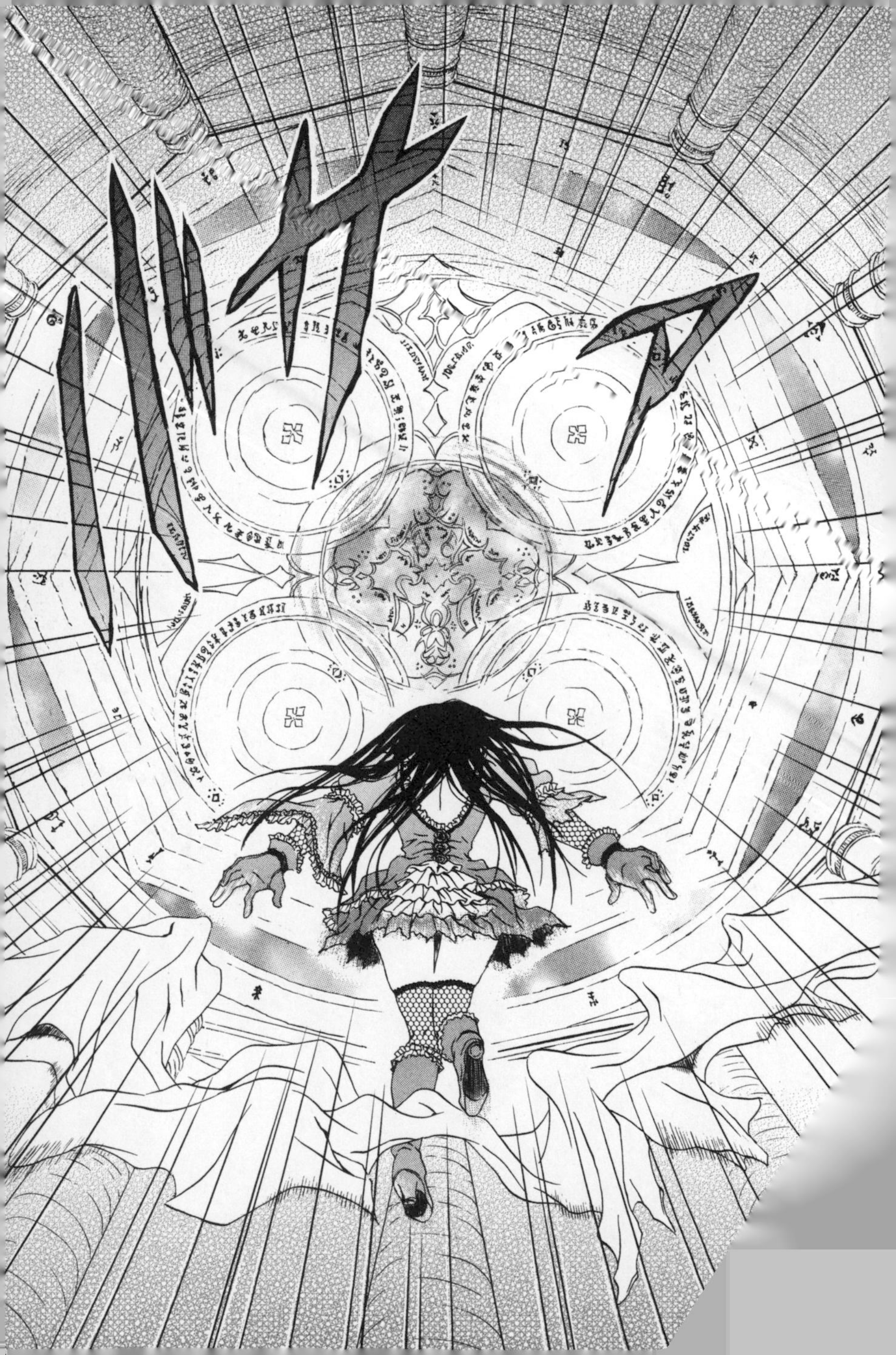

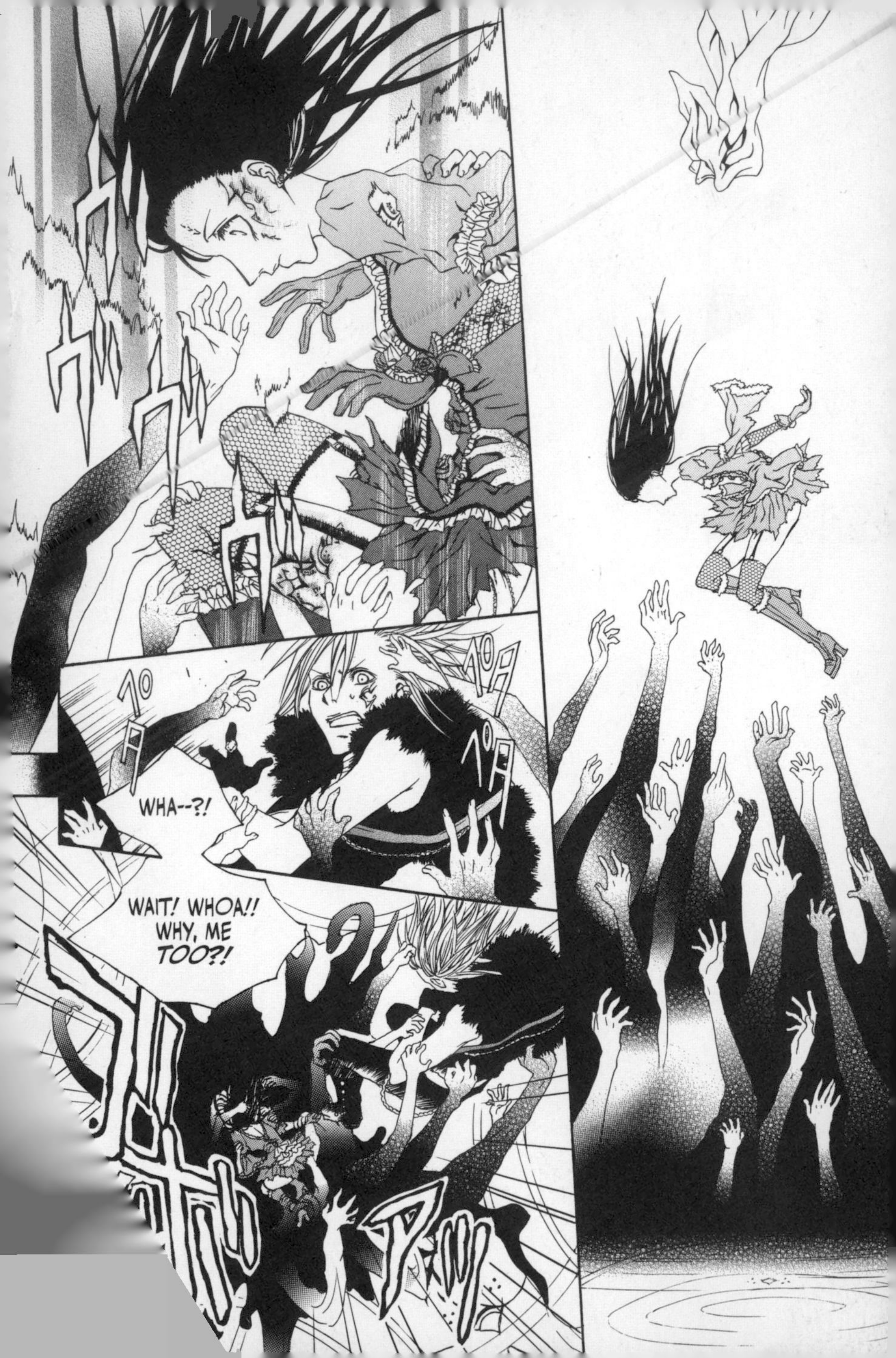
WHA--?!
WAIT! WHOA!! WHY, ME TOO?!

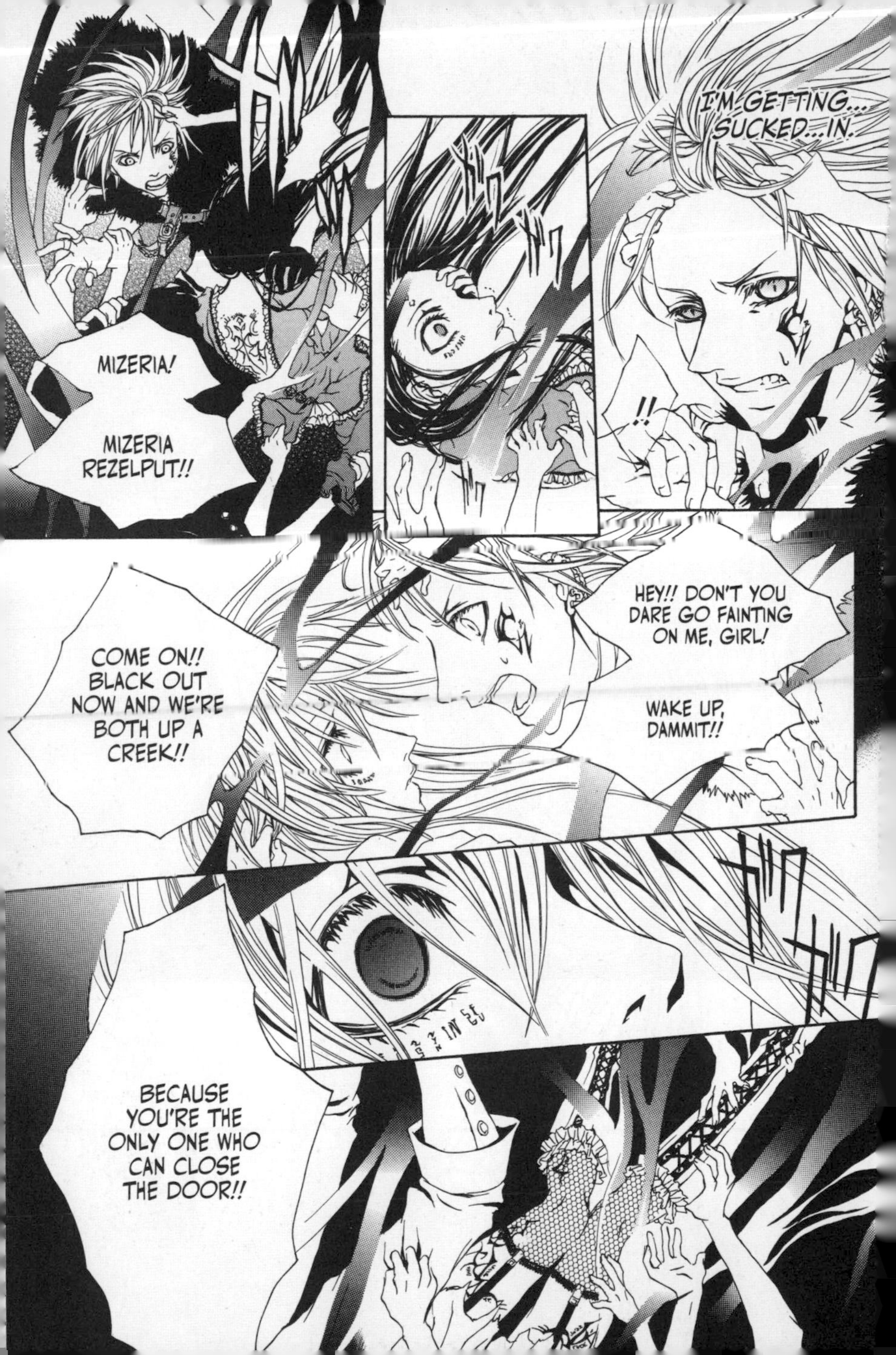
I'M GETTING... SUCKED...IN.
!!
MIZERIA!
MIZERIA REZELPUT!!
HEY!! DON'T YOU DARE GO FAINTING ON ME, GIRL!
WAKE UP, DAMMIT!!
COME ON!! BLACK OUT NOW AND WE'RE BOTH UP A CREEK!!
BECAUSE YOU'RE THE ONLY ONE WHO CAN CLOSE THE DOOR!!

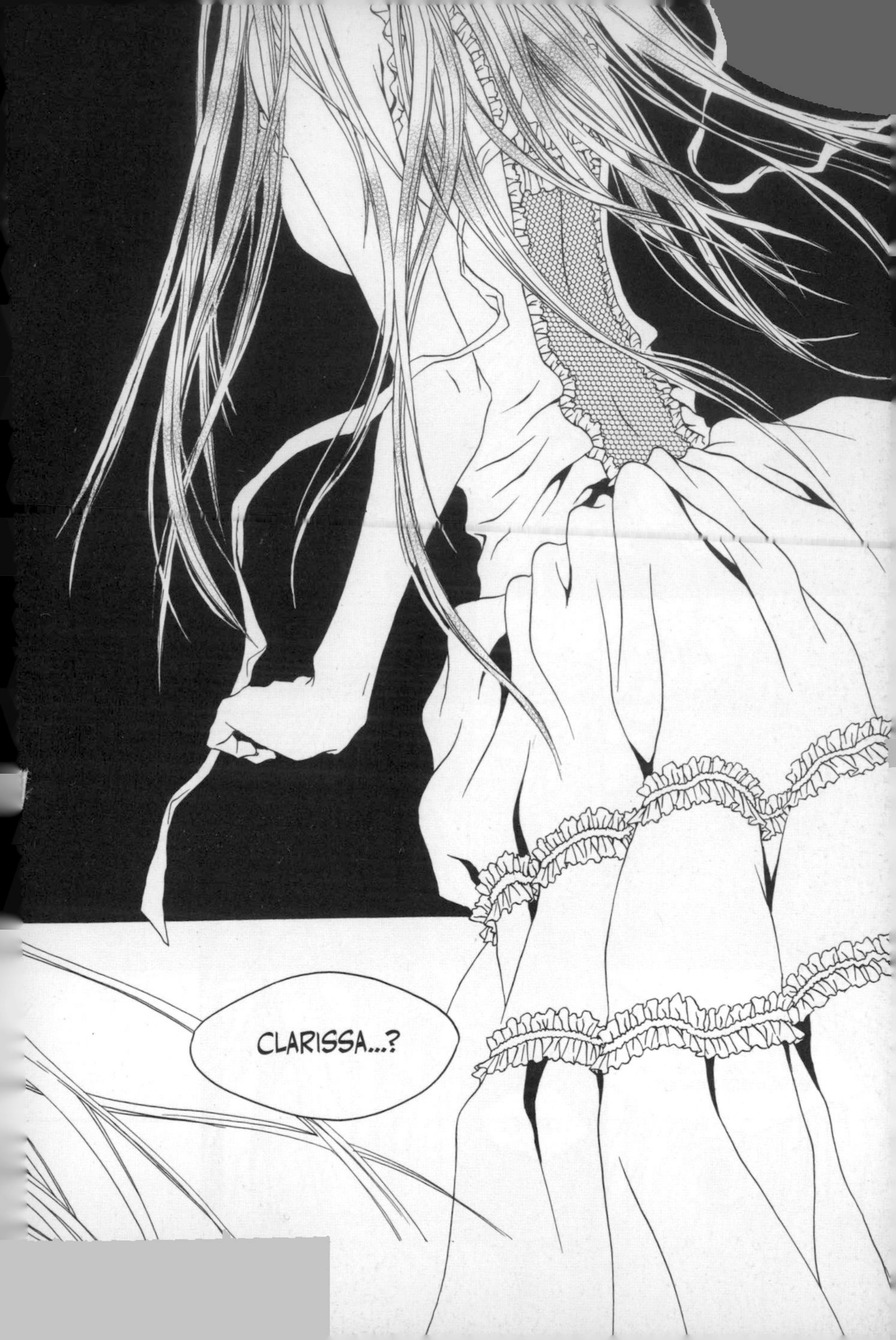
CLARISSA...?

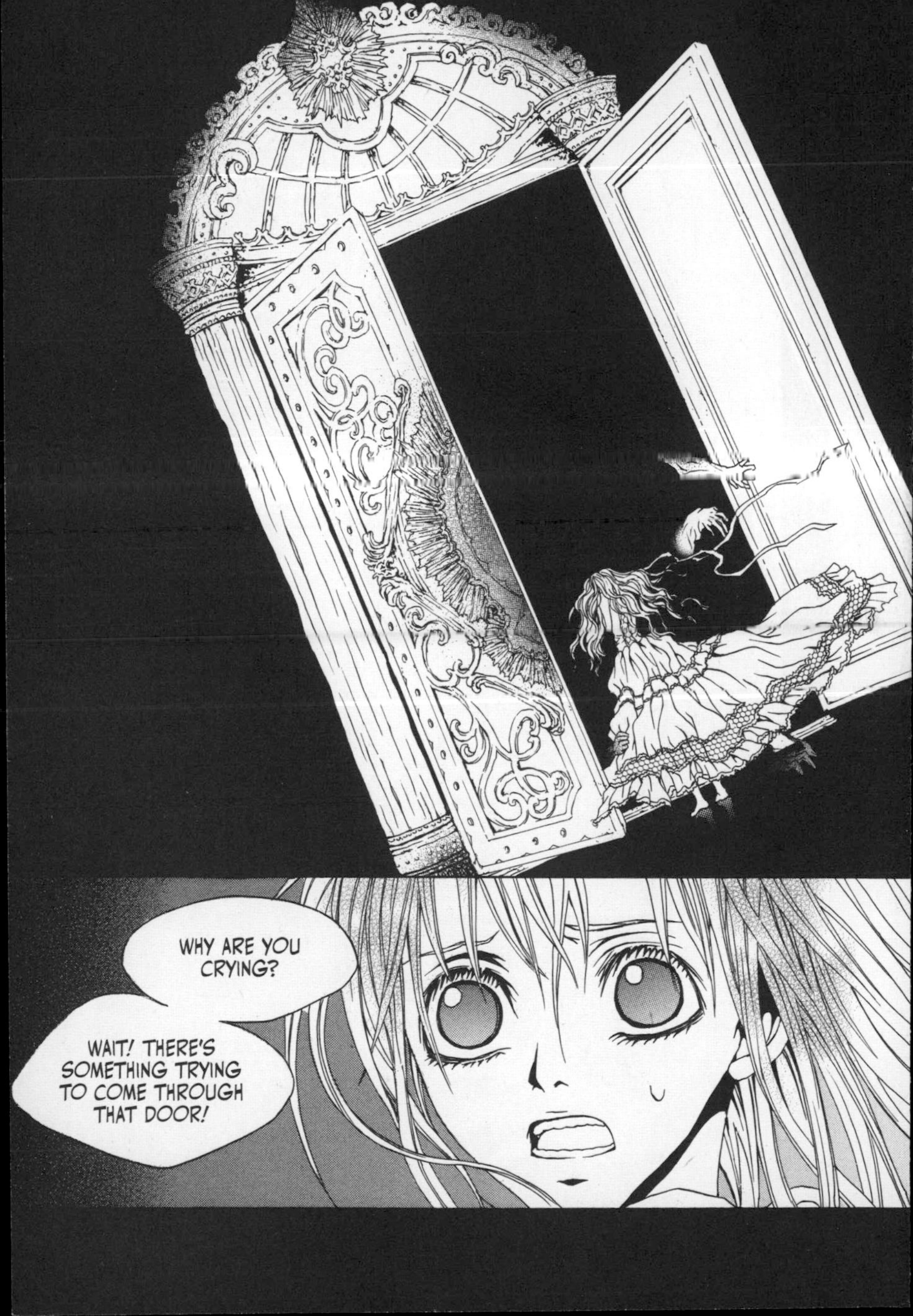
WHY ARE YOU CRYING?
WAIT! THERE'S SOMETHING TRYING TO COME THROUGH THAT DOOR!

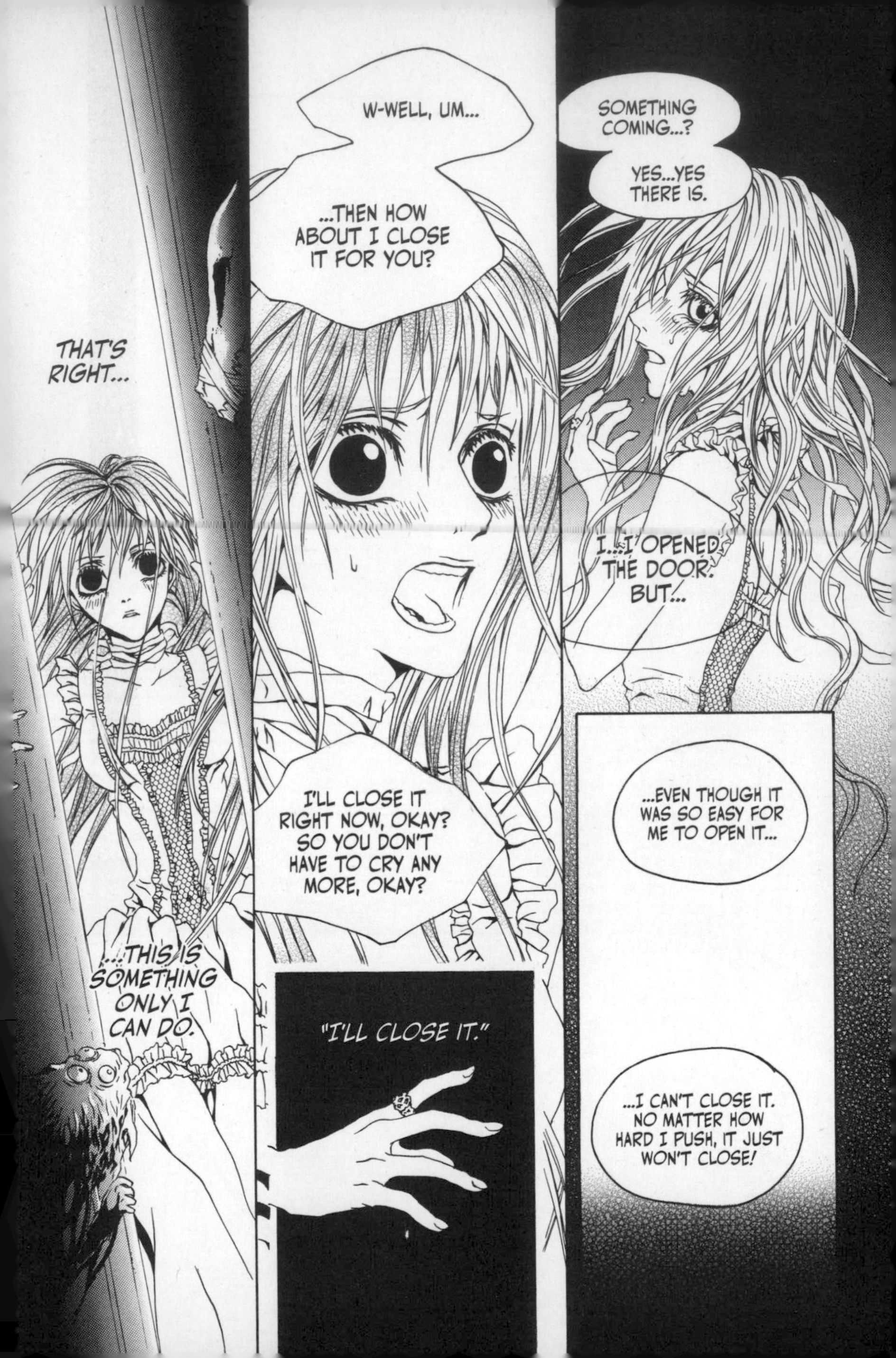
SOMETHING COMING...?
YES...YES THERE IS.
I...I OPENED THE DOOR. BUT...
...EVEN THOUGH IT WAS SO EASY FOR ME TO OPEN IT...
...I CAN'T CLOSE IT. NO MATTER HOW HARD I PUSH, IT JUST WON'T CLOSE!
W-WELL, UM...
...THEN HOW ABOUT I CLOSE IT FOR YOU?
I'LL CLOSE IT RIGHT NOW, OKAY? SO YOU DON'T HAVE TO CRY ANY MORE, OKAY?
"I'LL CLOSE IT."
THAT'S RIGHT...
...THIS IS SOMETHING ONLY I CAN DO.

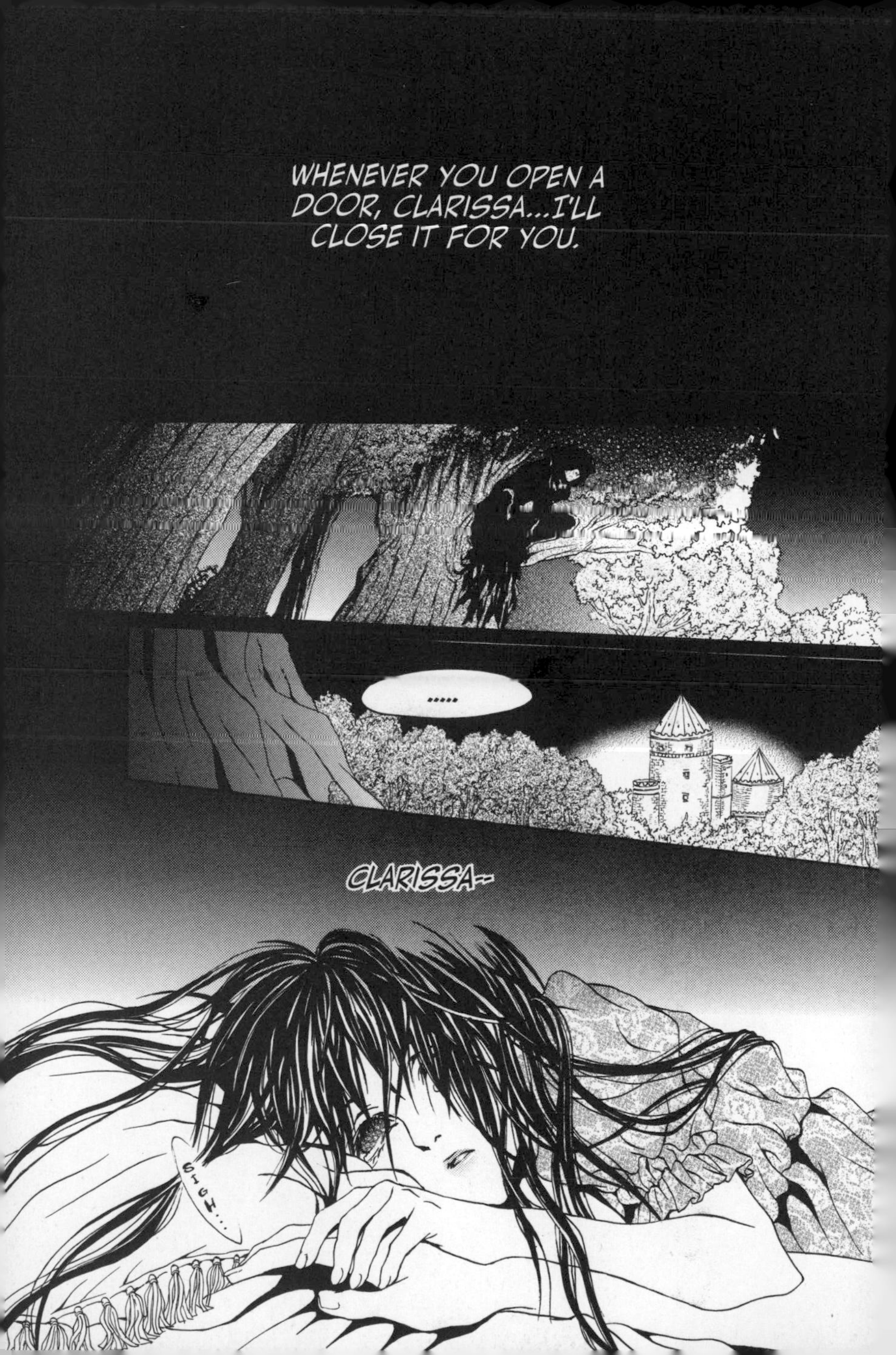
WHENEVER YOU OPEN A DOOR, CLARISSA...I'LL CLOSE IT FOR YOU.
.....
CLARISSA--
SIGH...

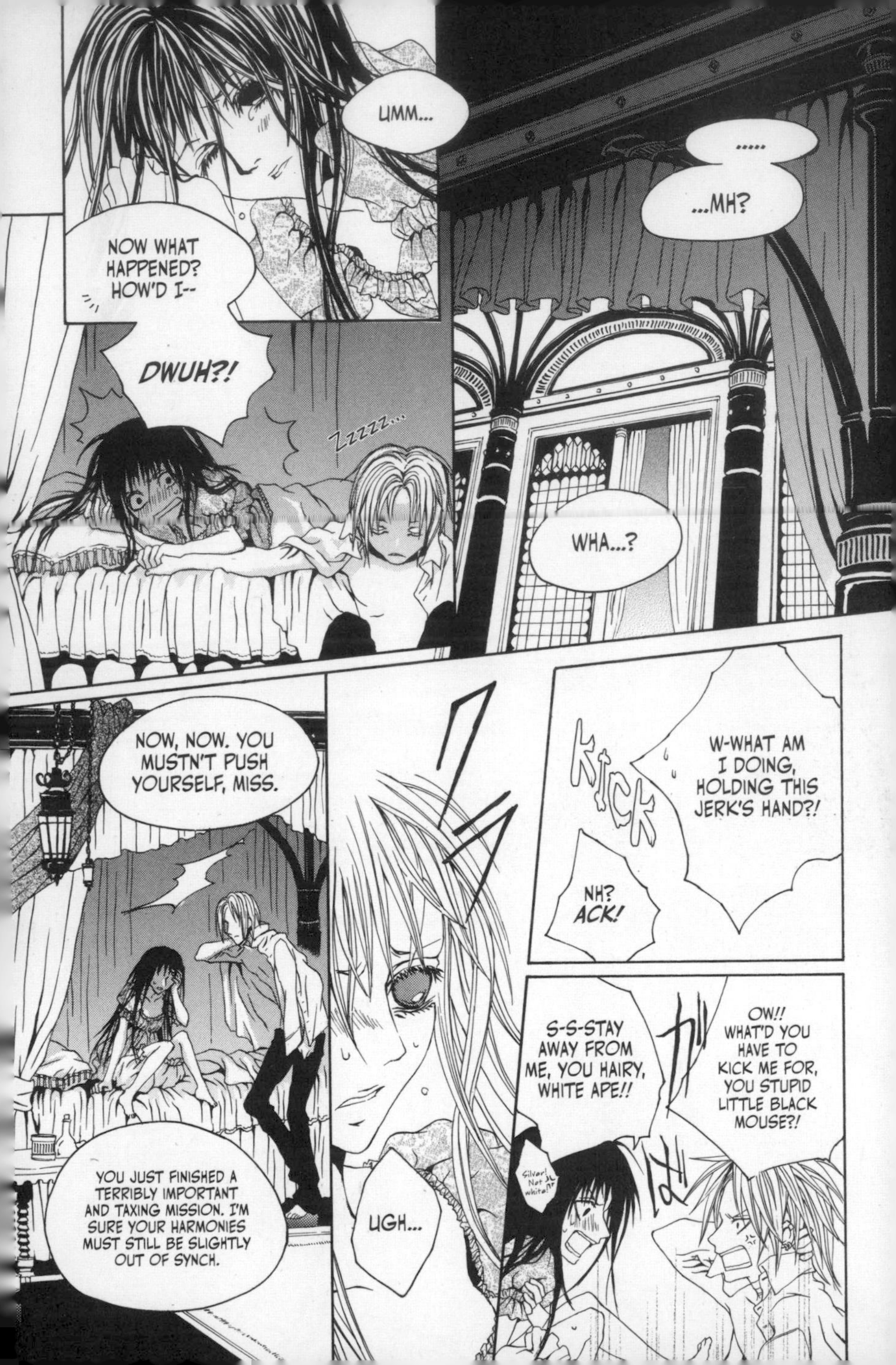
......
...MH?
WHA...?
UMM...
NOW WHAT HAPPENED? HOW'D I--
DWUH?!
Zzzzz...
KICK
W-WHAT AM I DOING, HOLDING THIS JERK'S HAND?!
NH? ACK!
OW!! WHAT'D YOU HAVE TO KICK ME FOR, YOU STUPID LITTLE BLACK MOUSE?!
S-S-STAY AWAY FROM ME, YOU HAIRY, WHITE APE!!
Silver! Not white!
UGH...
NOW, NOW. YOU MUSTN'T PUSH YOURSELF, MISS.
YOU JUST FINISHED A TERRIBLY IMPORTANT AND TAXING MISSION. I'M SURE YOUR HARMONIES MUST STILL BE SLIGHTLY OUT OF SYNCH.

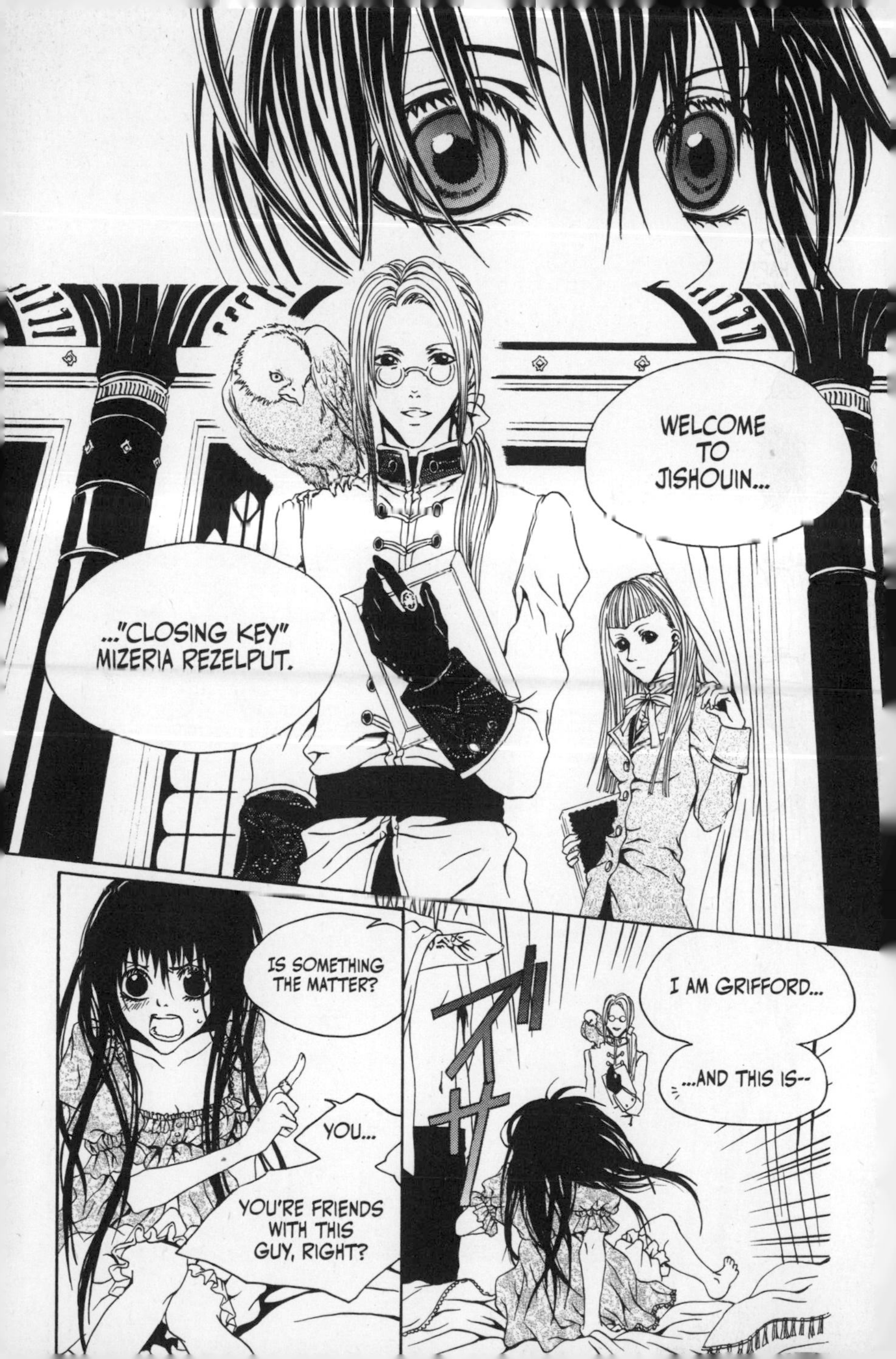
WELCOME TO JISHOUIN...
..."CLOSING KEY" MIZERIA REZELPUT.
I AM GRIFFORD...
...AND THIS IS--
IS SOMETHING THE MATTER?
YOU...
YOU'RE FRIENDS WITH THIS GUY, RIGHT?

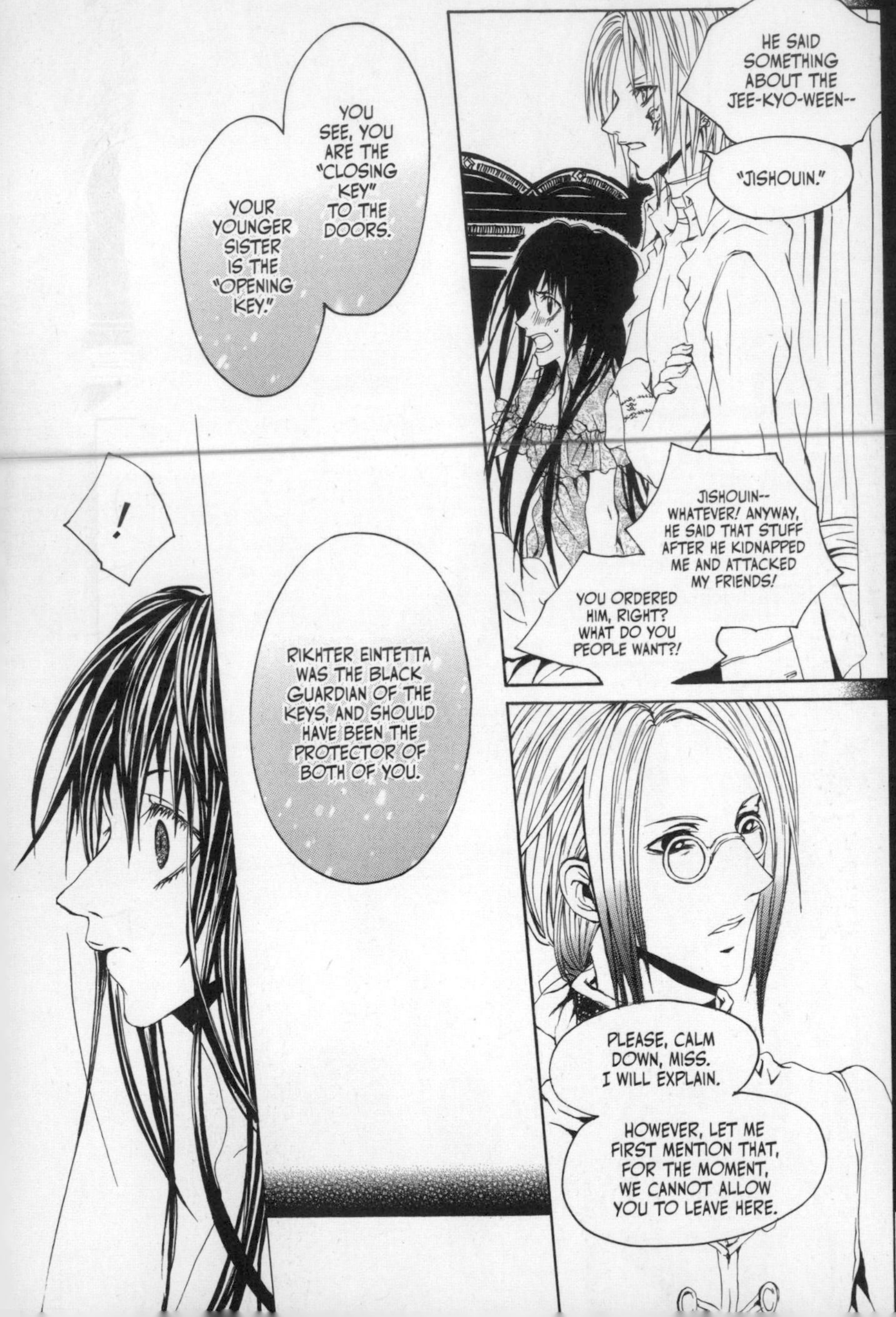
HE SAID SOMETHING ABOUT THE JEE-KYO-WEEN--
"JISHOUIN."
JISHOUIN-- WHATEVER! ANYWAY, HE SAID THAT STUFF AFTER HE KIDNAPPED ME AND ATTACKED MY FRIENDS!
YOU ORDERED HIM, RIGHT? WHAT DO YOU PEOPLE WANT?!
PLEASE, CALM DOWN, MISS. I WILL EXPLAIN.
HOWEVER, LET ME FIRST MENTION THAT, FOR THE MOMENT, WE CANNOT ALLOW YOU TO LEAVE HERE.
YOU SEE, YOU ARE THE "CLOSING KEY" TO THE DOORS.
YOUR YOUNGER SISTER IS THE "OPENING KEY."
!
RIKHTER EINTETTA WAS THE BLACK GUARDIAN OF THE KEYS, AND SHOULD HAVE BEEN THE PROTECTOR OF BOTH OF YOU.

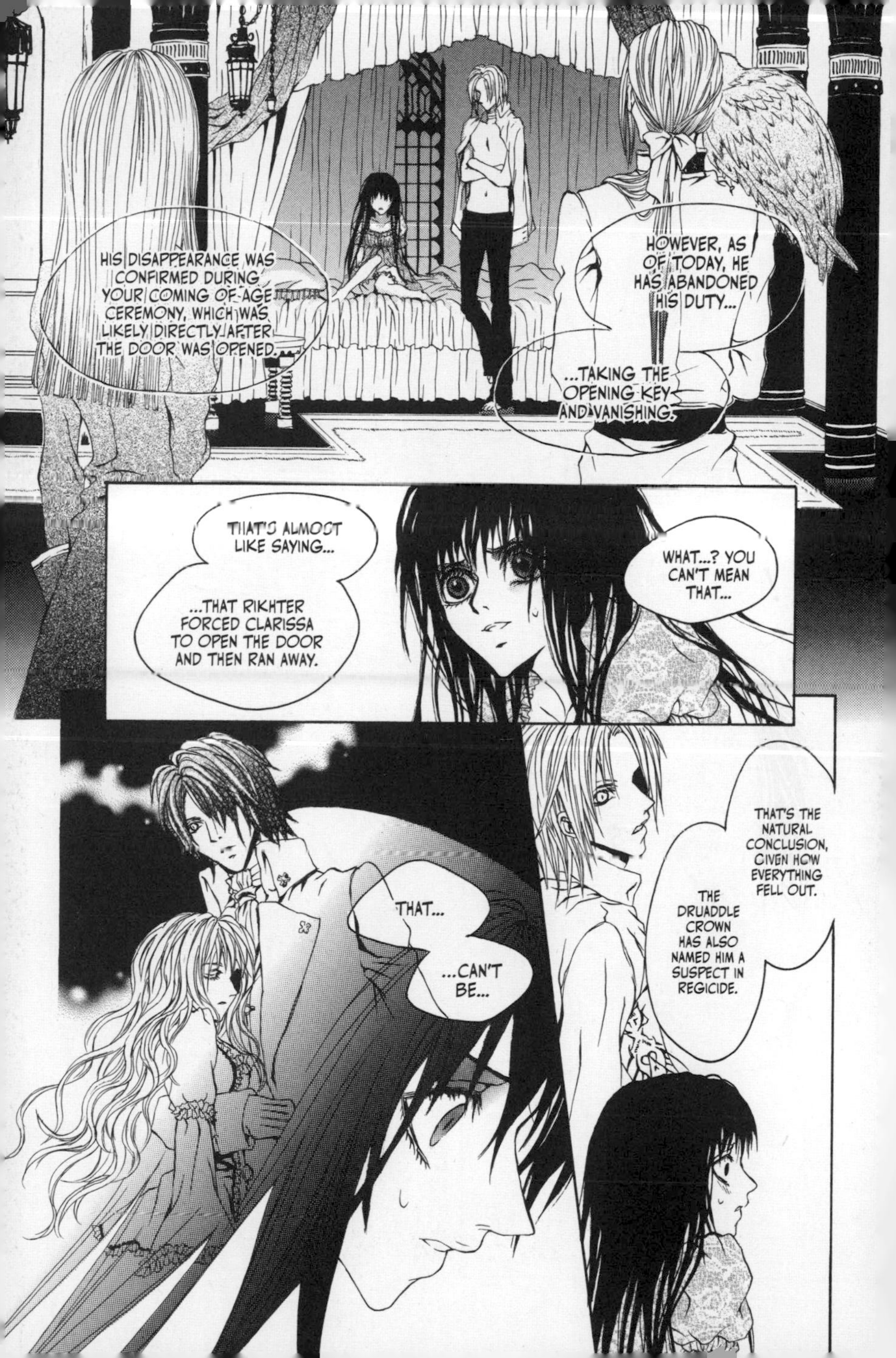
HOWEVER, AS OF TODAY, HE HAS ABANDONED HIS DUTY...
...TAKING THE OPENING KEY AND VANISHING.
HIS DISAPPEARANCE WAS CONFIRMED DURING YOUR COMING OF AGE CEREMONY, WHICH WAS LIKELY DIRECTLY AFTER THE DOOR WAS OPENED.
WHAT...? YOU CAN'T MEAN THAT...
THAT'S ALMOST LIKE SAYING...
...THAT RIKHTER FORCED CLARISSA TO OPEN THE DOOR AND THEN RAN AWAY.
THAT'S THE NATURAL CONCLUSION, GIVEN HOW EVERYTHING FELL OUT.
THE DRUADDLE CROWN HAS ALSO NAMED HIM A SUSPECT IN REGICIDE.
THAT...
...CAN'T BE...

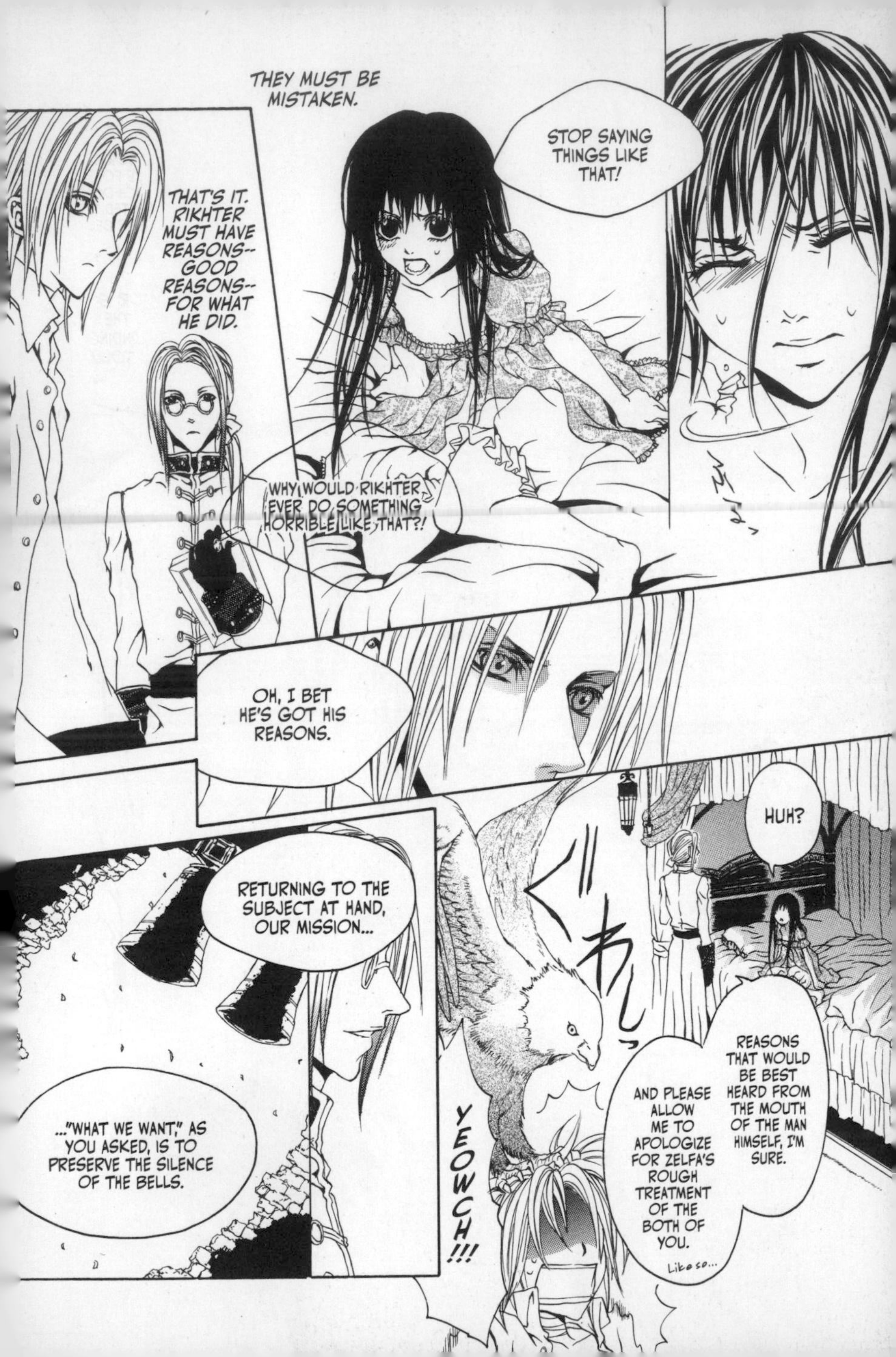
THEY MUST BE MISTAKEN.
STOP SAYING THINGS LIKE THAT!
WHY WOULD RIKHTER EVER DO SOMETHING HORRIBLE LIKE THAT?!
THAT'S IT. RIKHTER MUST HAVE REASONS-- GOOD REASONS-- FOR WHAT HE DID.
OH, I BET HE'S GOT HIS REASONS.
HUH?
REASONS THAT WOULD BE BEST HEARD FROM THE MOUTH OF THE MAN HIMSELF, I'M SURE.
AND PLEASE ALLOW ME TO APOLOGIZE FOR ZELFA'S ROUGH TREATMENT OF THE BOTH OF YOU.
Like so...
YEOWCH!!!
RETURNING TO THE SUBJECT AT HAND, OUR MISSION...
..."WHAT WE WANT," AS YOU ASKED, IS TO PRESERVE THE SILENCE OF THE BELLS.

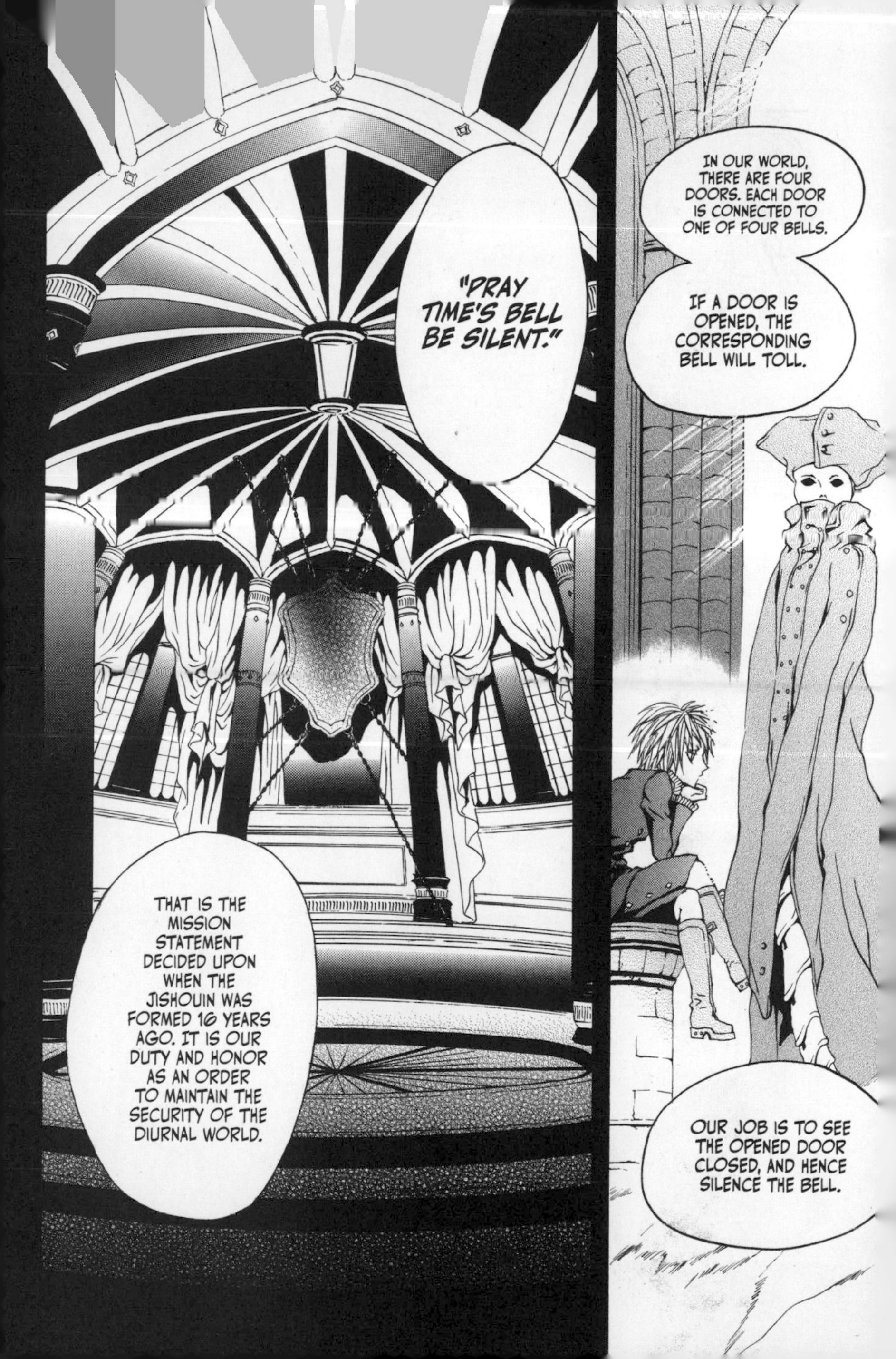
IN OUR WORLD, THERE ARE FOUR DOORS. EACH DOOR IS CONNECTED TO ONE OF FOUR BELLS.
IF A DOOR IS OPENED, THE CORRESPONDING BELL WILL TOLL.
OUR JOB IS TO SEE THE OPENED DOOR CLOSED, AND HENCE SILENCE THE BELL.
"PRAY TIME'S BELL BE SILENT."
THAT IS THE MISSION STATEMENT DECIDED UPON WHEN THE JISHOUIN WAS FORMED 16 YEARS AGO. IT IS OUR DUTY AND HONOR AS AN ORDER TO MAINTAIN THE SECURITY OF THE DIURNAL WORLD.

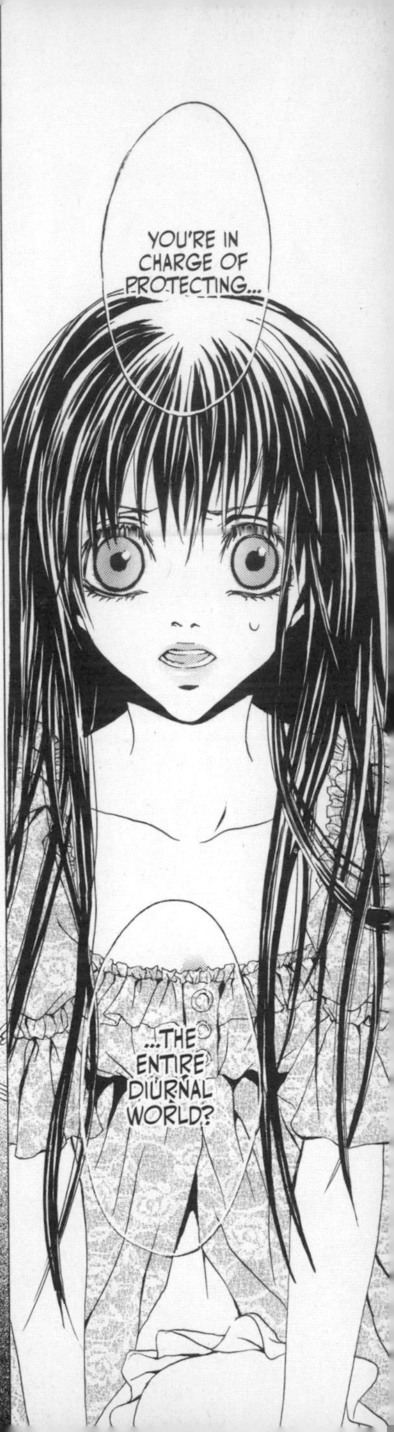
YOU'RE IN CHARGE OF PROTECTING...
...THE ENTIRE DIURNAL WORLD?

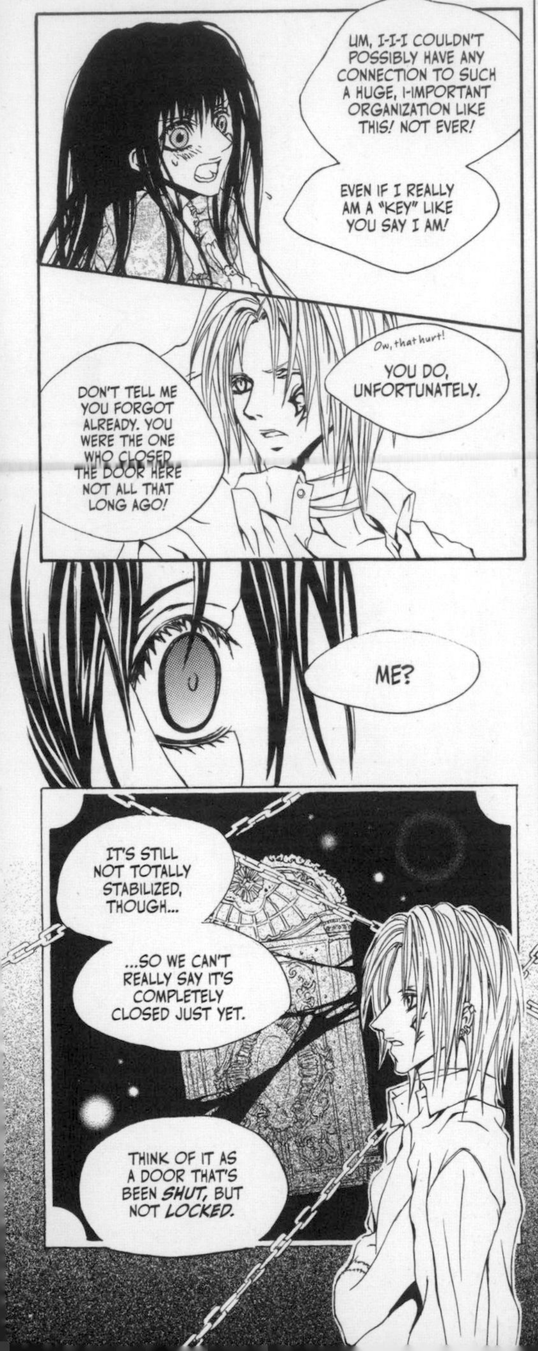
UM, I-I-I COULDN'T POSSIBLY HAVE ANY CONNECTION TO SUCH A HUGE, I-IMPORTANT ORGANIZATION LIKE THIS! NOT EVER!
EVEN IF I REALLY AM A "KEY" LIKE YOU SAY I AM!
Ow, that hurt!
YOU DO, UNFORTUNATELY.
DON'T TELL ME YOU FORGOT ALREADY. YOU WERE THE ONE WHO CLOSED THE DOOR HERE NOT ALL THAT LONG AGO!
ME?
IT'S STILL NOT TOTALLY STABILIZED, THOUGH...
...SO WE CAN'T REALLY SAY IT'S COMPLETELY CLOSED JUST YET.
THINK OF IT AS A DOOR THAT'S BEEN SHUT, BUT NOT LOCKED.

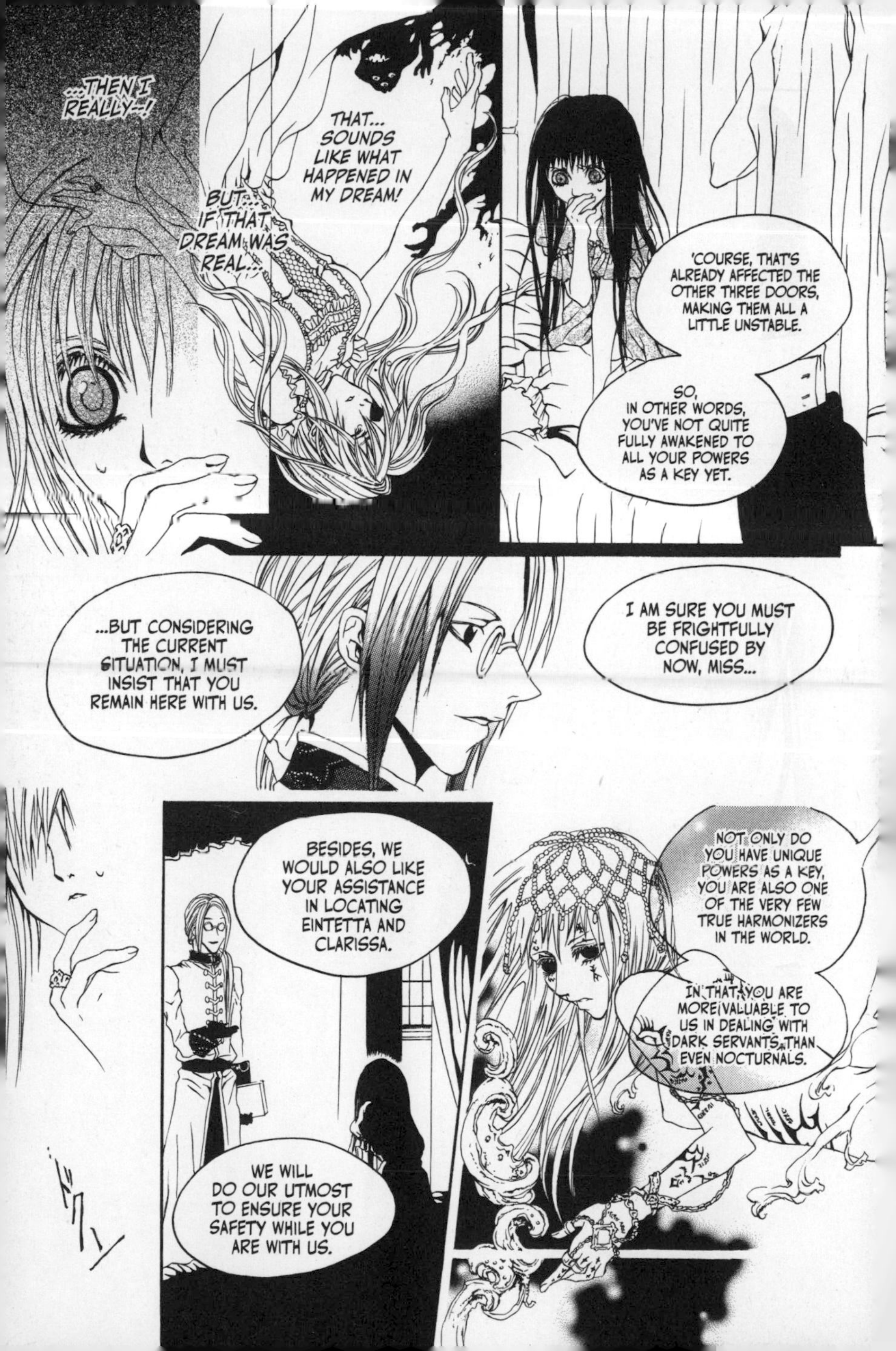
'COURSE, THAT'S ALREADY AFFECTED THE OTHER THREE DOORS, MAKING THEM ALL A LITTLE UNSTABLE.
SO, IN OTHER WORDS, YOU'VE NOT QUITE FULLY AWAKENED TO ALL YOUR POWERS AS A KEY YET.
THAT... SOUNDS LIKE WHAT HAPPENED IN MY DREAM!
BUT... IF THAT DREAM WAS REAL...
...THEN I REALLY--!
I AM SURE YOU MUST BE FRIGHTFULLY CONFUSED BY NOW, MISS...
...BUT CONSIDERING THE CURRENT SITUATION, I MUST INSIST THAT YOU REMAIN HERE WITH US.
NOT ONLY DO YOU HAVE UNIQUE POWERS AS A KEY, YOU ARE ALSO ONE OF THE VERY FEW TRUE HARMONIZERS IN THE WORLD.
IN THAT, YOU ARE MORE VALUABLE TO US IN DEALING WITH DARK SERVANTS THAN EVEN NOCTURNALS.
BESIDES, WE WOULD ALSO LIKE YOUR ASSISTANCE IN LOCATING EINTETTA AND CLARISSA.
WE WILL DO OUR UTMOST TO ENSURE YOUR SAFETY WHILE YOU ARE WITH US.
ドクン

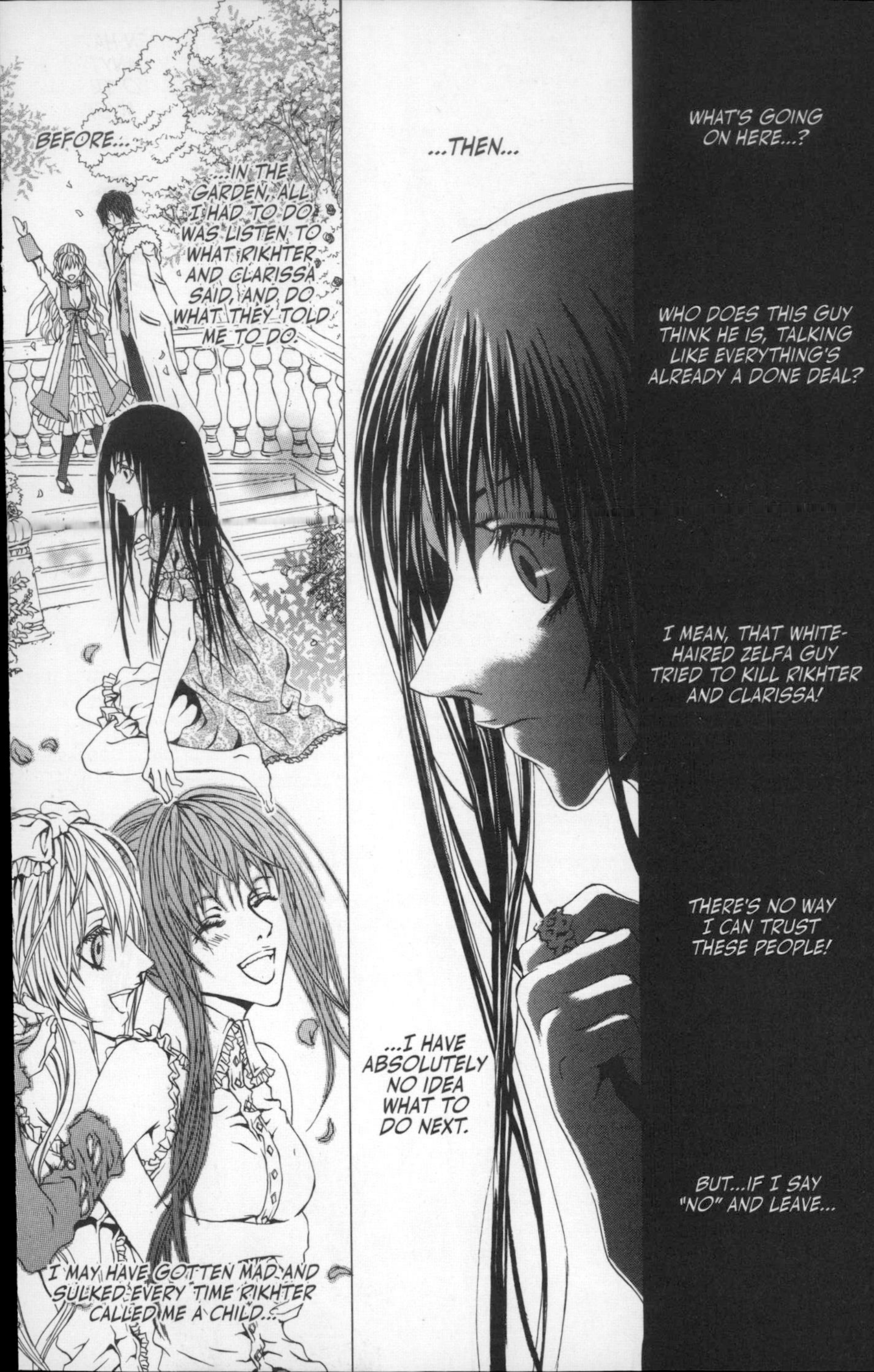
BEFORE...
...IN THE GARDEN, ALL I HAD TO DO WAS LISTEN TO WHAT RIKHTER AND CLARISSA SAID, AND DO WHAT THEY TOLD ME TO DO.
I MAY HAVE GOTTEN MAD AND SULKED EVERY TIME RIKHTER CALLED ME A CHILD...
...THEN...
...I HAVE ABSOLUTELY NO IDEA WHAT TO DO NEXT.
WHAT'S GOING ON HERE...?
WHO DOES THIS GUY THINK HE IS, TALKING LIKE EVERYTHING'S ALREADY A DONE DEAL?
I MEAN, THAT WHITE-HAIRED ZELFA GUY TRIED TO KILL RIKHTER AND CLARISSA!
THERE'S NO WAY I CAN TRUST THESE PEOPLE!
BUT...IF I SAY "NO" AND LEAVE...

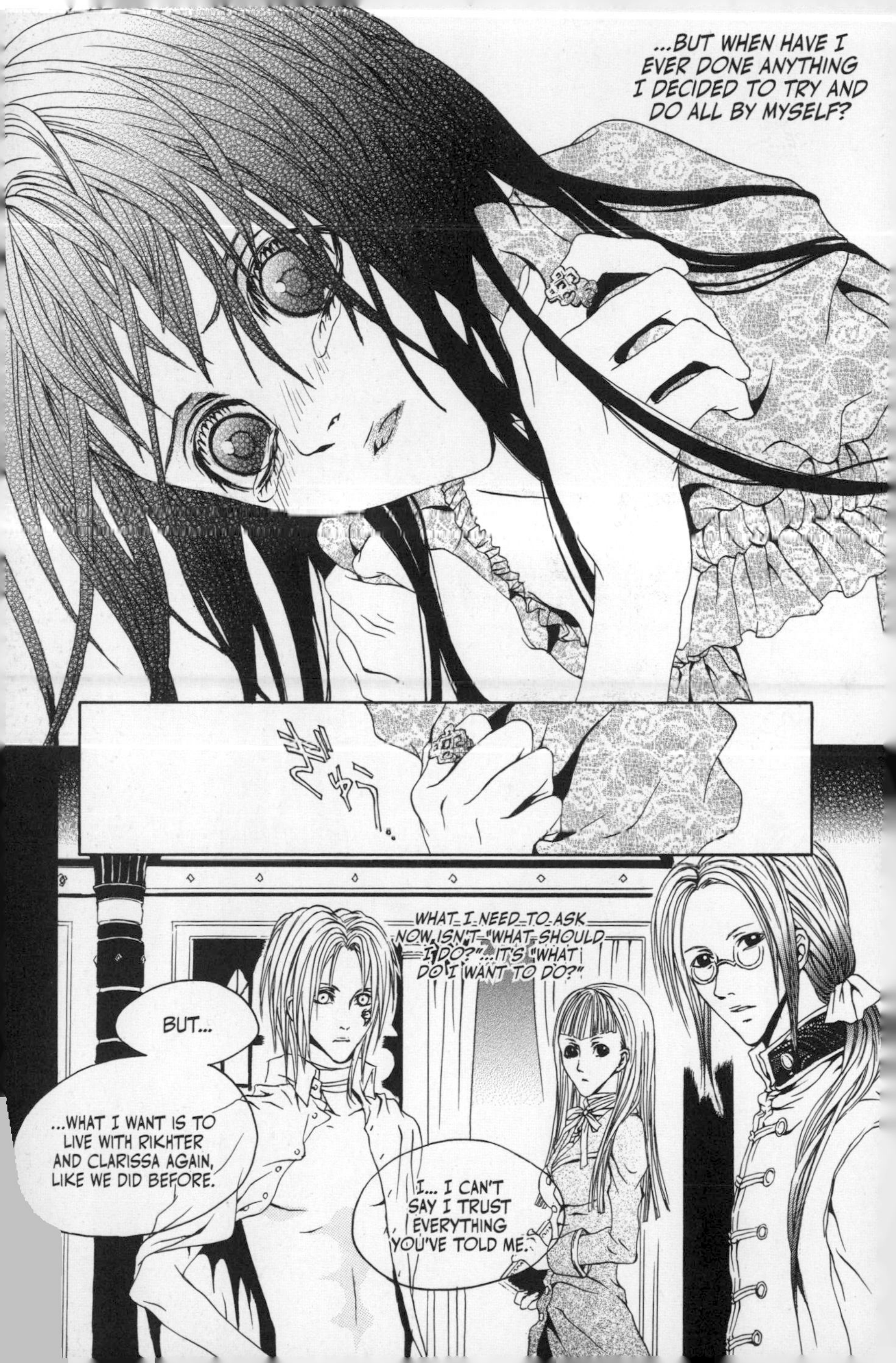
...BUT WHEN HAVE I EVER DONE ANYTHING I DECIDED TO TRY AND DO ALL BY MYSELF?
ぎゅっ
WHAT I NEED TO ASK NOW ISN'T "WHAT SHOULD I DO?"...IT'S "WHAT DO I WANT TO DO?"
BUT...
...WHAT I WANT IS TO LIVE WITH RIKHTER AND CLARISSA AGAIN, LIKE WE DID BEFORE.
I... I CAN'T SAY I TRUST EVERYTHING YOU'VE TOLD ME.

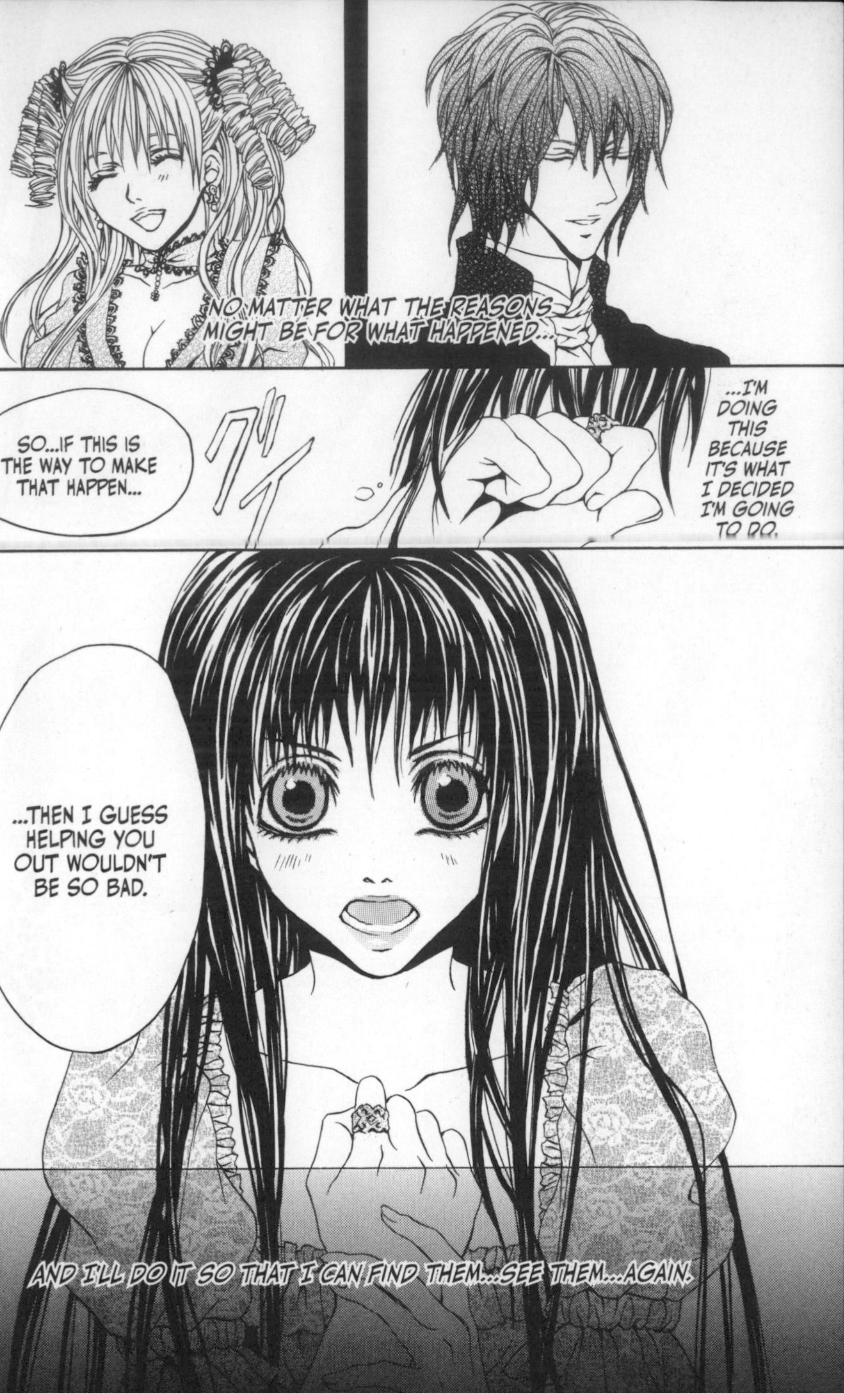
NO MATTER WHAT THE REASONS MIGHT BE FOR WHAT HAPPENED...
...I'M DOING THIS BECAUSE IT'S WHAT I DECIDED I'M GOING TO DO.
グイ
SO...IF THIS IS THE WAY TO MAKE THAT HAPPEN...
...THEN I GUESS HELPING YOU OUT WOULDN'T BE SO BAD.
AND I'LL DO IT SO THAT I CAN FIND THEM...SEE THEM...AGAIN.

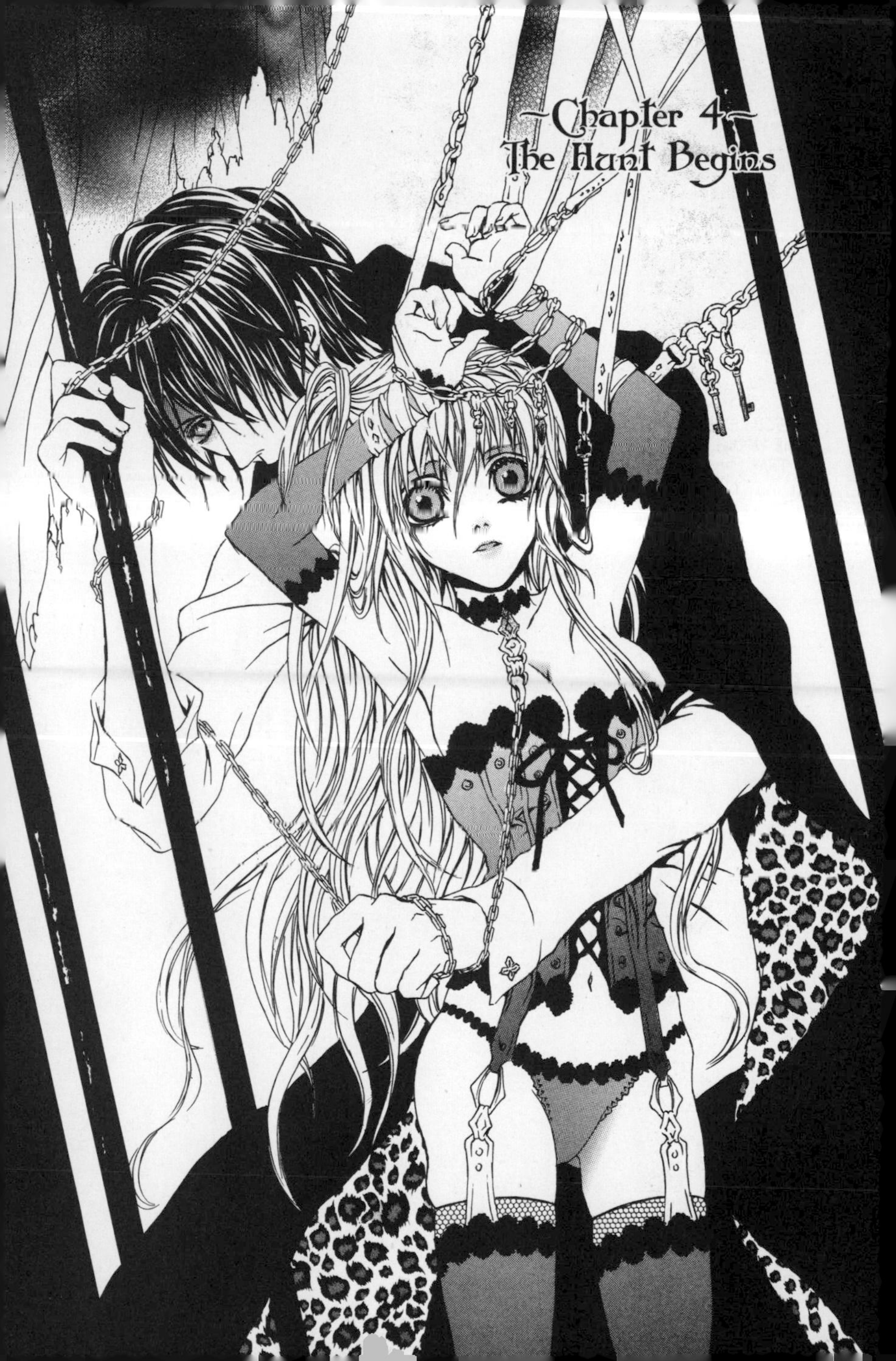
~Chapter 4~
The Hunt Begins

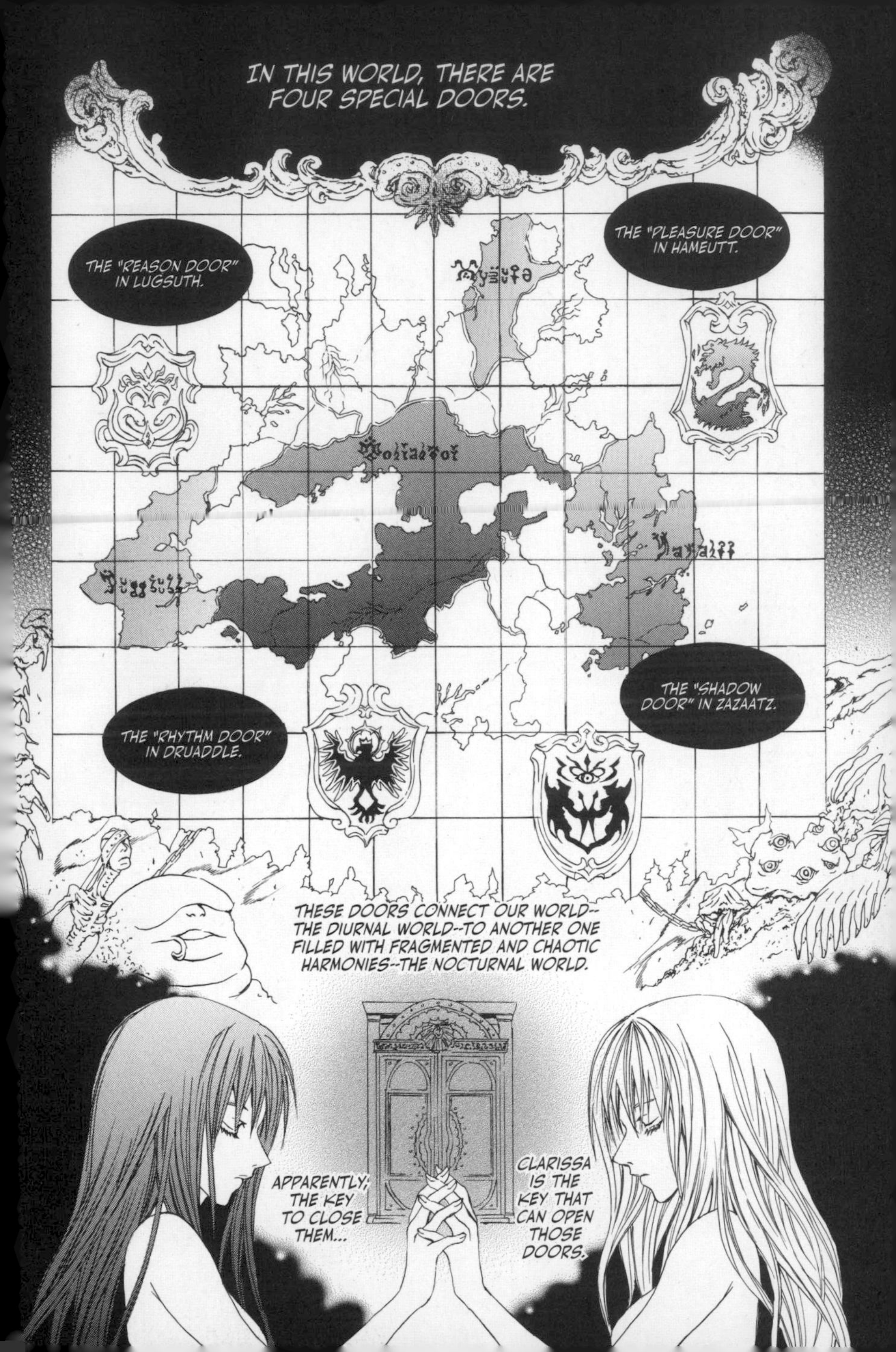
IN THIS WORLD, THERE ARE FOUR SPECIAL DOORS.
THE "PLEASURE DOOR" IN HAMEUTT.
THE "REASON DOOR" IN LUGSUTH.
THE "SHADOW DOOR" IN ZAZAATZ.
THE "RHYTHM DOOR" IN DRUADDLE.
THESE DOORS CONNECT OUR WORLD--THE DIURNAL WORLD--TO ANOTHER ONE FILLED WITH FRAGMENTED AND CHAOTIC HARMONIES--THE NOCTURNAL WORLD.
CLARISSA IS THE KEY THAT CAN OPEN THOSE DOORS.
APPARENTLY, THE KEY TO CLOSE THEM...

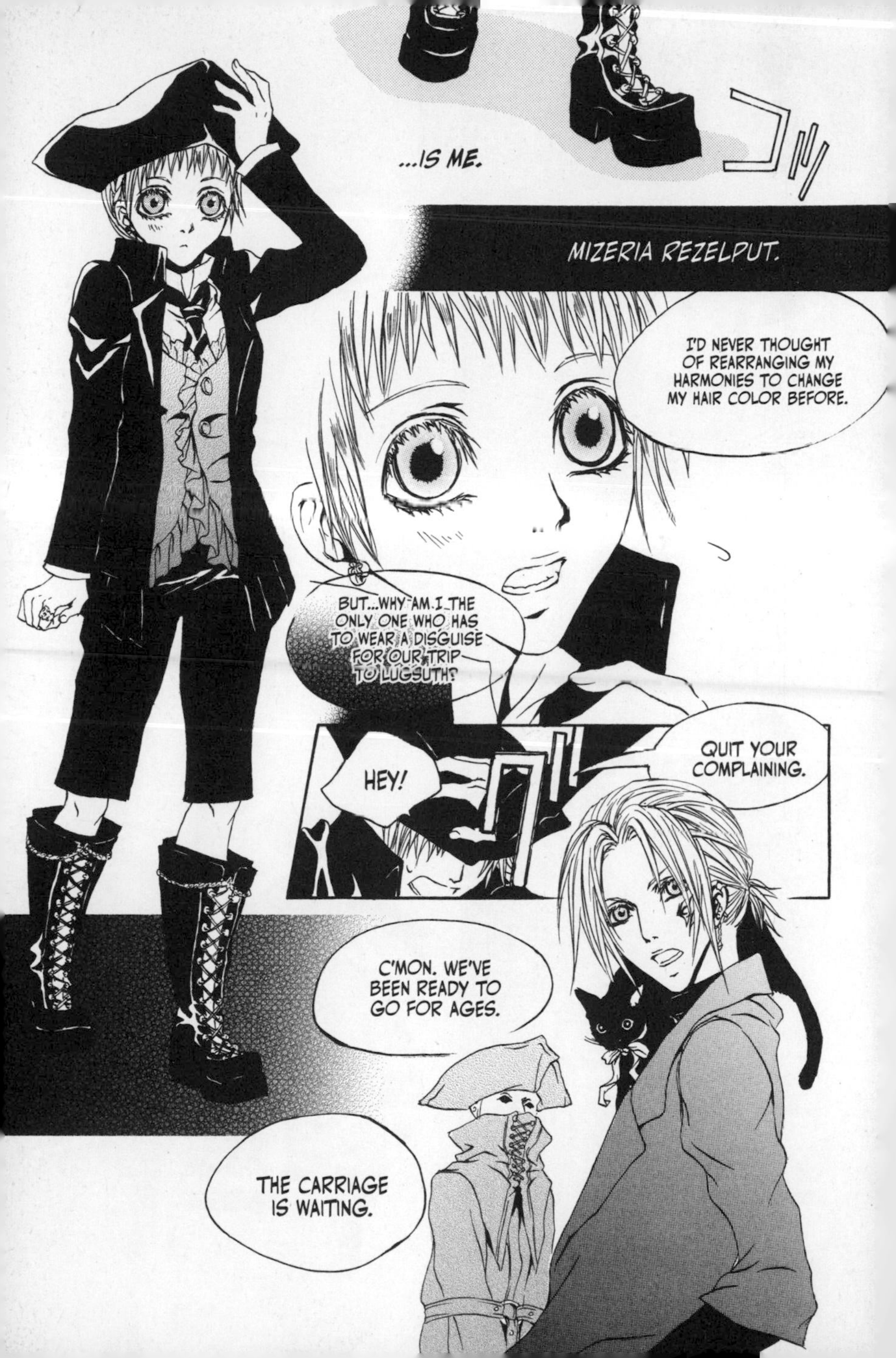
コツ
...IS ME.
MIZERIA REZELPUT.
I'D NEVER THOUGHT OF REARRANGING MY HARMONIES TO CHANGE MY HAIR COLOR BEFORE.
BUT...WHY AM I THE ONLY ONE WHO HAS TO WEAR A DISGUISE FOR OUR TRIP TO LUGSUTH?
QUIT YOUR COMPLAINING.
HEY!
C'MON. WE'VE BEEN READY TO GO FOR AGES.
THE CARRIAGE IS WAITING.

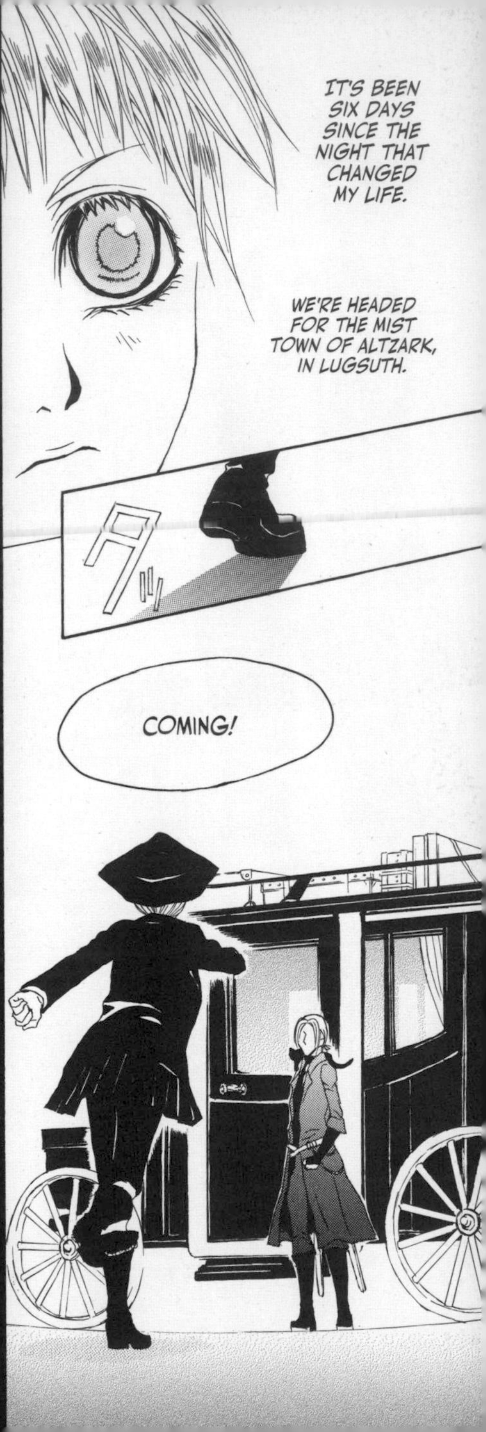
IT'S BEEN SIX DAYS SINCE THE NIGHT THAT CHANGED MY LIFE.
WE'RE HEADED FOR THE MIST TOWN OF ALTZARK, IN LUGSUTH.
COMING!

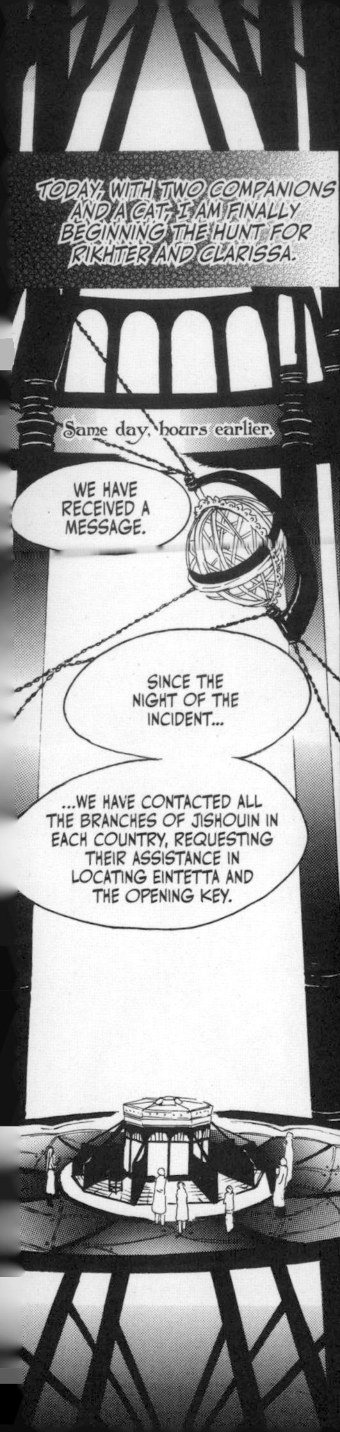
TODAY, WITH TWO COMPANIONS AND A CAT, I AM FINALLY BEGINNING THE HUNT FOR RIKHTER AND CLARISSA.
Same day, hours earlier.
WE HAVE RECEIVED A MESSAGE.
SINCE THE NIGHT OF THE INCIDENT...
...WE HAVE CONTACTED ALL THE BRANCHES OF JISHOUIN IN EACH COUNTRY, REQUESTING THEIR ASSISTANCE IN LOCATING EINTETTA AND THE OPENING KEY.

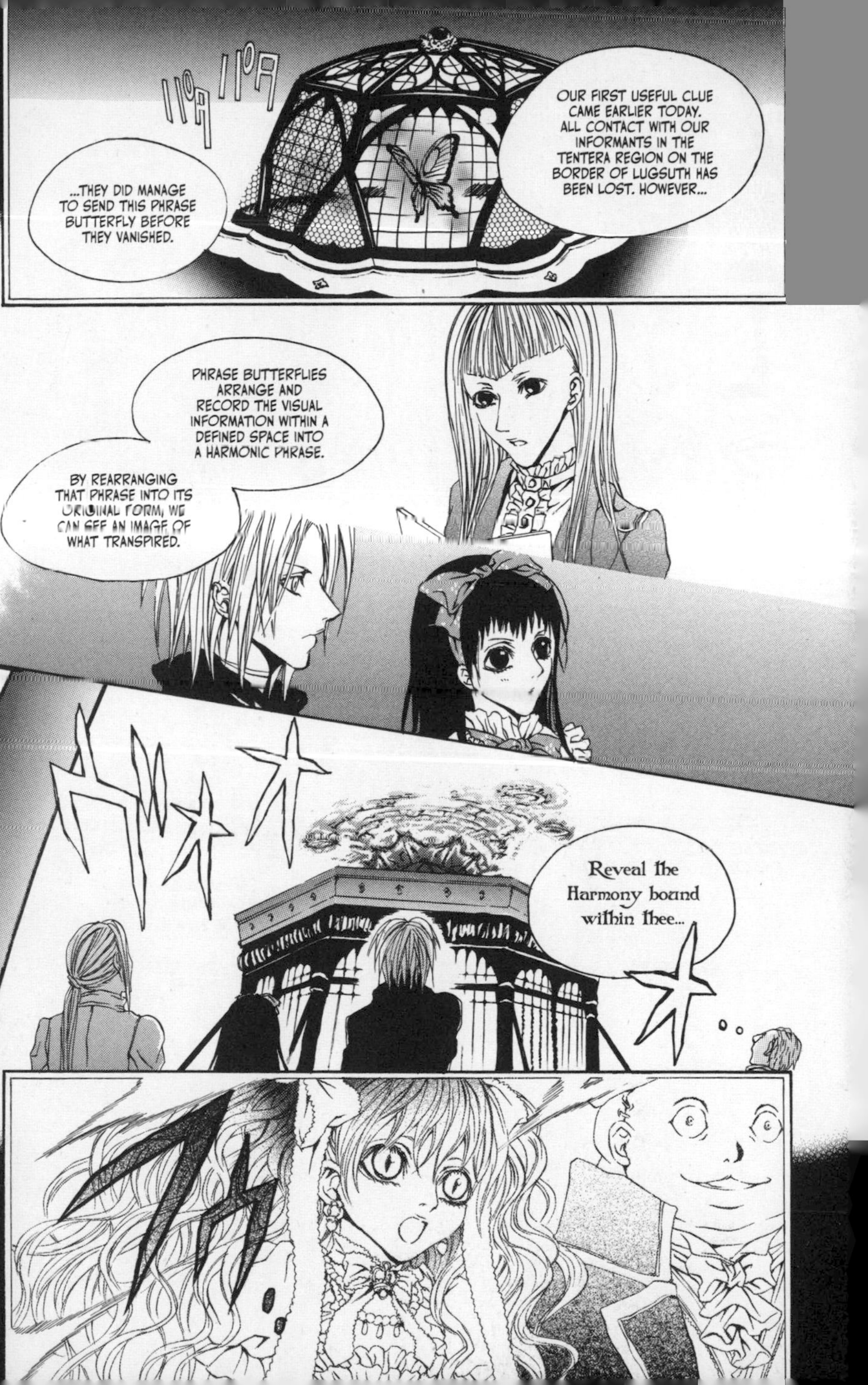
OUR FIRST USEFUL CLUE CAME EARLIER TODAY. ALL CONTACT WITH OUR INFORMANTS IN THE TENTERA REGION ON THE BORDER OF LUGSUTH HAS BEEN LOST. HOWEVER...
...THEY DID MANAGE TO SEND THIS PHRASE BUTTERFLY BEFORE THEY VANISHED.
PHRASE BUTTERFLIES ARRANGE AND RECORD THE VISUAL INFORMATION WITHIN A DEFINED SPACE INTO A HARMONIC PHRASE.
BY REARRANGING THAT PHRASE INTO ITS ORIGINAL FORM, WE CAN SEE AN IMAGE OF WHAT TRANSPIRED.
Reveal the Harmony bound within thee...

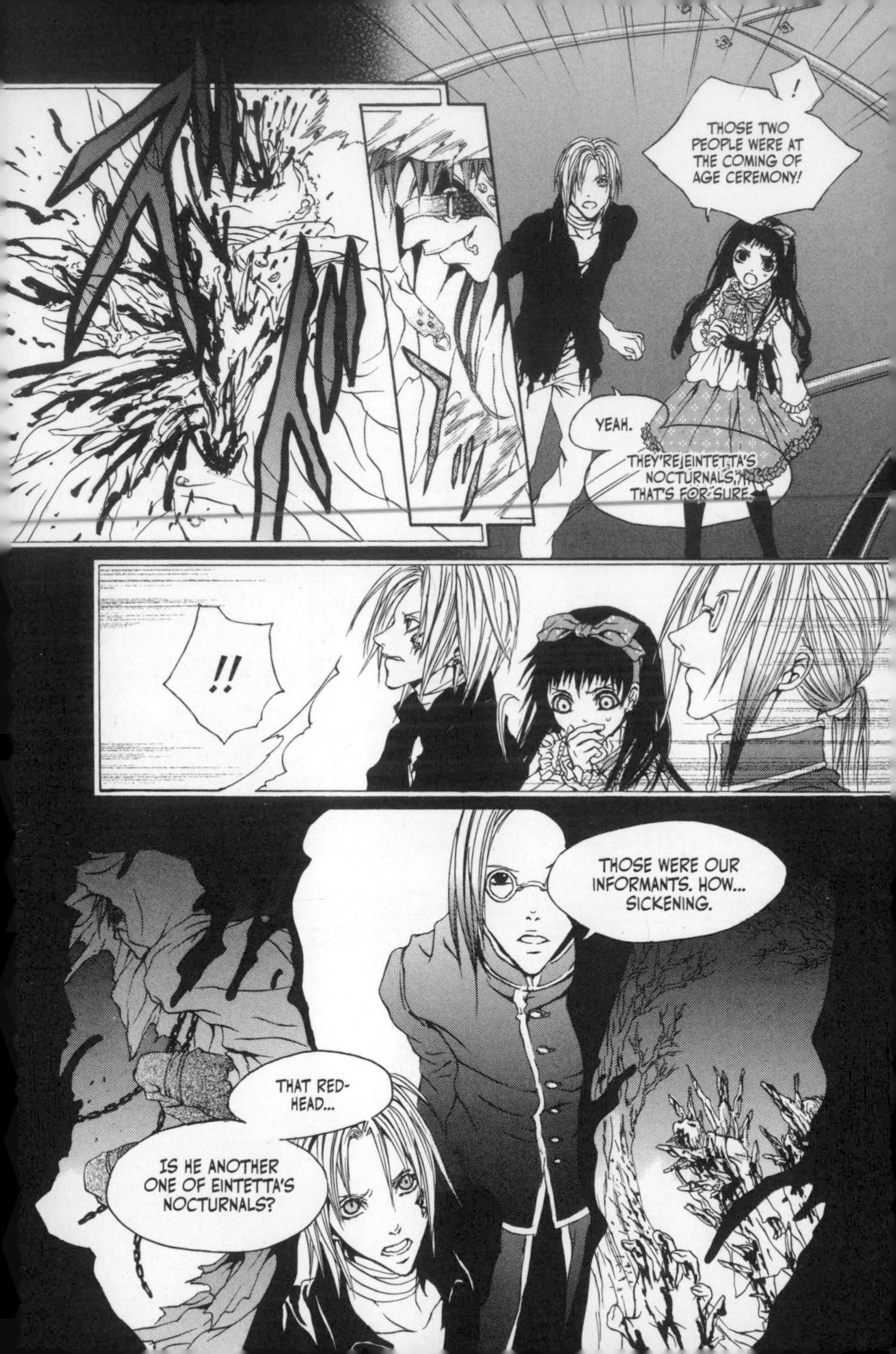
!
THOSE TWO PEOPLE WERE AT THE COMING OF AGE CEREMONY!
YEAH.
THEY'RE EINTETTA'S NOCTURNALS, THAT'S FOR SURE.
!!
THOSE WERE OUR INFORMANTS. HOW... SICKENING.
THAT RED-HEAD...
IS HE ANOTHER ONE OF EINTETTA'S NOCTURNALS?

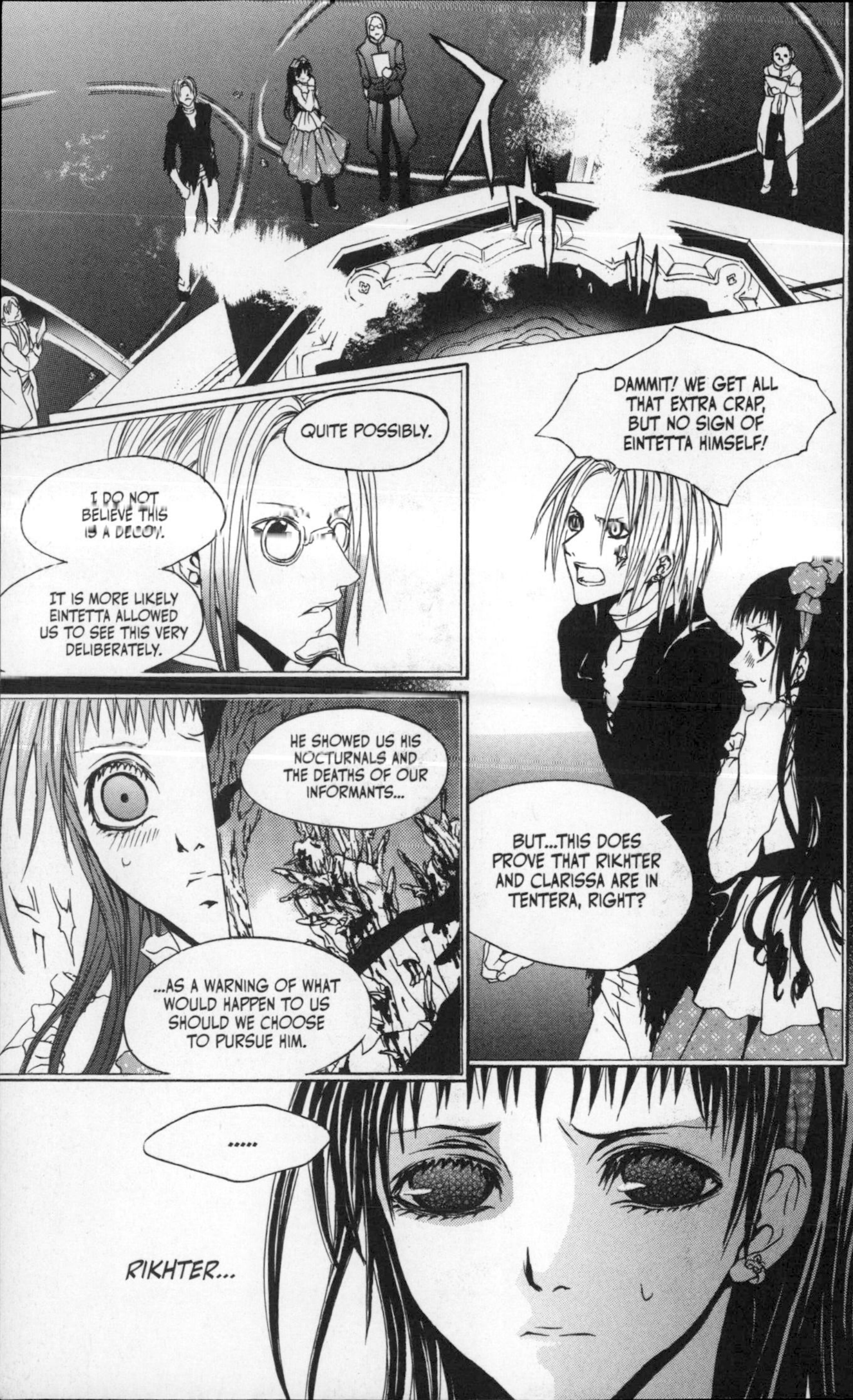

DAMMIT! WE GET ALL THAT EXTRA CRAP, BUT NO SIGN OF EINTETTA HIMSELF!
BUT...THIS DOES PROVE THAT RIKHTER AND CLARISSA ARE IN TENTERA, RIGHT?
QUITE POSSIBLY.
I DO NOT BELIEVE THIS IS A DECOY.
IT IS MORE LIKELY EINTETTA ALLOWED US TO SEE THIS VERY DELIBERATELY.
HE SHOWED US HIS NOCTURNALS AND THE DEATHS OF OUR INFORMANTS...
...AS A WARNING OF WHAT WOULD HAPPEN TO US SHOULD WE CHOOSE TO PURSUE HIM.
......
RIKHTER...

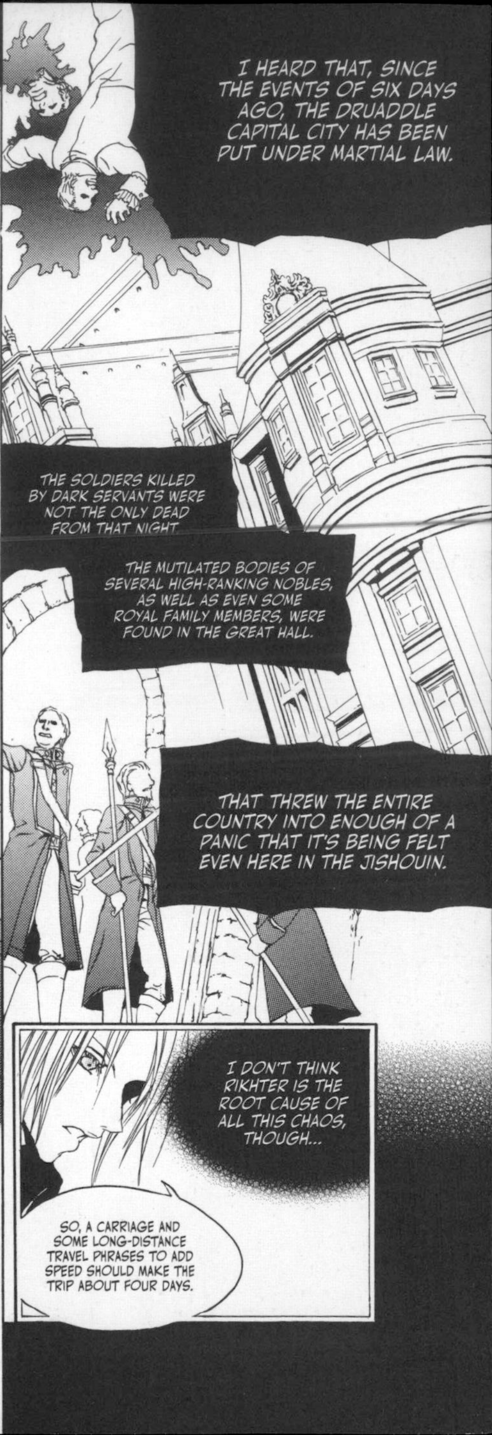
I HEARD THAT, SINCE THE EVENTS OF SIX DAYS AGO, THE DRUADDLE CAPITAL CITY HAS BEEN PUT UNDER MARTIAL LAW.
THE SOLDIERS KILLED BY DARK SERVANTS WERE NOT THE ONLY DEAD FROM THAT NIGHT.
THE MUTILATED BODIES OF SEVERAL HIGH-RANKING NOBLES, AS WELL AS EVEN SOME ROYAL FAMILY MEMBERS, WERE FOUND IN THE GREAT HALL.
THAT THREW THE ENTIRE COUNTRY INTO ENOUGH OF A PANIC THAT IT'S BEING FELT EVEN HERE IN THE JISHOUIN.
I DON'T THINK RIKHTER IS THE ROOT CAUSE OF ALL THIS CHAOS, THOUGH...
SO, A CARRIAGE AND SOME LONG-DISTANCE TRAVEL PHRASES TO ADD SPEED SHOULD MAKE THE TRIP ABOUT FOUR DAYS.
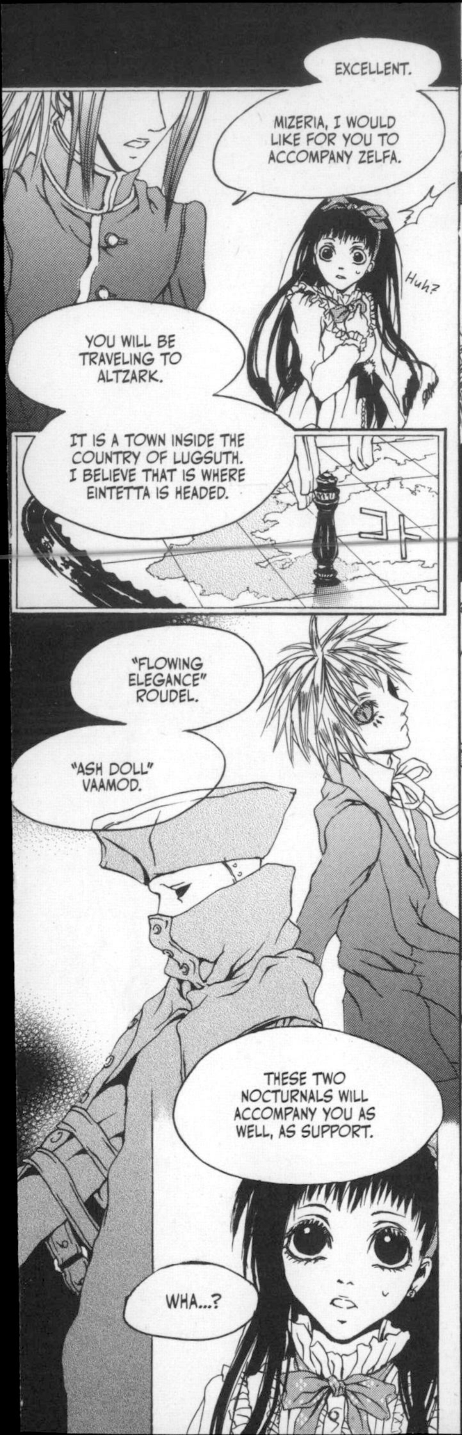
EXCELLENT.
MIZERIA, I WOULD LIKE FOR YOU TO ACCOMPANY ZELFA.
Huh?
YOU WILL BE TRAVELING TO ALTZARK.
IT IS A TOWN INSIDE THE COUNTRY OF LUGSUTH. I BELIEVE THAT IS WHERE EINTETTA IS HEADED.
"FLOWING ELEGANCE" ROUDEL.
"ASH DOLL" VAAMOD.
THESE TWO NOCTURNALS WILL ACCOMPANY YOU AS WELL, AS SUPPORT.
WHA...?

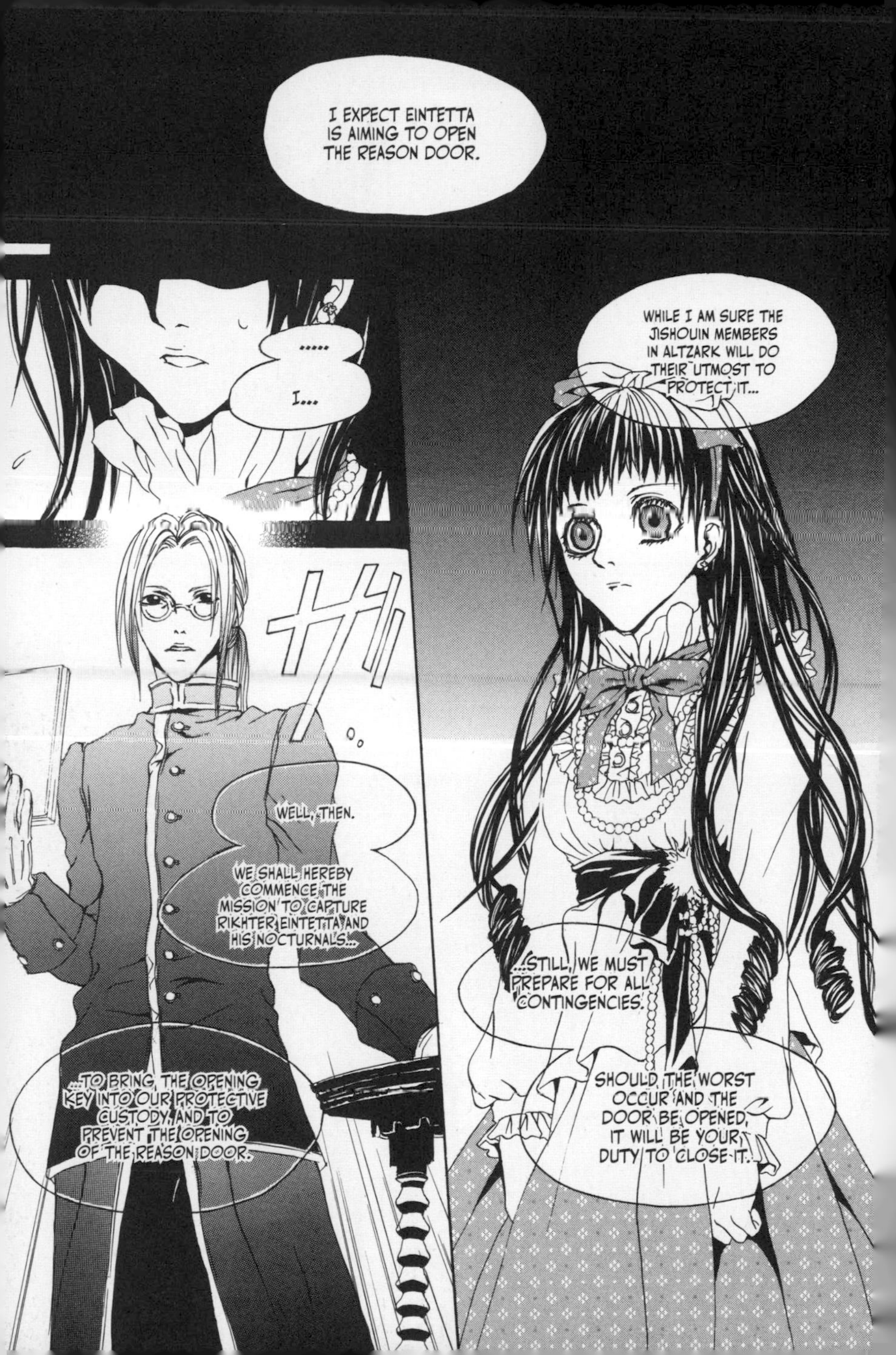
I EXPECT EINTETTA IS AIMING TO OPEN THE REASON DOOR.
WHILE I AM SURE THE JISHOUIN MEMBERS IN ALTZARK WILL DO THEIR UTMOST TO PROTECT IT...
...STILL, WE MUST PREPARE FOR ALL CONTINGENCIES.
SHOULD THE WORST OCCUR AND THE DOOR BE OPENED, IT WILL BE YOUR DUTY TO CLOSE IT.
......
I...
WELL, THEN.
WE SHALL HEREBY COMMENCE THE MISSION TO CAPTURE RIKHTER EINTETTA AND HIS NOCTURNALS...
...TO BRING THE OPENING KEY INTO OUR PROTECTIVE CUSTODY, AND TO PREVENT THE OPENING OF THE REASON DOOR.

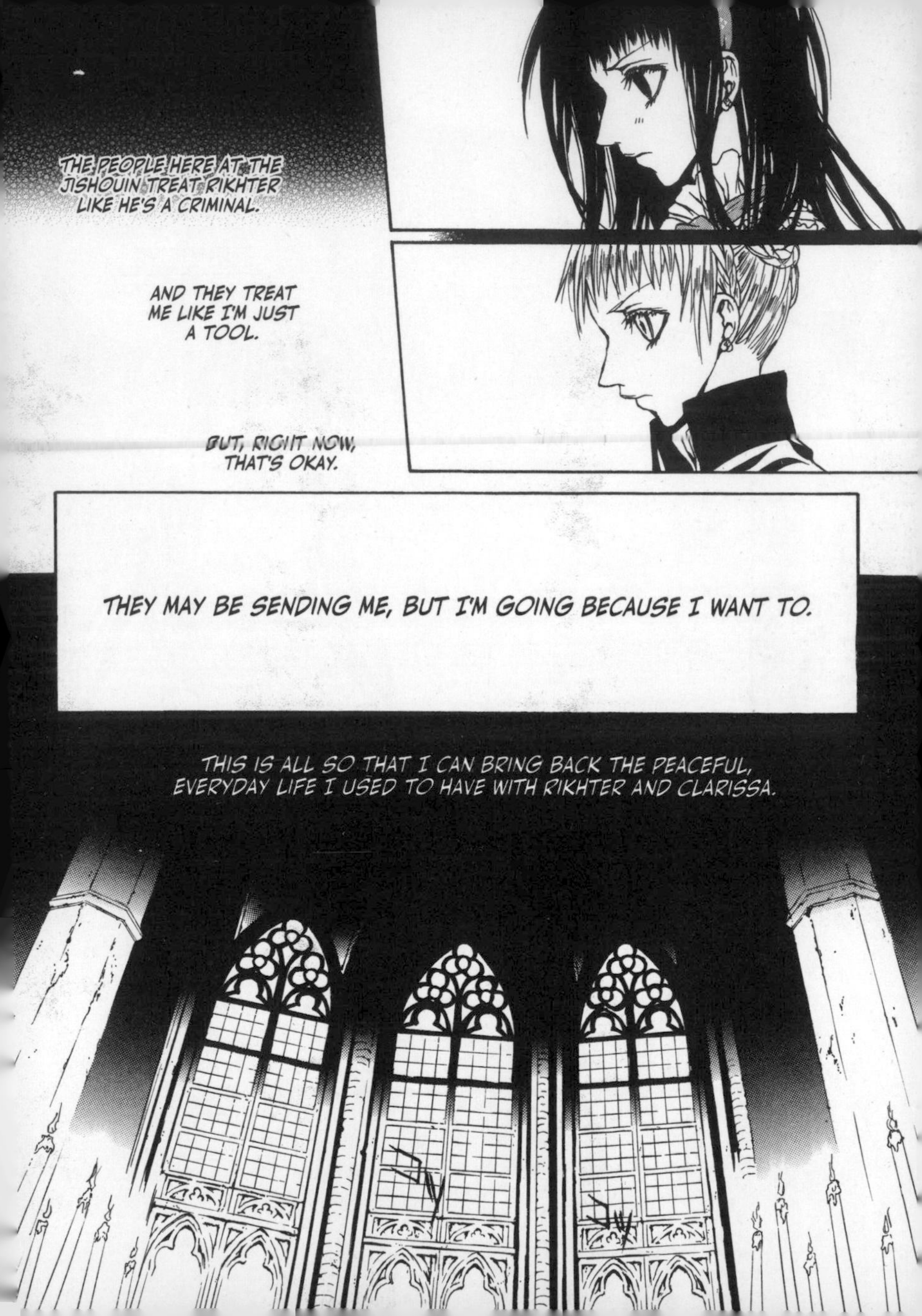
THE PEOPLE HERE AT THE JISHOUIN TREAT RIKHTER LIKE HE'S A CRIMINAL.
AND THEY TREAT ME LIKE I'M JUST A TOOL.
BUT, RIGHT NOW, THAT'S OKAY.
THEY MAY BE SENDING ME, BUT I'M GOING BECAUSE I WANT TO.
THIS IS ALL SO THAT I CAN BRING BACK THE PEACEFUL, EVERYDAY LIFE I USED TO HAVE WITH RIKHTER AND CLARISSA.

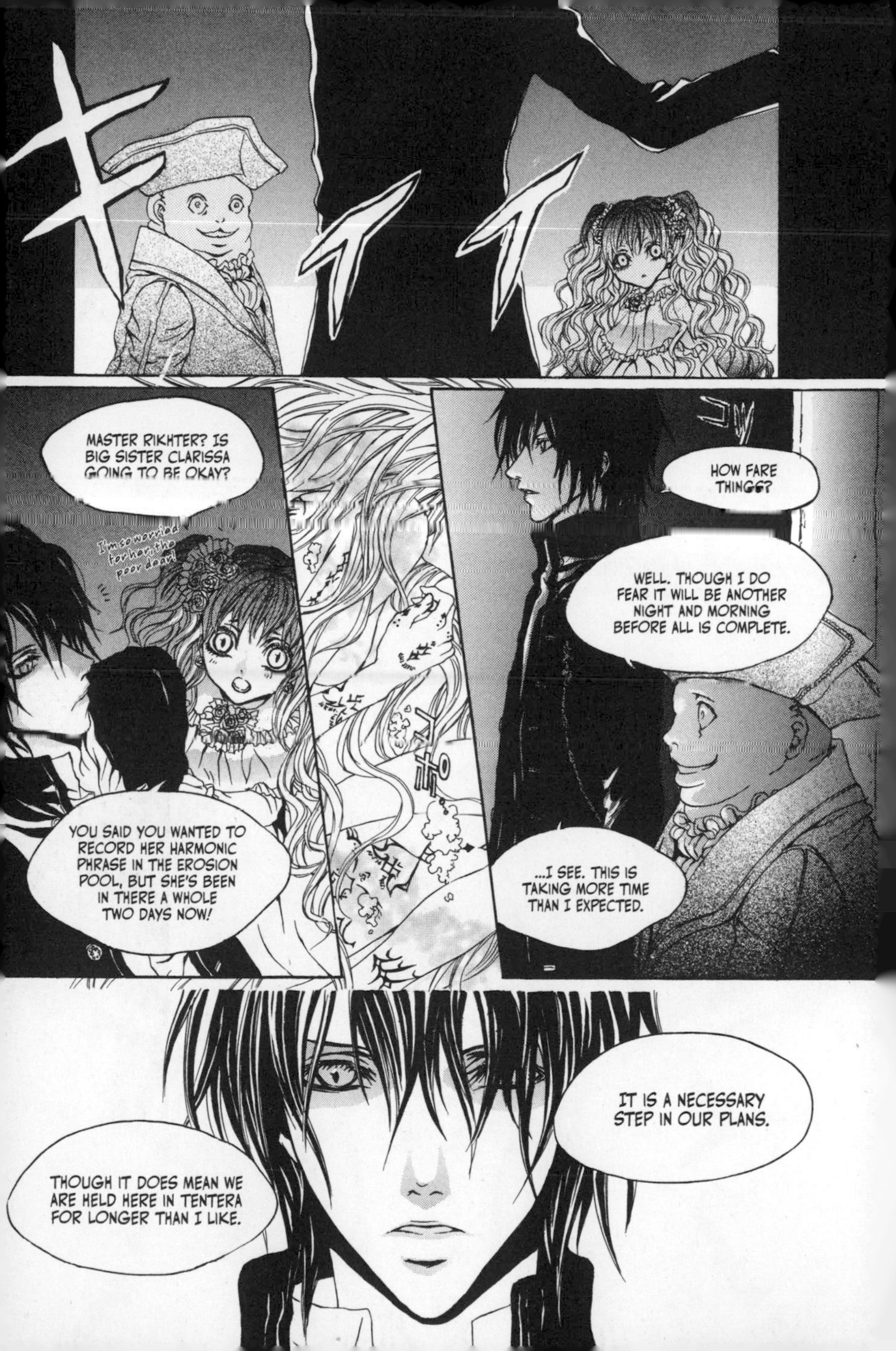
キイイ
HOW FARE THINGS?
WELL. THOUGH I DO FEAR IT WILL BE ANOTHER NIGHT AND MORNING BEFORE ALL IS COMPLETE.
...I SEE. THIS IS TAKING MORE TIME THAN I EXPECTED.
MASTER RIKHTER? IS BIG SISTER CLARISSA GOING TO BE OKAY?
I'm so worried for her, the poor dear!
YOU SAID YOU WANTED TO RECORD HER HARMONIC PHRASE IN THE EROSION POOL, BUT SHE'S BEEN IN THERE A WHOLE TWO DAYS NOW!
IT IS A NECESSARY STEP IN OUR PLANS.
THOUGH IT DOES MEAN WE ARE HELD HERE IN TENTERA FOR LONGER THAN I LIKE.

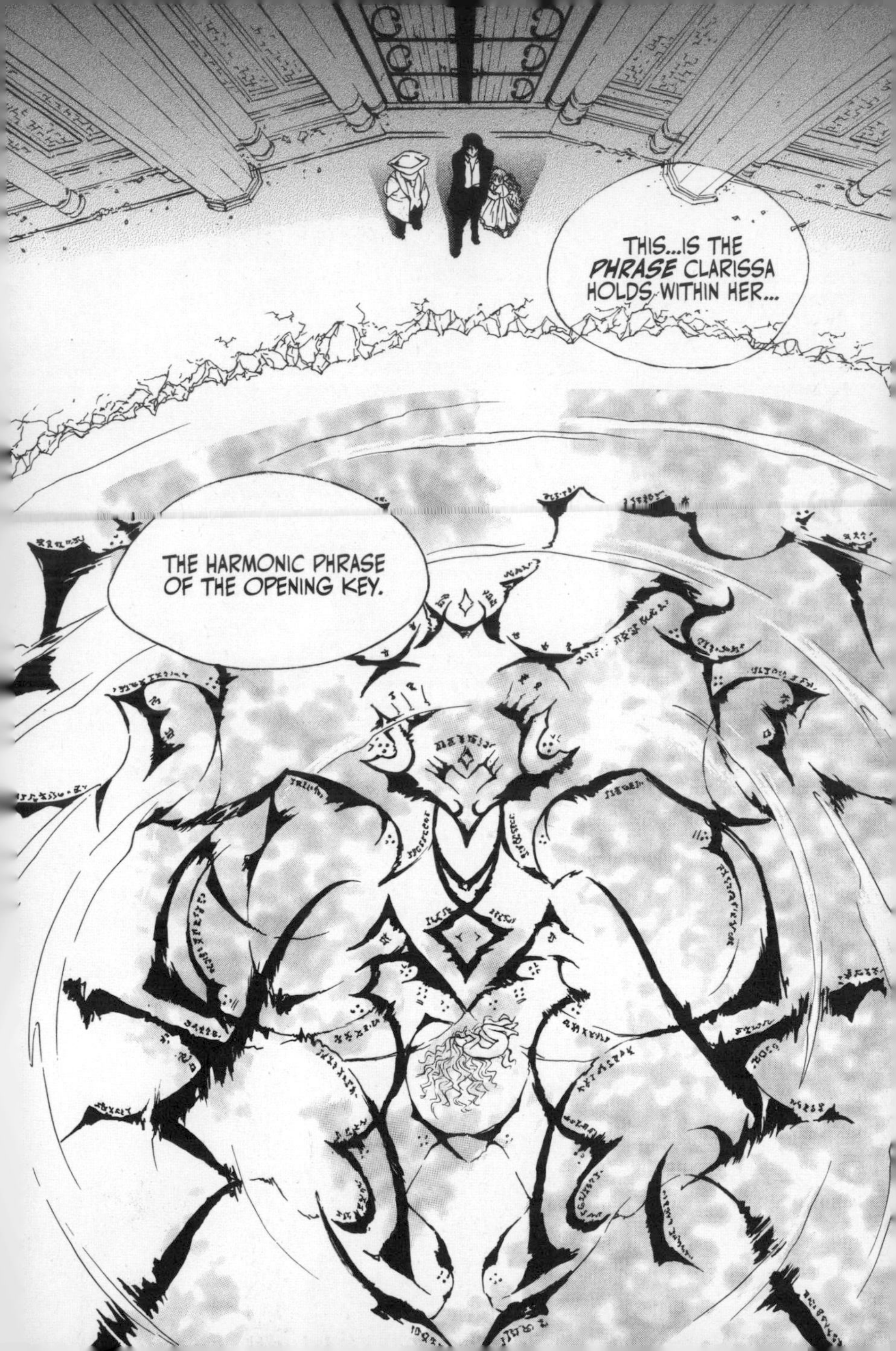
THIS...IS THE *PHRASE* CLARISSA HOLDS WITHIN HER...
THE HARMONIC PHRASE OF THE OPENING KEY.

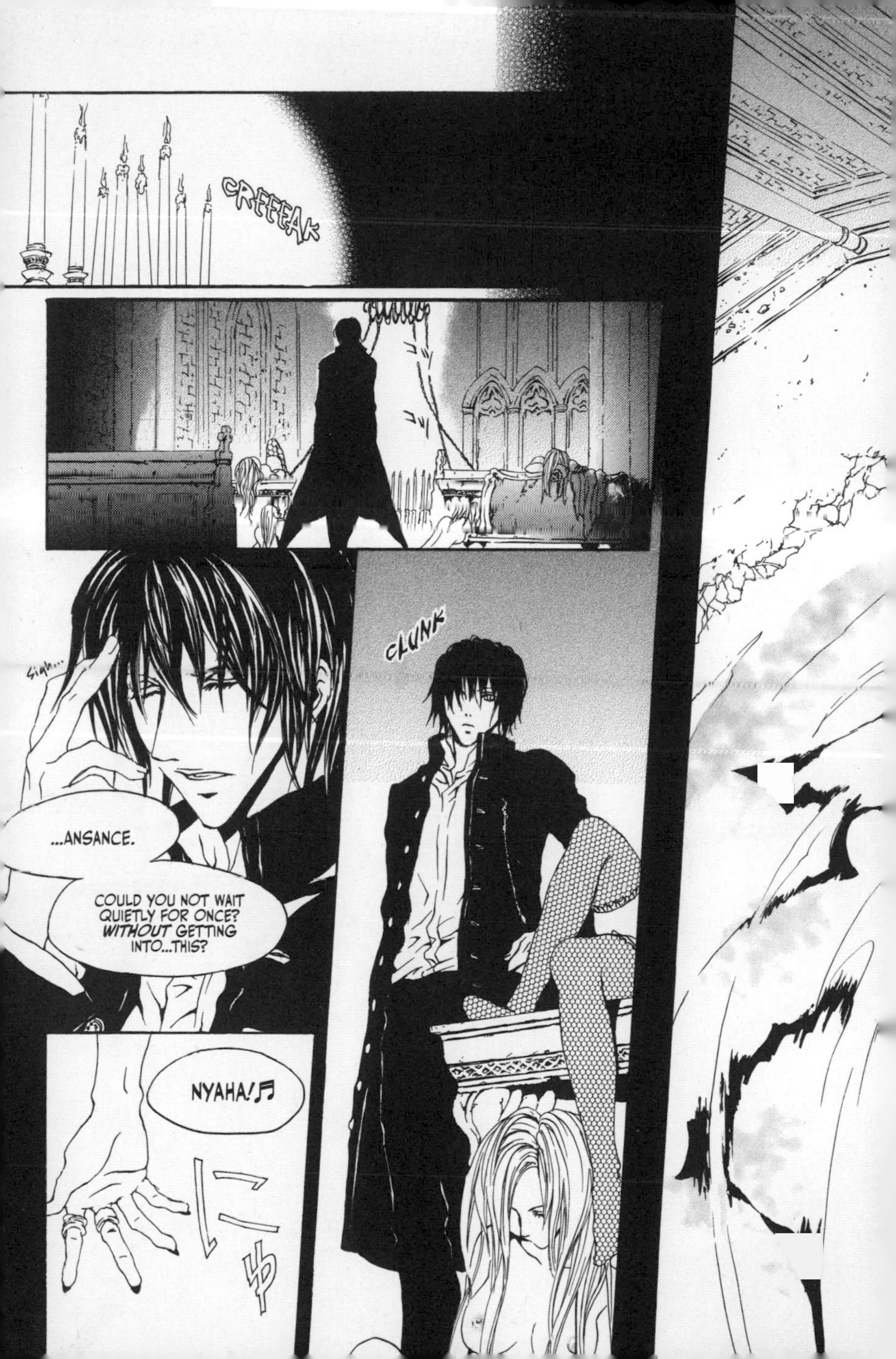
CREEEAK
CLUNK
Sigh...
...ANSANCE.
COULD YOU NOT WAIT QUIETLY FOR ONCE? *WITHOUT* GETTING INTO...THIS?
NYAHA!♬

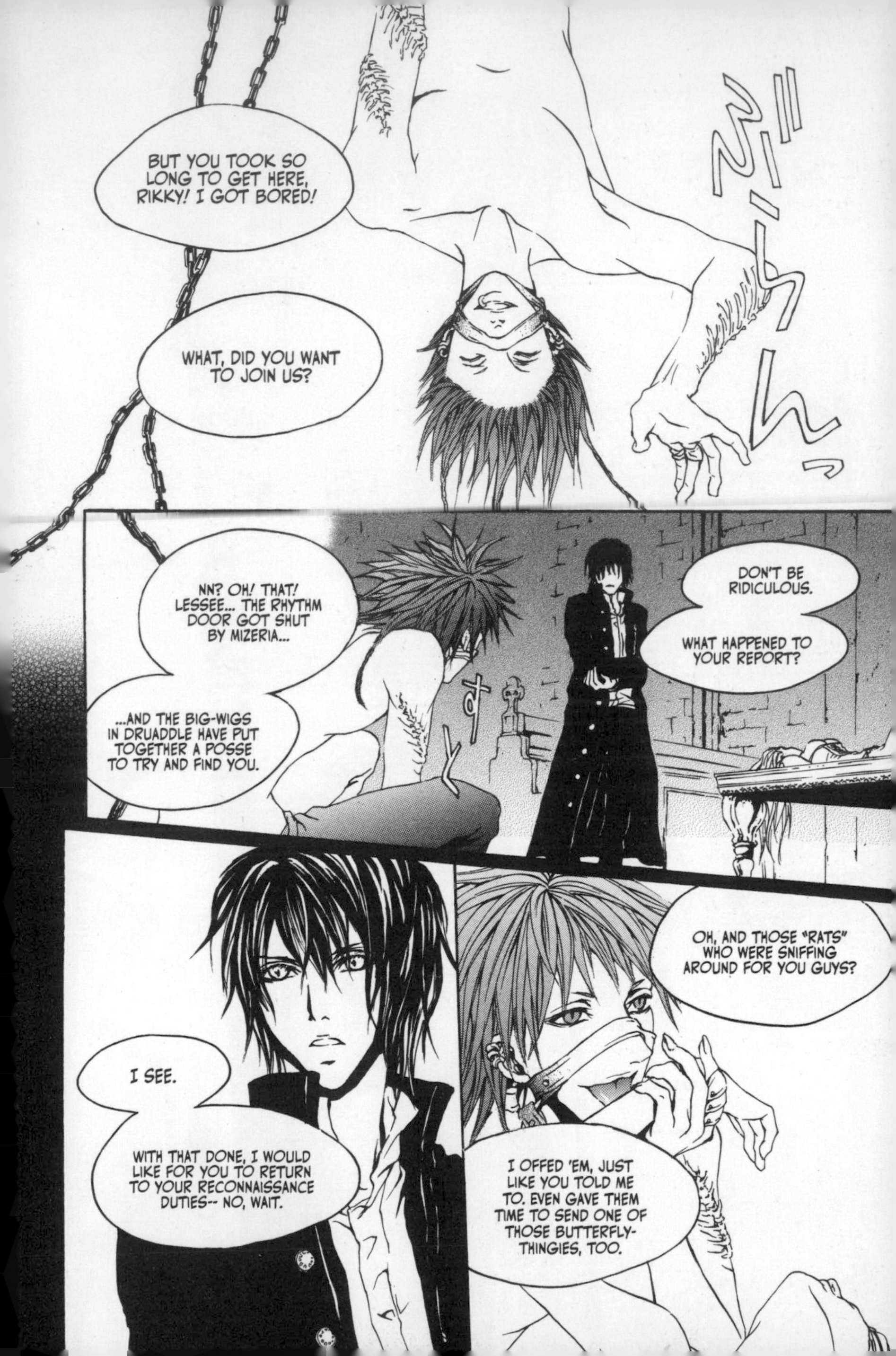
BUT YOU TOOK SO LONG TO GET HERE, RIKKY! I GOT BORED!
WHAT, DID YOU WANT TO JOIN US?
DON'T BE RIDICULOUS.
WHAT HAPPENED TO YOUR REPORT?
NN? OH! THAT! LESSEE... THE RHYTHM DOOR GOT SHUT BY MIZERIA...
...AND THE BIG-WIGS IN DRUADDLE HAVE PUT TOGETHER A POSSE TO TRY AND FIND YOU.
OH, AND THOSE "RATS" WHO WERE SNIFFING AROUND FOR YOU GUYS?
I OFFED 'EM, JUST LIKE YOU TOLD ME TO. EVEN GAVE THEM TIME TO SEND ONE OF THOSE BUTTERFLY-THINGIES, TOO.
I SEE.
WITH THAT DONE, I WOULD LIKE FOR YOU TO RETURN TO YOUR RECONNAISSANCE DUTIES-- NO, WAIT.

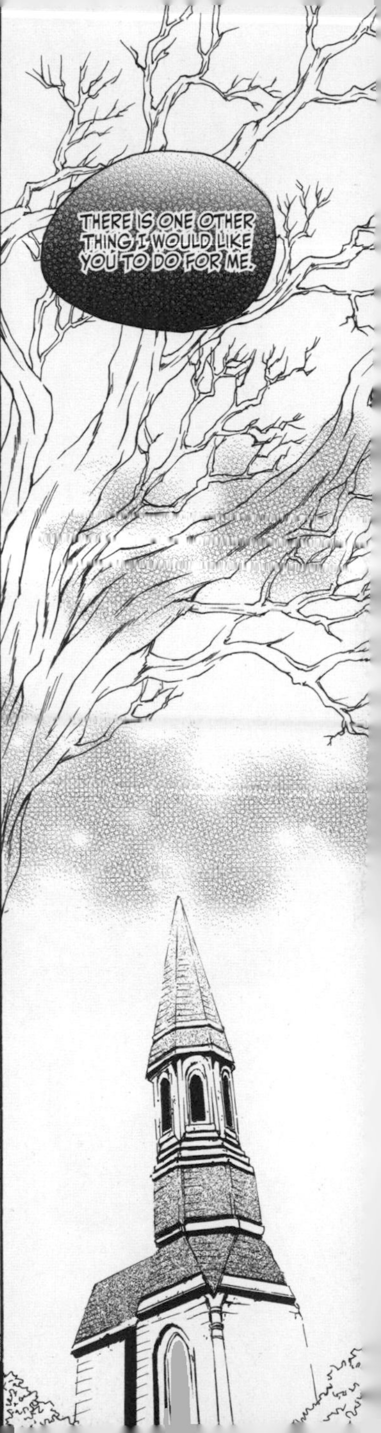
THERE IS ONE OTHER THING I WOULD LIKE YOU TO DO FOR ME.

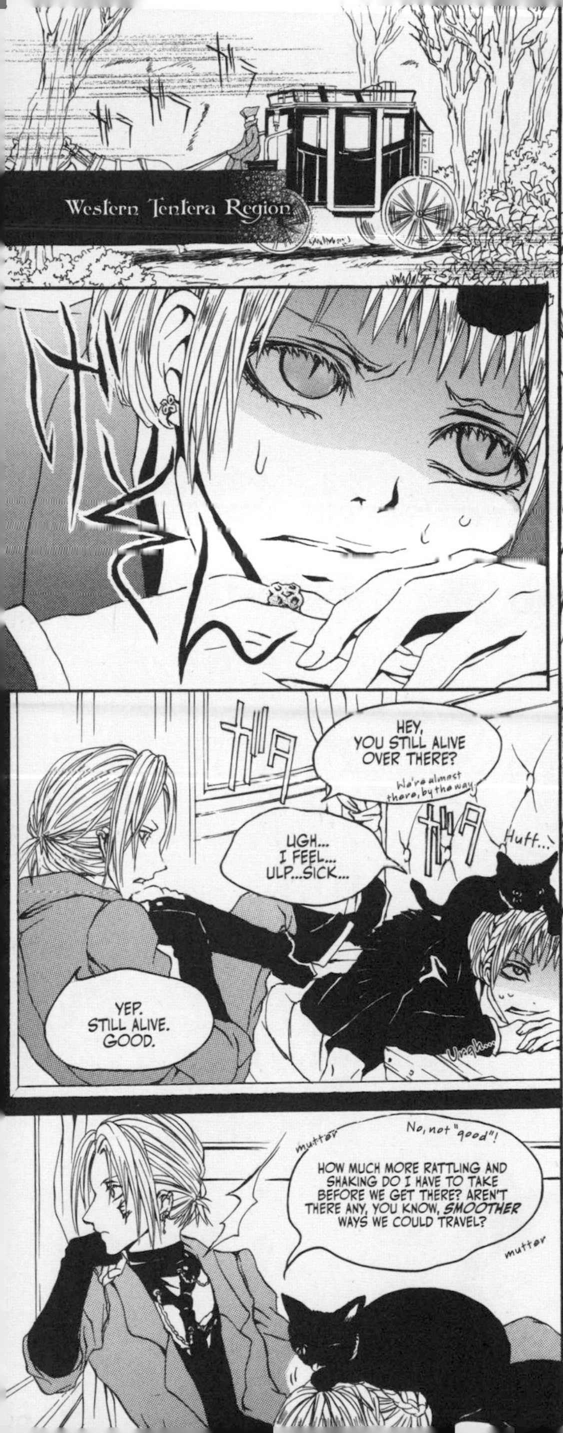
Western Tentera Region
ガタ
HEY, YOU STILL ALIVE OVER THERE?
We're almost there, by the way.
Huff...
ガタ
UGH... I FEEL... ULP...SICK...
Ungh...
YEP. STILL ALIVE. GOOD.
No, not "good"!
mutter
HOW MUCH MORE RATTLING AND SHAKING DO I HAVE TO TAKE BEFORE WE GET THERE? AREN'T THERE ANY, YOU KNOW, SMOOTHER WAYS WE COULD TRAVEL?
mutter

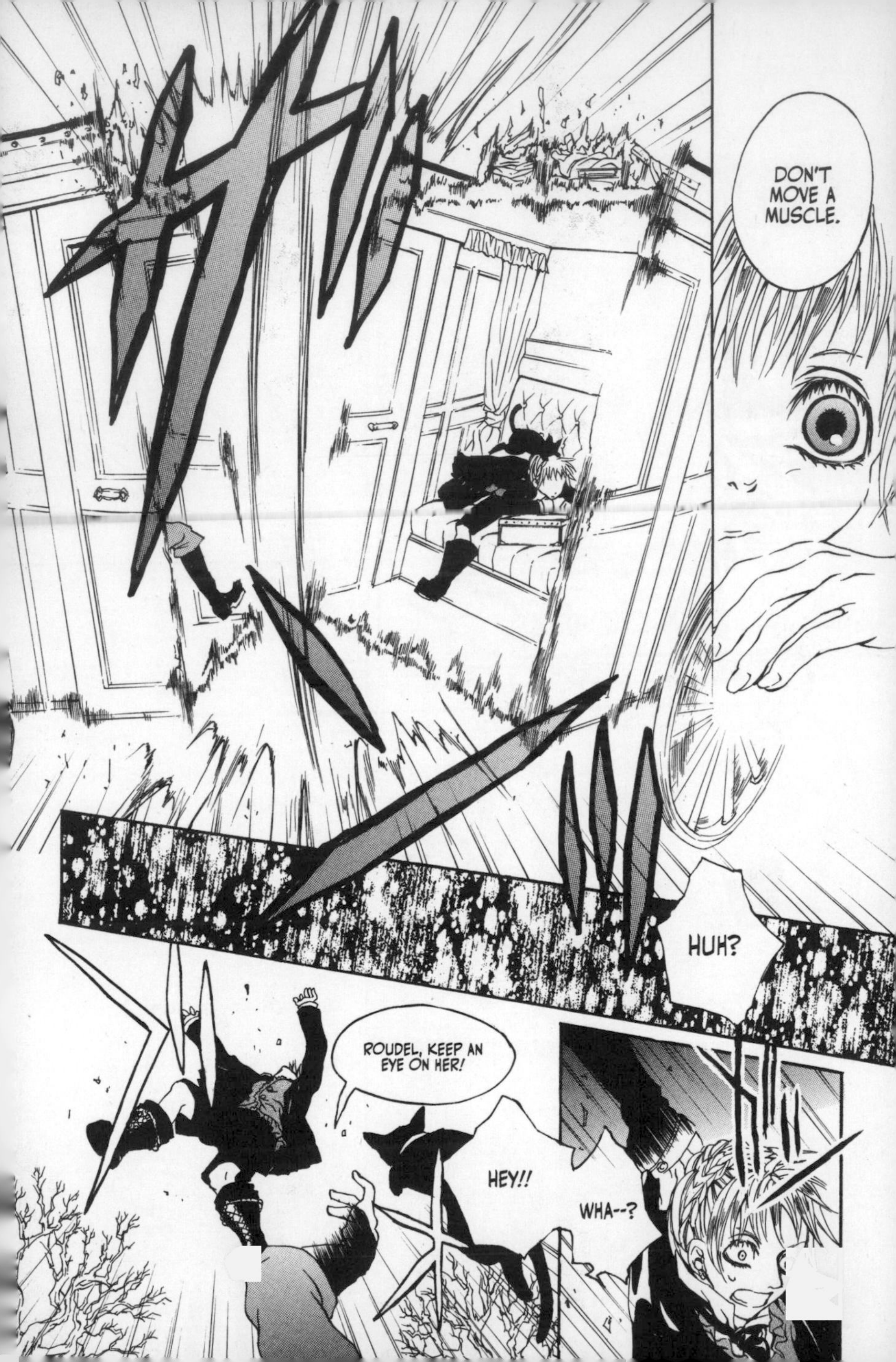
DON'T MOVE A MUSCLE.
HUH?
WHA--?
HEY!!
ROUDEL, KEEP AN EYE ON HER!

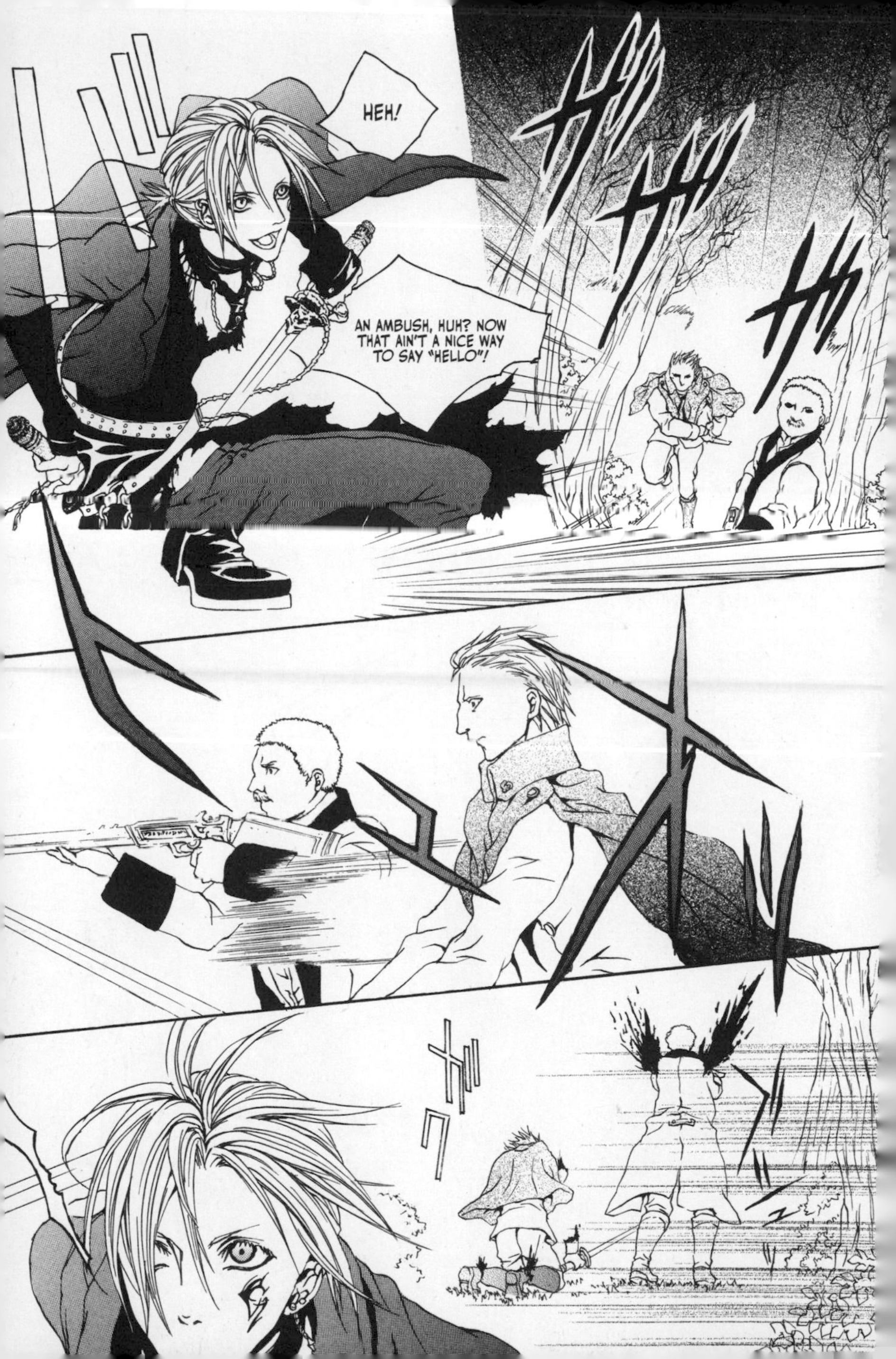
HEH!
AN AMBUSH, HUH? NOW THAT AIN'T A NICE WAY TO SAY "HELLO"!

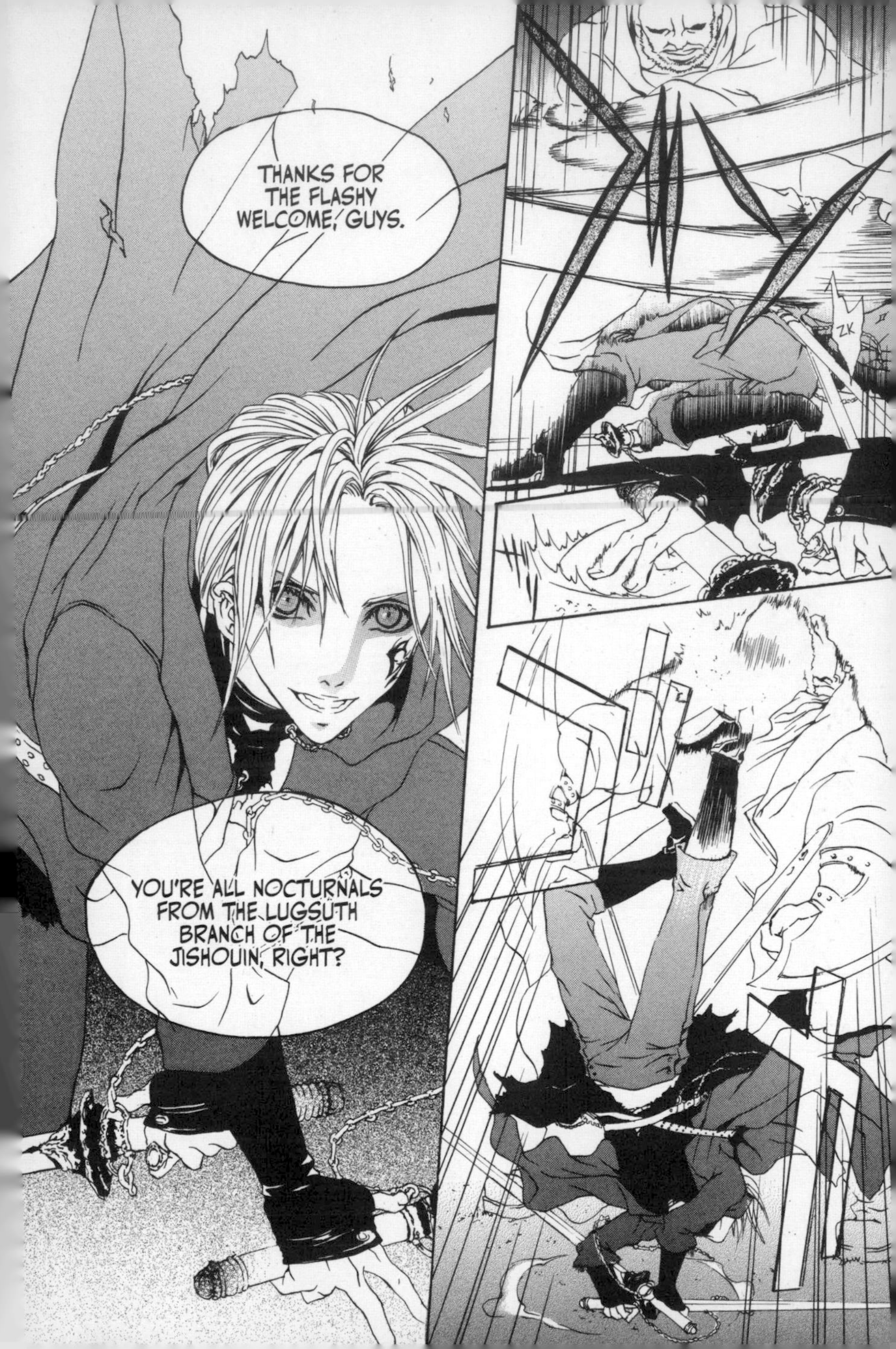
ZK
THANKS FOR THE FLASHY WELCOME, GUYS.
YOU'RE ALL NOCTURNALS FROM THE LUGSUTH BRANCH OF THE JISHOUIN, RIGHT?

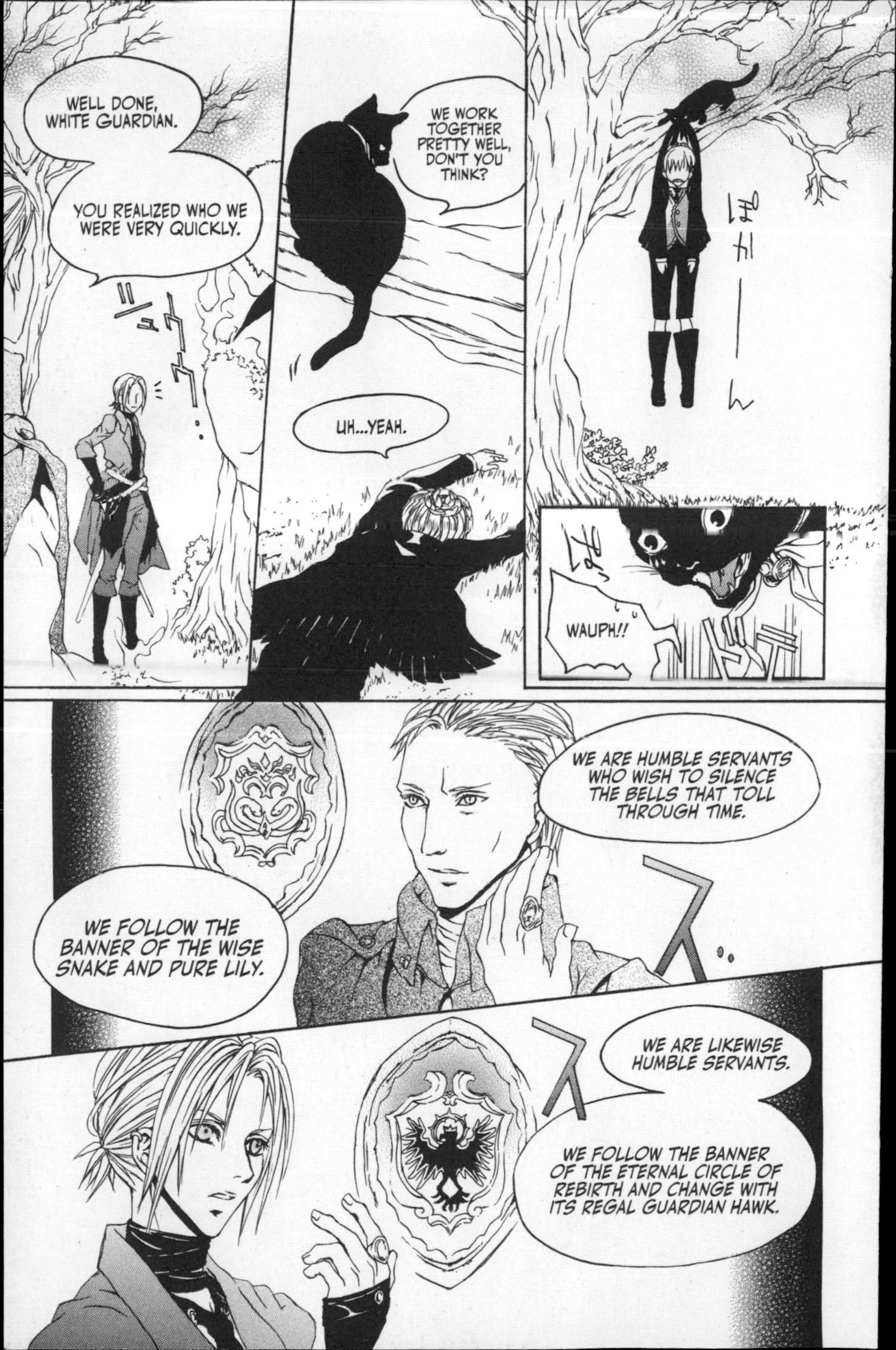
WAUPH!!
WE WORK TOGETHER PRETTY WELL, DON'T YOU THINK?
UH...YEAH.
WELL DONE, WHITE GUARDIAN.
YOU REALIZED WHO WE WERE VERY QUICKLY.
WE ARE HUMBLE SERVANTS WHO WISH TO SILENCE THE BELLS THAT TOLL THROUGH TIME.
WE FOLLOW THE BANNER OF THE WISE SNAKE AND PURE LILY.
WE ARE LIKEWISE HUMBLE SERVANTS.
WE FOLLOW THE BANNER OF THE ETERNAL CIRCLE OF REBIRTH AND CHANGE WITH ITS REGAL GUARDIAN HAWK.

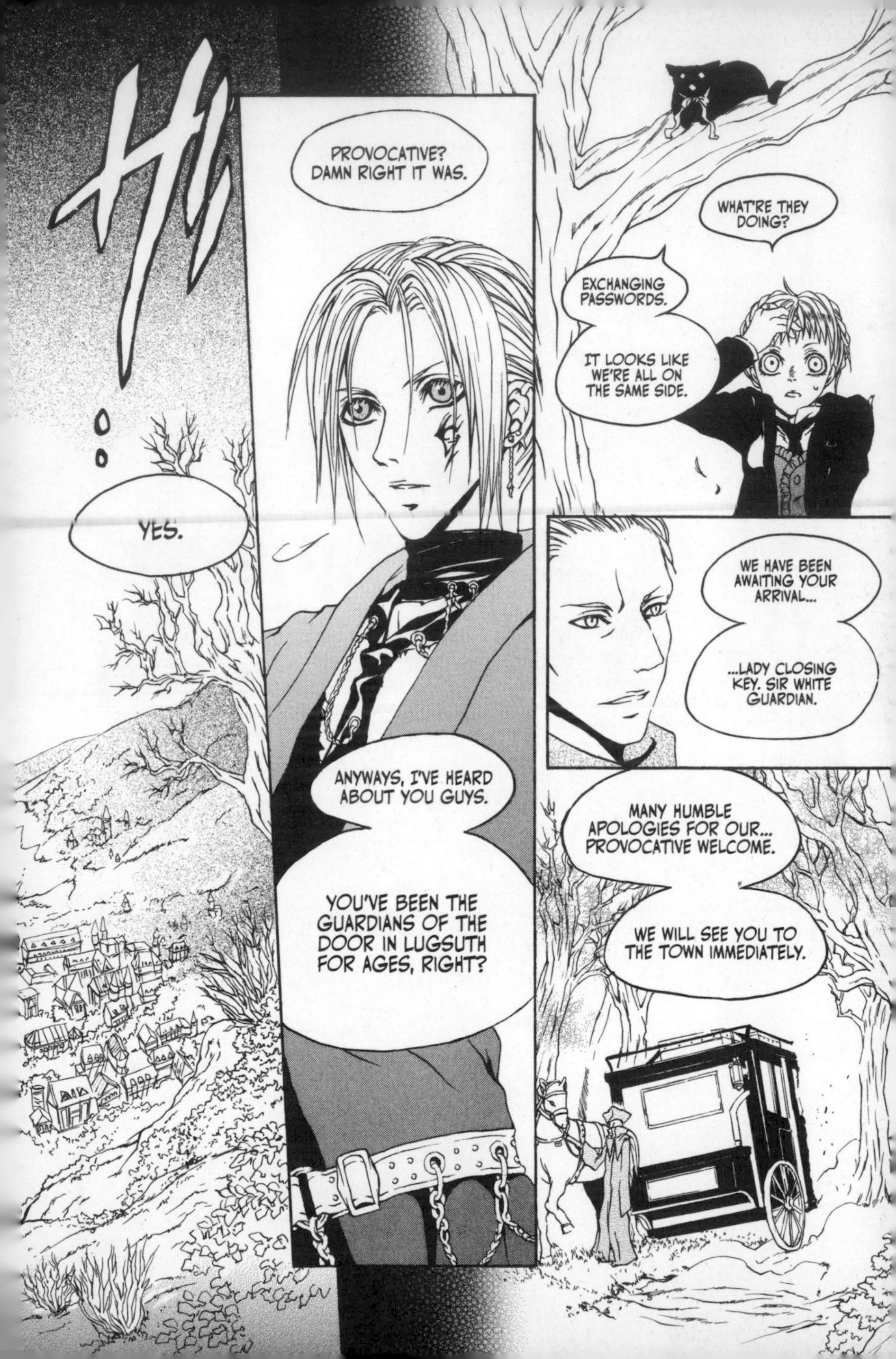

WHAT'RE THEY DOING?
EXCHANGING PASSWORDS.
IT LOOKS LIKE WE'RE ALL ON THE SAME SIDE.
WE HAVE BEEN AWAITING YOUR ARRIVAL...
...LADY CLOSING KEY. SIR WHITE GUARDIAN.
MANY HUMBLE APOLOGIES FOR OUR... PROVOCATIVE WELCOME.
WE WILL SEE YOU TO THE TOWN IMMEDIATELY.
PROVOCATIVE? DAMN RIGHT IT WAS.
ANYWAYS, I'VE HEARD ABOUT YOU GUYS.
YOU'VE BEEN THE GUARDIANS OF THE DOOR IN LUGSUTH FOR AGES, RIGHT?
HI
YES.

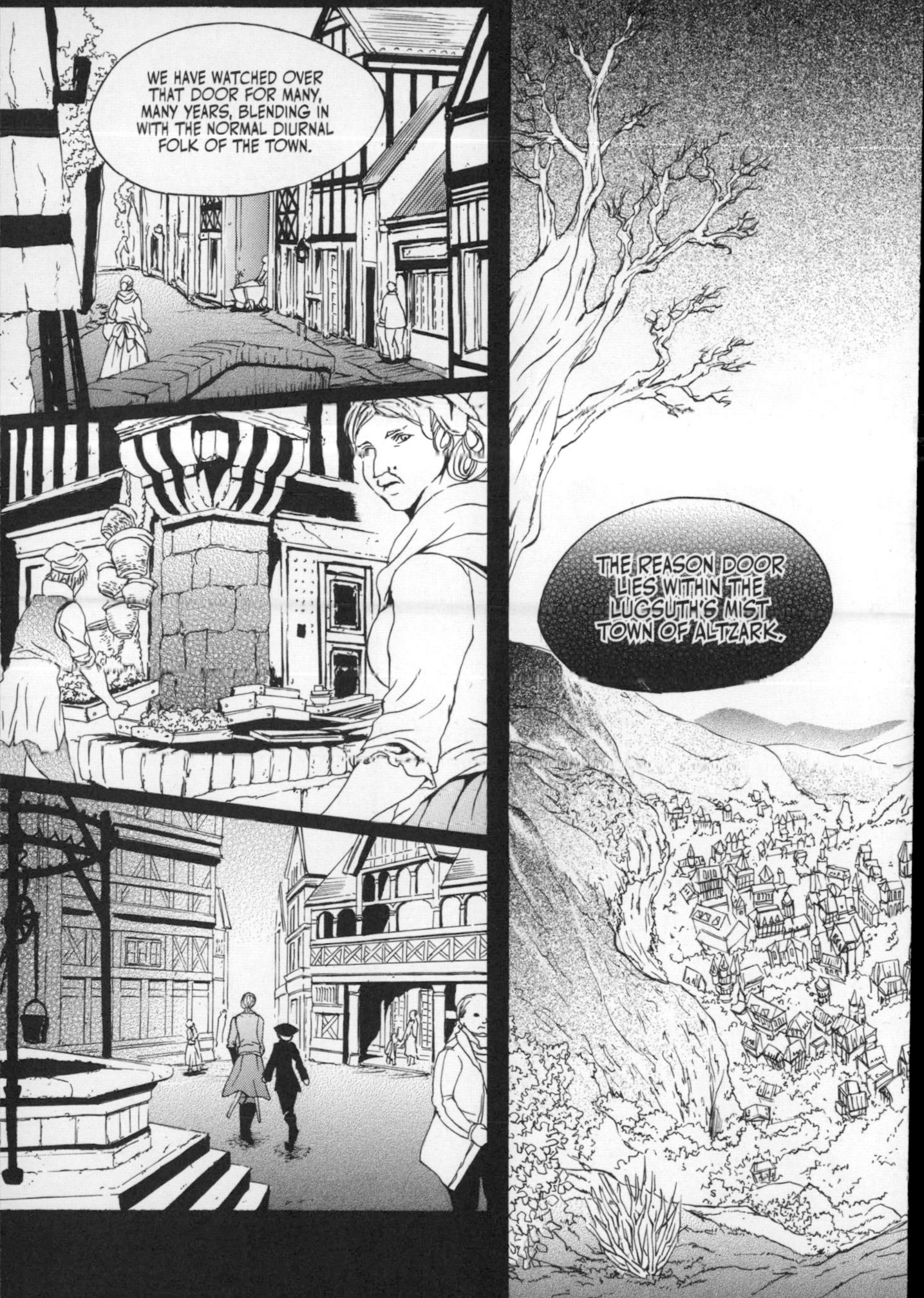
THE REASON DOOR LIES WITHIN THE LUGSUTH'S MIST TOWN OF ALTZARK.
WE HAVE WATCHED OVER THAT DOOR FOR MANY, MANY YEARS, BLENDING IN WITH THE NORMAL DIURNAL FOLK OF THE TOWN.

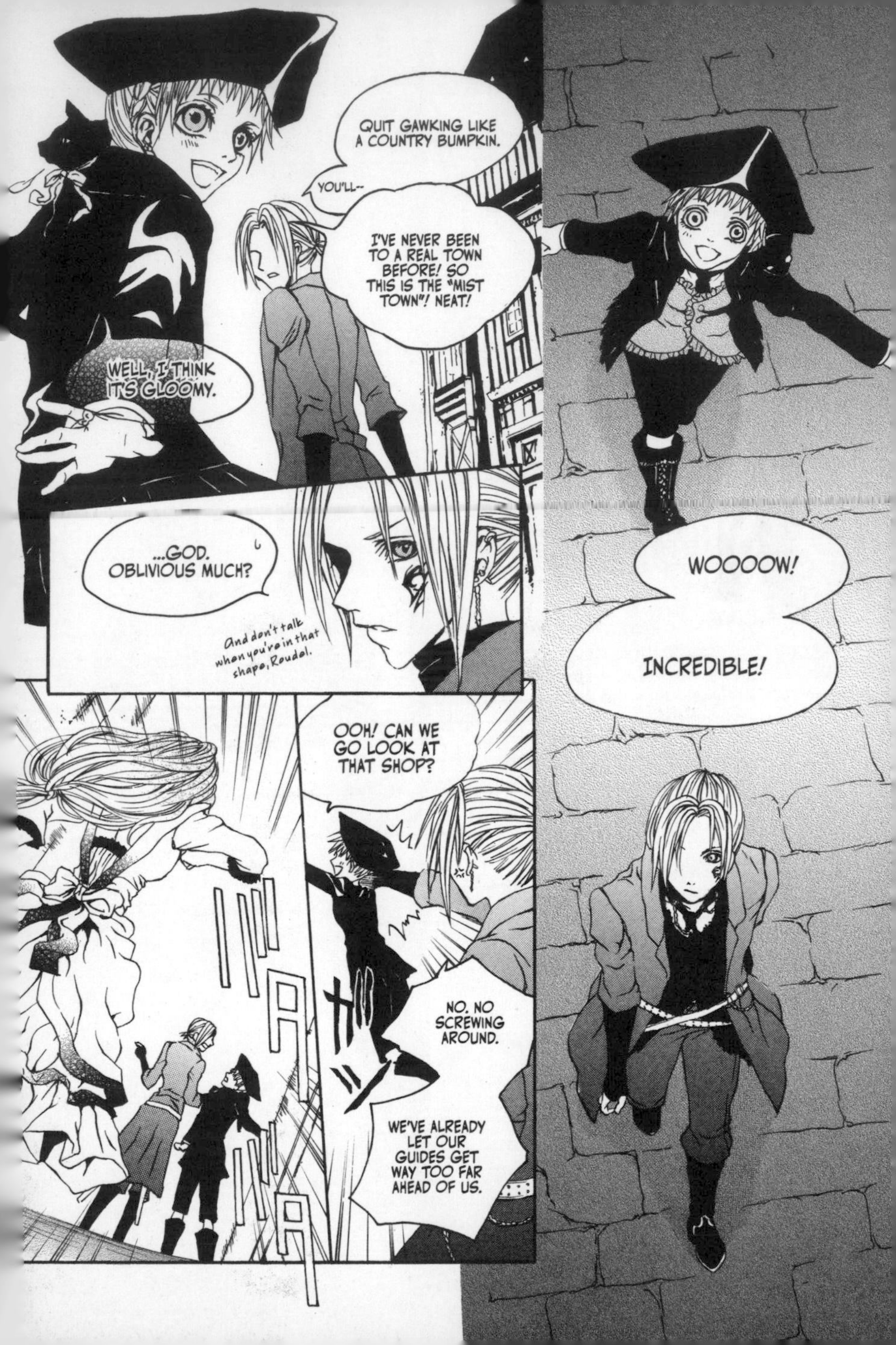
WOOOOW!
INCREDIBLE!
QUIT GAWKING LIKE A COUNTRY BUMPKIN.
YOU'LL--
I'VE NEVER BEEN TO A REAL TOWN BEFORE! SO THIS IS THE "MIST TOWN"! NEAT!
WELL, I THINK IT'S GLOOMY.
...GOD. OBLIVIOUS MUCH?
And don't talk when you're in that shape, Roudel.
OOH! CAN WE GO LOOK AT THAT SHOP?
NO. NO SCREWING AROUND.
WE'VE ALREADY LET OUR GUIDES GET WAY TOO FAR AHEAD OF US.

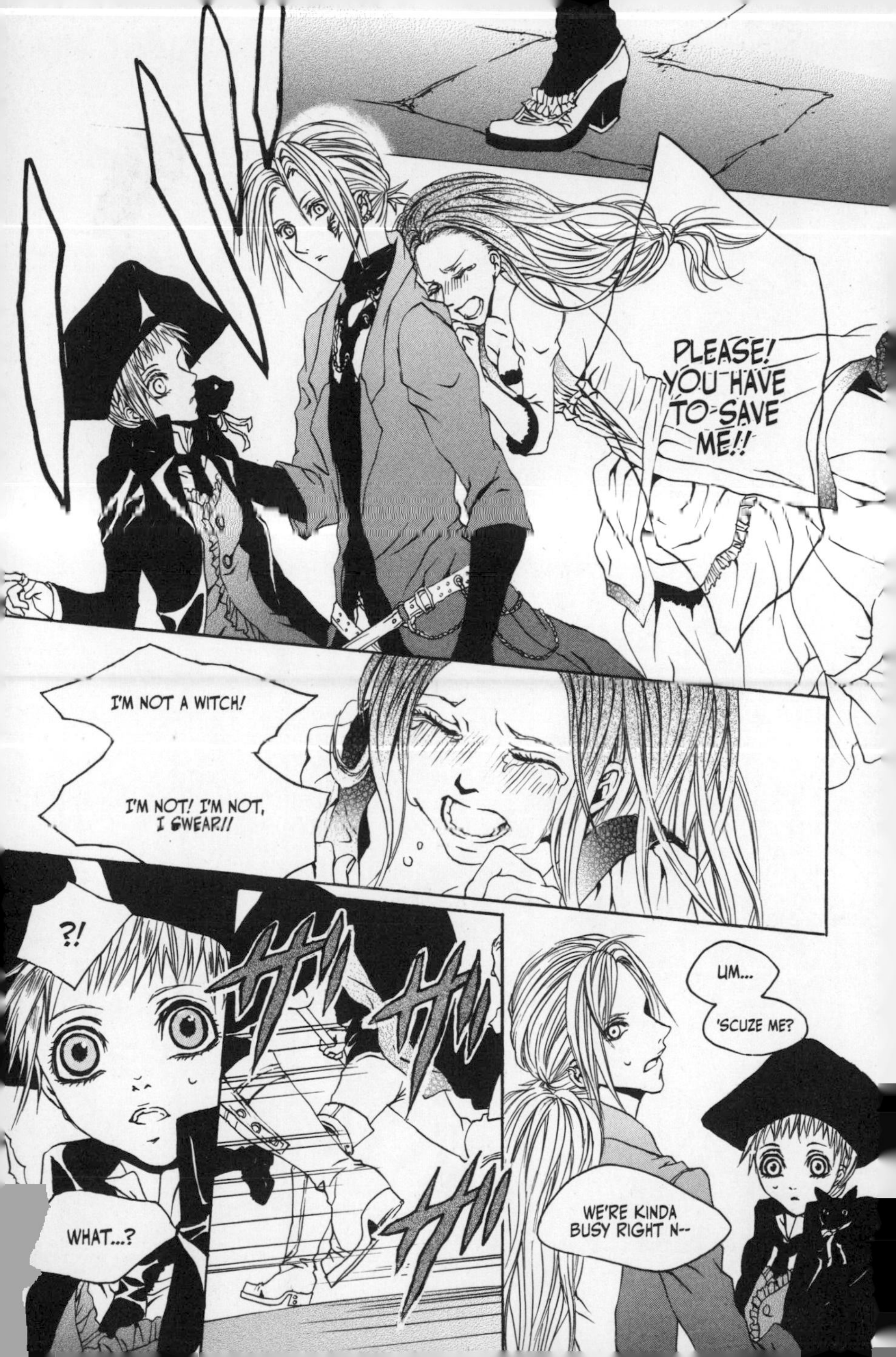
PLEASE! YOU HAVE TO SAVE ME!!
I'M NOT A WITCH!
I'M NOT! I'M NOT, I SWEAR!!
UM...
'SCUZE ME?
WE'RE KINDA BUSY RIGHT N--
?!
WHAT...?

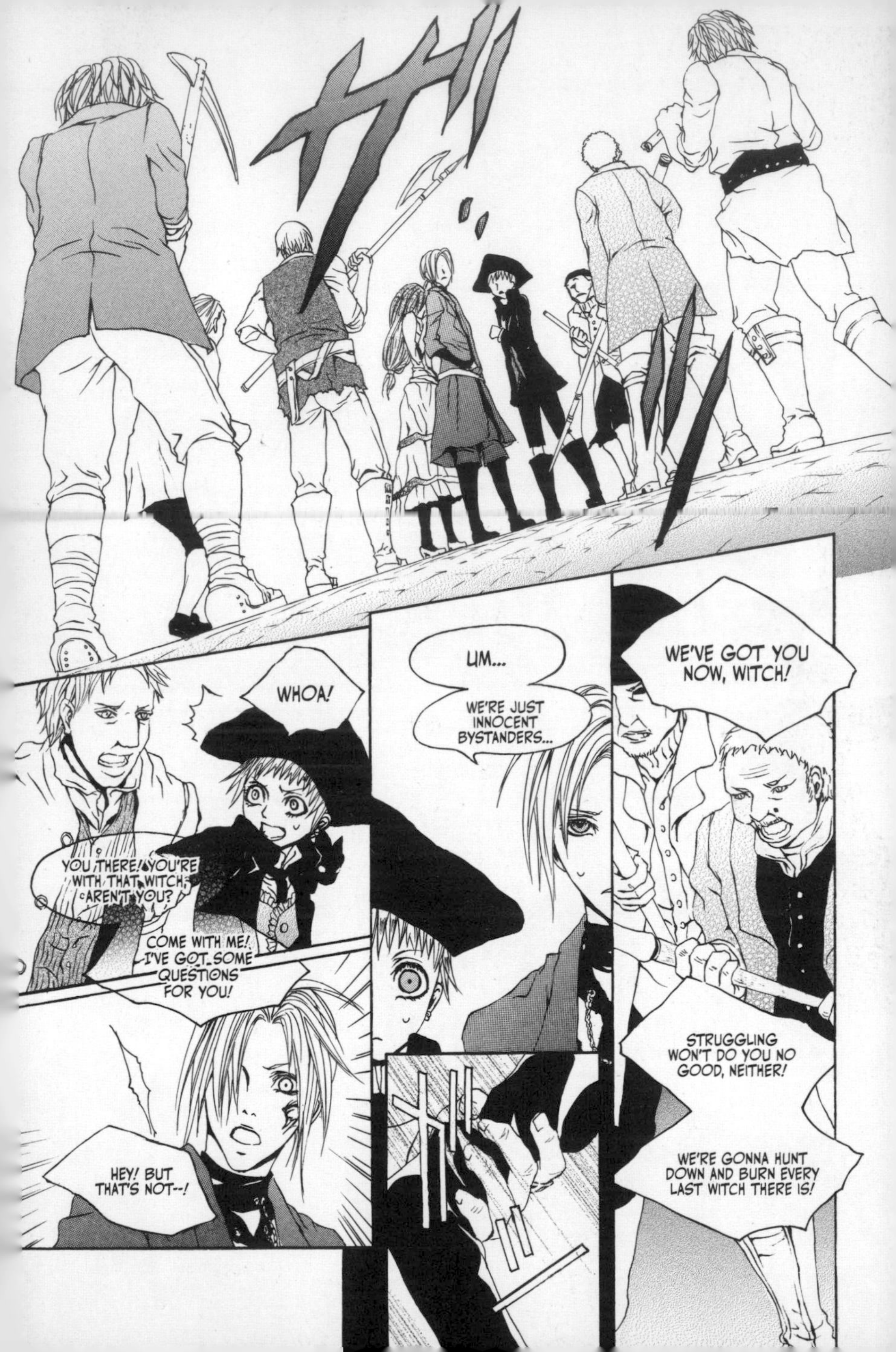

WE'VE GOT YOU NOW, WITCH!
STRUGGLING WON'T DO YOU NO GOOD, NEITHER!
WE'RE GONNA HUNT DOWN AND BURN EVERY LAST WITCH THERE IS!
UM...
WE'RE JUST INNOCENT BYSTANDERS...
WHOA!
YOU THERE! YOU'RE WITH THAT WITCH, AREN'T YOU?
COME WITH ME! I'VE GOT SOME QUESTIONS FOR YOU!
HEY! BUT THAT'S NOT--!

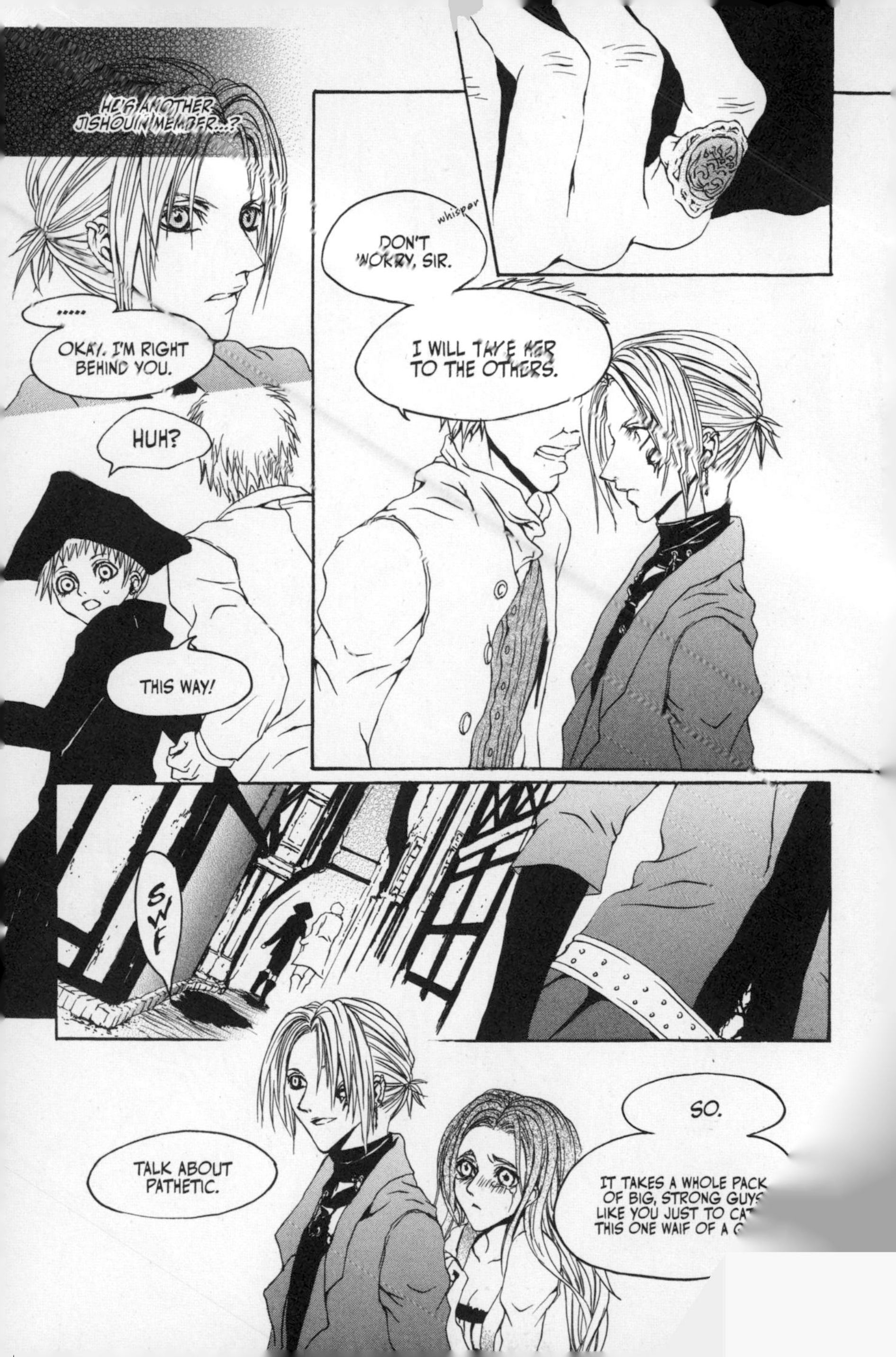
whisper
DON'T WORRY, SIR.
I WILL TAKE HER TO THE OTHERS.
HE'S ANOTHER JISHOUIN MEMBER...?
......
OKAY. I'M RIGHT BEHIND YOU.
HUH?
THIS WAY!
SWF
SO.
IT TAKES A WHOLE PACK OF BIG, STRONG GUYS LIKE YOU JUST TO CAT THIS ONE WAIF OF A G
TALK ABOUT PATHETIC.

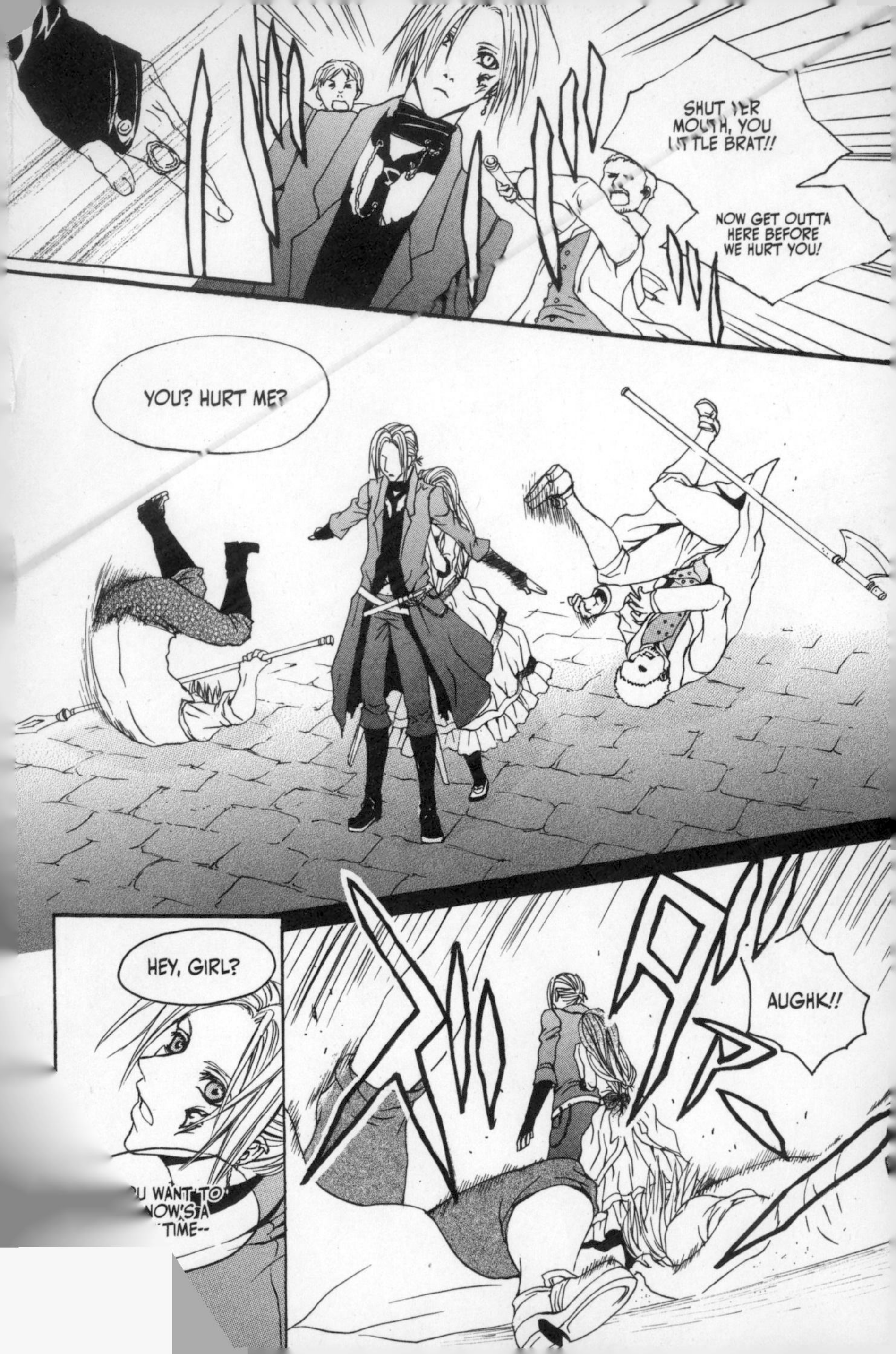
SHUT YER MOUTH, YOU LITTLE BRAT!!
NOW GET OUTTA HERE BEFORE WE HURT YOU!
YOU? HURT ME?
AUGHK!!
HEY, GIRL?
U WANT TO NOW'S A TIME--

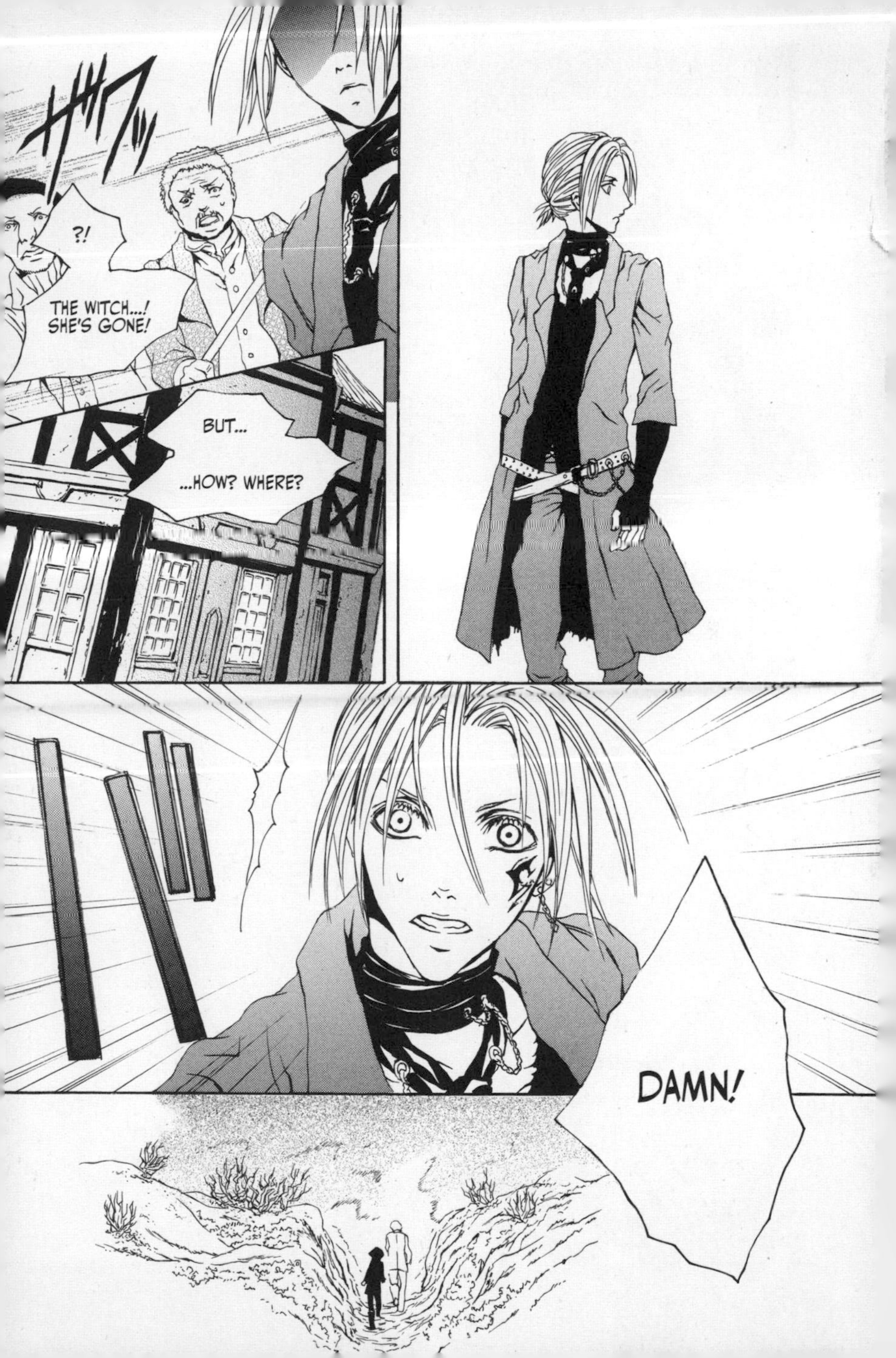
?!
THE WITCH...! SHE'S GONE!
BUT...
...HOW? WHERE?
DAMN!

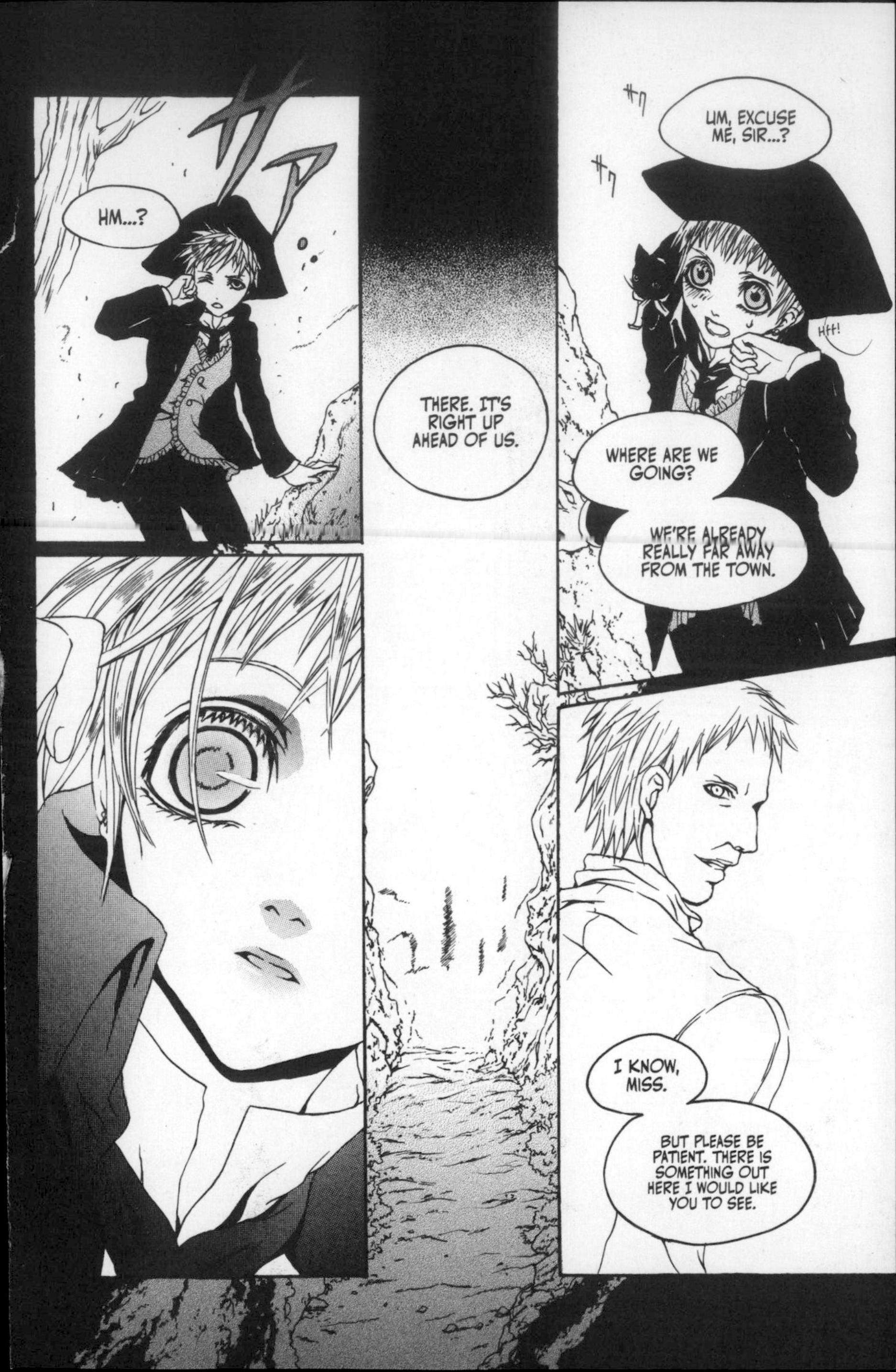
UM, EXCUSE ME, SIR...?
Hff!
WHERE ARE WE GOING?
WE'RE ALREADY REALLY FAR AWAY FROM THE TOWN.
I KNOW, MISS.
BUT PLEASE BE PATIENT. THERE IS SOMETHING OUT HERE I WOULD LIKE YOU TO SEE.
THERE. IT'S RIGHT UP AHEAD OF US.
HM...?

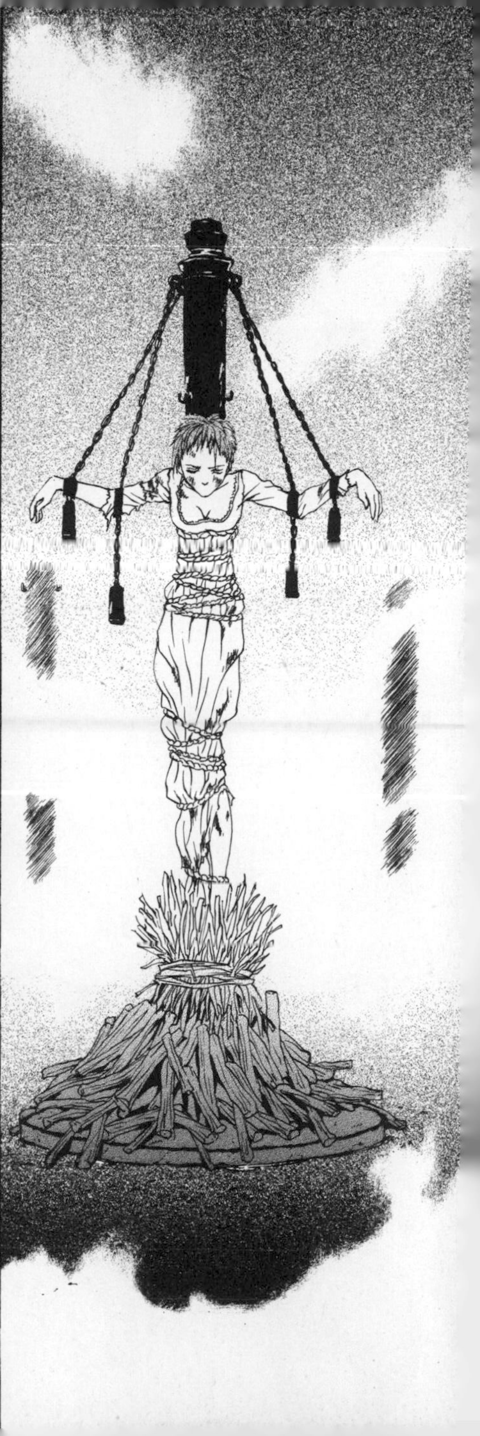

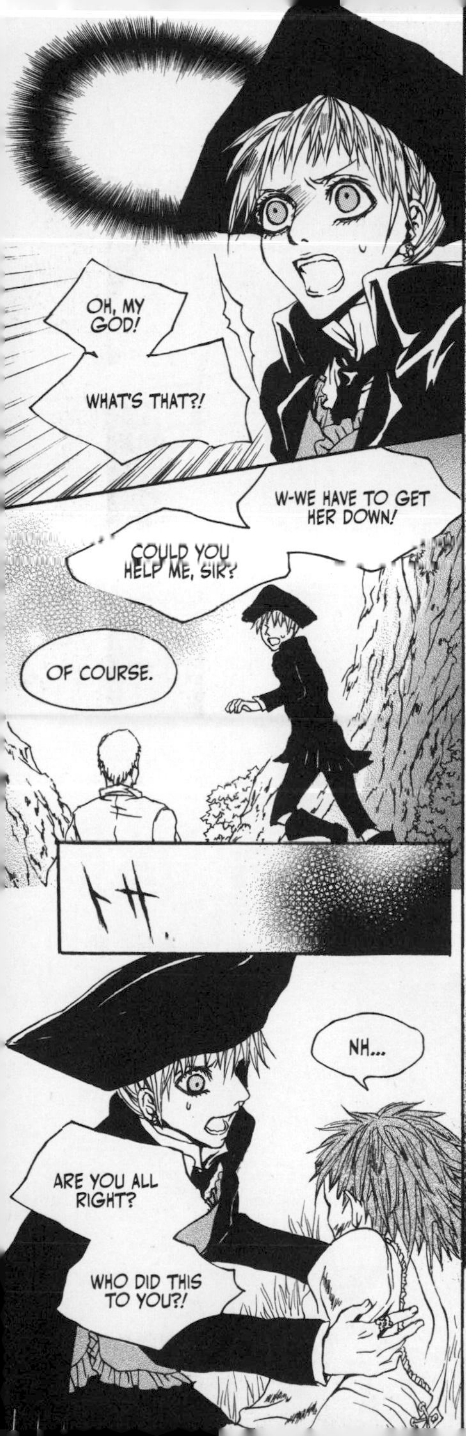
OH, MY GOD!
WHAT'S THAT?!
W-WE HAVE TO GET HER DOWN!
COULD YOU HELP ME, SIR?
OF COURSE.
NH...
ARE YOU ALL RIGHT?
WHO DID THIS TO YOU?!

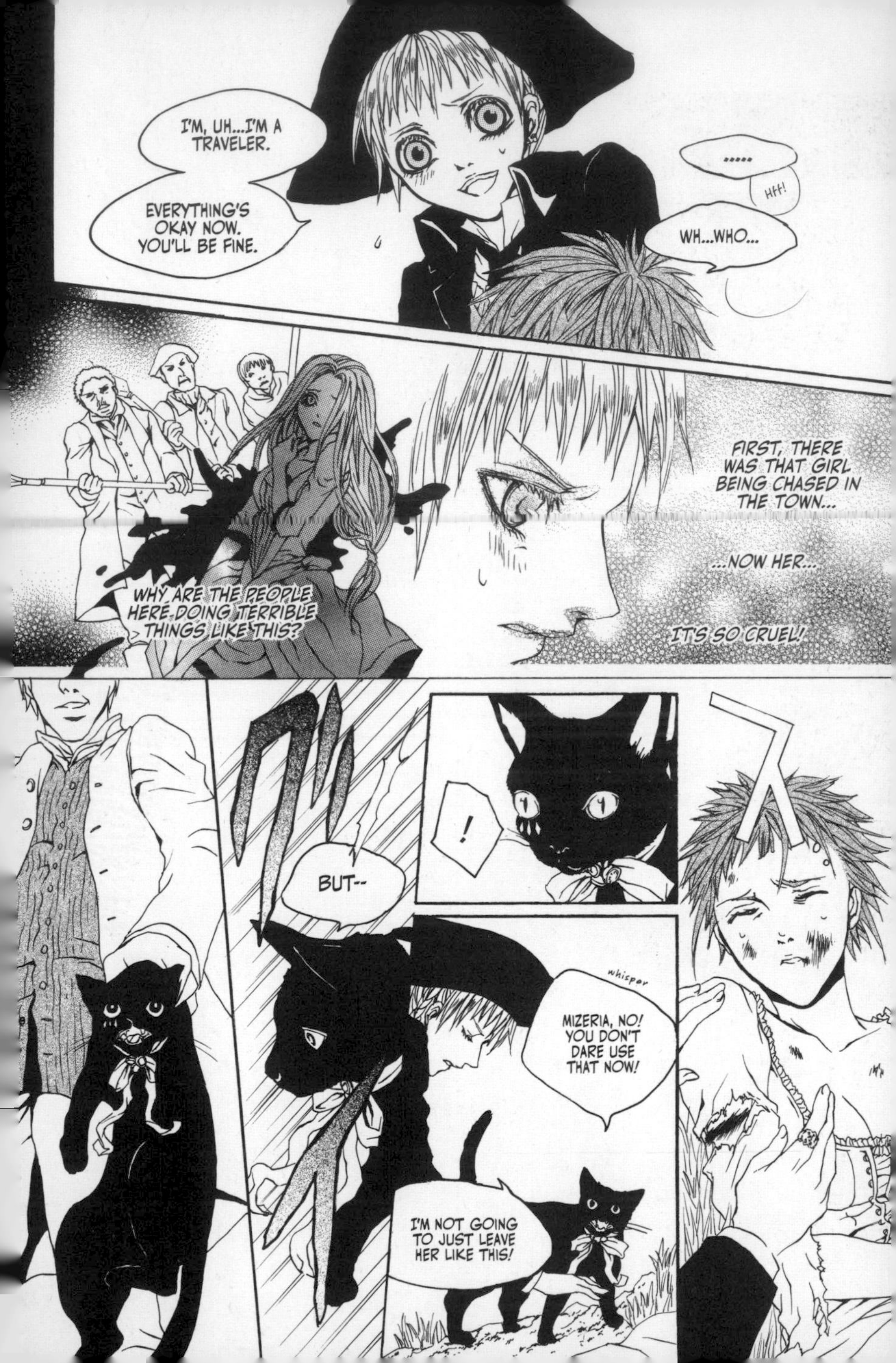
......
Hff!
WH...WHO...
I'M, UH...I'M A TRAVELER.
EVERYTHING'S OKAY NOW. YOU'LL BE FINE.
FIRST, THERE WAS THAT GIRL BEING CHASED IN THE TOWN...
...NOW HER...
IT'S SO CRUEL!
WHY ARE THE PEOPLE HERE DOING TERRIBLE THINGS LIKE THIS?
!
whisper
MIZERIA, NO! YOU DON'T DARE USE THAT NOW!
I'M NOT GOING TO JUST LEAVE HER LIKE THIS!
BUT--

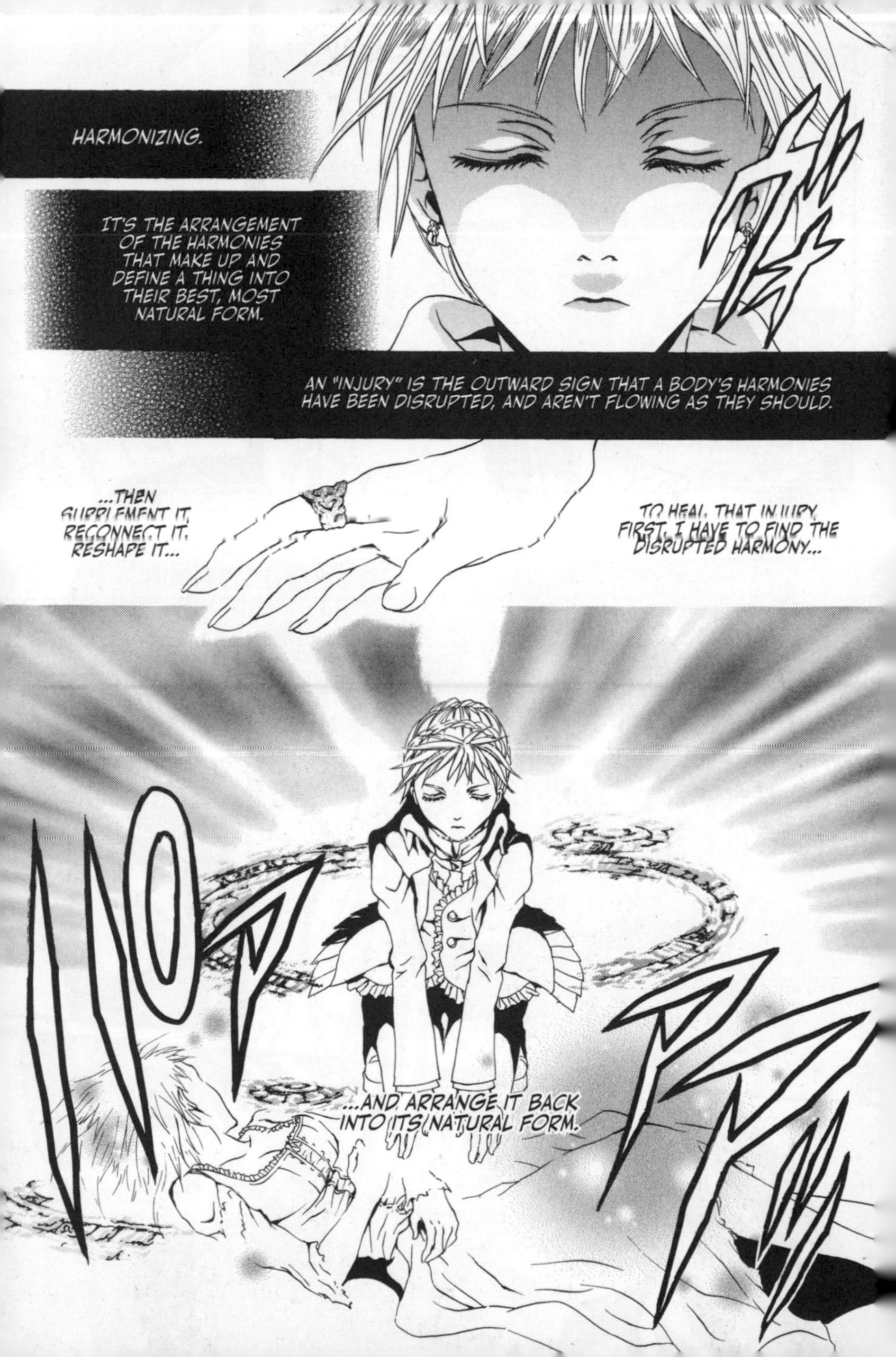
HARMONIZING.
IT'S THE ARRANGEMENT OF THE HARMONIES THAT MAKE UP AND DEFINE A THING INTO THEIR BEST, MOST NATURAL FORM.
AN "INJURY" IS THE OUTWARD SIGN THAT A BODY'S HARMONIES HAVE BEEN DISRUPTED, AND AREN'T FLOWING AS THEY SHOULD.
TO HEAL THAT INJURY, FIRST, I HAVE TO FIND THE DISRUPTED HARMONY...
...THEN SUPPLEMENT IT, RECONNECT IT, RESHAPE IT...
...AND ARRANGE IT BACK INTO ITS NATURAL FORM.

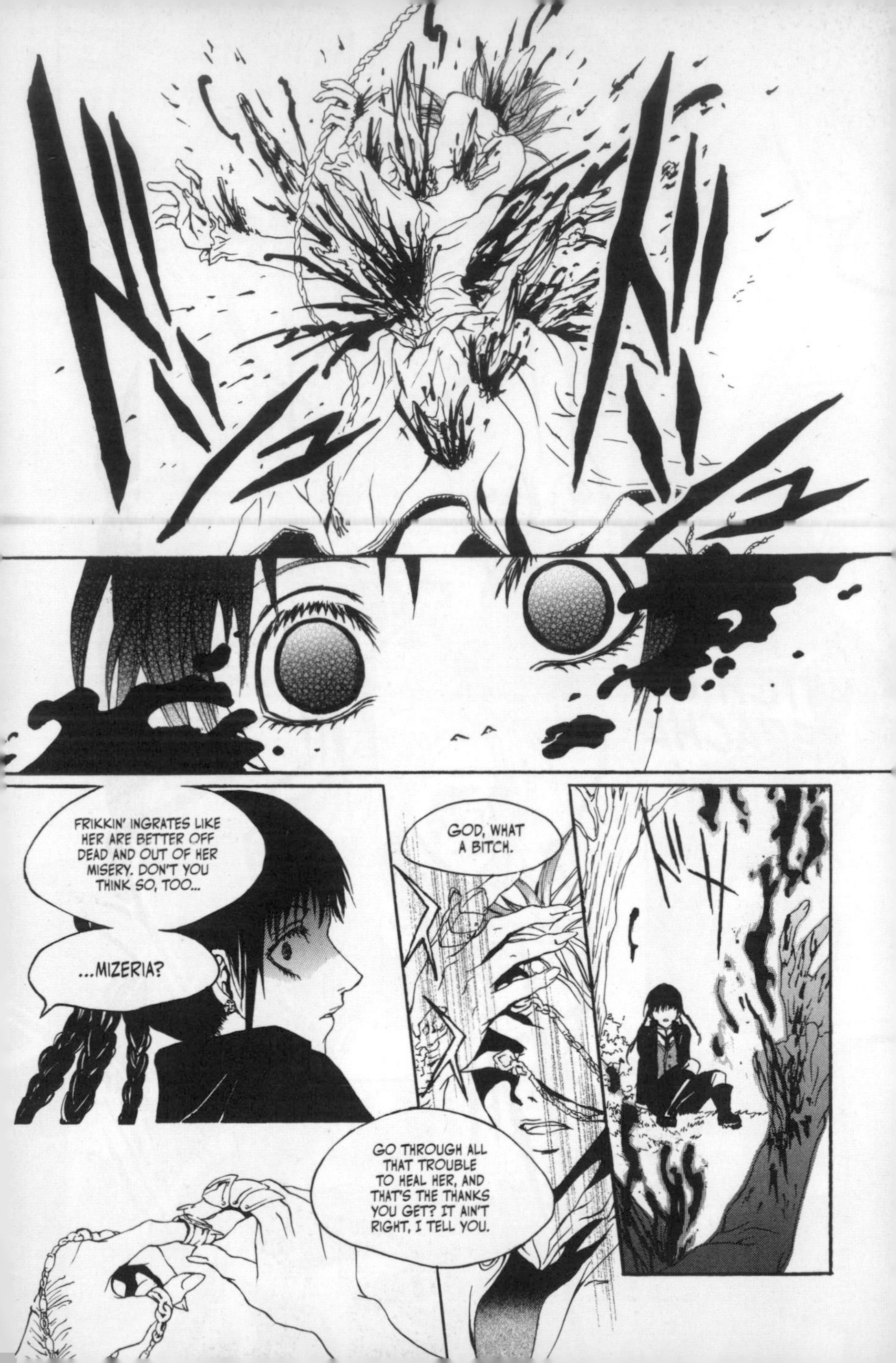
GOD, WHAT A BITCH.
GO THROUGH ALL THAT TROUBLE TO HEAL HER, AND THAT'S THE THANKS YOU GET? IT AIN'T RIGHT, I TELL YOU.
FRIKKIN' INGRATES LIKE HER ARE BETTER OFF DEAD AND OUT OF HER MISERY. DON'T YOU THINK SO, TOO...
...MIZERIA?

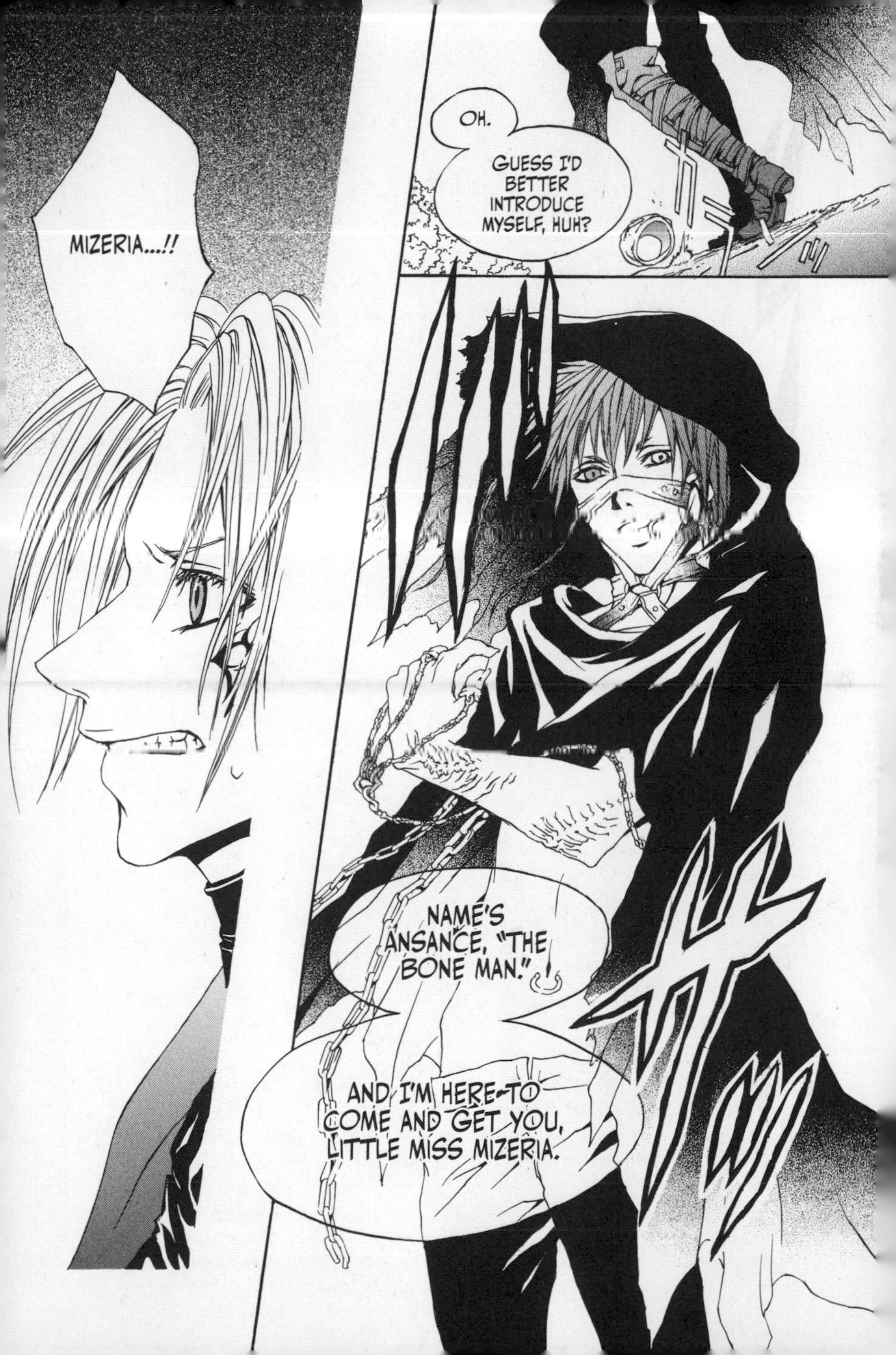
OH.
GUESS I'D BETTER INTRODUCE MYSELF, HUH?
NAME'S ANSANCE, "THE BONE MAN."
AND I'M HERE TO COME AND GET YOU, LITTLE MISS MIZERIA.
MIZERIA...!!

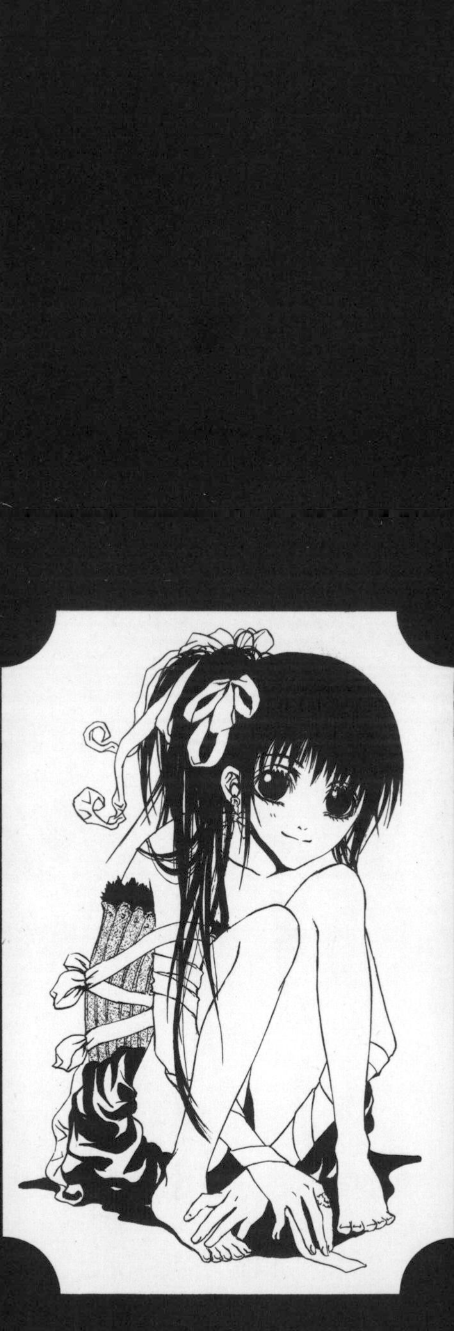

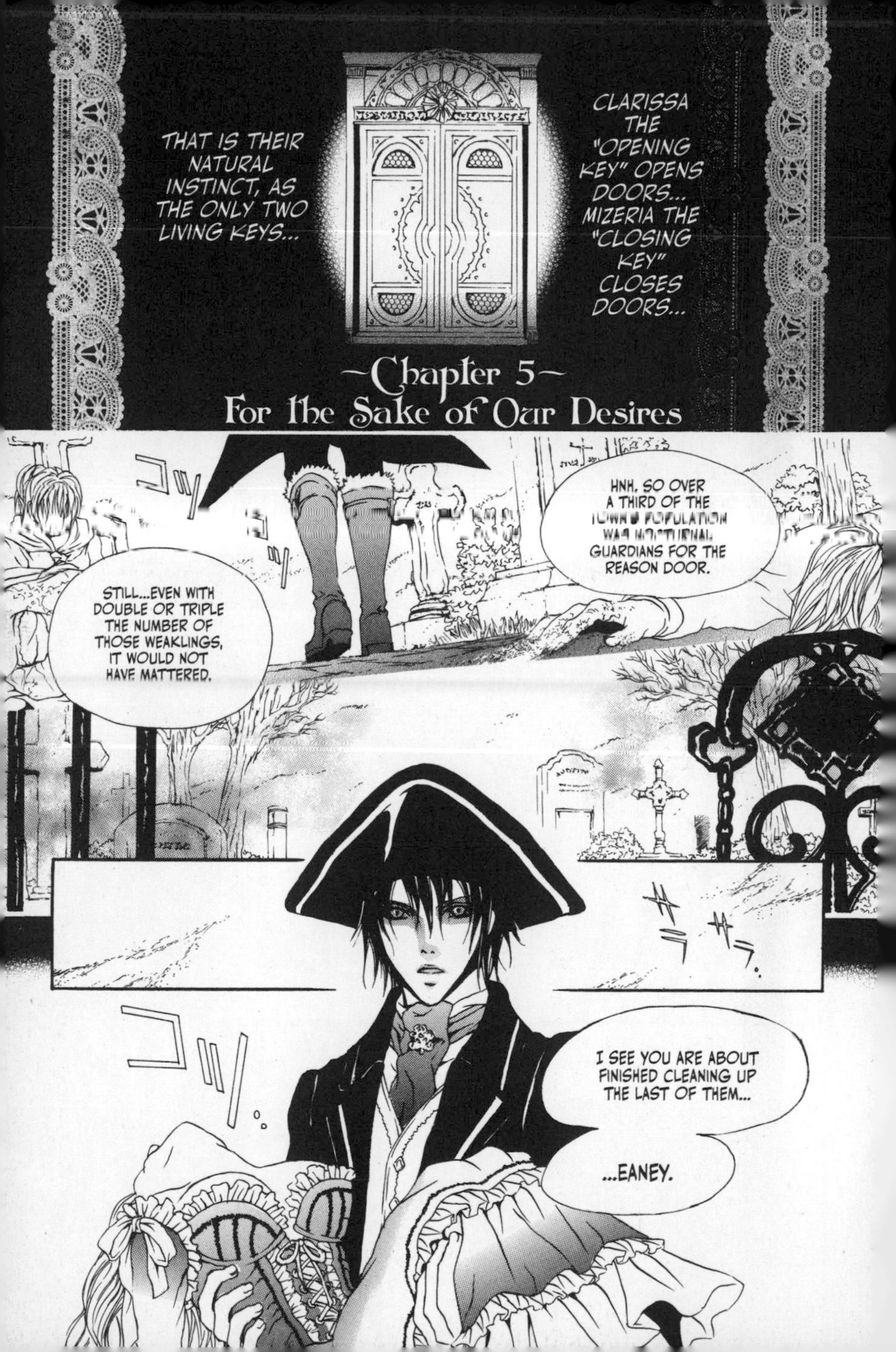
CLARISSA THE "OPENING KEY" OPENS DOORS... MIZERIA THE "CLOSING KEY" CLOSES DOORS...
THAT IS THEIR NATURAL INSTINCT, AS THE ONLY TWO LIVING KEYS...
~Chapter 5~
For the Sake of Our Desires
HNH. SO OVER A THIRD OF THE TOWN'S POPULATION WAS NOCTURNAL GUARDIANS FOR THE REASON DOOR.
STILL...EVEN WITH DOUBLE OR TRIPLE THE NUMBER OF THOSE WEAKLINGS, IT WOULD NOT HAVE MATTERED.
I SEE YOU ARE ABOUT FINISHED CLEANING UP THE LAST OF THEM...
...EANEY.

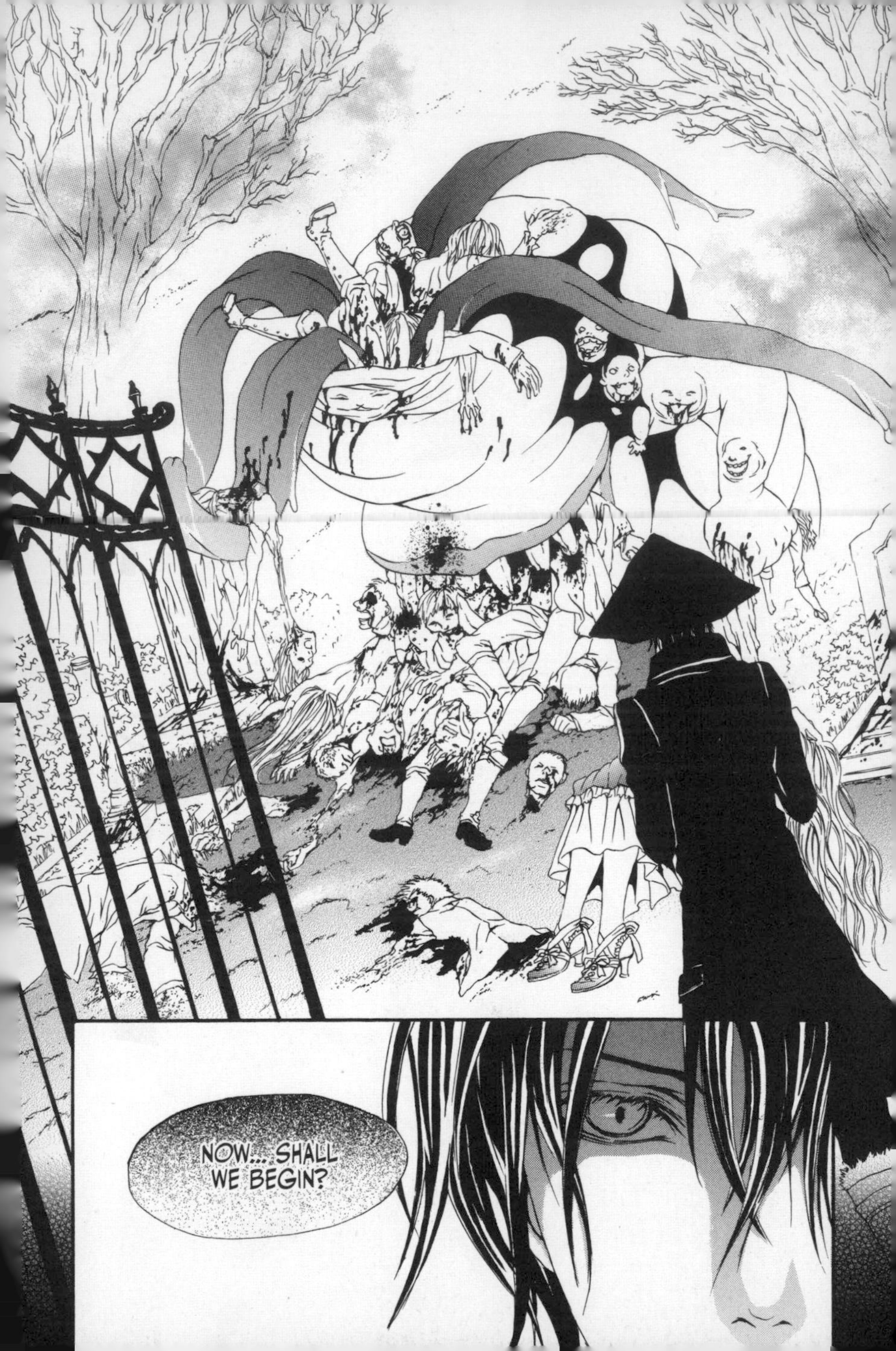
NOW... SHALL WE BEGIN?

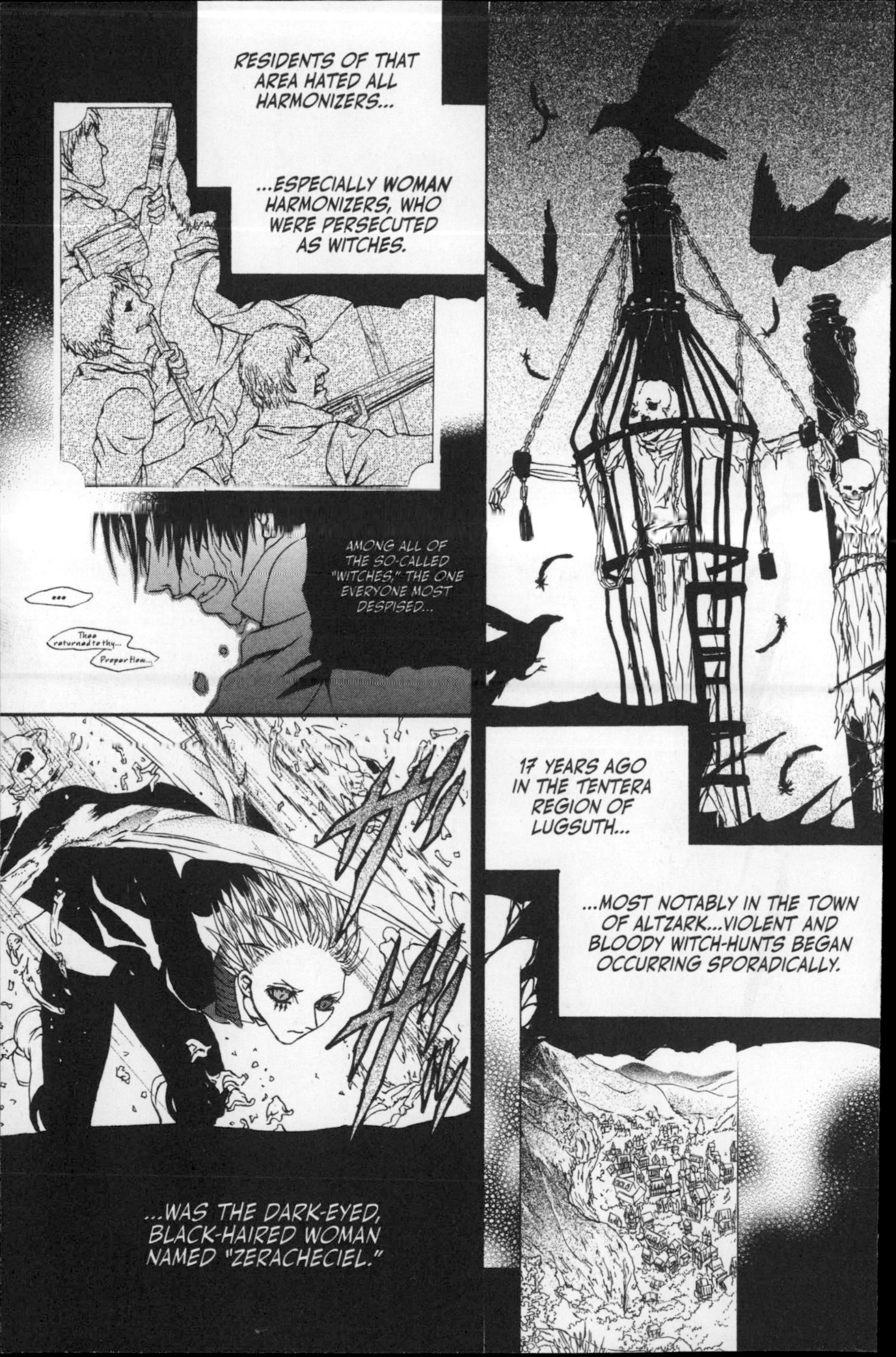

17 YEARS AGO IN THE TENTERA REGION OF LUGSUTH...
...MOST NOTABLY IN THE TOWN OF ALTZARK...VIOLENT AND BLOODY WITCH-HUNTS BEGAN OCCURRING SPORADICALLY.
RESIDENTS OF THAT AREA HATED ALL HARMONIZERS...
...ESPECIALLY WOMAN HARMONIZERS, WHO WERE PERSECUTED AS WITCHES.
AMONG ALL OF THE SO-CALLED "WITCHES," THE ONE EVERYONE MOST DESPISED...
...
Thee returned to thy...
Proper Flow...
...WAS THE DARK-EYED, BLACK-HAIRED WOMAN NAMED "ZERACHECIEL."

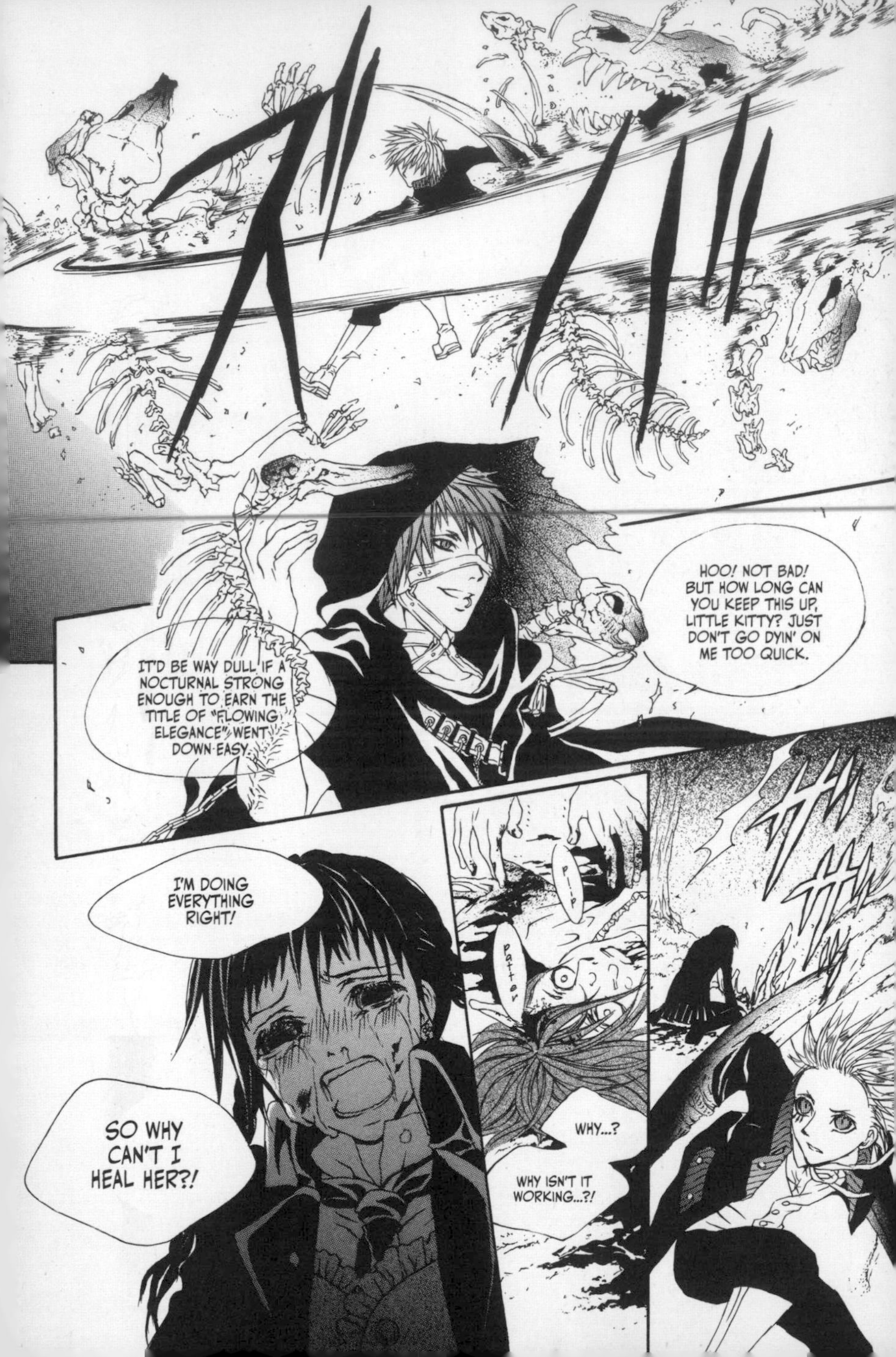
HOO! NOT BAD! BUT HOW LONG CAN YOU KEEP THIS UP, LITTLE KITTY? JUST DON'T GO DYIN' ON ME TOO QUICK.
IT'D BE WAY DULL IF A NOCTURNAL STRONG ENOUGH TO EARN THE TITLE OF "FLOWING ELEGANCE" WENT DOWN EASY.
plip
patter
WHY...?
WHY ISN'T IT WORKING...?!
I'M DOING EVERYTHING RIGHT!
SO WHY CAN'T I HEAL HER?!

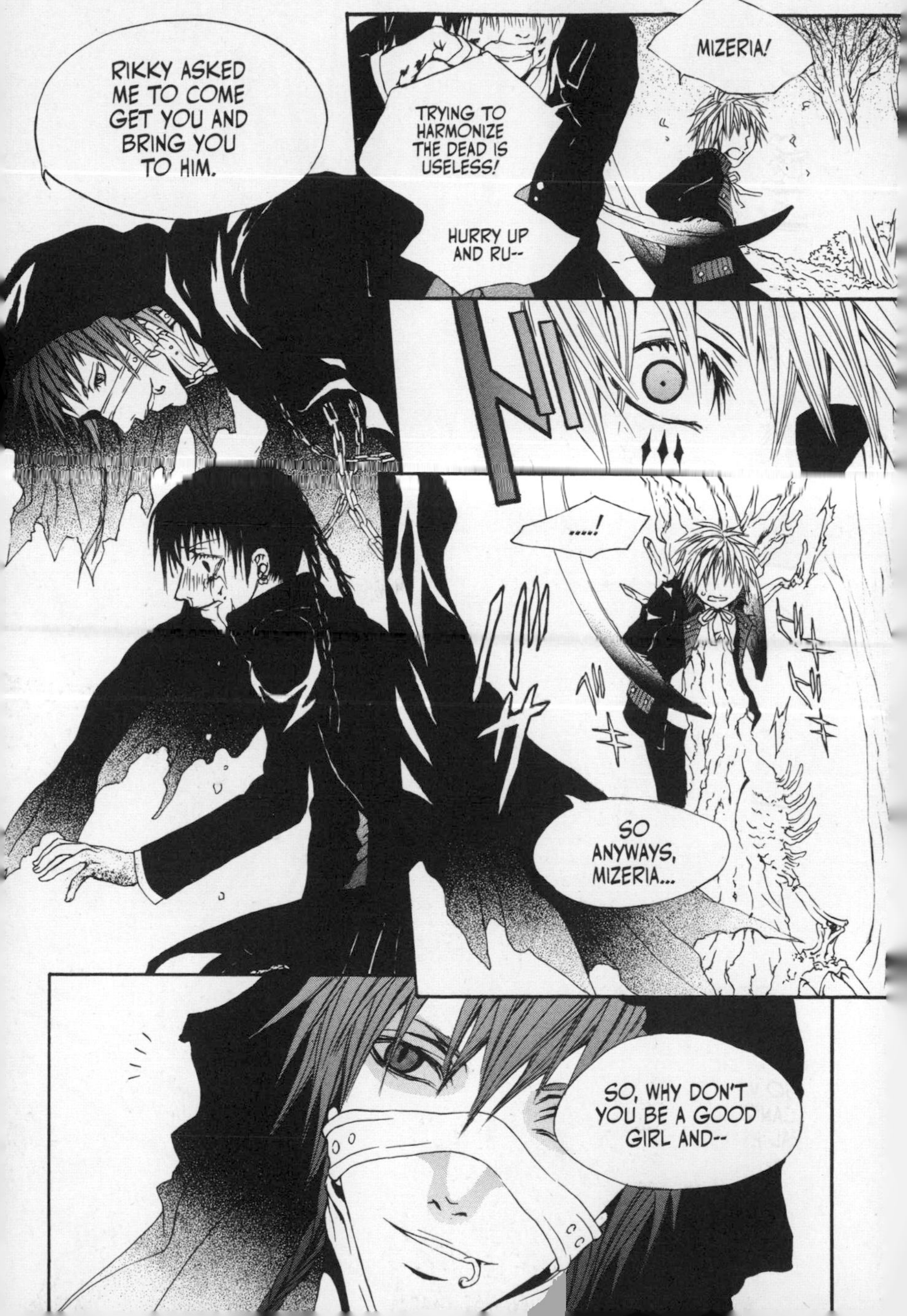
MIZERIA!
TRYING TO HARMONIZE THE DEAD IS USELESS!
HURRY UP AND RU--
HII
RIKKY ASKED ME TO COME GET YOU AND BRING YOU TO HIM.
.....!
SO ANYWAYS, MIZERIA...
SO, WHY DON'T YOU BE A GOOD GIRL AND--

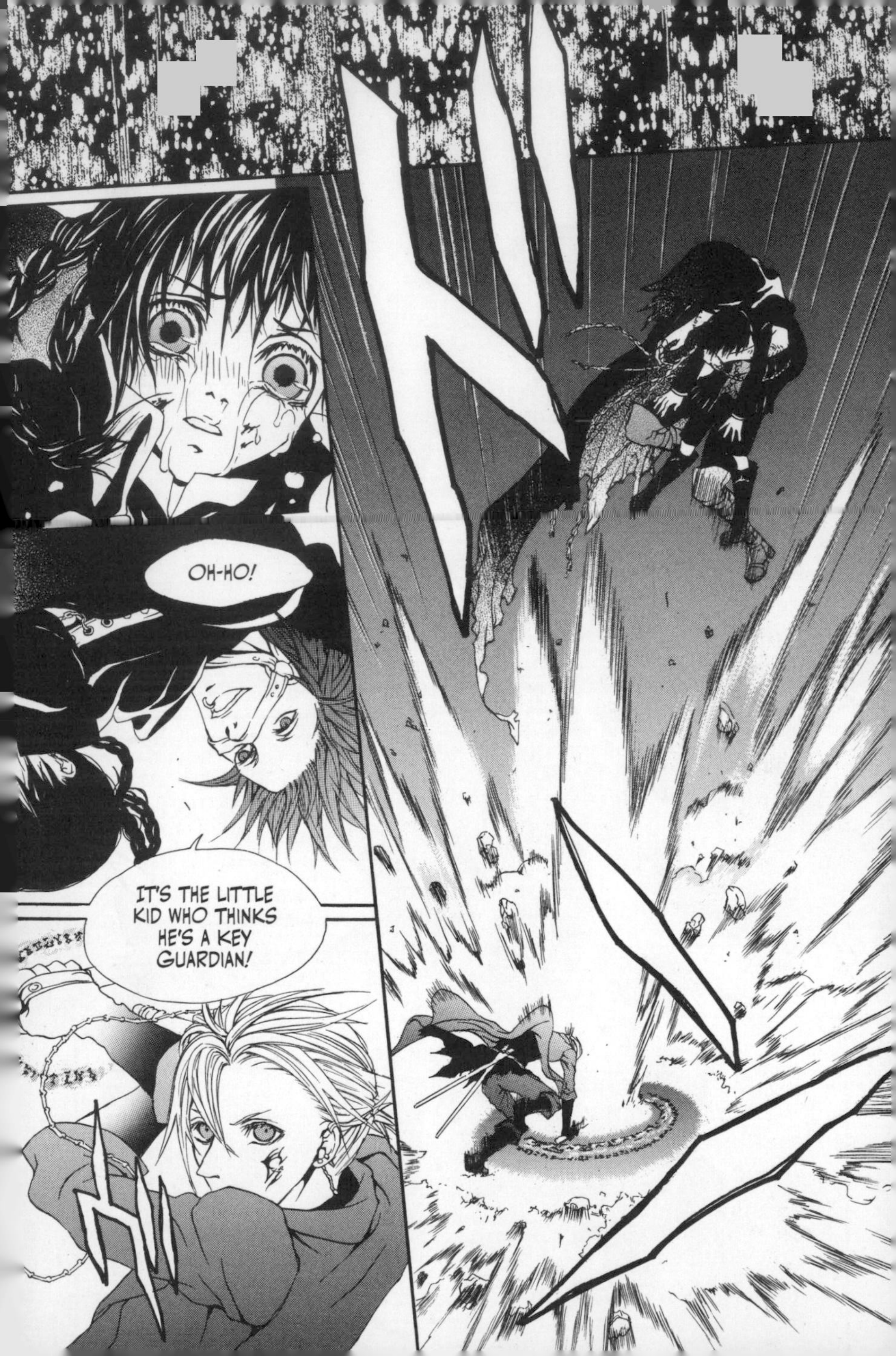
OH-HO!
IT'S THE LITTLE KID WHO THINKS HE'S A KEY GUARDIAN!

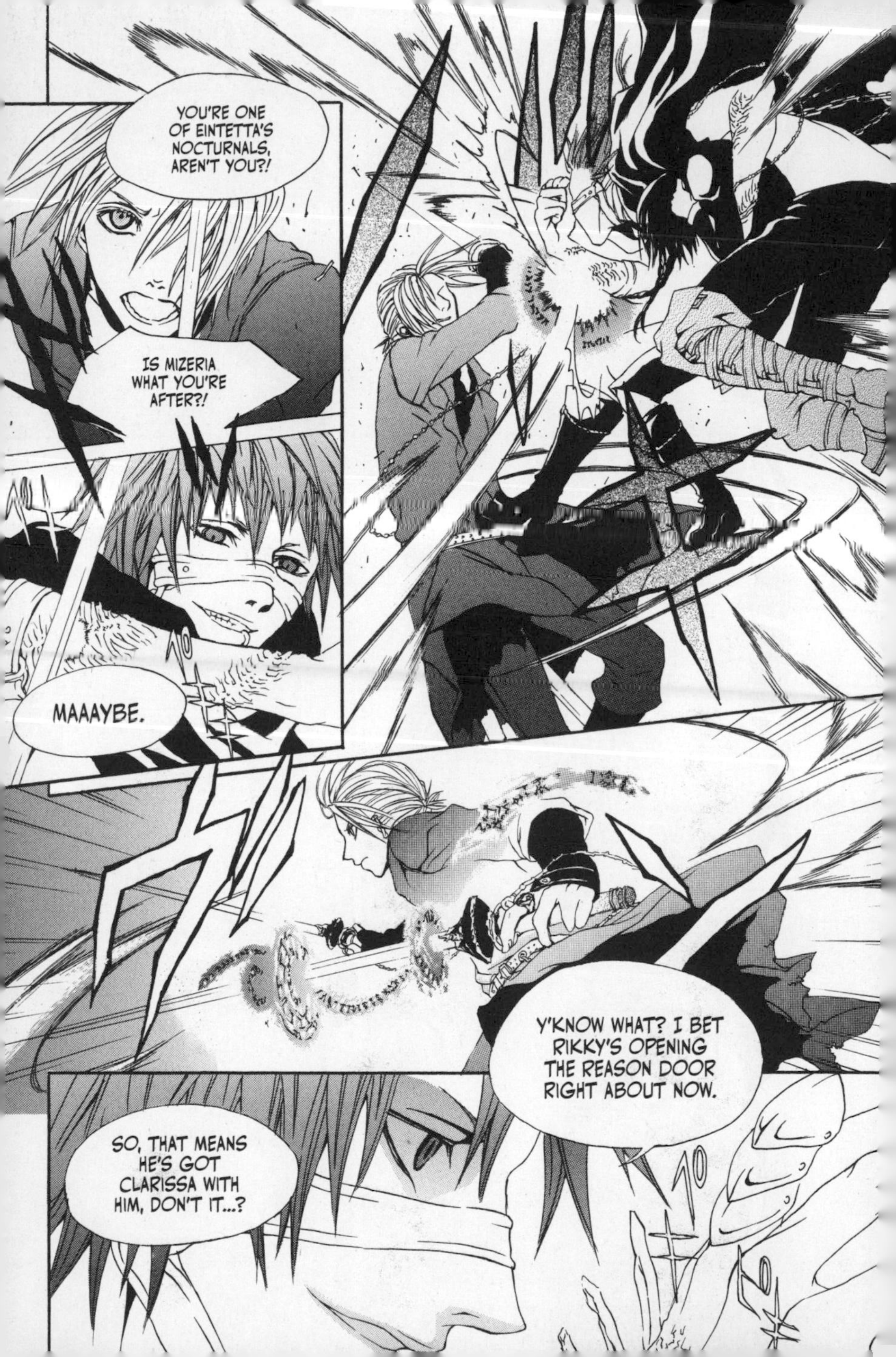
YOU'RE ONE OF EINTETTA'S NOCTURNALS, AREN'T YOU?!
IS MIZERIA WHAT YOU'RE AFTER?!
MAAAYBE.
Y'KNOW WHAT? I BET RIKKY'S OPENING THE REASON DOOR RIGHT ABOUT NOW.
SO, THAT MEANS HE'S GOT CLARISSA WITH HIM, DON'T IT...?

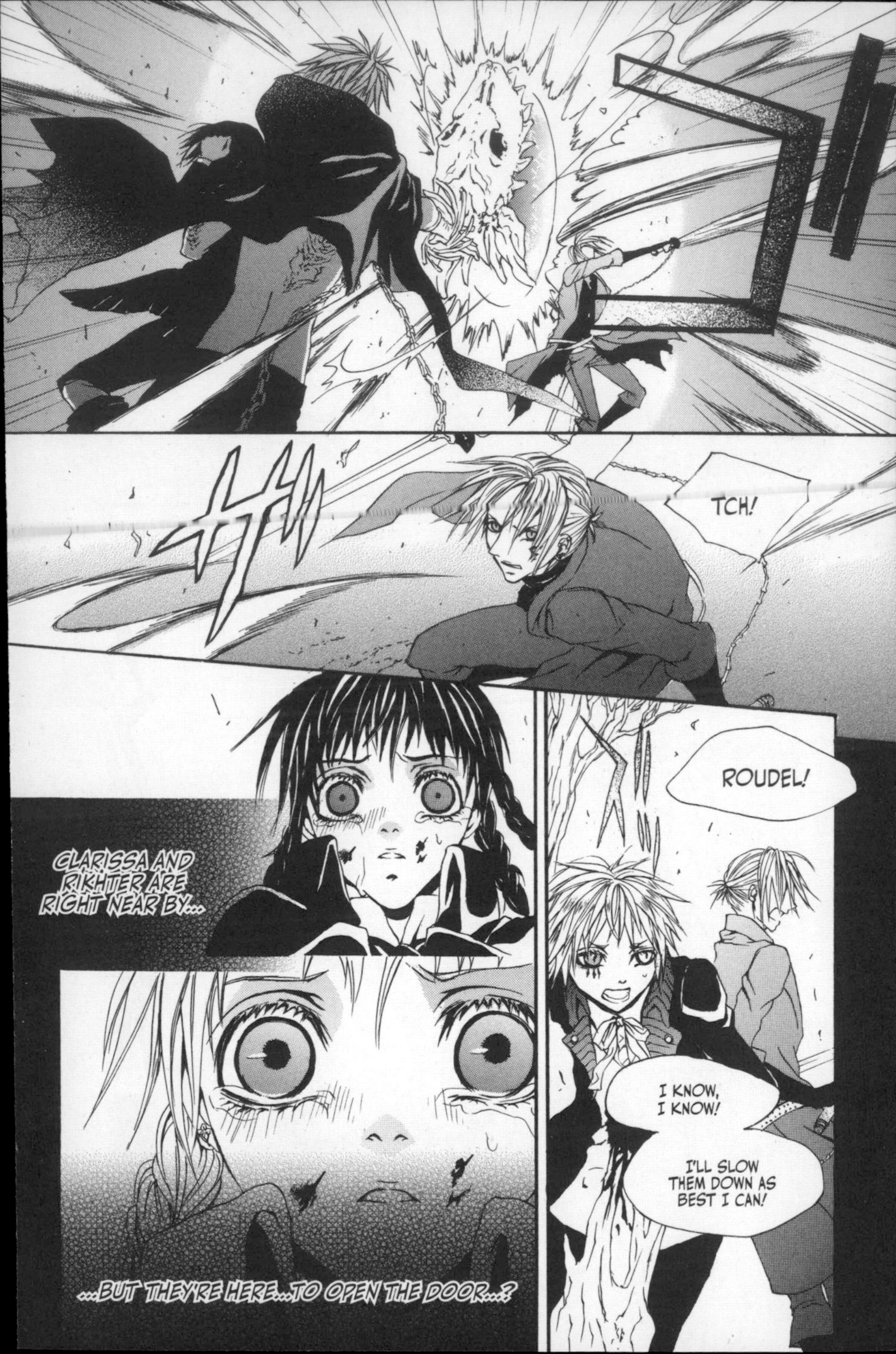
TCH!
ROUDEL!
I KNOW, I KNOW!
I'LL SLOW THEM DOWN AS BEST I CAN!
CLARISSA AND RIKHTER ARE RIGHT NEAR BY...
...BUT THEY'RE HERE...TO OPEN THE DOOR...?

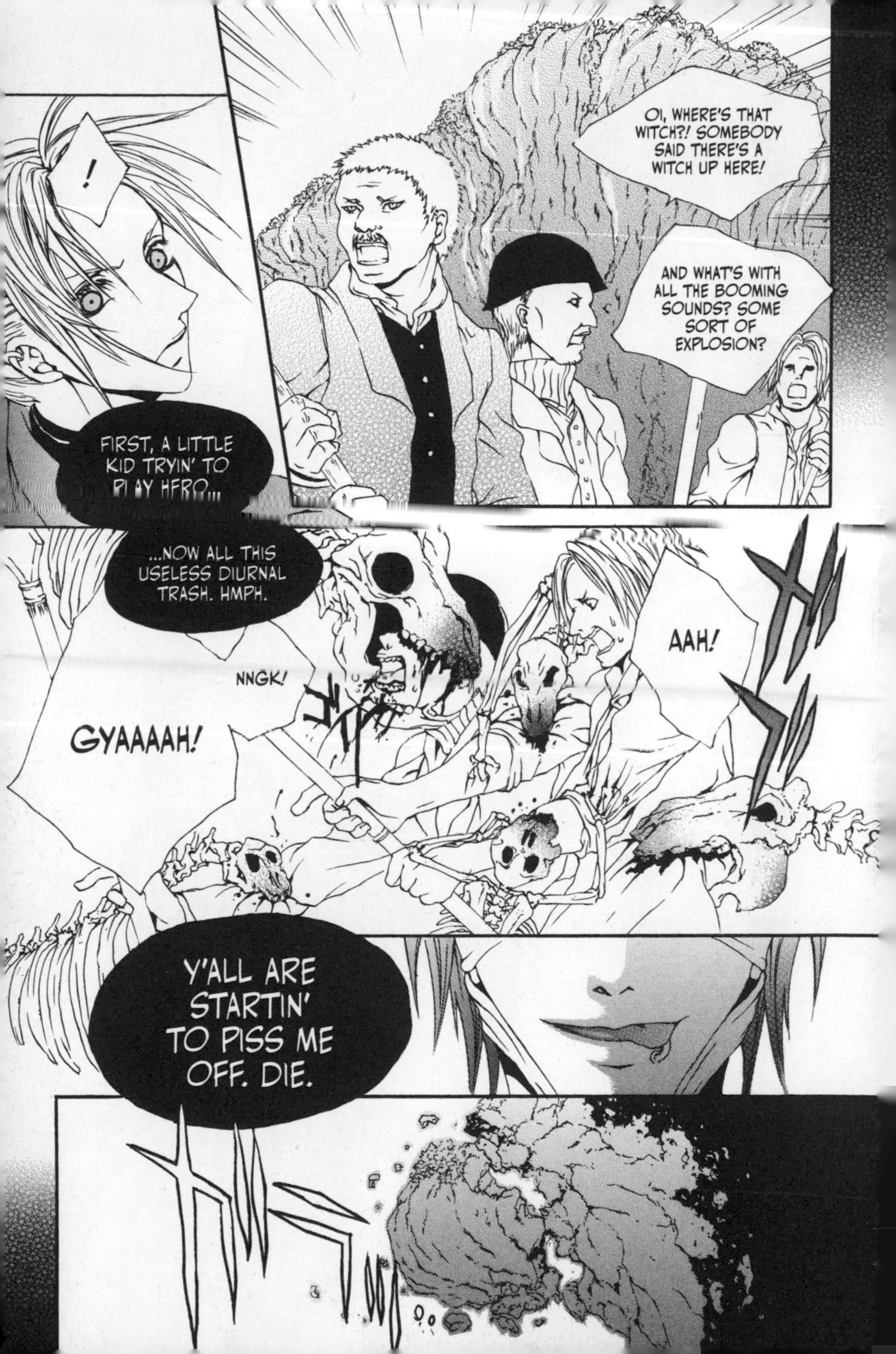
OI, WHERE'S THAT WITCH?! SOMEBODY SAID THERE'S A WITCH UP HERE!
AND WHAT'S WITH ALL THE BOOMING SOUNDS? SOME SORT OF EXPLOSION?
!
FIRST, A LITTLE KID TRYIN' TO PLAY HERO...
...NOW ALL THIS USELESS DIURNAL TRASH. HMPH.
AAH!
NNGK!
GYAAAAH!
Y'ALL ARE STARTIN' TO PISS ME OFF. DIE.

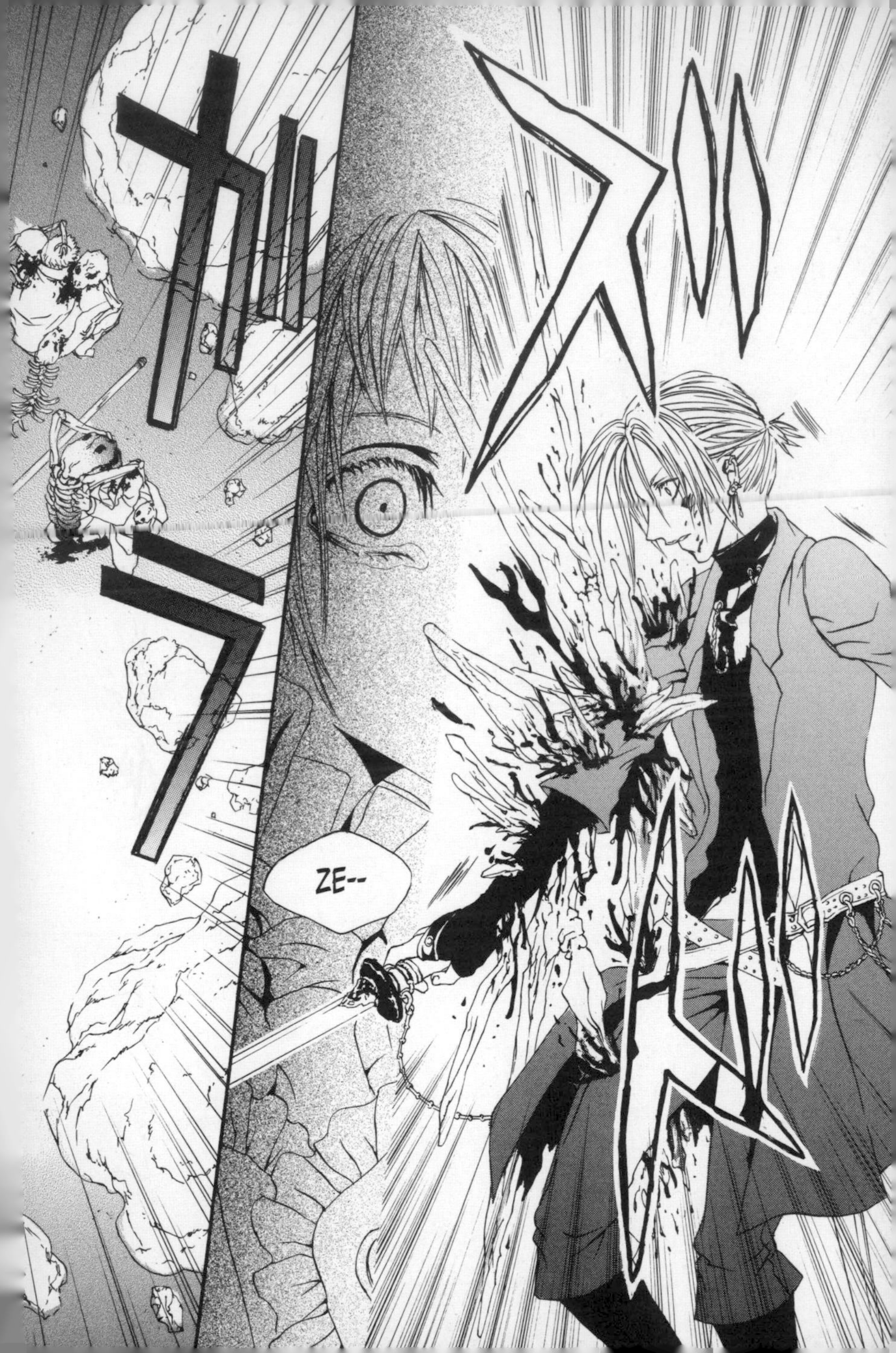
ZE--

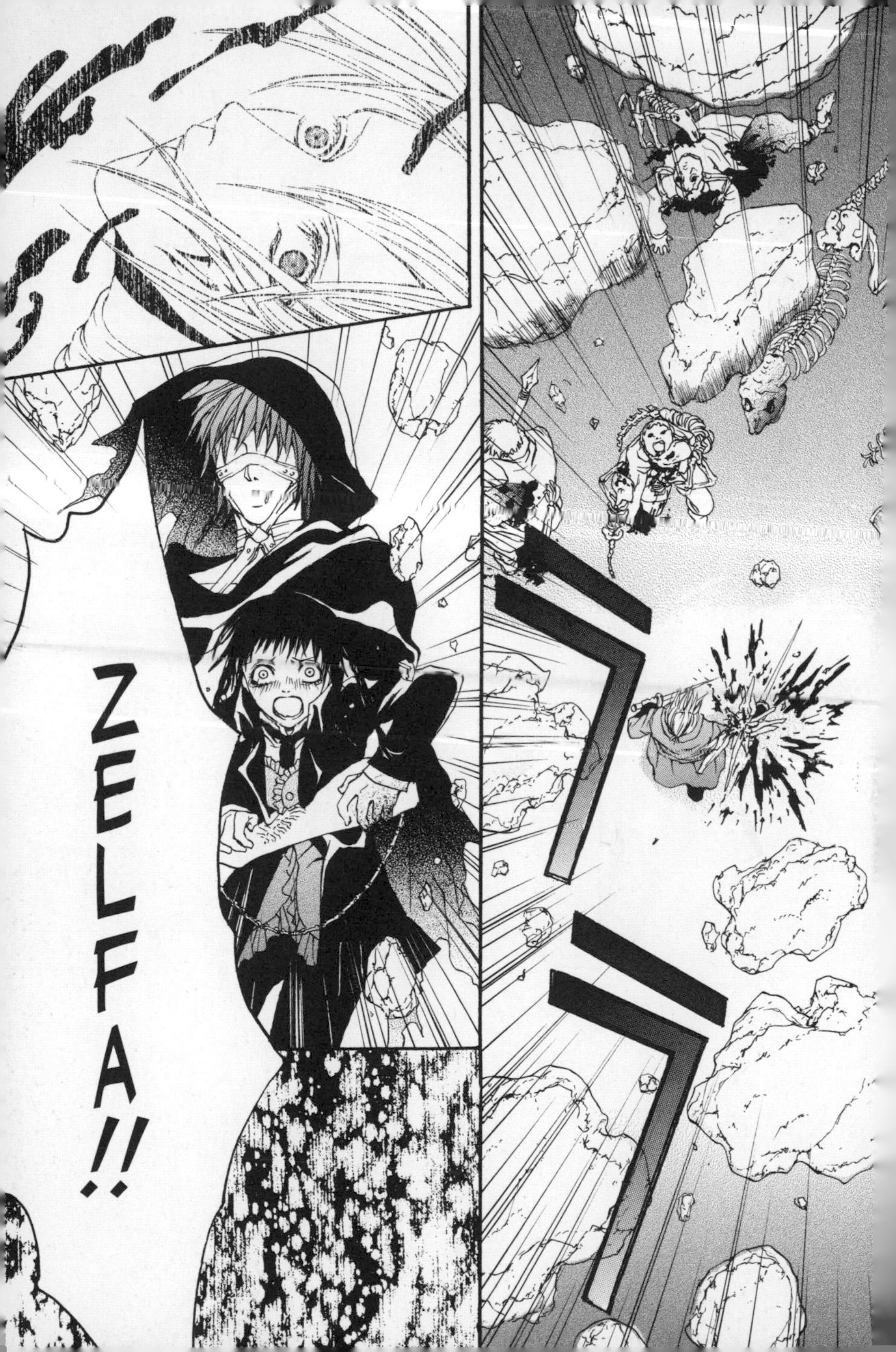
ZELFA!!

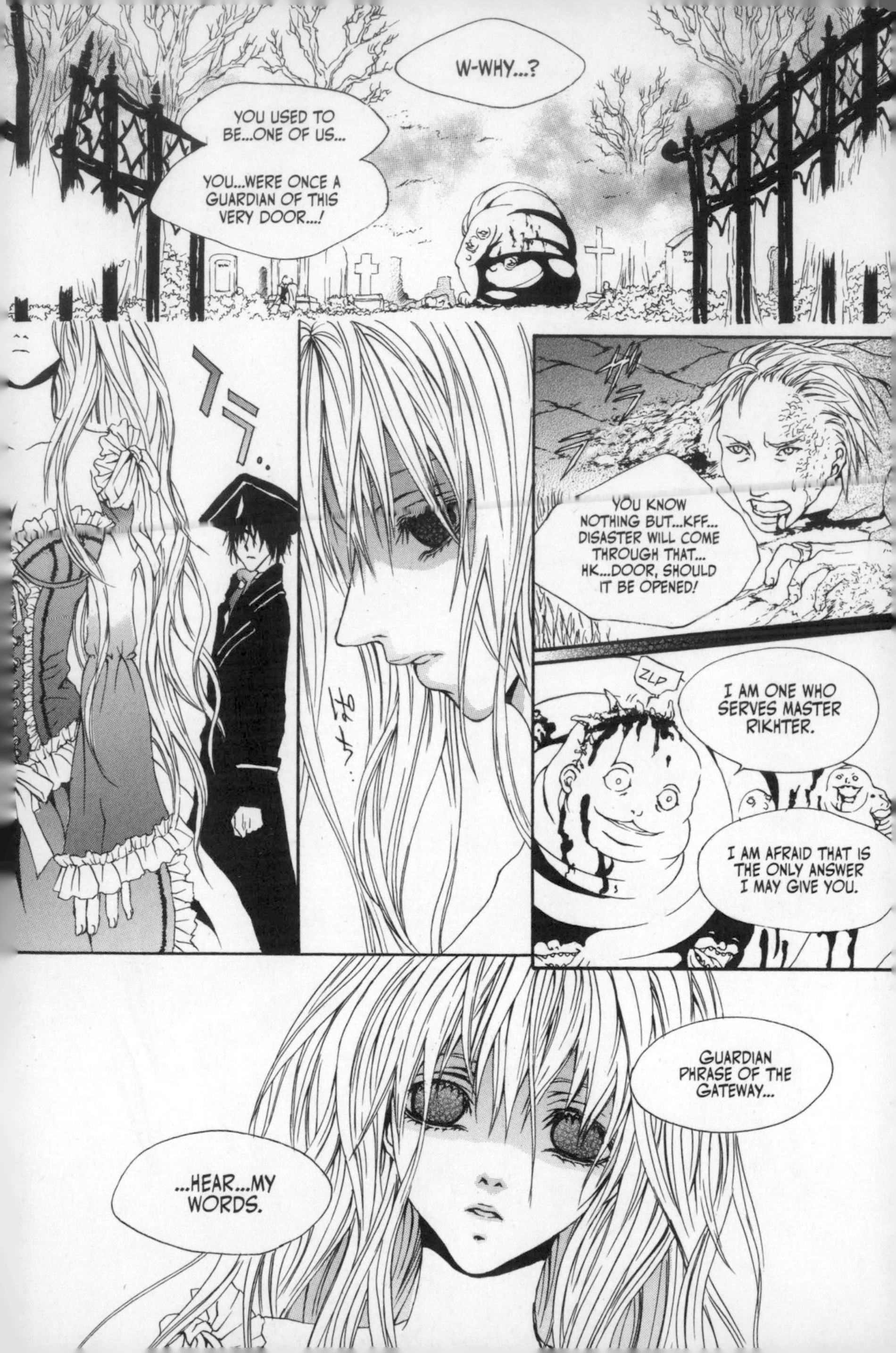
W-WHY...?
YOU USED TO BE...ONE OF US...
YOU...WERE ONCE A GUARDIAN OF THIS VERY DOOR...!
YOU KNOW NOTHING BUT...KFF... DISASTER WILL COME THROUGH THAT... HK...DOOR, SHOULD IT BE OPENED!
ZLP
I AM ONE WHO SERVES MASTER RIKHTER.
I AM AFRAID THAT IS THE ONLY ANSWER I MAY GIVE YOU.
GUARDIAN PHRASE OF THE GATEWAY...
...HEAR...MY WORDS.

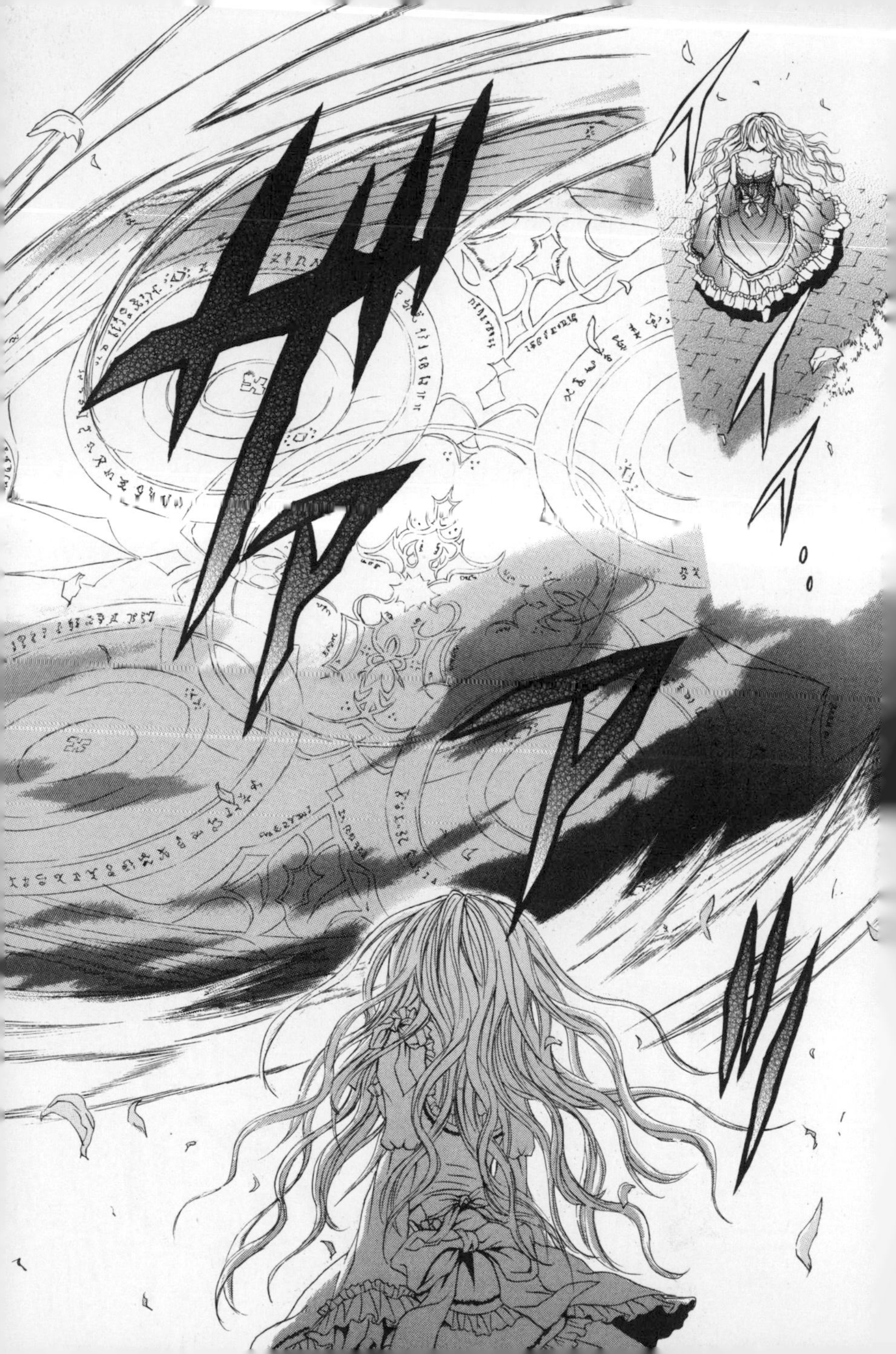

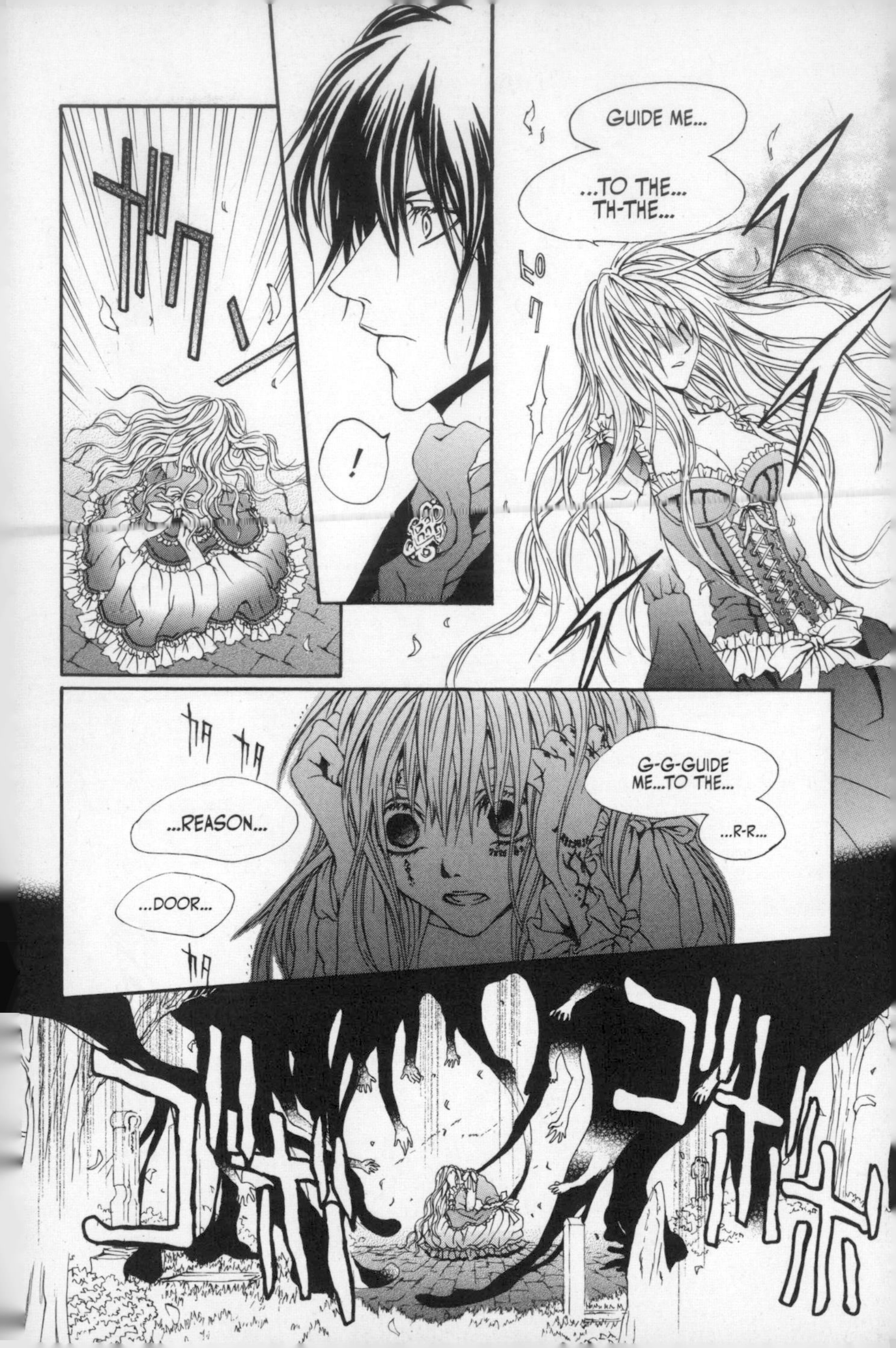
GUIDE ME...
...TO THE... TH-THE...
!
G-G-GUIDE ME...TO THE...
...R-R...
...REASON...
...DOOR...

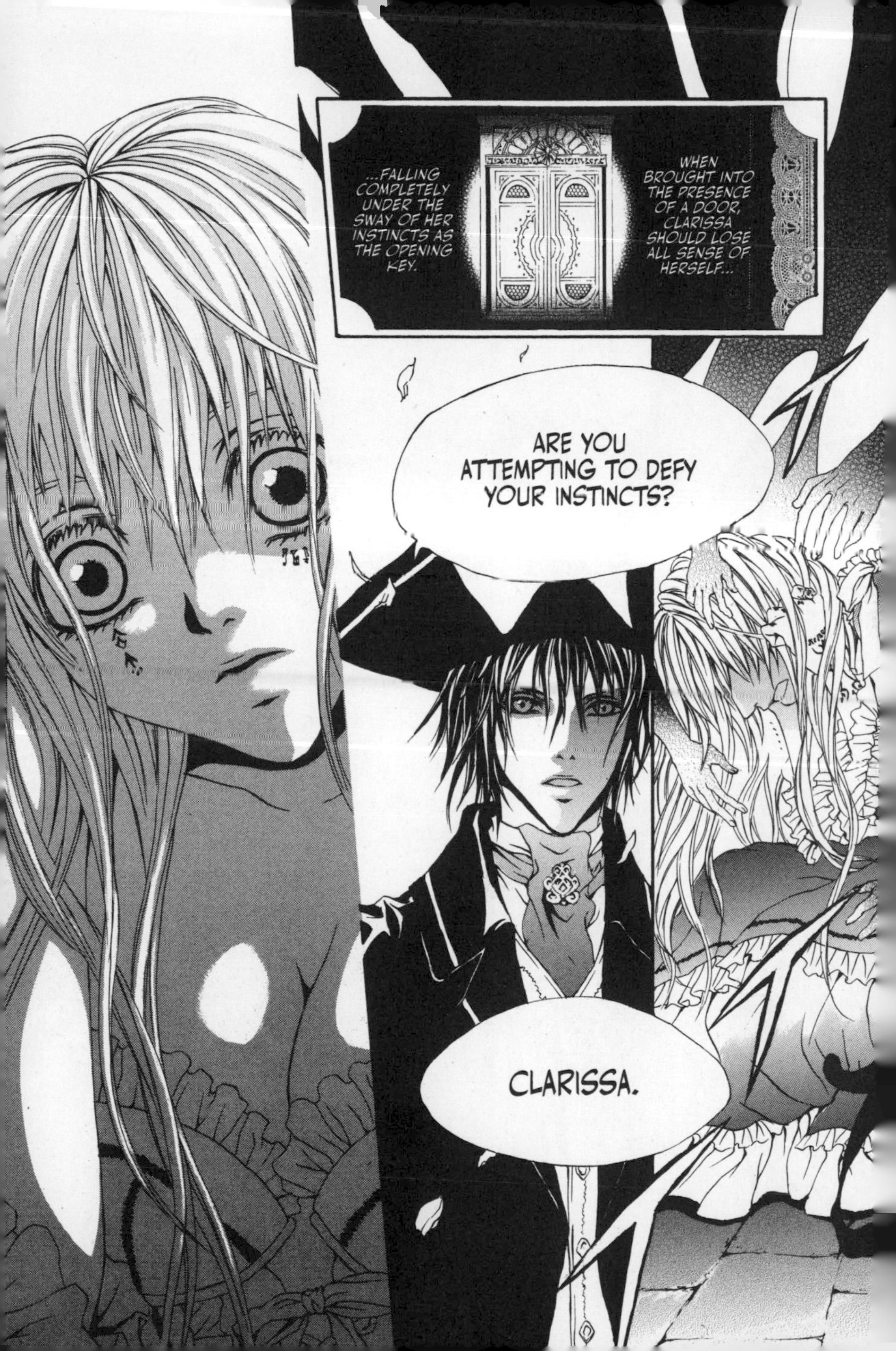
WHEN BROUGHT INTO THE PRESENCE OF A DOOR, CLARISSA SHOULD LOSE ALL SENSE OF HERSELF...
...FALLING COMPLETELY UNDER THE SWAY OF HER INSTINCTS AS THE OPENING KEY.
ARE YOU ATTEMPTING TO DEFY YOUR INSTINCTS?
CLARISSA.

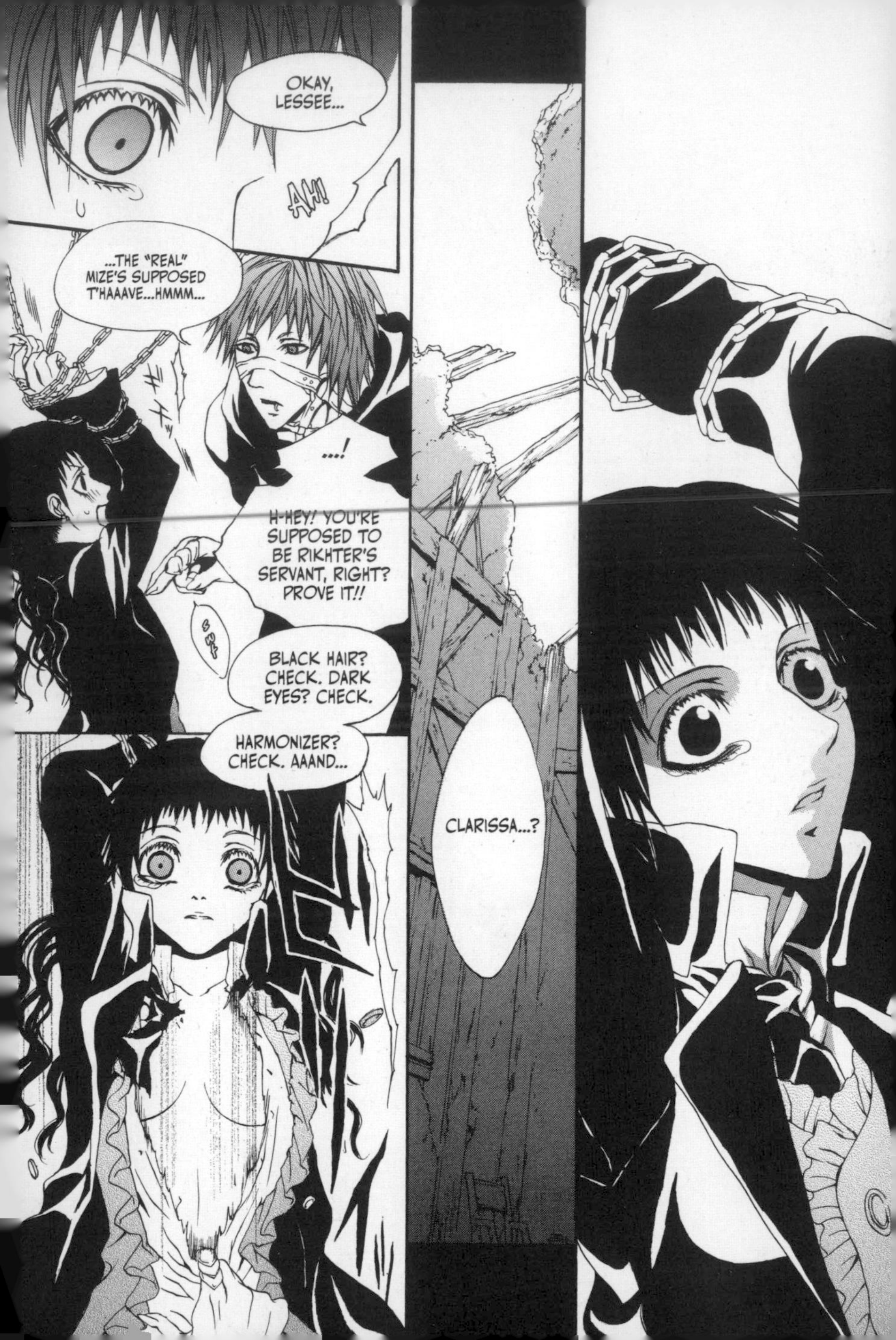
CLARISSA...?
OKAY, LESSEE...
AH!
...THE "REAL" MIZE'S SUPPOSED T'HAAAVE...HMMM...
...!
H-HEY! YOU'RE SUPPOSED TO BE RIKHTER'S SERVANT, RIGHT? PROVE IT!!
BLACK HAIR? CHECK. DARK EYES? CHECK.
HARMONIZER? CHECK. AAAND...

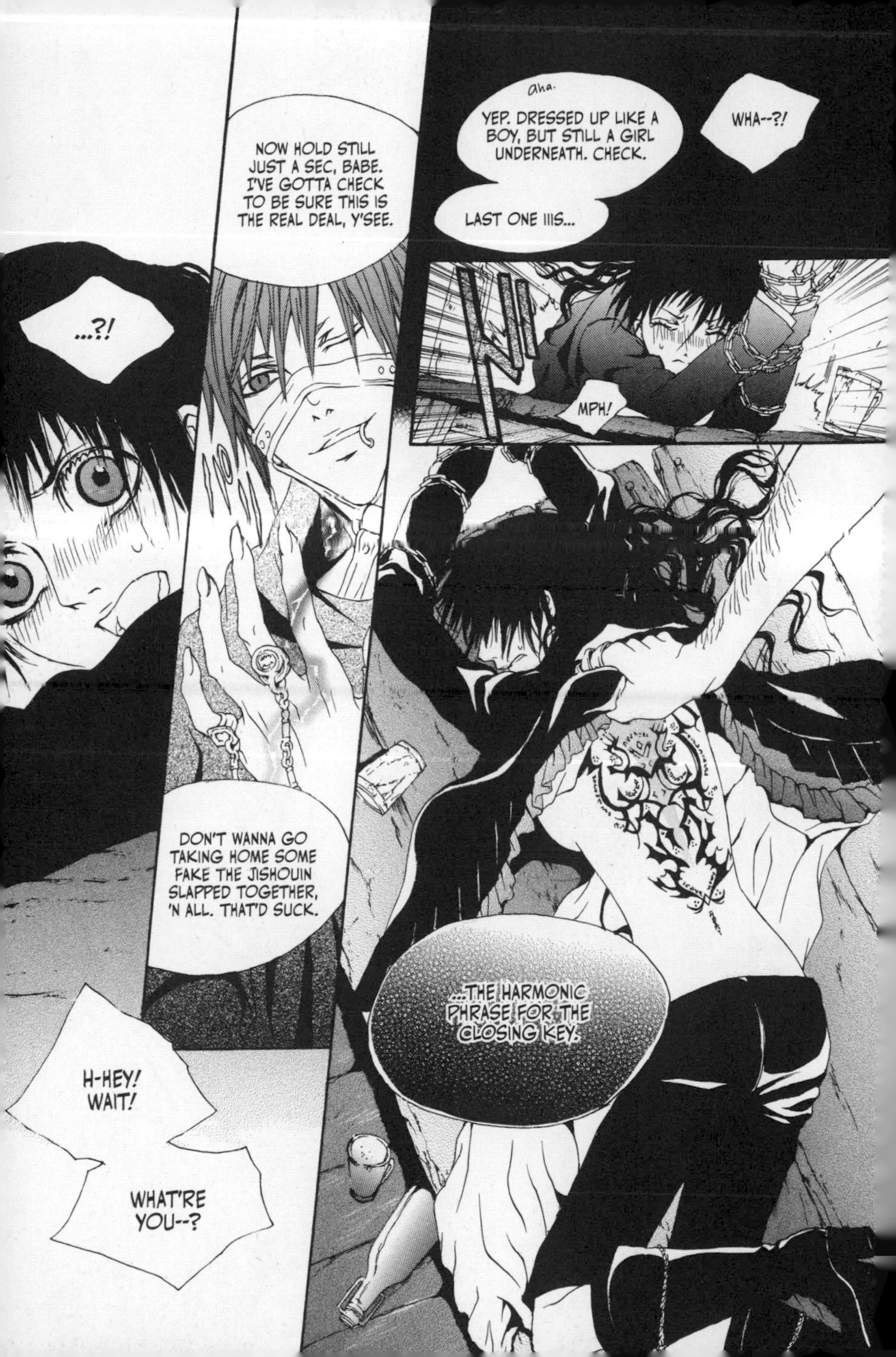
WHA--?!
aha.
YEP. DRESSED UP LIKE A BOY, BUT STILL A GIRL UNDERNEATH. CHECK.
LAST ONE IIIS...
MPH!
...THE HARMONIC PHRASE FOR THE CLOSING KEY.
NOW HOLD STILL JUST A SEC, BABE. I'VE GOTTA CHECK TO BE SURE THIS IS THE REAL DEAL, Y'SEE.
DON'T WANNA GO TAKING HOME SOME FAKE THE JISHOUIN SLAPPED TOGETHER, 'N ALL. THAT'D SUCK.
...?!
H-HEY! WAIT!
WHAT'RE YOU--?

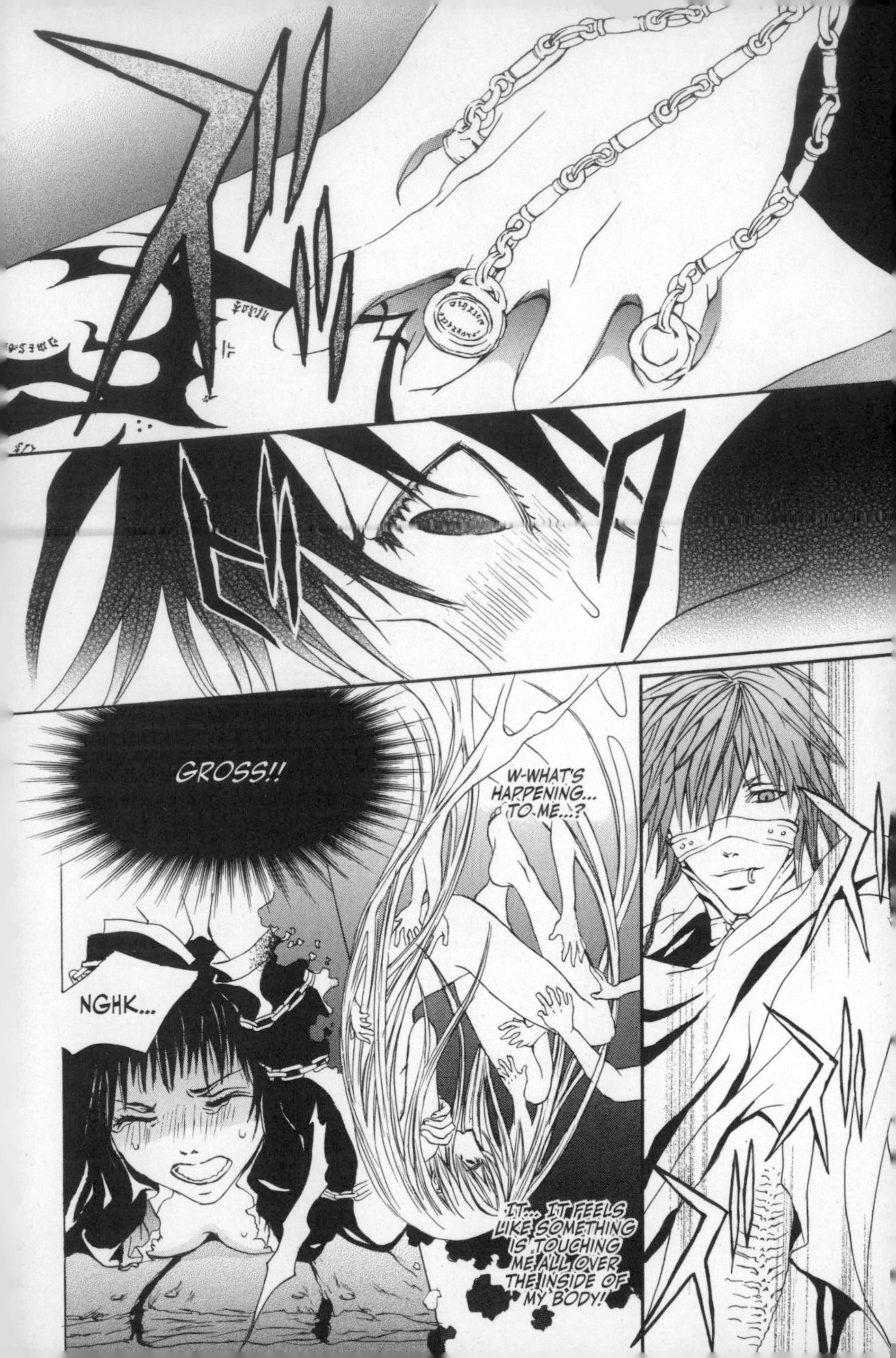
W-WHAT'S HAPPENING... TO ME...?
IT... IT FEELS LIKE SOMETHING IS TOUCHING ME ALL OVER THE INSIDE OF MY BODY!
GROSS!!
NGHK...

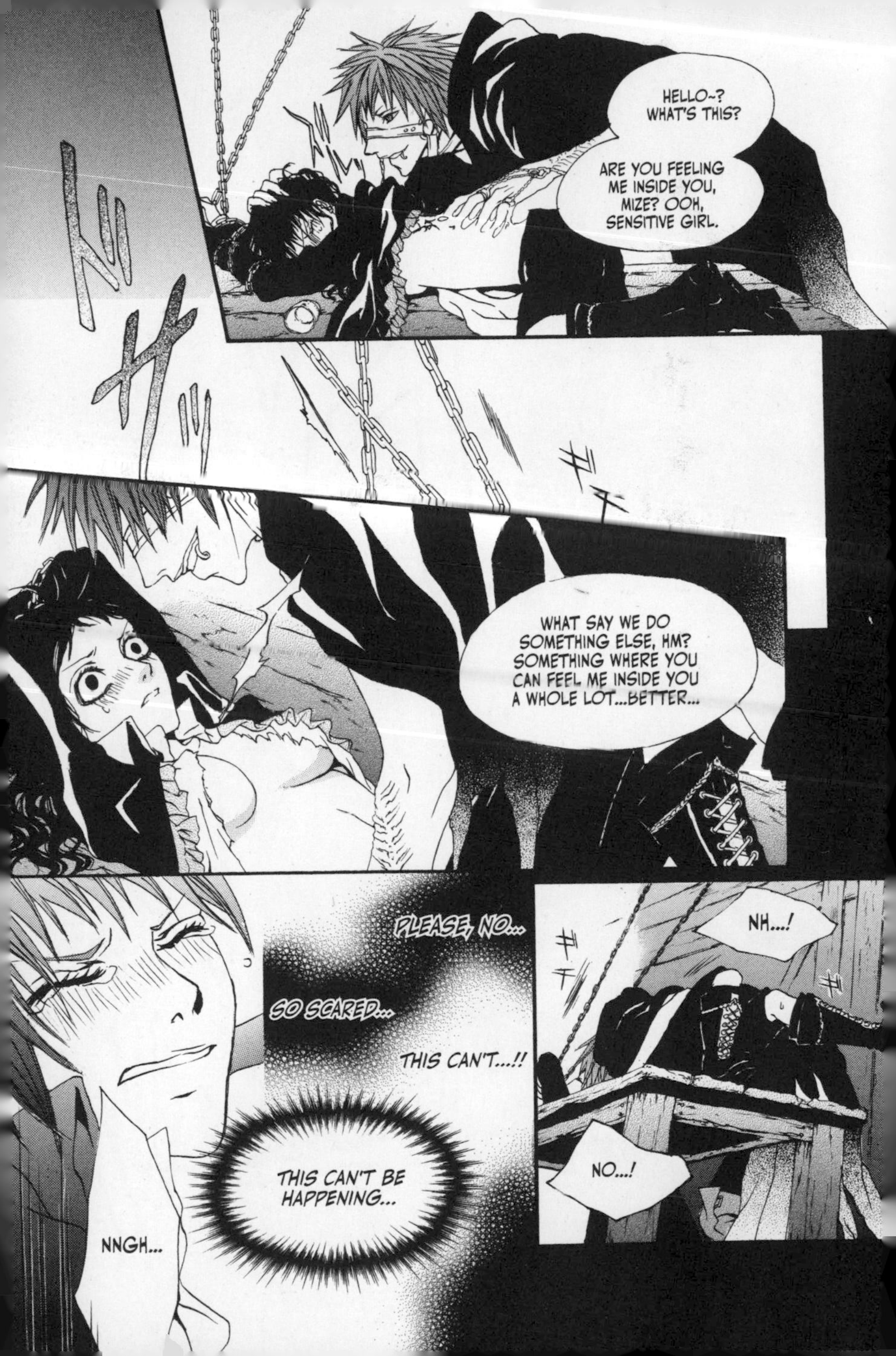
HELLO~? WHAT'S THIS?
ARE YOU FEELING ME INSIDE YOU, MIZE? OOH, SENSITIVE GIRL.
WHAT SAY WE DO SOMETHING ELSE, HM? SOMETHING WHERE YOU CAN FEEL ME INSIDE YOU A WHOLE LOT...BETTER...
NH...!
NO...!
PLEASE, NO...
SO SCARED...
THIS CAN'T...!!
THIS CAN'T BE HAPPENING...
NNGH...

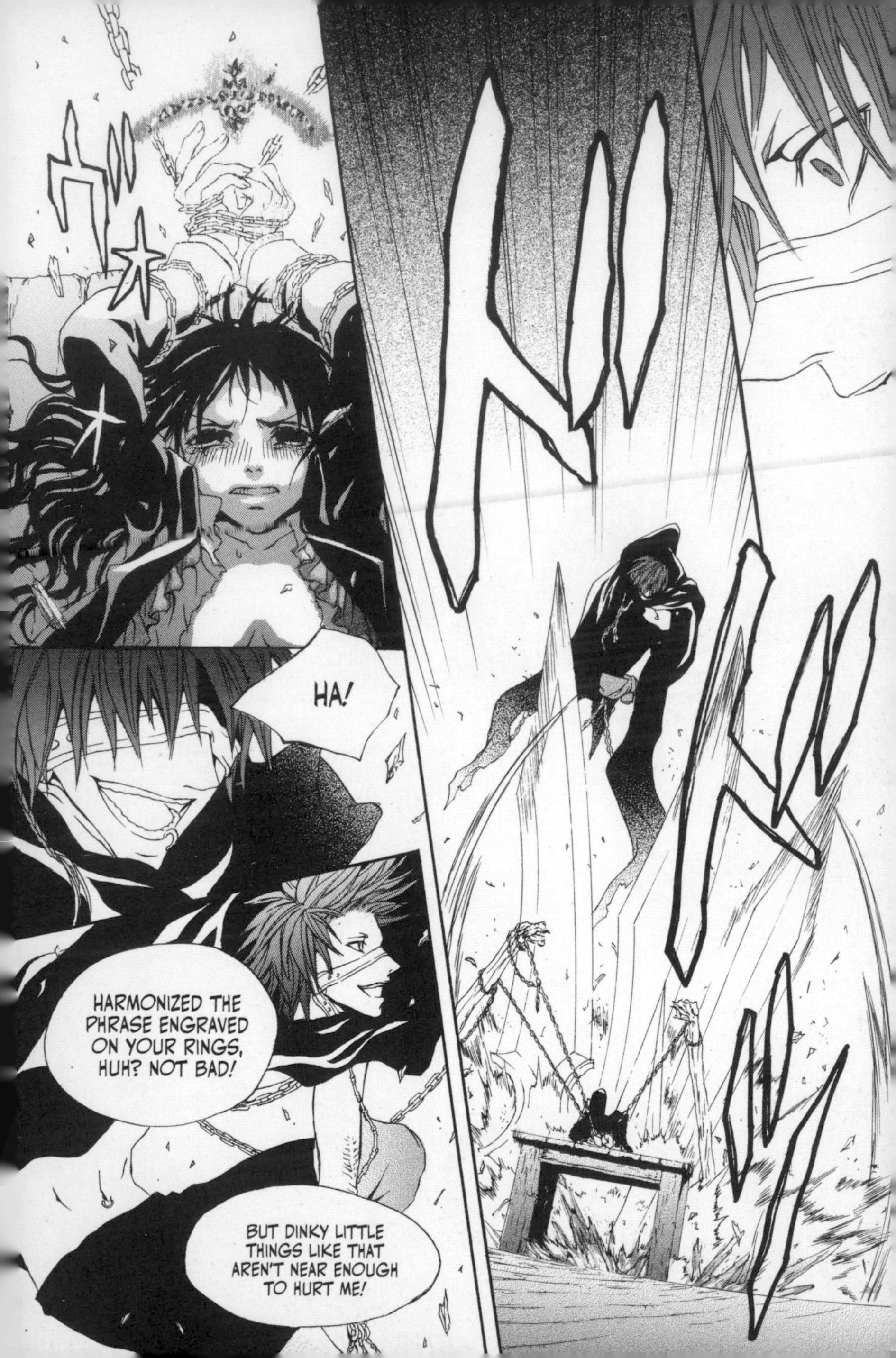
HA!
HARMONIZED THE PHRASE ENGRAVED ON YOUR RINGS, HUH? NOT BAD!
BUT DINKY LITTLE THINGS LIKE THAT AREN'T NEAR ENOUGH TO HURT ME!

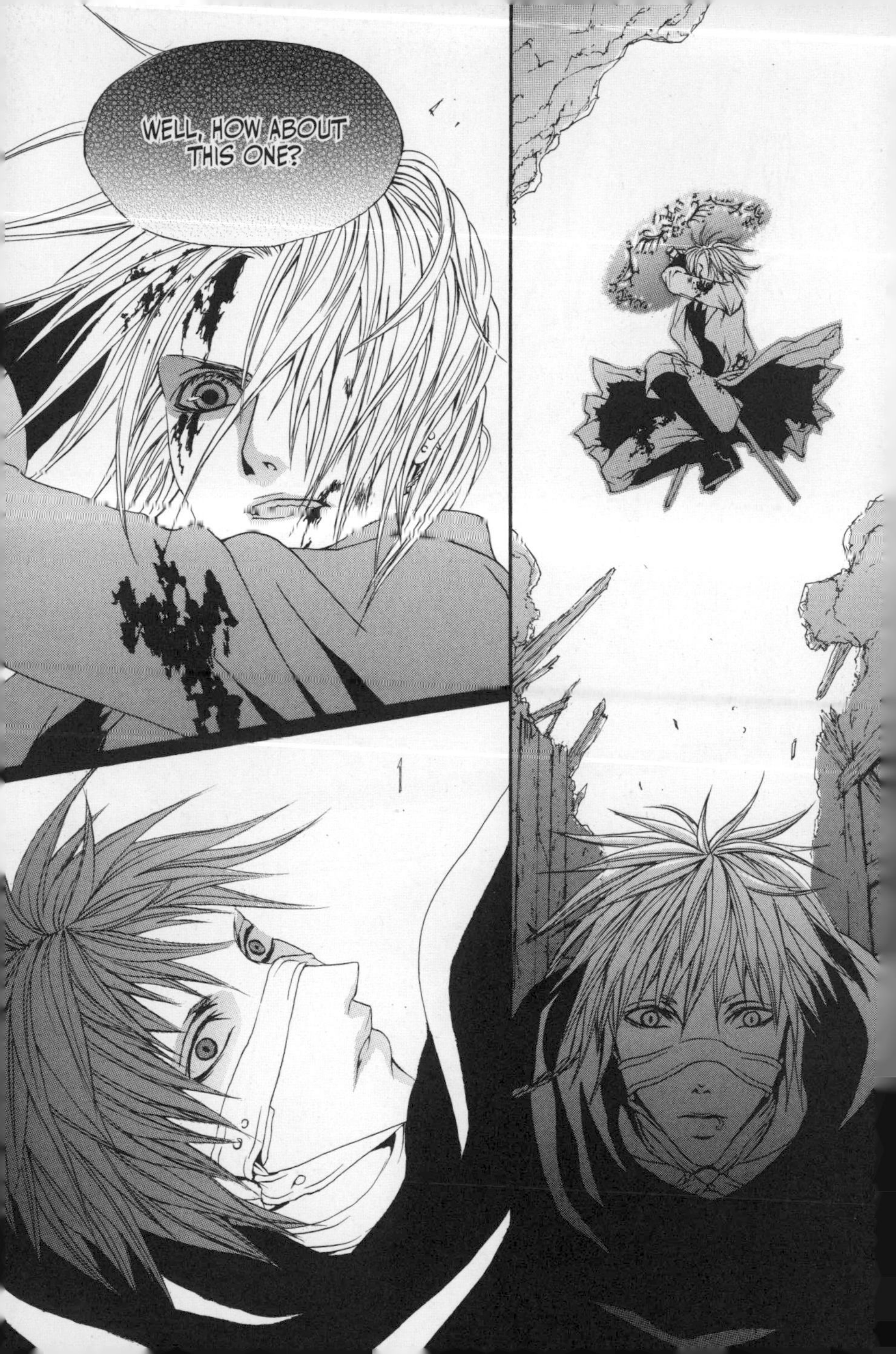
WELL, HOW ABOUT THIS ONE?

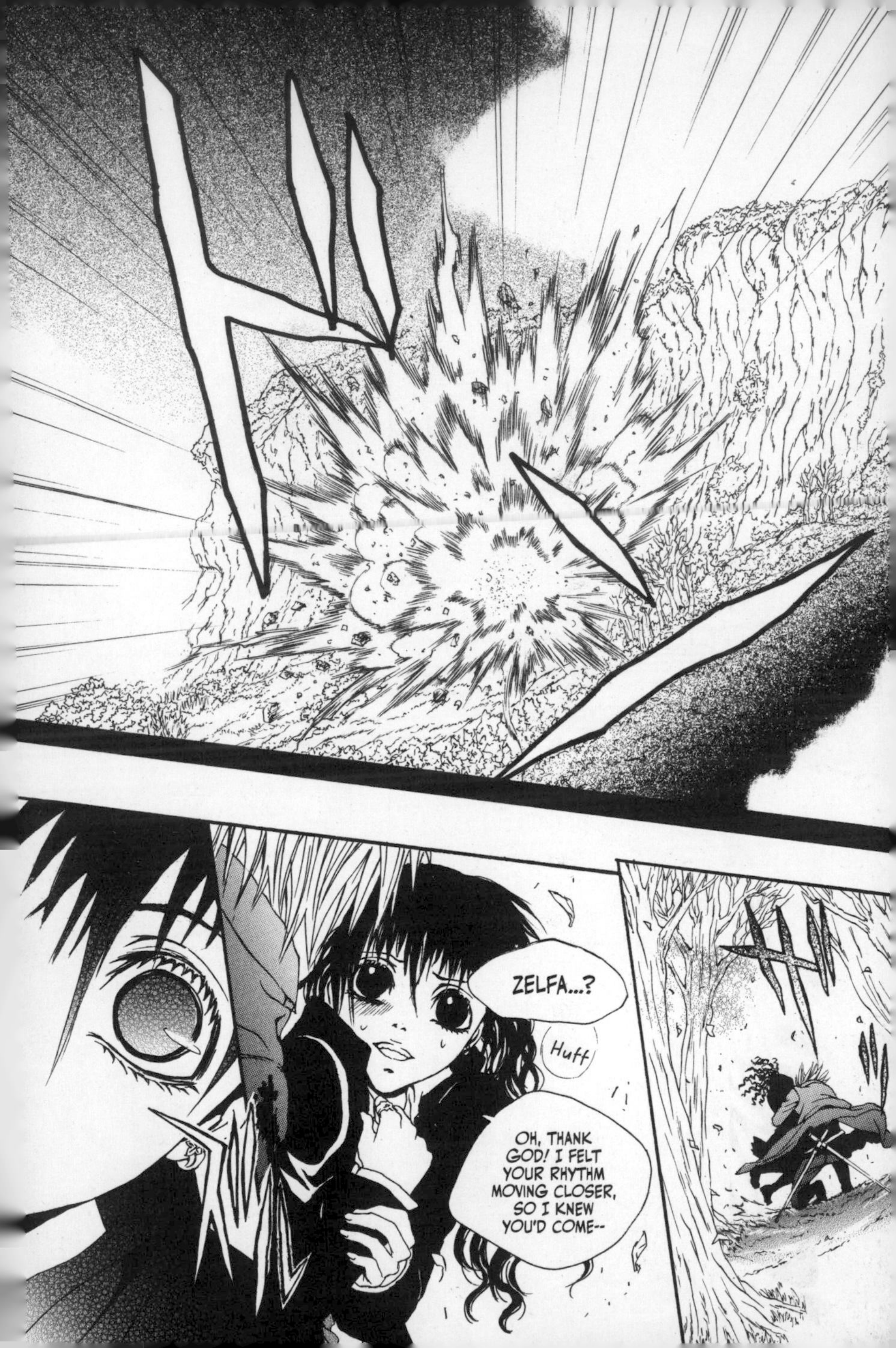
ZELFA...?
Huff
OH, THANK GOD! I FELT YOUR RHYTHM MOVING CLOSER, SO I KNEW YOU'D COME--

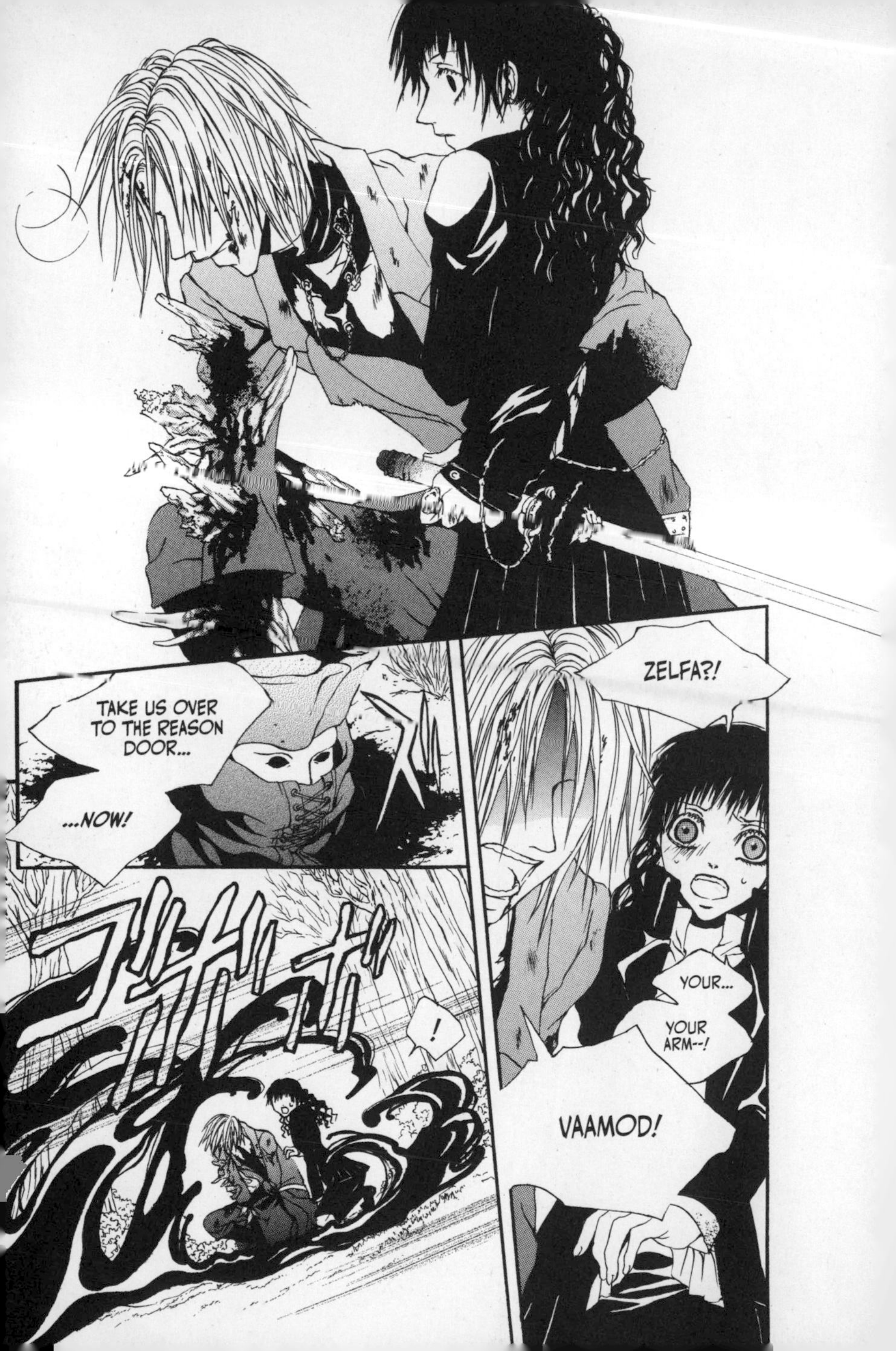
ZELFA?!
YOUR...
YOUR ARM--!
VAAMOD!
TAKE US OVER TO THE REASON DOOR...
...NOW!
!

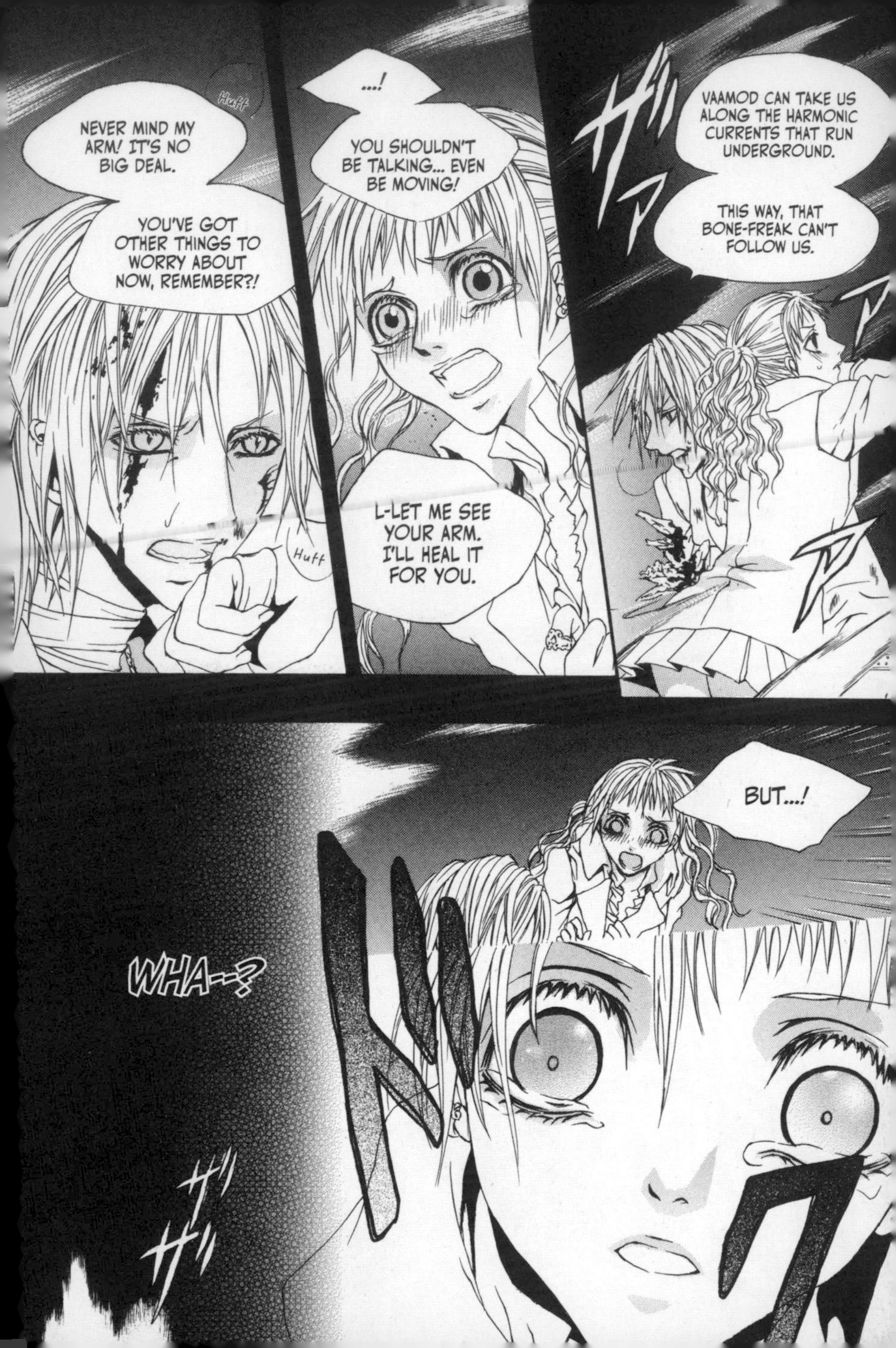
VAAMOD CAN TAKE US ALONG THE HARMONIC CURRENTS THAT RUN UNDERGROUND.
THIS WAY, THAT BONE-FREAK CAN'T FOLLOW US.
...!
YOU SHOULDN'T BE TALKING... EVEN BE MOVING!
L-LET ME SEE YOUR ARM. I'LL HEAL IT FOR YOU.
Huff
NEVER MIND MY ARM! IT'S NO BIG DEAL.
YOU'VE GOT OTHER THINGS TO WORRY ABOUT NOW, REMEMBER?!
Huff
BUT...!
WHA--?

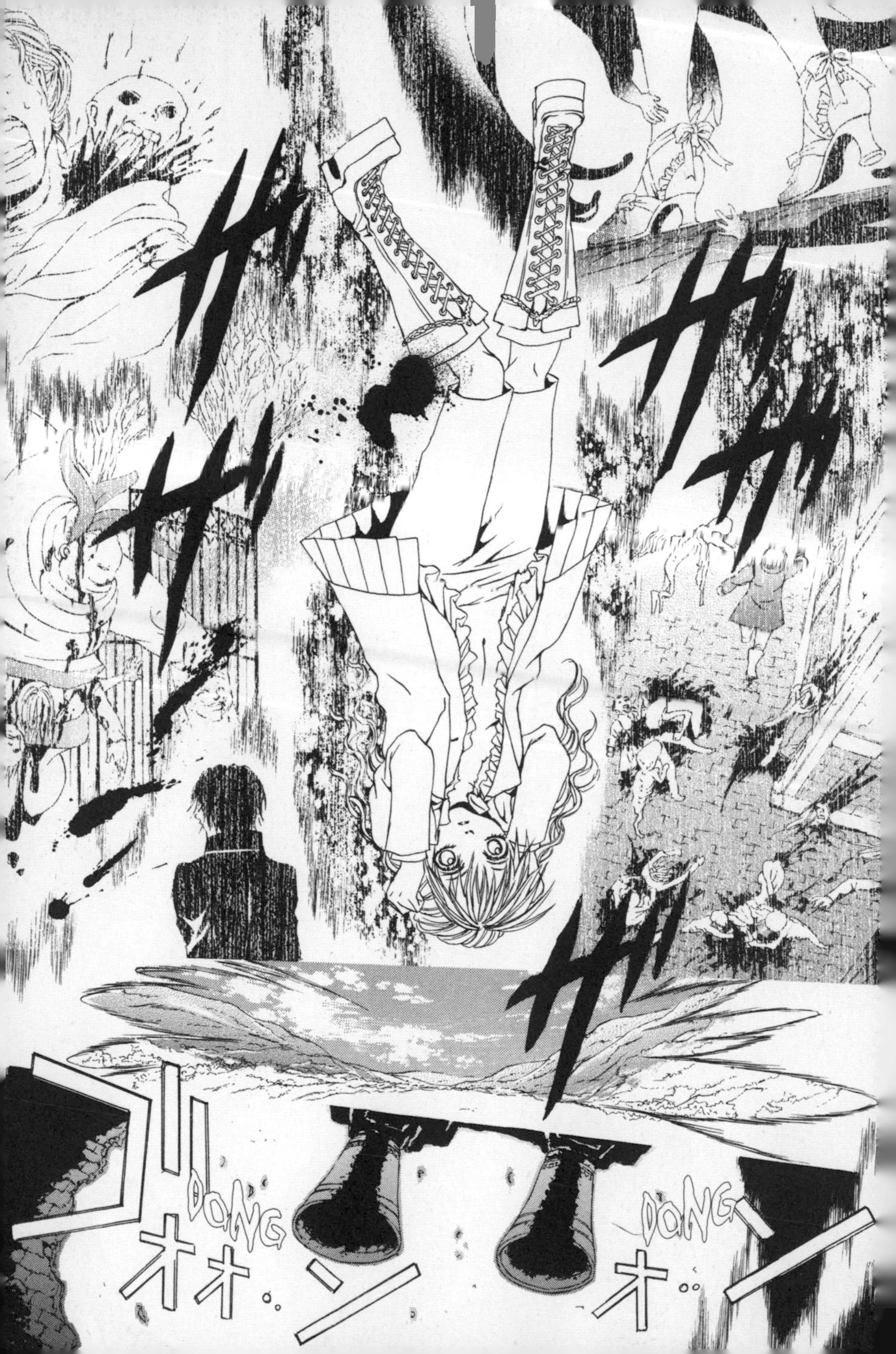
DONG
DONG

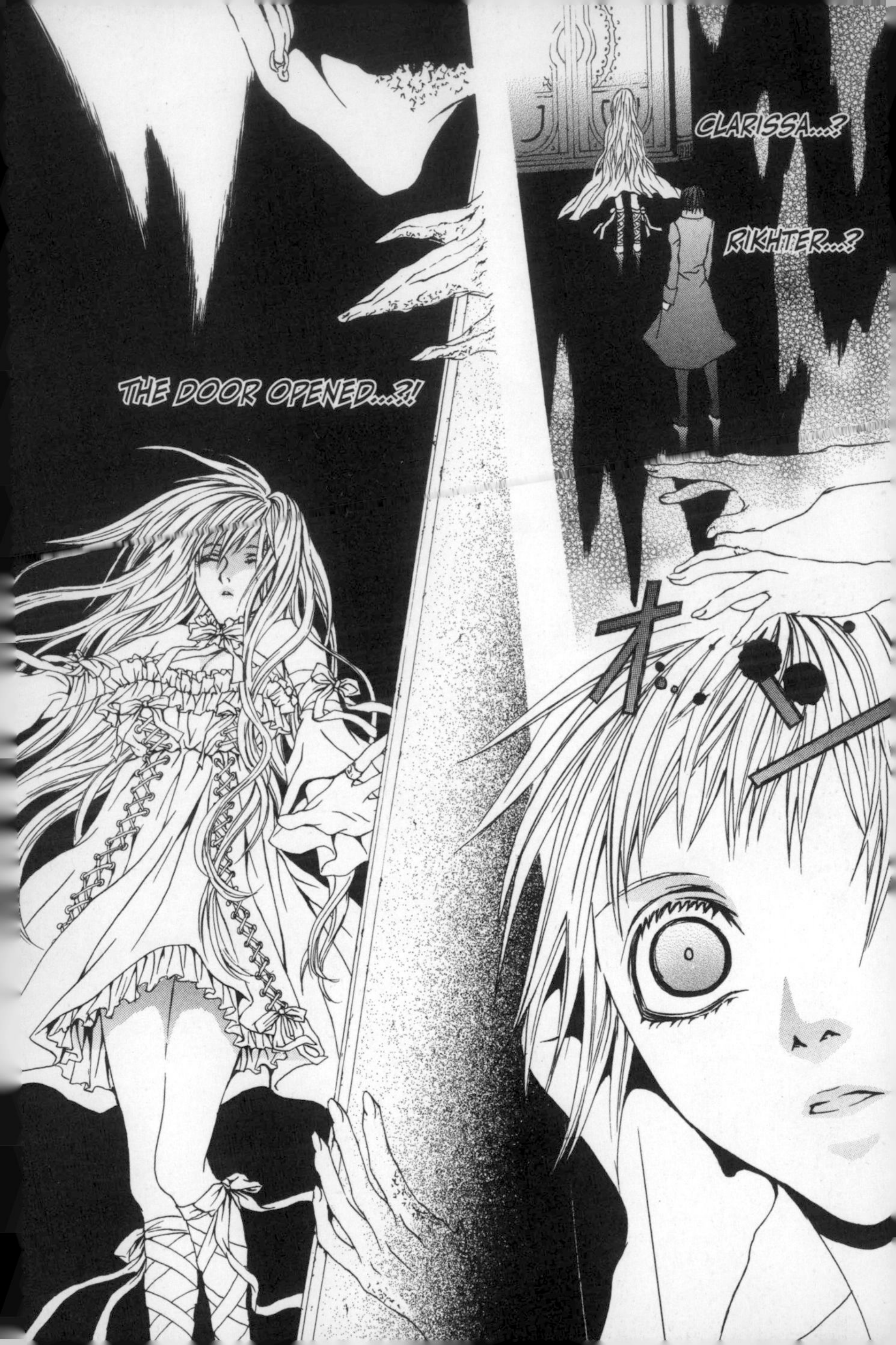
CLARISSA...?
RIKHTER...?
THE DOOR OPENED...?!

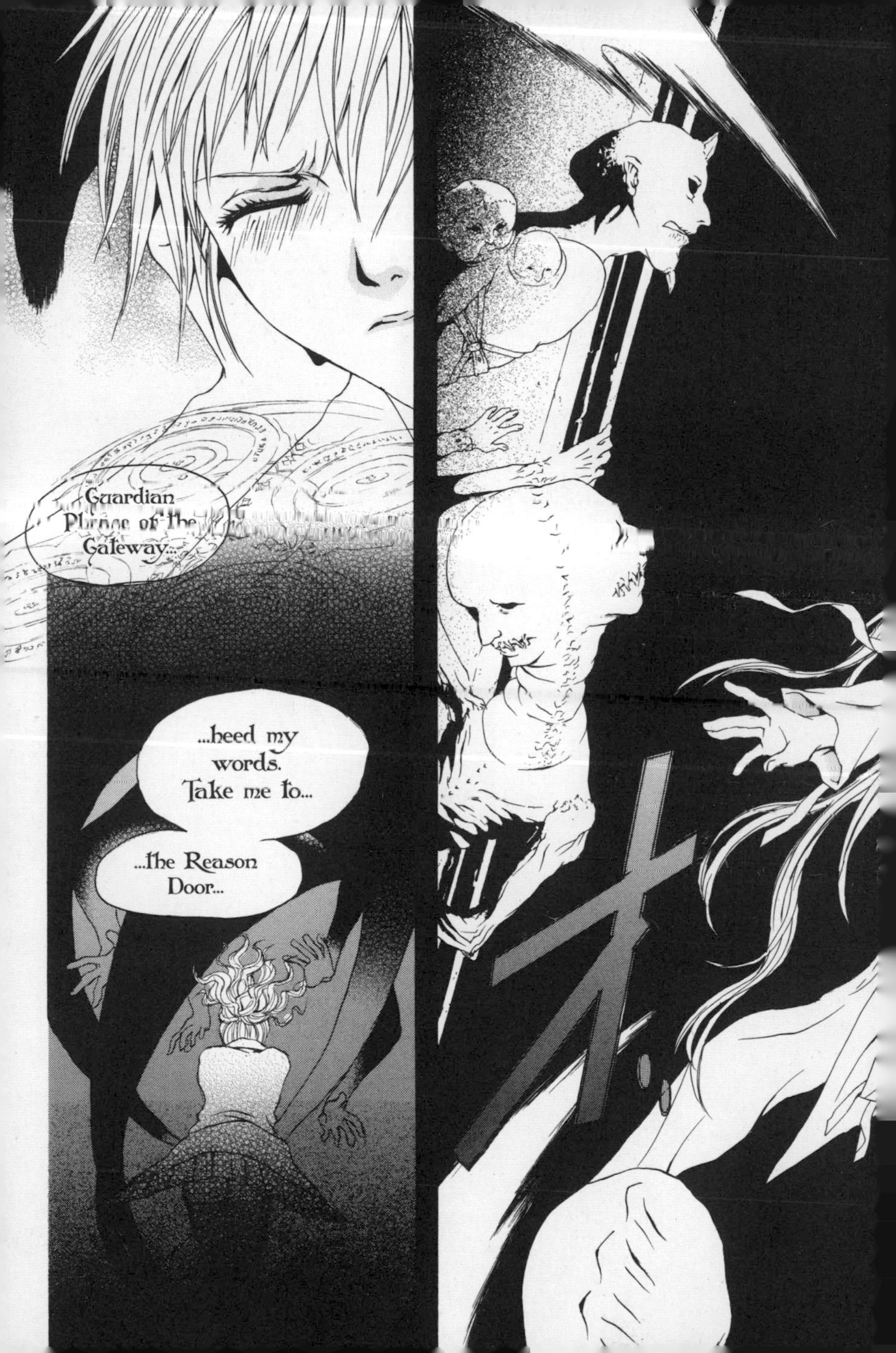

Guardian Prince of the Gateway...
...heed my words. Take me to...
...the Reason Door...

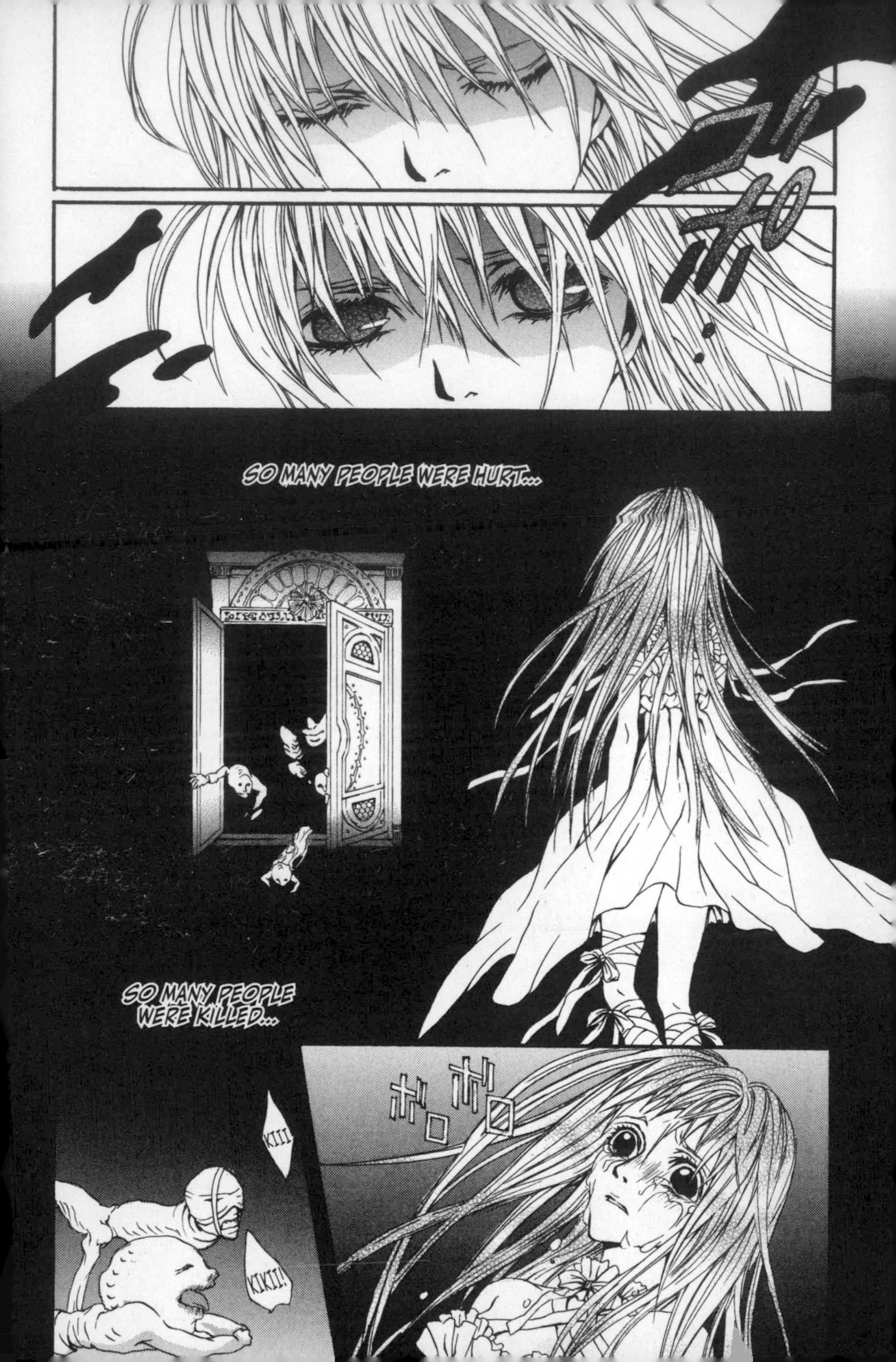
SO MANY PEOPLE WERE HURT...
SO MANY PEOPLE WERE KILLED...
ポロ ポロ
KIII!
KIKII!

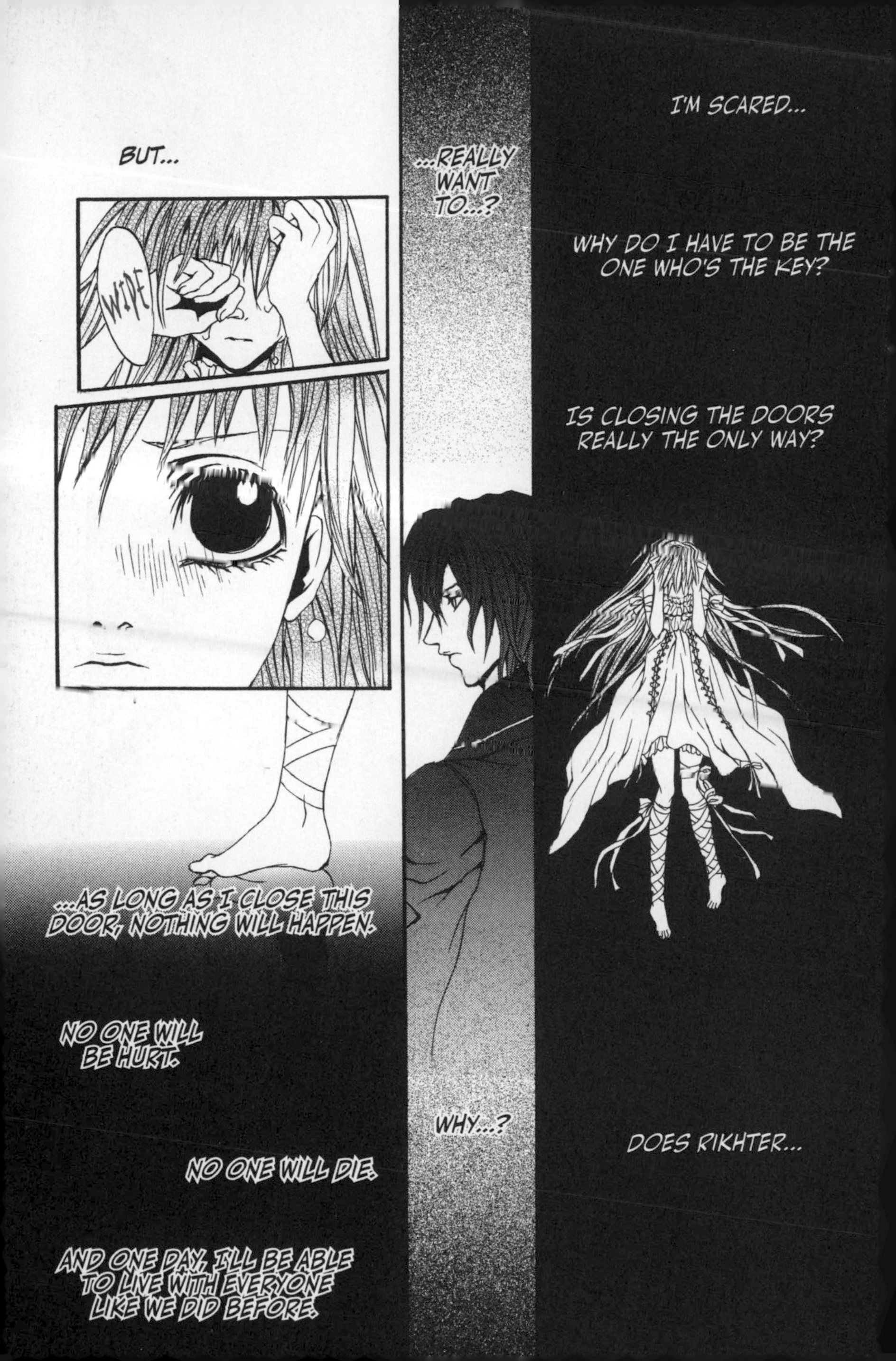
I'M SCARED...
WHY DO I HAVE TO BE THE ONE WHO'S THE KEY?
IS CLOSING THE DOORS REALLY THE ONLY WAY?
DOES RIKHTER...
...REALLY WANT TO...?
WHY...?
BUT...
WIPE
...AS LONG AS I CLOSE THIS DOOR, NOTHING WILL HAPPEN.
NO ONE WILL BE HURT.
NO ONE WILL DIE.
AND ONE DAY, I'LL BE ABLE TO LIVE WITH EVERYONE LIKE WE DID BEFORE.

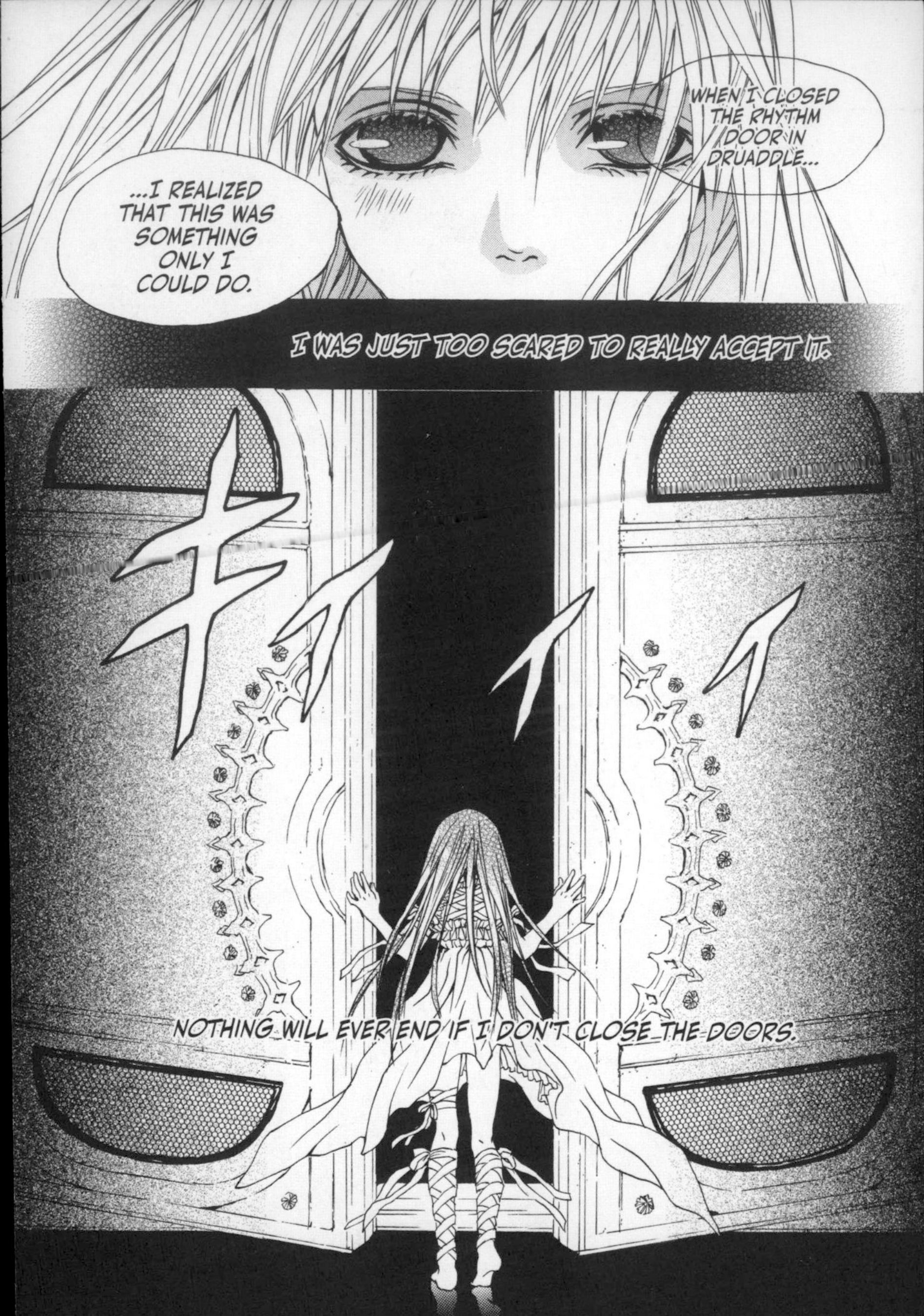

WHEN I CLOSED THE RHYTHM DOOR IN DRUADDLE...
...I REALIZED THAT THIS WAS SOMETHING ONLY I COULD DO.
I WAS JUST TOO SCARED TO REALLY ACCEPT IT.
ギイイイ
NOTHING WILL EVER END IF I DON'T CLOSE THE DOORS.

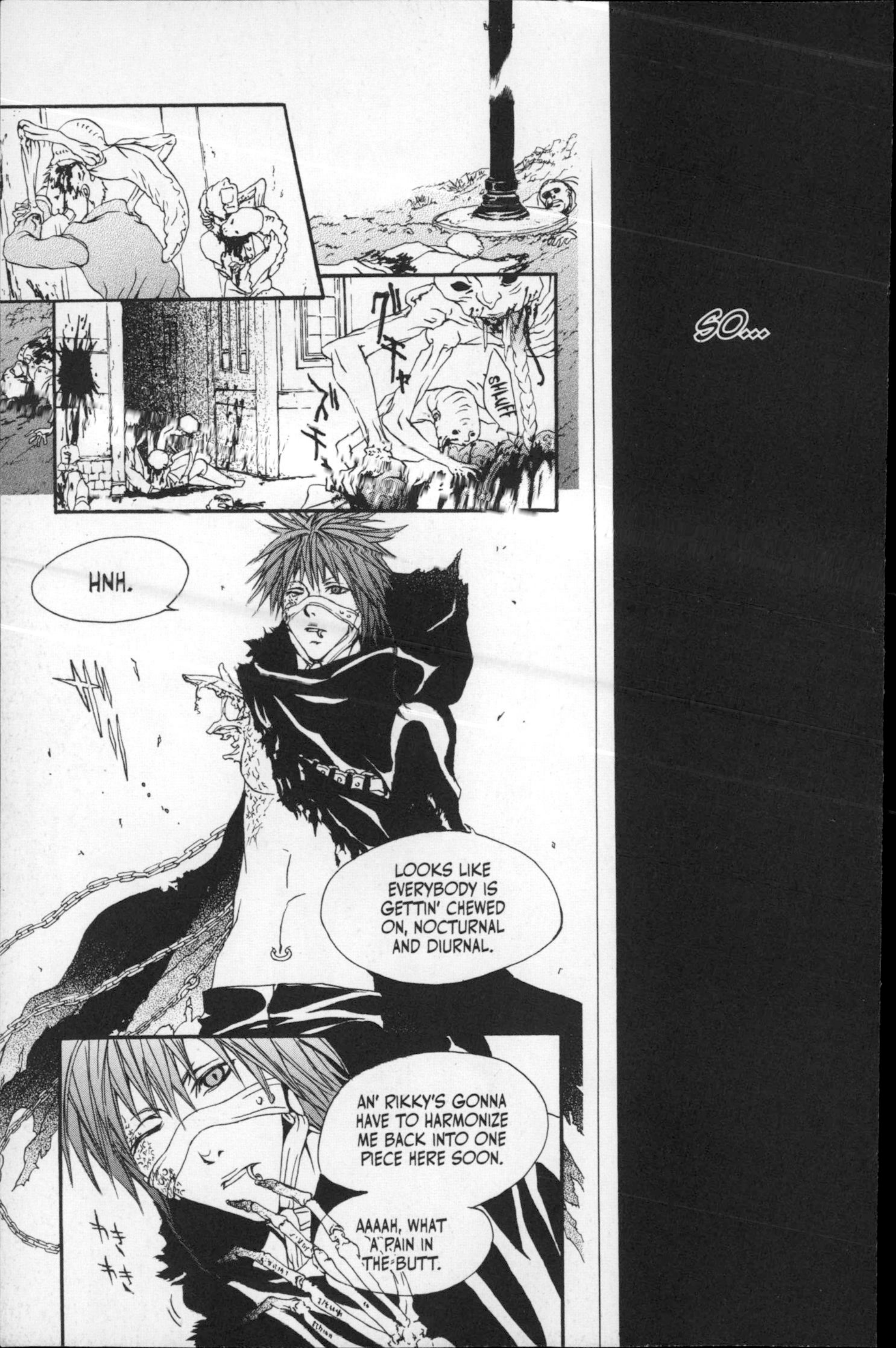
SO...
SHLUFF
HNH.
LOOKS LIKE EVERYBODY IS GETTIN' CHEWED ON, NOCTURNAL AND DIURNAL.
AN' RIKKY'S GONNA HAVE TO HARMONIZE ME BACK INTO ONE PIECE HERE SOON.
AAAAH, WHAT A PAIN IN THE BUTT.

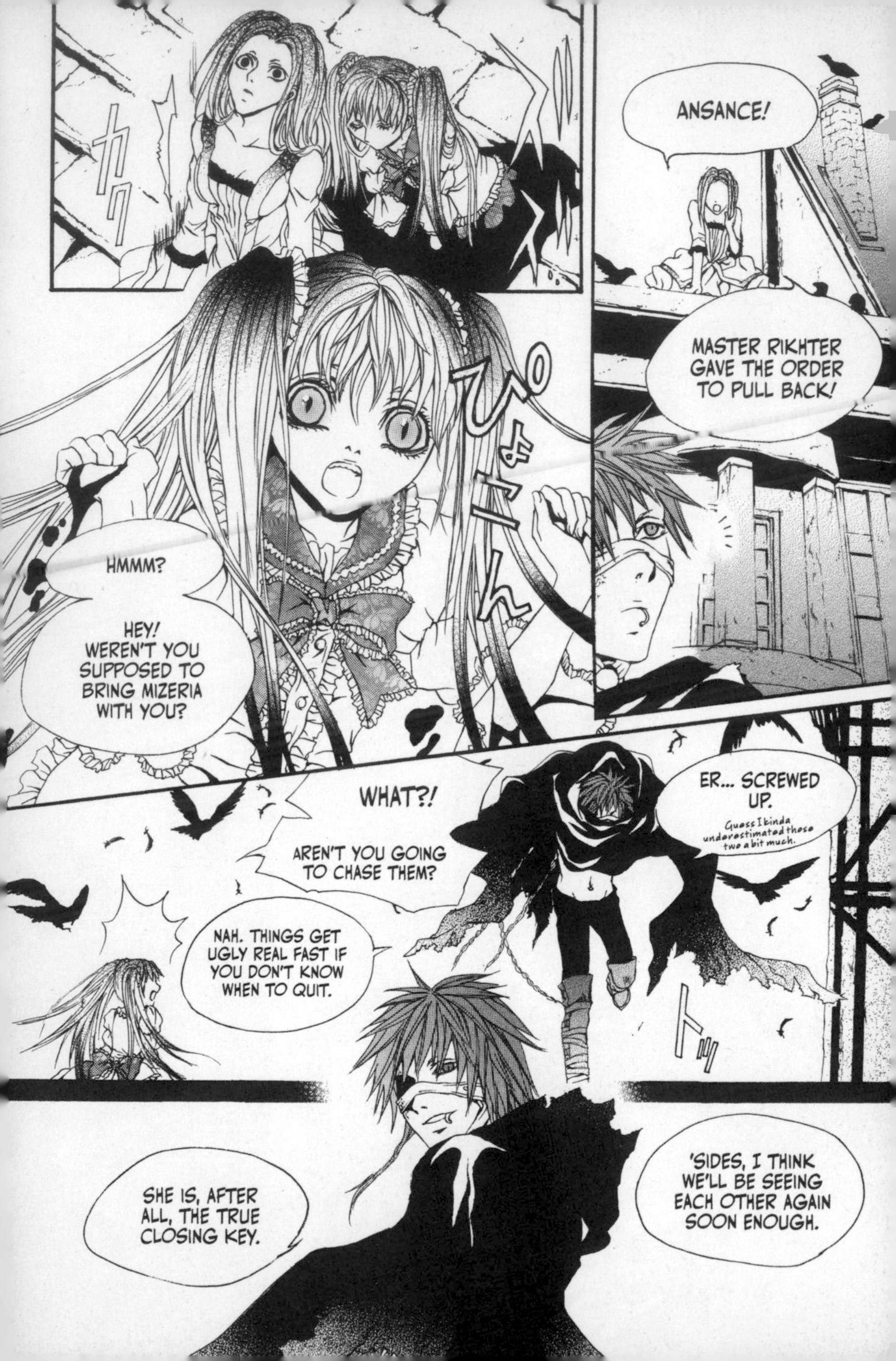
ANSANCE!
MASTER RIKHTER GAVE THE ORDER TO PULL BACK!
HMMM?
HEY! WEREN'T YOU SUPPOSED TO BRING MIZERIA WITH YOU?
ER... SCREWED UP.
Guess I kinda underestimated those two a bit much.
WHAT?!
AREN'T YOU GOING TO CHASE THEM?
NAH. THINGS GET UGLY REAL FAST IF YOU DON'T KNOW WHEN TO QUIT.
'SIDES, I THINK WE'LL BE SEEING EACH OTHER AGAIN SOON ENOUGH.
SHE IS, AFTER ALL, THE TRUE CLOSING KEY.

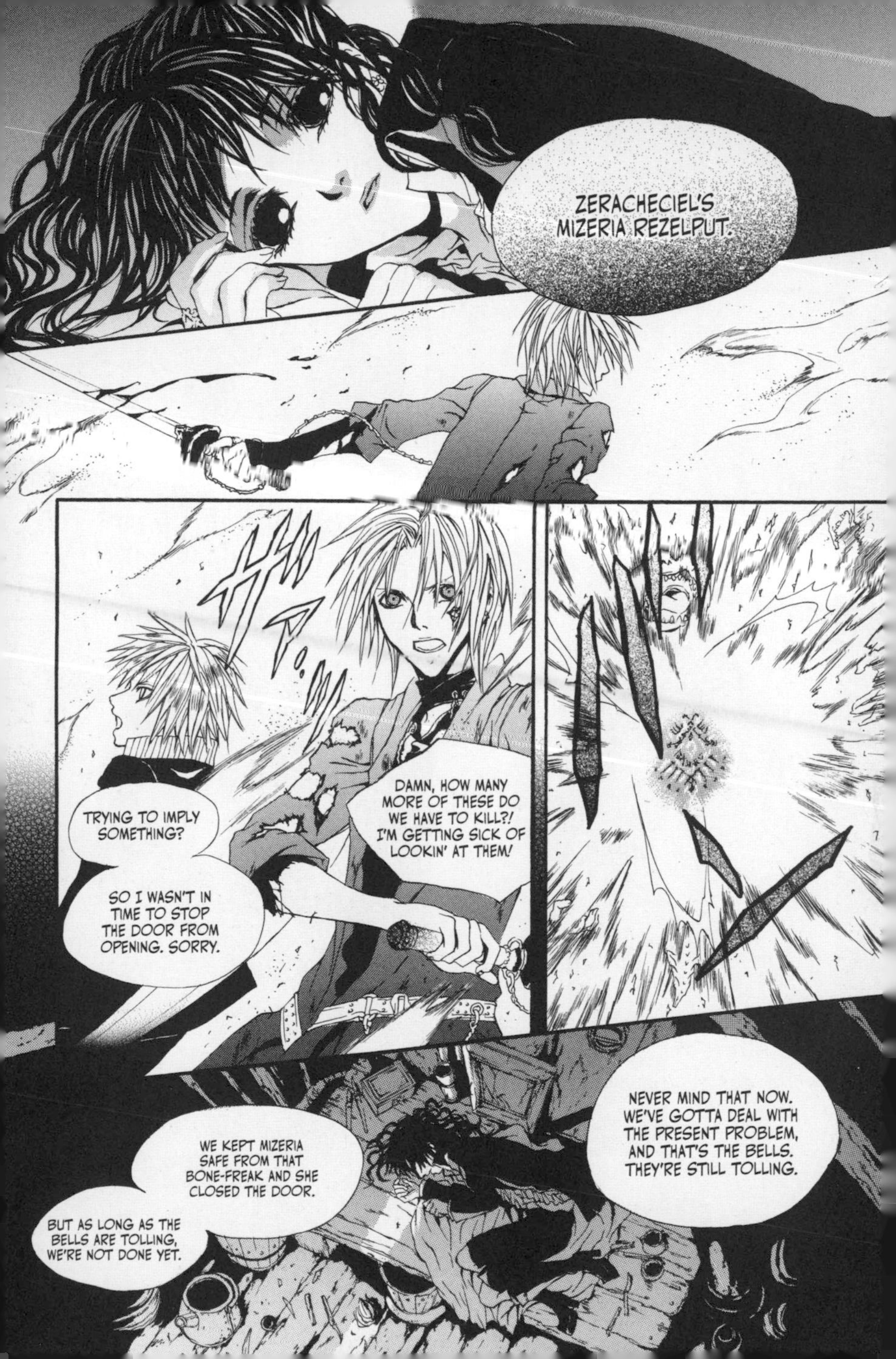
ZERACHECIEL'S MIZERIA REZELPUT.
DAMN, HOW MANY MORE OF THESE DO WE HAVE TO KILL?! I'M GETTING SICK OF LOOKIN' AT THEM!
TRYING TO IMPLY SOMETHING?
SO I WASN'T IN TIME TO STOP THE DOOR FROM OPENING. SORRY.
NEVER MIND THAT NOW. WE'VE GOTTA DEAL WITH THE PRESENT PROBLEM, AND THAT'S THE BELLS. THEY'RE STILL TOLLING.
WE KEPT MIZERIA SAFE FROM THAT BONE-FREAK AND SHE CLOSED THE DOOR.
BUT AS LONG AS THE BELLS ARE TOLLING, WE'RE NOT DONE YET.

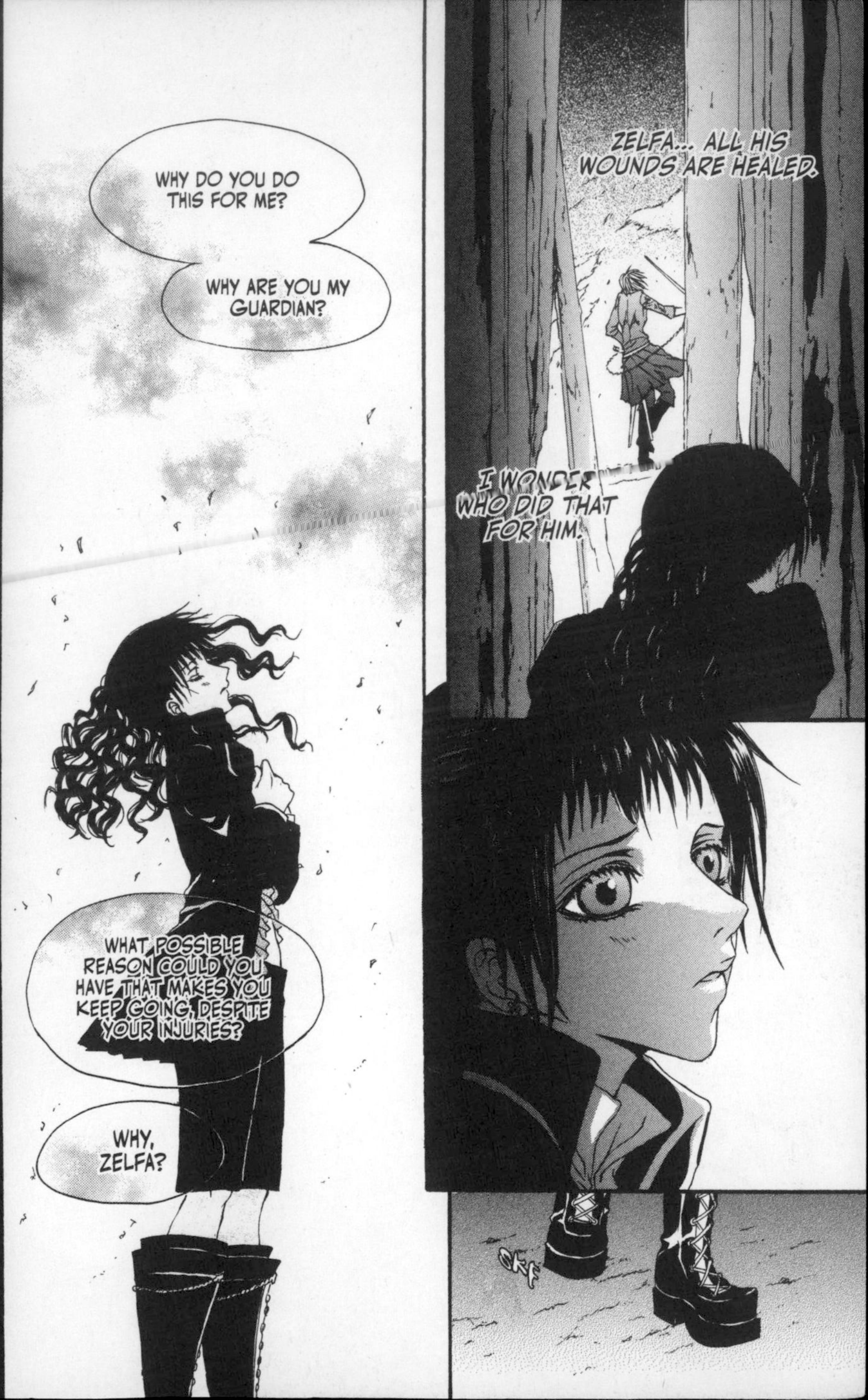
ZELFA... ALL HIS WOUNDS ARE HEALED.
I WONDER WHO DID THAT FOR HIM.
SKF
WHY DO YOU DO THIS FOR ME?
WHY ARE YOU MY GUARDIAN?
WHAT POSSIBLE REASON COULD YOU HAVE THAT MAKES YOU KEEP GOING, DESPITE YOUR INJURIES?
WHY, ZELFA?

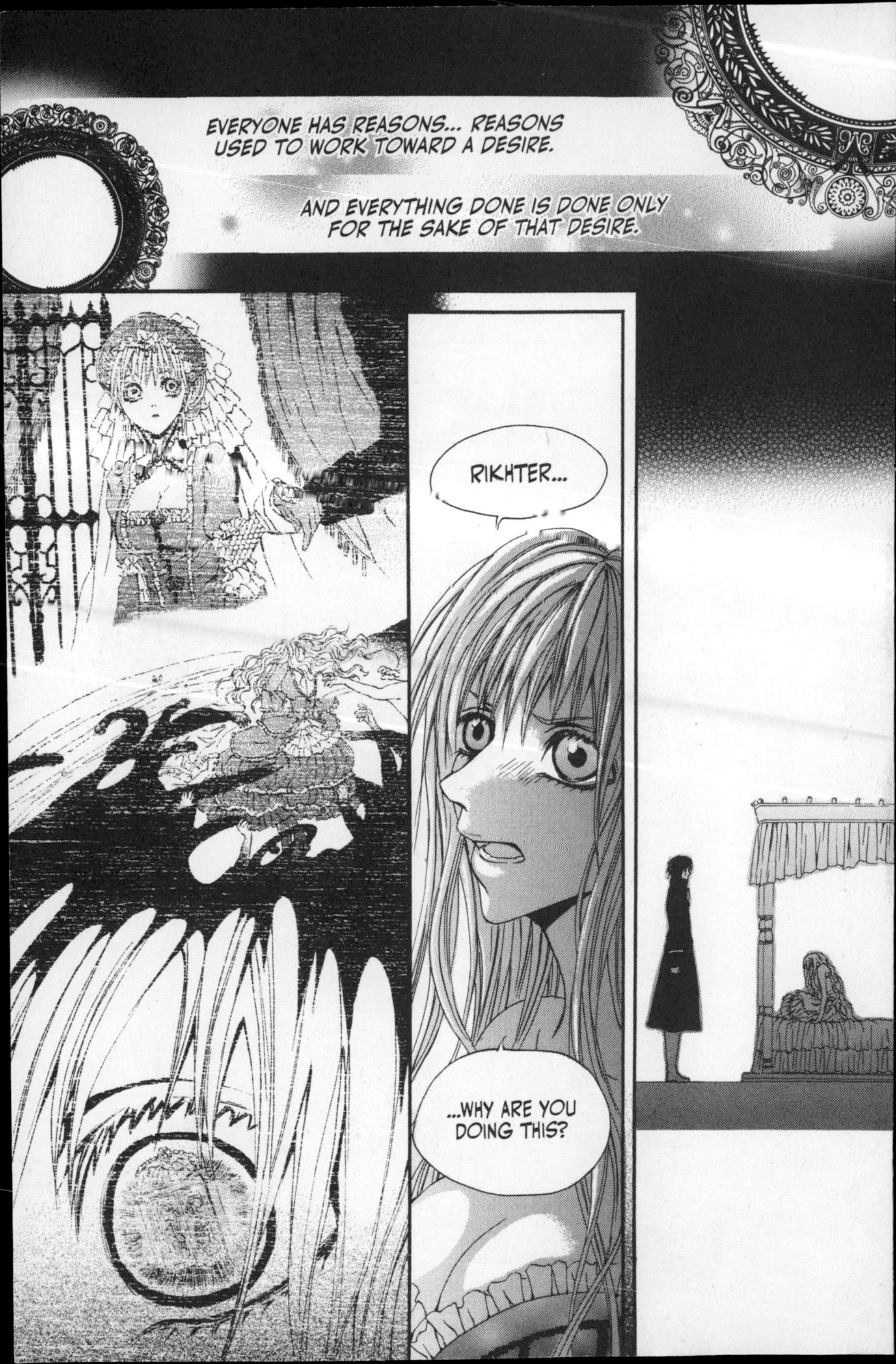
EVERYONE HAS REASONS... REASONS USED TO WORK TOWARD A DESIRE.
AND EVERYTHING DONE IS DONE ONLY FOR THE SAKE OF THAT DESIRE.
RIKHTER...
...WHY ARE YOU DOING THIS?

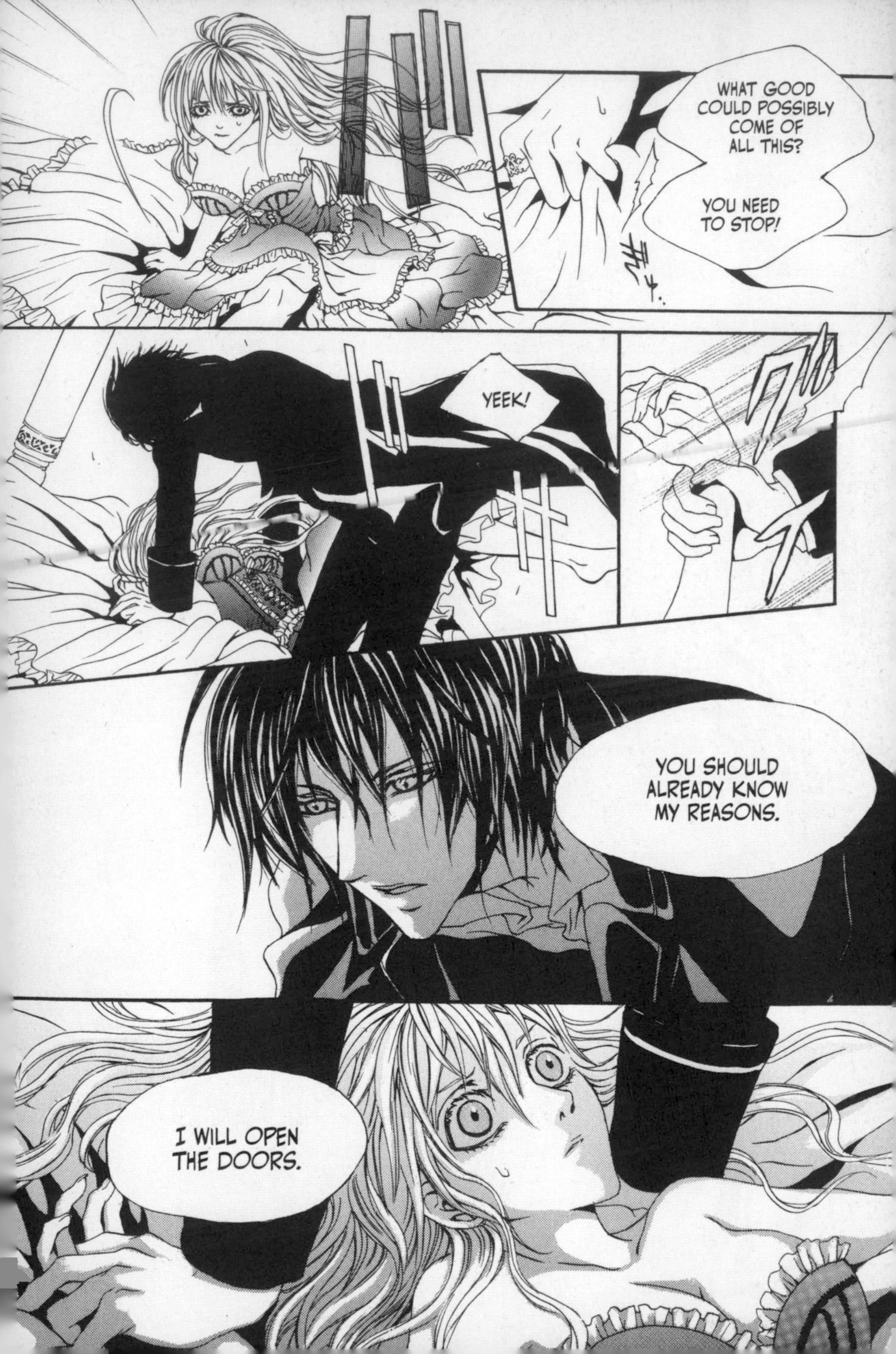
WHAT GOOD COULD POSSIBLY COME OF ALL THIS?
YOU NEED TO STOP!
YEEK!
YOU SHOULD ALREADY KNOW MY REASONS.
I WILL OPEN THE DOORS.

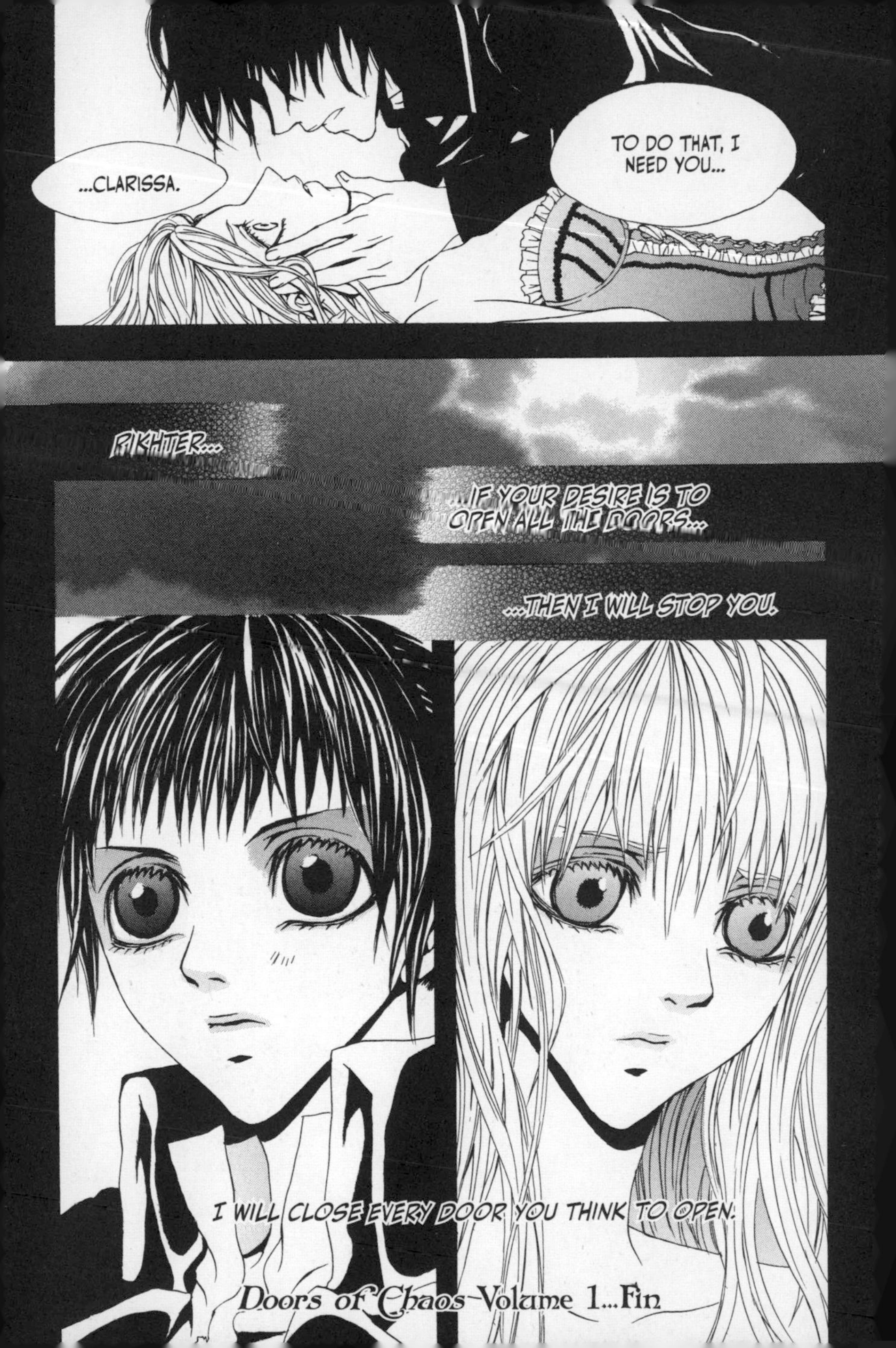
TO DO THAT, I NEED YOU...
...CLARISSA.
RIKHTER...
...IF YOUR DESIRE IS TO OPEN ALL THE DOORS...
...THEN I WILL STOP YOU.
I WILL CLOSE EVERY DOOR YOU THINK TO OPEN.
Doors of Chaos Volume 1...Fin

Postscript...

Nice to meet you. This is Ryoko Mitsuki, thanking you for picking up this *Doors of Chaos* book. Because this is actually my first published book, I'd like to give a big thanks to the publisher TOKYOPOP for giving me this chance.

(Just so you know, the Japanese choice for the title is *Grenzen Tur*, which is German for *Doors of the Border*.)

The artwork and story still have a long way to go, and there are some places I can't even stand to look at!
Still, I put in my all every step of the way, so I know they're full of love.

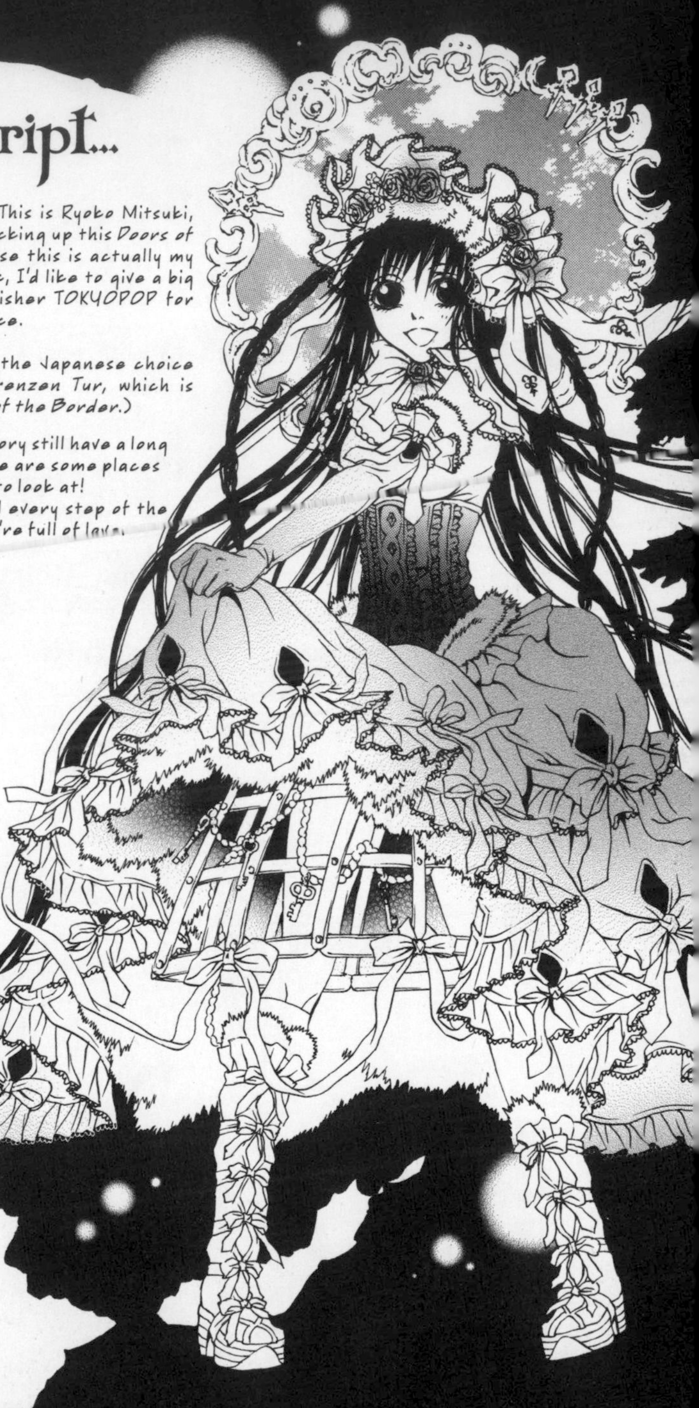

Caricature of Mitsuki

Thank you very much!

- My assistants
  - Akane-san, Tadashi-san
- Helpers
  - Hori, Mom
- Editor
  - Shiramizu
- Consultants
  - Tounon, Oqi
- Readers

I still don't know how long this story will continue, but I hope you stick around for at least the next volume.

2007.10
Ryoko Mitsuki

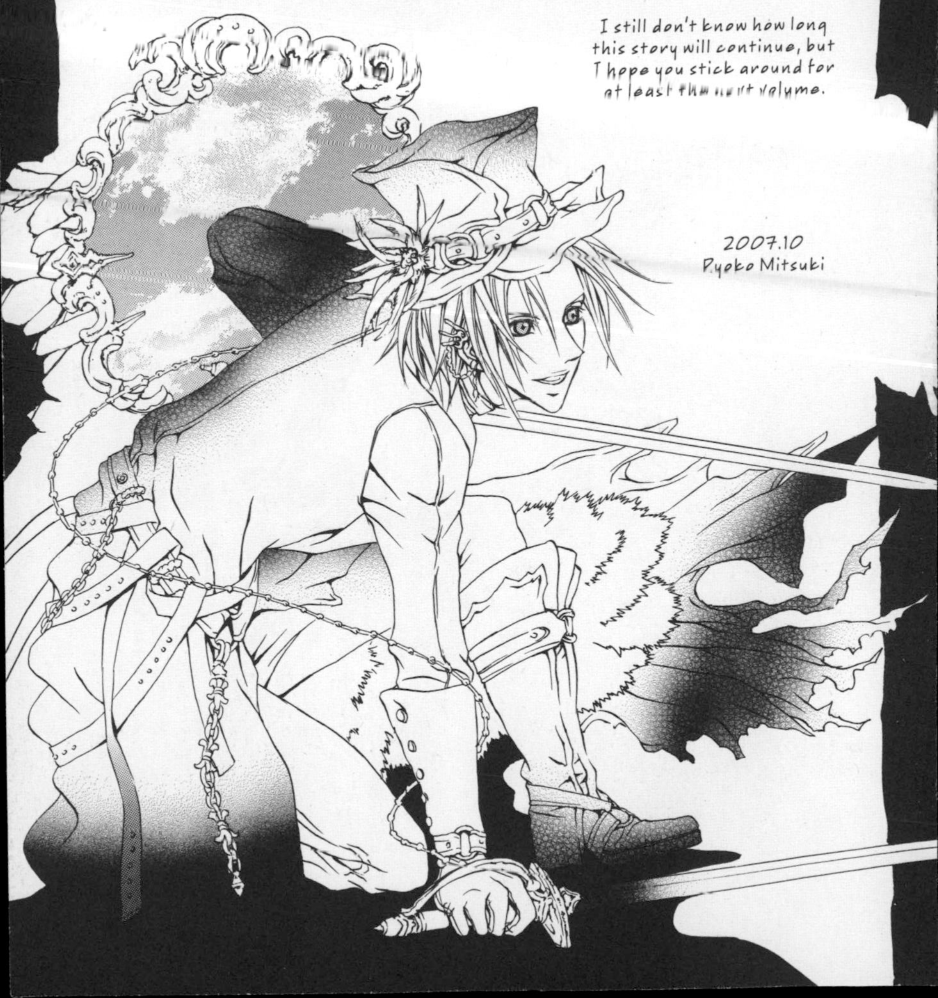

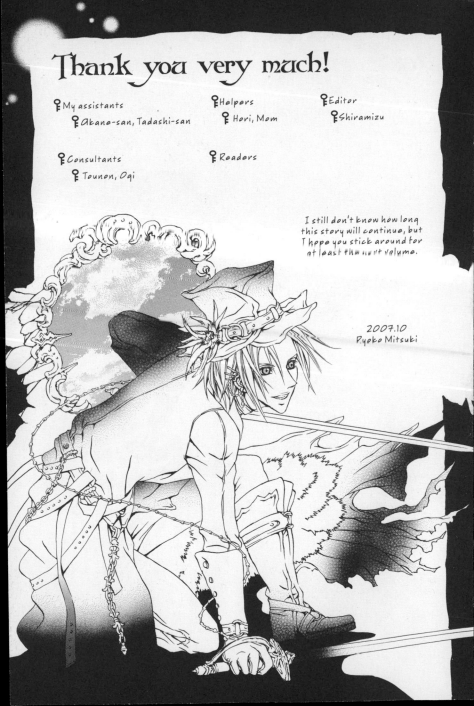

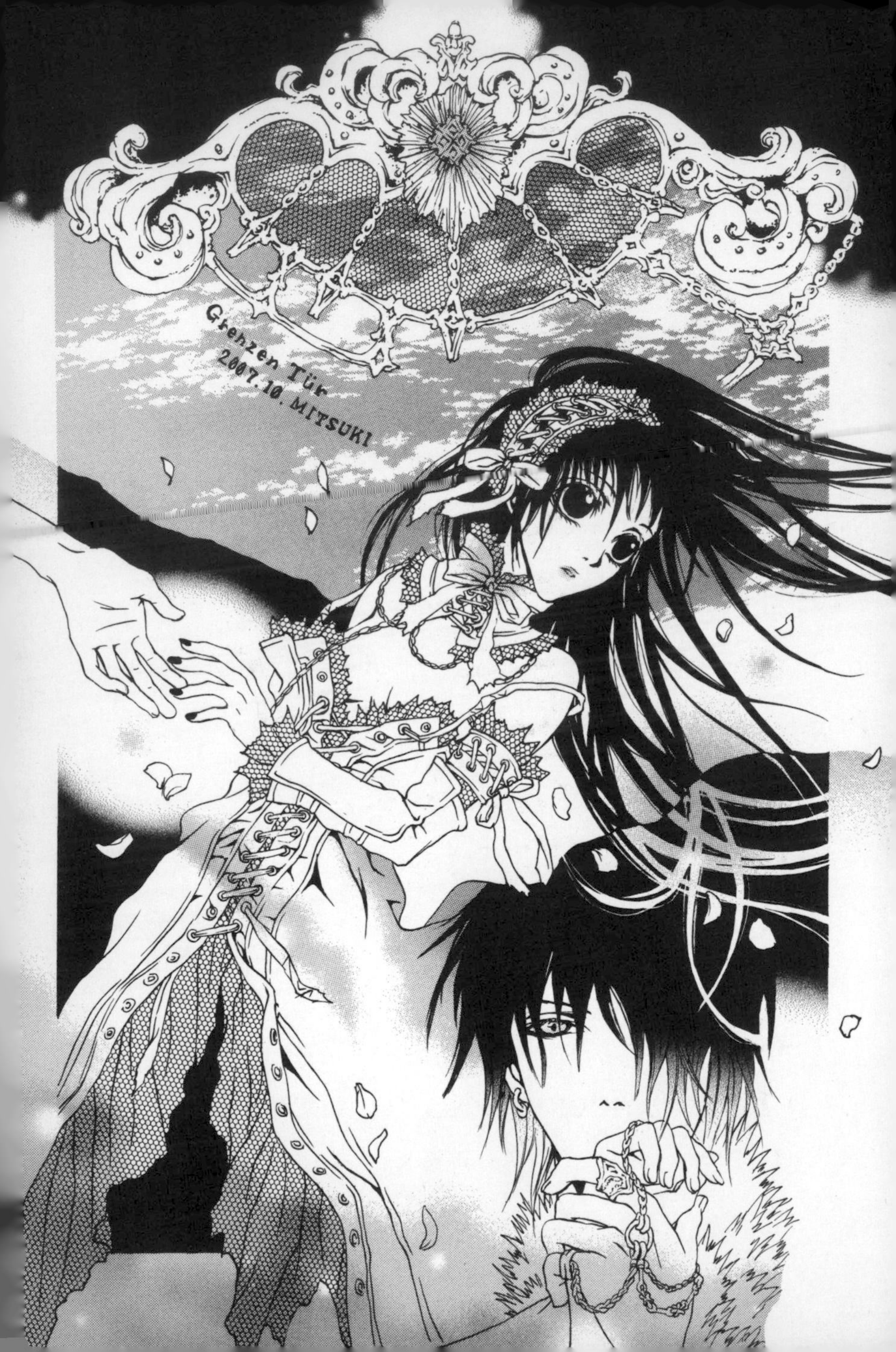
Grenzen Tür
2007.10. MITSUKI

In the next volume of...

After the tragedy at Altzark,
Mizeria and Zelfa travel north to
the city of Zazaatz, in pursuit of
Rikhter and his captive, Clarissa.
There, a festive carnival tempts
our heroine to forget her worries,
but danger lurks in the crowd...

STOP!

This is the back of the book.
You wouldn't want to spoil a great ending!

This book is printed "manga-style," in the authentic Japanese right-to-left format. Since none of the artwork has been flipped or altered, readers get to experience the story just as the creator intended. You've been asking for it, so TOKYOPOP® delivered: authentic, hot-off-the-press, and far more fun!

DIRECTIONS

If this is your first time reading manga-style, here's a quick guide to help you understand how it works.

It's easy... just start in the top right panel and follow the numbers. Have fun, and look for more 100% authentic manga from TOKYOPOP®!

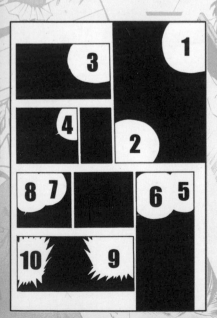